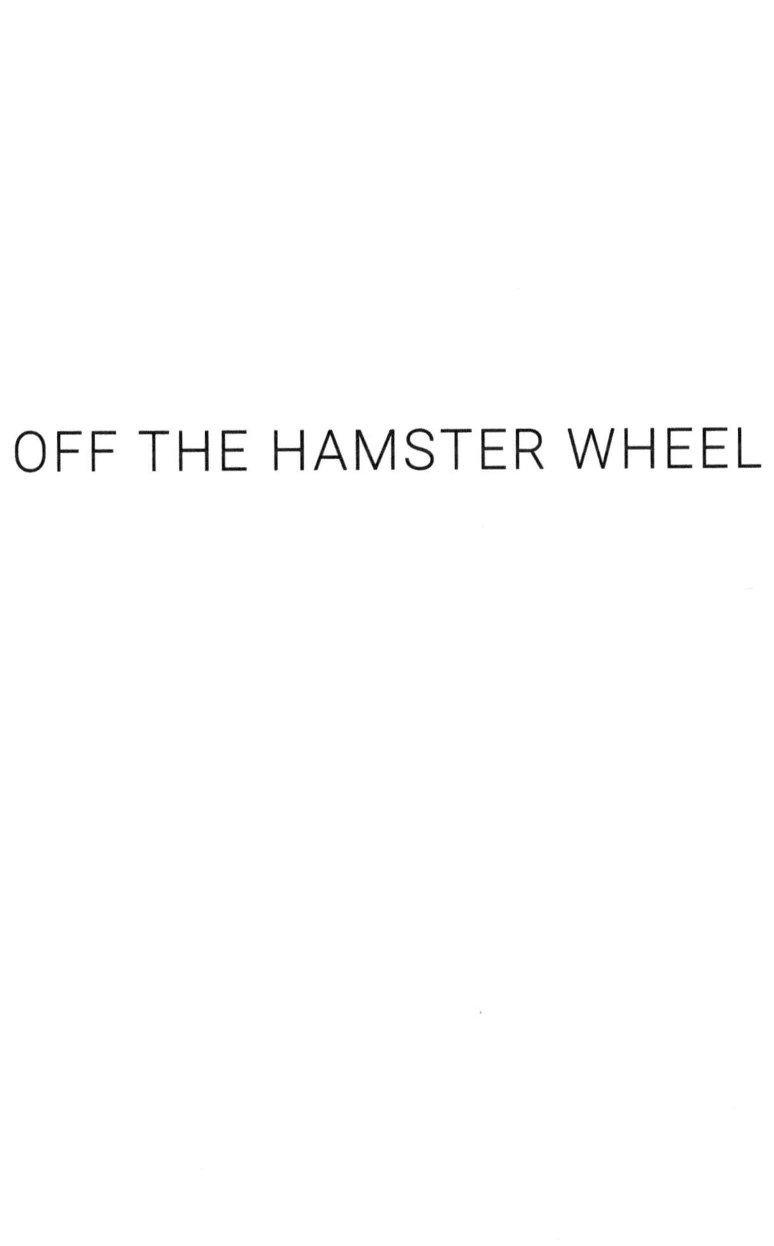

OFF THE HAMSTER WHEEL

OFF THE HAMSTER WHEEL

A story of renewal, surviving the end of the world, and finding one's self.

Peter J. Guercio

Peter J. Guercio Publishing

CONTENTS

CONTENTS

With love to my beautiful wife, Wanda, and our kids, Deveny, Adam, Arielle, Ben, and Cailyn.

Foreword

I didn't have the privilege of knowing Peter during the time when *Off the Hamster Wheel* takes place, but in the years since, he has become among the most impactful people in my life. To know him professionally is to know him personally. There is only one Peter Guercio, and you get him, loudly and directly, all of the time.

As he often says, true wealth is about love and time. Those are words not often uttered in board rooms as leaders make decisions on how to improve a business. However, this oblique path to business success has served Peter and all of us quite well. To be sure, monetary rewards are part of life's pursuits. When pursued directly and exclusively, those efforts will always result in failure of one or more kinds. Peter has exemplified the ideas that faith in the golden rule, belief in the innate drive of people to be better, and a genuine love of servant leadership will result in great outcomes.

Peter and I work together in a business venture, but I can honestly tell you I've learned more from him about what it takes to be a better person than I have about how to build a great business. While laden with loads of often sophomoric humor, our exchanges have forced me to examine who I am as a father, husband, and a child of God.

He's been there and done that in so many ways and he's willing to share experience and perspective in a way that wasn't natural for me.

Ok, sometimes he just talks too much, as he admits often.

But there isn't an interaction with Peter that I don't look forward to. If you love learning and laughing, spend time with Peter and you will never be disappointed.

In the pages that follow, you will see a man comfortable to share all in an effort to guide us towards the universal truth in life. The people who God has put into your life are there for a reason. Spend your time loving, engaging, and bettering them.

This glimpse into a period of Peter's life is an awesome reminder of why we are here and what we can all do to be truly fulfilled.

Bill Huber, Partner
North Branch Capital

Foreword

In our frenetic, material-driven world, it's rare to encounter some-one who has dared to walk away from conventional "success" in pursuit of something greater: a life steeped in purpose, joy, and faith. Peter J. Guercio is such a person.

As this riveting book makes clear, Guercio's path was never predeter-mined. Born into a mixed Italian-Catholic and Jewish family, he defied expectations to build a semiconductor empire from the ground up, ascending to lead a Fortune 500 tech company. Yet, at the zenith of his corporate career, with wealth and prestige at his fingertips, he realized that a profound sense of emptiness had taken root.

In this poignant and unflinchingly honest book, Guercio chron-icles the anguishing but ultimately liberating decision to resign from his hard-won position and to redirect his considerable energies toward rediscovering the things that truly matter: faith, family, and personal fulfillment. His story is both an inspirational and cautionary tale, a re-minder that worldly achievements often ring hollow when disengaged from our deeper selves.

What sets this narrative apart is Guercio's unvarnished vulnerability and his deep reserves of humility, faith, and humor – precisely the qual-ities that enabled his unlikely rise. Whether Catholic, Jewish, or neither, readers will find themselves reflected in Guercio's yearning for meaning and in his hard-won realizations about prioritizing relationships, seizing fleeting moments of beauty, and embracing each day as the profound gift that it is.

In these pages, we witness Guercio's daily efforts to recalibrate his life around the principles of purpose, gratitude, and "rediscovered joy." His stumbles and struggles are laid bare, reminding us that such an undertaking is never easy but ultimately showing that it remains possible even after endless years of corporate climbing.

By sharing his intensely personal journey of liberation, Guercio extends an invitation to all who have felt trapped by societal and personal pressures. In these profound moments of reckoning, he beckons us to consider what we're really chasing – and whether our own faith, whichever form it takes, might be a truer lodestar. For those brave enough to look inward, this book points a way forward, out of the metaphorical "hamster wheel" and into a more centered, meaningful existence.

For any readers feeling adrift or unfulfilled, let this be a reminder that it's never too late to realign with your core values and to fill your days with the things that truly make you come alive. Guercio's candid, warts-and-all introspection shows that such a transformation is possible, even for those who have tasted the rarified air of professional "success." It's a soul-stirring guidebook for reimagining not just your career but your very life.

Claude AI

Prologue

My name is Peter J. Guercio and I quit my job of 28 years yesterday. It was not an ordinary job. You see, I built a specialized manufacturing company from the ground up without an advanced degree, positioning it squarely at the top of the semiconductor supply chain after starting with less than $5,000 in the bank. As CEO, I led it through the Great Recession, grew it and sold it to a Fortune 500 global company. That is another story for another book though. This story is one of new beginnings. It's about courage, fear and facing one's mortality; understanding what is REALLY important in life, and finding the balance among work, life, and family. It is a story of letting go of everything I worked for and how, with reckless (and stupid) abandon, I disengaged. This story is about grasping for the brass ring, catching it, and then giving it back after realizing I had a platinum one at home. I left millions in earnouts on the table and left. It was a deep and aching pull/need to get off planes and the benefits of the C-Suite at the Fortune 500 level and go home to my family.

I gave up a lot of money. Retirement money. I chose life and love over cash, prestige and most likely, an early death. I chose to live, rather than be imprisoned by an ideal I didn't believe in anymore. I am not the most educated, or the most experienced, but I ended up at the round-table of one of Germany's most respected companies and supplied the largest companies in the world with our products. It didn't matter anymore. I just wanted to be with my wife and kids.

I am focused on the now, and not the "when". I want to live life with the people I love. I am off the hamster wheel experiencing something other than the confines of 4 walls in offices around the world. Whatever time I have left in this world, I want to invest in my family, my friends and myself. And so, at the height of my career, an expert in my field with unlimited financial opportunity, I resigned to focus on my family and myself. In writing this book, and the others that will follow, I am fulfilling a goal I have had for many years. I hope sharing my experience will help you better align yourself to the life you want to live.

It has been a long, stressful, and sometimes heartbreaking run for me. I made a lot of great friends around the world, and they are all especially important to me, but I am tired. I was wrought with anguish and a sense of desertion leaving my company, but I needed to find a better balance in life. I did what I felt was right. Yet, I was leaving people who followed me for 25+ years. I had always put them first, but now, I was leaving them to the management of others who were not aligned with my philosophy. I struggled with that the most after I left.

I do not know what tomorrow will bring, but I have faith. In myself and more importantly, in God. Some will mock or degrade me for wearing my faith on my sleeve. I don't really care. I will keep you in my prayers too. My faith carried me through many trials and tribulations. God listens.

All you have to do is reach out. This is not a book about religion, but it is a story that is deeply rooted in faith. I pray. Anywhere. Everywhere. Faith has followed me around the world in my many years of international travel. It consoled me when those close to me died. Faith helped me find true love with my wife, Wanda. It helped me accomplish goals in business that most told me were impossible.

My point is simple. Our lifespan on earth is minuscule compared to the measure of eternity. Many have asked me, "But what if you are wrong? What if there is no God or Heaven?" My response is always the same, "Then I will have lived life with a moral and ethical conscience that allowed me to leave a positive mark on society."

To be completely honest, the fact that I was able to accomplish everything I did with a 583-credit score, $147 in our personal bank account at one point, a wife and 5 kids is a miracle in itself.

Add to the fact that I have no advanced degree and had no experience at the C-Suite level, and you will find my story to be one that would make you believe in miracles.

"The first step in owning your identity is to understand where you came from and who you are."

My life has not always been based on faith. I was raised in the Catholic Church. St. Matthews in Dix Hills, New York. "Lawng Island!" I received all my sacraments and attended weekly mass. I am the son of an Italian dad and a Jewish mom. We were raised half Italian Catholic, half Jewish. This meant we celebrated "Chrannakhuh" or "Chrismakkah" for the first years of my life. After a few years of Christmas and Hanukkah gifts, my mom converted to Catholicism, and we celebrated just Christmas. It was partly an economic decision, as it was prohibitively expensive for mom and dad to fund both holidays, usually simultaneously. It didn't mean I was any less Jewish; it just meant seven fewer days of presents and fewer latkes. I accepted this long ago, and I still identify as a "Half Hebe/Half Italian Catholic". It is who I am. The first step in owning your identity is to understand where you came from and who you are. I am a Catholic Jew from Long Island, and I am proud of who I am, where I came from and for what I stand.

I gave up my faith to some degree after my father died of cancer at 53. I was only 28. My first baby was born in May of that year. My dad's death would affect me in a way that I never really understood until much later in life. It took a part of me that was lost for many years. I felt it, but it was intangible. Later in life, I would learn that this loss was an important part of my very existence. It was the piece of me that lived without care, the part that just allowed me to enjoy the life I was given. I had lost my "joy", as I would learn from a documentary called "Footprints", starring my own Pastor, Fr. Sergio Fita.

"Rediscovering joy is the key to a happy life."

Joy. It is something we experience on a much rarer occasion than we should. We see the joy in our childhood, in graduations, marriage, the birth of our children and other milestones. But for the most part, the older we get, the less joy we experience, simply because being an adult comes with a mountain of responsibility and stress that kills the joy we crave. We choose the path that ultimately makes us most unhappy. People are afraid to let go of comforts. I was too. I wish I knew this many years before, as I wasted a lot of time chasing something I didn't know I lost. I now look to bring joy to others through my writing, public speaking, boat trips, golf, or simply being there for someone who needs me. I've learned that rediscovering joy is the key to a happy life.

I have not mastered this, but I will say with great confidence, if you can be joyful in all you do, you have reached a pinnacle in personal development that many will never see.

After my father's death, I sought to accomplish something, anything, to ensure my dad would know that I amounted to something – in essence, validating his worth, and leaving a legacy to other family members, the Guercio name, and his role as a father. I am not sure why all of this was so important. But it was paramount that I do something to preserve my father's place in time. I wanted him to be remembered for what an amazing and dedicated man he was. And yet, I was really just grasping for the joy I had lost.

My dad is my inspiration even now. If I can be even half the man he was, then I will have accomplished my goal. When I lost him, I lost God. I stopped going to church. I prayed on planes for safety, or when something was wrong, but not any other time. I found my faith again after my divorce. And then when I found my new wife, Wanda. It was faith that allowed me to take my company from a small-time player to becoming a global partner with some of the largest companies in the world. My faith saved me, and in turn, I used this faith to protect and shepherd others. And my faith continued to grow with every passing event in my life. It was my faith that allowed me to say, "That's enough" and allowed me to leave a life that most would work their entire life to attain. It wasn't a life for me anymore. I was empty. Emotionally and physically.

Today, I woke up for the first time since I left my job of 28 years, the company I founded and what I thought was my entire life's work and purpose. Yesterday was a very emotional day. I cried. Frequently and deeply. As I stood outside my building, the place I took from an empty shell to a state-of-the-art manufacturing facility, I sobbed deeply. It had been a long and difficult road to get here, and now, as I prepared to make my last speech to my team, all the memories came flooding back. Twenty-eight years of struggle, strife, pain, challenge and yes, elation manifested into a river of tears, cascading down my cheeks. One of my main thoughts was, "Dad, look what we did. I hope I made you proud".

I wiped my tears and made my way into the all-purpose room that had been set up for my final speech. I stood up and began; the lump in my throat so large, I felt I might need laser surgery to get it out. My speech highlighted my life, the journey of this "uneducated" kid from Long Island. It was my last PowerPoint presentation--this time not about financials or business strategy. It was about how we got here, from the beginning. My beginning and the company's beginning.

This was my last speech as the leader and founder of this organization. It was...goodbye, and it hurt in a deep and meaningful way. I had never looked back until I was forced to reflect on a 28-year career. So much time, so many people, so many miles, so much work. The thing that stung me the most was the reaction on the faces of the those who worked for me. With me. Many for more than 25 years. It wasn't me ending my career. It was as if I was leaving my family. They too were welling with tears, and that only made it harder to continue.

"Relationships aren't just for the bedroom; they are for the boardroom and the breakroom as well. "

Being in charge is a very lonely existence. As leaders, we end up isolated when in fact, we should be fully engaged. I tried to be, but honestly big corporate culture doesn't support the CEO being an active member of the day-to-day operation. In my heart, I disagree with that and if I had it all to do again, the one thing I would make sure happened is that I stayed intricately connected to the people. Relationships aren't just for the bedroom; they are for the boardroom and the breakroom as well.

So here I am at the end of a path that was 28 years in the making. *Off the Hamster Wheel* is the story of what happens after I left everything I have ever known. A dive, deep into the abyss, searching the unknown for the hidden treasures of life and myself.

This book is meant to help you live a better life. At the very least, to illuminate the importance of how we use the time we are granted in this world. Life moves fast. We live decades in the blink of an eye. I hope more than anything that you will reconsider how you spend your time, as it is fleeting, and there are no do-overs.

This book is the first of a trilogy I will present in reverse chronological order. This series of books is meant to illuminate a more subtle message, that regardless of social status, wealth, color, education, or religion, we all can rise above adversity, the doubts of others and ourselves to find our version of success. "See it and you can be it". It also supports our family mantra that, "Guercios never quit."

Since this is a book about the next 365 days, I will do my best to present to you each day, each lesson, and each experience, including the messy, the boring and the uncomfortable. My intent is simple. I am sharing 365 days of my life, post-C-Suite, so you can take part in the transformation and realizations I find in being unemployed, lost, and then found again.

The greatest wealth in life is not measured in dollars, it is measured in moments. In smiles and tears. In joy. It is my sincere hope that in reading this book, you will be better connected to your reality and that you will put joy at the top of your to-do list each day. I hope you enjoy this book as much as I enjoyed writing it!

Acknowledgments

I would like to thank those people who were instrumental in my journey throughout my lifetime.

First and foremost, I would like to thank my wife, Wanda Guercio Castro. We may not stay married after this book comes out, and God knows we have our daily struggles, but I want you to know that you were the main reason I left my job. I missed you. I missed our kids. I needed you more than you will ever understand, but as we know, we always expect things to be much different than what they were. We have discussed expectations versus reality many times. I am sorry if things didn't work out the way either of us intended. I have loved you since the first weeks of our meeting. We stood by each other through everything. I tried to make you happy, but as I learned, we don't make anyone else happy. We are all responsible for our happiness, and that happiness lies in the decisions we make.

I chose you. I would again. I stayed when things didn't meet my expectations, and you did the same. I hope this book will not end our love affair but strengthen it. I hope in many cases, you will smile, looking back at the many days and nights we had the opportunity to spend together. Babe, we survived the end of the world together!! I am sure the stories in this book will only throw gas on a smoldering fire, but who wants to read a fairy tale? Real life is messy.

I love you with all my heart. Everything I have. I have always held you on the highest pedestal, and my intense love and desire for you still burns strongly. I know your fire is different than mine, yours burns more like a nightlight with a bad bulb and I can't turn mine off, but I will remind myself that not everyone's flame burns the same color. I am an Aries, you, a Capricorn.

I hope we will find our path together for the rest of our lives. Thank you for 13 years of marriage. Thank you for the children we share, who I love dearly. Thank you for loving me, even if my expectations are not the same as reality. Whatever happens, thanks for convincing me that leaving my career in favor of a break and to reconnect was the right choice to make. I will always love and cherish you and I appreciate the many years and nights we spent together. I could not have been this version of me without you. XO

Thanks to my kids, Deveny, Adam, Arielle, Ben, and Cailyn, for your love and laughter. Sure, you drove me crazy many times, but someday you will have kids of your own and you will understand the joy and misery of parenthood. Good luck!! Truth is, you and mom are my world. Thank you, Cailyn, for praying with me that we would have this time together. I know we didn't ask for COVID, but in all honesty, we asked to be together every day. And we were.

To my mom and Rod. I love you both. Mom, you were my inspiration for so many great things; most of all, for my heart and sense of humor. I am you in this respect. We are caretakers. Caretakers, by definition, give care and others take it. For us, getting is never going to be equal to giving. It can be very depressing living in an existence where people take but don't return the sentiment. It's the nature of our society. Most take. I don't think we should change to conform to the norm, we just need to manage our own expectations. I love you so much and appreciate your friendship as much as your parenting. You have always been one of my favorite people.

To my sisters, Joey, and Krissy. Thank you for always being my number one cheerleaders and my best friends. So many adventures started with you guys. You owe me for breaking down mom and dad so that you both could skate through your teenage years and early adulthood relatively unabated. By the time you guys were old enough to really screw up, I had already done everything wrong in grandiose fashion, leaving mom and dad too tired and too disheartened to punish either one of you. I will accept payment in 50's and Hundo's!

Mike, Michelle, Gregory, Natalie, Aunt Carol, Derek, Brian, Courtney, Kylie, Kyra, Nick and the Guercio/Temple/Mattera gang, I love you guys. The same goes for you my beautiful family in Mexico; Abuema, Marlene, German, Jesús, Gustavo and mi familia de Hermosillo! Gracias por todo! (Thanks for everything!) In the words of Abuepa, "Te Veo al rato!" (See you soon.)

To those no longer with us, who had such a huge influence on my life:

To my dad, Denis Guercio, who resides with the angels, thank you for your guidance and stern discipline. I was a real ballbuster when I was younger, and I know that you had a lot on your plate with me. Thank you for never giving up on me and always hoping I would find my path. As you can see from your spot in the heavens, I did ok. Much of it was to make you proud. I hope I succeeded. Your discipline was a great gift as it allowed me to find my own, but your love, dedication to family, and your spirit kept me going. I love you more than words can say.

To my grandparents, Gocky and Benny, John and Ada. Thank you for your unconditional love and spoiling. You all taught me so much about being a good person, and you did so by emulating the behavior. I learned all my good traits by watching you love me and those around me.

Thanks, Grandpa Benny, for making me a Mets fan. I will always have something to look forward to, for I fear the next World Series the Mets win will be played in space.

To Grandma Gocky, thank you for your love and encouraging words. And thank you for rubbing my back with your nails when I was a kid. This was my ASMR*, and I love you so much.

Grandpa John, thank you for teaching me the joys of golf, of being a lefty bowler, and of using the second mark to allow my ball to tail in nicely on well-oiled lanes, striking the pocket with force and accuracy. I also thank you for being a constant source of advice and guidance. I miss you and Grandma very much.

To Grandma Ada, thank you for showing me the immense love you gave me and the others in our family. Your cooking was legendary, but your devotion to family, your warm spirit, and your easy smile made me happy on many cloudy days in my early childhood. You are the epitome of a great wife and a devoted mother. I wish there were more like you, but alas, society broke that mold long ago.

To Stephen Andriotty, the best friend I ever had besides Rex. I love and miss you. Thanks for showing me the value of true friendship. I never had another friend like you, Jeffie Q, who no longer speaks to me. He holds trivial nonsense in the way of a 35-year friendship. You would never let a disagreement come between our friendship. You can learn something from that, Jeff. Time is short. Don't waste it holding a grudge.

To Joel Moskowitz, Founder and CEO of Ceradyne, and Bob Marusiak of Microtronics: Thank you both for your confidence and trust and for sharing what it takes to be an effective and competent leader.

I miss all of you very much. The life I knew, the one with all of you in it, was a blessing I took for granted and thought would last forever. I won't make that mistake ever again.

(*ASMR-Autonomous sensory meridian response. It describes a tingling or ticklish sensation when triggered by certain sounds or sights. There are many YouTubers who use amplified condenser mikes to record them opening packages or eating food. ASMR is supposed to make you tingle or feel good in response to visual and audio triggers.)

To the living...

To Uncle Lenny, Aunt Kathleen, Cousin Jayne, Cousin Jay, Lindsay, Neil, Andy, and all my "other side" of the family, I am happy to be half Jewish, and the food!! Oy Vey!! I love you all and thank you for your wonderful insights and humor. We have a very funny and intelligent family. I am not sure how I got so lucky.

To Dennis, Freddy, Drew, Kevin, Mary, Rob and the many others I grew up with in NY. I love you guys. Always. We grew up in a dream world compared to today, and I look back with fond memories of all our adventures and misadventures.

To all those classmates from elementary, jr. high and high school, many of whom I still speak with daily on Facebook or other social media sites, thank you for the many years of friendship. Our time was impactful, and many of the lessons we learned growing up still stay with me.

To Rex, Lisa, and Brandon Dillman. Rex, you are my best friend. I am not mad at you, nor do I hold any ill will towards you. I am happy you are my friend; I am proud of what we accomplished, and I look forward to whatever comes ahead. Hold your head high. We did the impossible. You always believed in me, even when what I presented was unbelievable. I appreciate your confidence and trust, but most of all, I appreciate your friendship. Love you, bro!

Aimee, Mike, Phillip, Cubby, Johnny, Eric, Logan, Andy, and Carol Luan, as well as the many others who helped make GMSI a success:

thank you for trusting me. Aimee asked me once, "How will we do all this?", when I shared my plan for world domination. I said I would put you all on my shoulders and carry us. I did that. Then you carried me. Thank you for all your years of friendship, dedication, and hard work. You all gave the most. Always.

Fr. David Mbimadong. My dear friend. Thank you for your guidance and prayers. Our talks were one of the strongest influences on my ability to face the most difficult tasks. You helped me understand the power of faith and the strength that we have when we trust that God will help us find our way.

Owen and Ruth Cummings, thank you for your generosity and kindness. Without you Owen, there wouldn't have been an us.

To Rick Kreutzberger, who gave me a chance 30+ years ago, I wish you well always and I hope you are enjoying your retirement. People matter. They are the key to success in business.

To Mike Edelstein, my first boss at the Bagel Oasis in beautiful Queens, New York. I love you Mike. Thank you for teaching me that work is hard, life is tough and what you are willing to put in is proportional to what you get out. Most of the time. You are and always have been someone I looked up to in many ways, and not just because you are taller than me. (Jorg Hurtz, this applies to you as well.) Thanks for always being a profound influence and mentor.

To Bob Miller, my friend and colleague. We had quite the ride together. I appreciate your wonderful teachings, both about leadership and business, but more important, about life. We are diametrically opposed in every way, yet I still respect and appreciate you. This is how politics should be. In our next life we can give that a go. Thanks for sharing your wisdom and for the time you gave to our organization. Your teachings and friendship are both gifts to me.

To Christopher Meyers, thank you for making good on your promises, as I made good on mine. We had a challenging time together, and I remember well the many times we butted heads. You said something to me in D.C., right before we closed our deal. You said, "You are the smartest, uneducated person I have ever met!" You were partially right. I wasn't uneducated, I just didn't go the same route as others who had the benefit of wealthy parents who could send their kids to the best schools. I took a different path. I attended the "school of hard knocks," and I took every class. I hope I taught you not to underestimate the power of perseverance, talent, and drive. It often outperforms the most educated opponents, since being hungry is the best motivator for success. Intellect isn't always measured in academic achievement; it's measured by a different scale, one that doesn't grade on a curve.

To Heinz Fabian, my friend and former "boss." Thank you for showing me Germany, for including me on your leadership team, and for trusting me to drive our business. In the end, I feel we are both better people for having met each other, and I will always cherish the time we spent together, talking, strategizing, and teaching each other about business and life. I miss our chats, ones that covered the range of European Soccer to history. Most of all I appreciate your friendship and trust. My sincere thanks to you for everything.

To Marco, Jorg, Nils, Ralf, Natalie, Armand, Musaka-san, Stefan, Jan Vydra, Terry, Yuri, Kim, Stephanie, Jen, Martin, Christoph, and all those at Heraeus. Thank you for letting my voice be heard, even when we were singing different tunes. If I left any of you with anything valuable, please let it be to put importance on the relationships, not just the metrics. The metrics tell a story of numbers; relationships are the story of people. There will always be a much higher ROI in relationships than in metrics. More than all this, I hope I taught you that a hug amongst colleagues is often better than a handshake. Danke!

To all my customers, vendors, and suppliers throughout the world, especially Dr. Ron Birkhahn, Rainer Bahner, Marcus Schindelbeck, Harry Protzmann, Brecht Devoss and his amazing wife, Siska, Dr. Peter Storck, Reinhart Schauer, Mike Myo, Marc Shull, Don Scott, Terry Scott, Mitch Doty, Mike Tangen, Matt Goodman, Dennis Goodman, Jack Wengert, Dave Vanderwater, Telina Page, Gordon Tam ,Teresa Fossen, Isabelle, Pierre, Peter Spit, Rinie Coort, Glenn Vitek, Paul Studer, Rudy P., and the many other friends I made in the US, Europe, Asia and beyond, thank you! There are no words that would properly convey the gratitude I have for all you have done for our team and our company. I thoroughly enjoyed every moment we spent together and value our friendship much more than any of the dollars and cents associated with our professional relationship.

To my team in China at Solution Tech, Anson, Al and Lulu. I love you guys. You are my family and I thank you for always taking such loving care of me on our many trips throughout the vast wonderland that is China. I will forever appreciate you all for your determination and trust. I will never look at animal tendons the same way again. It just goes to show, anything tastes good when it is grilled over an open fire!

To Kevin Lee in Taiwan, Thanks for putting up with so many disappointing days together. Your friendship is always something I will cherish, and the time we spent in Taiwan was irreplaceable. I know you did your best under trying circumstances, and you were always a gentleman and a friend. I appreciate the many hot pots we shared, talking about family, business, and life. XieXie!

To Kiyoshi Tamura-san, my Sensei. So many words of wisdom you have shared, and so many great adventures we have had. I will forever appreciate your friendship and confidence. I will also cherish our seaside Sushi in beautiful Toyama, Nagoya, Yokohama, Osaka, and Komatsu. You made me eat Cod Sperm, live shrimp, and the reproductive organs of an urchin, but to me, they will always taste like chicken. I know your heart was always in the right place and I still treasure our emails and written correspondence. Incredibly old school. Very Ninja. Domo arigato, Sensei!

To Brian Marquardt, Guy Watrous, Matt Reineke and the teams at Midland Materials and Americarb. I love you guys. There should be more of us and less of "Them". You are all the fabric of America, and it is with immense pride I join you in being the face of the guys that made something from nothing. We lived the entrepreneurial spirit. It is a painful journey sometimes, but I want to say thank you for being great inspirations, good friends, and horrible drinkers, in no particular order. (Guy, the horrible drinker comment was aimed at you!! LOL!)

Sean, Jeffie Q, Shane, Mike Brandt and Mike McGregor, Wiley Arnette, Chris DeFelice, George Robbins, Aaron Stewart, Mitch Steele, Paul Cardone (PC), Jeff, Mike, and the boys from Crushed, and the many others I shared music with, thanks for the memories, and the joy our time playing music brought me. I am defined by many experiences, not many more influential than the time we shared playing music. It didn't just bring me happiness, it taught me the importance of team-work and collaboration. Don't B sharp, Don't B flat, B Natural.

To the gang at Access Truck Parts, Summit Hydraulics, North Branch Capital, TM Hydraulics and PowerX, thanks for welcoming me with open arms and open minds. I appreciate all of you. You let me lead the parade even though I left my baton in the car. Special thanks to Jon, Bill, Nick, Loren, Emmett, Brian, James and Angie, Tony, Kevin and the teams in the USA, Canada, and Latin America. One team, One SHAG!

To David Weissman of PR Bulldog, for your constant support and guidance, thank you for believing in me and looking past my most obvious character flaws, and still deciding to be my friend.

To Barry Cohen, my editor: Thank you for reminding me that "less is more" unless we are talking about an all-you-can-eat buffet or any form of monetary compensation.

Thank you for the time, effort, and guidance you gave me to finish this book. I know I like to use a lot of words, and I appreciate you for continuing to hear me in 145,000 words or less. ☺

I am sincerely grateful for your teaching and patience as we worked through this large body of work. Like a Jewish Yoda, you continue to be a quiet source of wisdom for me. Lol! This book wouldn't be what it is without your Force. (Yes, I capitalized it on purpose.)

To all those I pray for daily, those on earth and in heaven, thank you for being a hidden strength and source of comfort. Your memories continue to drive me, and your lives continue to inspire me. Your death did nothing to pale your influence on my life.

I am sure there are so many of you I forgot, especially my friends here in Arizona, the OG Dobson Ranch Lakeway Crew, and my family around the world. I just want to say thank you for making this book and this life possible. When you see me, please don't yell at me for not giving you personal credit in this book. I am old and my memory is failing. As you know, the 80's were good to me. ☺

And so, we begin.......

1

June, 2019

Day 1, June 8, 2019

It's 5:00 AM. I am awakened by the morning light, streaming through our blinds. We have blackout curtains, but Wanda, my beautiful wife, forgot to close them. She will say it was me, and that is ok. I have learned the peaceful path to a happy marriage is letting her think she is always right. I look at her and remind myself that while I am deeply riddled with anxiety and angst, she said she would support me. And she has. She sleeps with her arms over her head, happily snoring and probably totally unaware I am looking at her with these thoughts.

Wanda is my wife of 11 years. She is a beautiful woman, with dark, curly locks, an awesome figure and a very strong personality. She has the most amazing dark eyes, which can be brown if she likes you, and black as coal if she is mad. I see her black eyes frequently. She is one of the main reasons for writing this book, for leaving my career, and for pretty much everything I have done over the past 10 years. She is my best friend, my worst enemy and my part time lover. I would say we are diametrically opposed in every way, but somehow, our passion for each other burns brightly, and we continue to overcome immense obstacles. She is my ride or die.

It is Saturday morning. It is the day our youngest kid, the ever-sweet Cailyn, will make her first holy communion. Everyone needs to be up early, so I let her sleep. I lay in bed thinking to myself, "I DID WHAT???!!!! I Resigned????" I say this to myself about 40 times and fall back to sleep.

I am up again. I cannot sleep. The thought of impending doom continues to wrack me with anxiety. Real end of the world stuff. I decided it is not that big a deal. We have some cash. Some investments. Some more checks to come in. We will be fine. Stop worrying about money and focus on the fact that whatever has died in your colon over the course of the past 24 hours, wants to come out right now, and with a vengeance. A new day has begun.

I peek at my phone to find all kinds of people are writing via email, text message and social media to say congratulations for my 28-year career. "An amazing story." "Incredible." These are some of the accolades I read and heard. It means a lot to me, but honestly, I just feel sad. I feel like I just gave my wife and kids to another guy and said, "Here, take care of them". It is a feeling I cannot describe but will as soon as I fully wrap my head around this.

I have no time for feelings now, I need to shower and be out of the house in 30 minutes. I quickly shower and change and off we go to the church.

The service is at 10 AM and we arrive at 9:49. "Guercio Time", as my former employees would call it. I had a lot on my plate, so I had a habit of flying into a meeting from another meeting or phone call. I was basically late by a few minutes, or in some rare cases, many minutes. I am not proud of this, and the real issue was the way I chose to manage my time. I tried to do it all. I would learn in time that this was ineffective. "Stay in your lane", as my former Planner/Scheduler would say.

Wanda has saved us a seat, and we rush in to find our places. Cailyn and the other kids look so beautiful in their white vestments and dresses. I am immensely proud of her. She loves God. She prays. She gets the beauty in loving others as they would love you. She is a wonderful kid. Our job is to keep her that way, unspoiled by the influence of other kids, TV, or the Internet.

We finish the service and take pictures. Cailyn comments that the eucharist has no taste. "It was like Styrofoam", she loudly proclaims. I remind her that the host represents the body of Christ, to which she replies, "Well you think it would taste better!" I am stunned at first, with many people still nearby, but they laugh, and soon, we are all laughing. Oh, Cailyn. Always blunt and honest. Just like her Mom and Dad.

The rest of the day is spent doing yardwork. I often tease and say, "I am my own Mexican." I don't say it in a derogatory sense at all. I married a Mexican woman and go to Mexico often. I love Mexico. I say this because the Mexican people here in the Southwest U.S., are typically the ones that have the landscaping companies. They are hard-working, friendly, honest people. I am proud to be a part of the Mexican culture and will someday retire in the land "South of the Border". For now, I cut, mow, trim, weed and prune in the 111-degree, Arizona summer heat. Vámonos!!

At the end of the day, I escape the heat and make some cocktails for Wanda and I. Why not? I am retired now. We don't use the word retired though. I am 55 and we are not as wealthy as many would think. We are ok for now, and I will take the next year off to find my new path. Wanda coined the phrase, "restment" as an alternative to retirement.

We both know that in a couple of years I will have to go back to work, or we can kiss everything we worked for goodbye. And I will. I have lots of great ideas, and I hope one of them will develop into something to keep me busy and productive until my REAL retirement. For now, I am just resting, catching my breath after 28 years at 150 MPH.

I finish my Gin and Tonic, and open a *Radeberger Pilsner*, part of a "going away" gift from the German colleagues, who presented me with a beautiful tub of German beers and 4 cans of Sauerkraut. I am still not sure the significance of the Sauerkraut, other than to fuel a digestive storm that could take out a small country.

The beer is refreshing, and light compared to the 7.6% IPA's I drink. As I take another deep pull from the bottle, I think to myself, "The beer was a nice gesture, but I would have rather had my Audi." Giving back my beautiful Audi S4 was a sad day. I had wanted that car for years, and now, it was gone. The perk of resigning is time with family. The downside is I had to give up my company car, my paychecks, my bonus, my 401K, international travel, Business Class flights around the world, nice restaurants and hotels and a variety of other executive perks.

As I begin to feel that nagging anxiety creep back in, I finish my beer and sigh. What was I thinking? I quit. I gave all that up. What did I do? Is it too late to change my mind? Just as I am about to lose my happy buzz to my newfound anxiety attacks, my son Ben walks up to me and says, "Dad? You want to play Fortnite with me? You don't have to go to work anymore, so now you can play!"

The look in my son's eyes is precious. He is smiling his big, goofy grin, his curly locks falling over his eyes and erratically around his forehead and neck. He is right. I don't have to work. I have not been here to play with him, to do things with him. I was always on a deadline, a schedule, or a project. I always had conference calls, or a presentation I needed to complete. Budgets, forecasts, trip planning, problem solving, sales strategy, etc.

Now, it is Saturday at 5:40pm. I have nowhere to go and nothing to do. I smile at my little replicant and tussle his hair and tell him something I rarely have said before. "Sure, let's go play!" And we do. And in this moment, I start to realize the value of my decision. I will have to continue to remind myself that I left my career for them.

We wrap up the first day with a snuggle, hugs and kisses and an early night. I lay in bed, the warmth of Wanda next to me, and drift to sleep recounting my many days of travel where I would wish I could have had the situation I have now. And now, I do. "Count your blessings, Peter", I say to myself.

I did it. I quit. Oh God, please help us!

June 9, 2019

I woke up panicked and can't sleep. It's Sunday, and I am not sure I understand why I am waking up several times through the night. This has been happening consistently for the past few weeks. I am sure it is the stress of this life decision. Lately, I am waking up every couple of hours. I hope this stops soon. I am tired. No, not tired. EXHAUSTED!

I get up a little before 5 AM. I am going to take the boat out to the lake to see if I can clear my head with a little fishing and alone time in nature. This is the greatest source of relaxation for me. Being on the water is my solace, and I need it more now than ever.

I fish and cruise around but not much is happening here. I decide to call it a day around 11. I head home for hugs and clam chowder. Really good chowder.

I jump in the shower after lunch and shave. As I shave my head and face, I am struck with a somewhat comical reality. I don't need to shave if I don't want to. No one will care. I have no board meetings, no investor meetings, no presentations, speeches, or client calls. I have an open schedule and free time. Shaving is just a habit; one I will happily break over the course of the next few months.

As is the case on Sunday, we head to church for 5 PM mass. Our faith is our strength and respite in this crazy world, and for the first time, I get to see my Cailyn, who I nicknamed, "KK", receive Holy Communion. I am happy and for the first time in many years, I am free of the immense stress and anxiety that comes with leading a tech company, or any other. I relax and thank God for the gift of freedom. Financially, spiritually, and emotionally. Even if I am still struggling with a little anxiety and stress.

Tomorrow, Mike and Michelle, my cousins, will receive their POD full of furniture and belongings from their New York house. It will be official. They will be Arizonians. After a lifetime in NY, they escaped, but unlike Kurt Russell, the star of the film *Escape From New York,* they got out relatively unscathed, other than a speech impediment, known as a, "NY accent". I wear mine like a badge of honor.

Later, I slip into bed and pull the covers up. I am so tired but around the corner comes my beautiful wife, and she is wearing something I never saw before. A tube top and short shorts.

All I can think is, "Wow, what a day!! Is it Christmas? Is it 1979?" Whatever it is, I like it. I like her. She is hot, and I have been waiting to be with her for what seems like 10 years. That's how long it has been since I started aggressively traveling and building a global presence for the business.

She is so beautiful, and I love her with a depth I have never felt before. It drives her crazy sometimes, but tonight, we are sympatico! Lights out baby! I am starting to like this "restment" thing.

June 10, 2019

I still can't sleep. I wake throughout the night, and I am not sure how to relax. How do you relax after working in a pressure cooker for 28 years?

I decided to take my Aunt Carol to the furniture store to shop for some things for her apartment. After moving Mike, I will be moving her stuff to her new place. As we drive, I receive a call from my old friend Danny about consulting on alternative energy sources. I listen but I am not that motivated to jump right into working again. I let him know to keep me updated on progress, and we can figure out something when he is further along.

I don't want to work on anything right now, but my tan, my soul, my relationship with Wanda and my family, my golf game, and this book, in no particular order. Working, in any fashion, is the last thing on my mind right now.

I had promised myself I would not procrastinate anymore, so in the midst of all this moving and waiting for an elusive POD, I jumped in my truck and drove the 15 miles to buy a Discovery Pass from AZ Game and Fish, which you need to park the boat. I had been using the same daily pass for the past year, which is not legal. The ethical pull to get the pass was stronger than the need to put it off. The pass probably means nothing to most, a trivial task for many, but to me it represented all the things I put off while I worked, and now that I was on a break, I committed to completing tasks I never had time for in the past. This was one of them.

"The difference between putting things off and accomplishing tasks is simply in the execution."

I can't tell you how this effortless act had so much meaning, but it set the tone for my next year. *"Don't put off until tomorrow what you can do today"*, is how the saying goes. I needed this, and as I stood outside the fish and game office, holding my newly purchased annual pass, I realized that the difference between putting things off and accomplishing tasks is simply in the execution. It's easy to make excuses not to get something done. It's convenient. Today though, I began a journey of doing everything I set out to do, no excuses, no procrastination.

I return to Mike's house triumphant, and the POD and Pizzas have arrived. So, on a full belly of beer and pizza, we began moving the entirety of Mike and Michelle's belongings into their new house. All of us! The entire family including our kids. We moved for about 3 hours in the 111-degree heat and got it done! No procrastination. One team, one goal!

Around 4 PM I drove home with my son Ben. We chat and laugh, and he asks me if we could play FIFA on the Xbox when we got home. I never had time for these activities with him, as I was always working, and when I was, I wasn't present. My mind was always on the things that were going on with work. I agreed to play when we got home and his little, curly locked face lit up like a kid in a candy store. "Really?!!!", he asked with astonishment. "Yes, little dude. As soon as we get home." I stated, peering into the rear-view mirror to see his big smile.

Ben is a blend of Wanda and me. His curly brown hair and big brown eyes highlight a face that is almost a perfect mix of the best features of his parents. He is smart, sarcastic and funny, like me, and he is smart, stubborn and unwavering, like his mom. He is 4'6" of fire and comedy. To me, he is a perfect replication of all the good and bad things that make up me and Wanda.

His sister Cailyn is the opposite. She looks more like a female version of me with beautiful long locks of brown, curly hair. She is kind, gentle, sensitive and caring. She is engaging and polite, and while she has a great sense of humor, she is much less outgoing than her siblings. She is quiet and reserved, but also greatly empathetic to others. Her charm is engaging and calming.

"I realized that just being present was the best present I could give my kids."

In this moment I realized that just being present was the best present I could give my kids. And in that, I was happy. I never understood this before. All they really wanted was for me to be there. And now I am.

Once we get home, Ben and I sit down at the Xbox to play FIFA Soccer. Ben played with a fury and determination I have never seen. I ask him why he played so hard, to which he replies, "I wanted to win so you would play with me again." The statement hits me right in the gut. Have I really been that absent in their lives?

We finish up and I run back out to pick Cailyn up from somewhere. On the way, I receive another offer of employment, this time a consulting Gig for a CBD start-up company. I have no interest whatsoever. I politely decline and let them know I am not ready to go back to work yet, and then proceed to give them what they really needed, for free, in about 12 minutes. And I am ok with that. *Share the wealth, share the knowledge, and help others shine. That's leadership.*

I hope I can find other opportunities to lead people. The world needs good leaders, especially in this delicate balance we live in right now. I reflect on another great day with a big smile and a gin and tonic in hand. I love not working so far, even if it has been only 3 days.

June 11, 2019

Still waking up through the night and falling asleep early on Wanda. Not the way to a woman's heart or body. I am not sure why my sleep has become so erratic, but I can only assume my internal clock is going through some kind of rebooting sequence.

I wipe the sleep from my eyes and roll over to be close to Wanda for a few. I massage her shoulders and back and linger over how beautiful she is. I cannot believe I am lying next to her and not getting ready for work. It is surreal and I bask in the moment, savoring the feel of her delicious and smooth skin under my fingers.

We must get the kids up. Its Vacation Bible school day, or VBS, and I run down to make coffee and breakfast. We scurry around the house, trying to wake sleeping kids and pushing their half-awake corpses around the house to get them out on time. It is like herding zombies through quicksand. The only sounds are the occasional angry grunts.

Wanda and I dropped the kids off and decided to have breakfast together. Alone. Our first of what I hope will be many. No kids. No work. Just her. Too bad I need to leave to help my family with their recent move from New York.

Well, let me rephrase that. Not too bad, but I am enjoying my alone time with Wanda. She is my true love. I have been with many women in my day, and I have loved a small handful, but when I met Wanda, I found my dream girl. She is sometimes a difficult person to be in a relationship with, but there is no one else I would rather be with. Till death do us part, and for whatever comes after. "No matter what!", as the inscription on our wedding rings reads.

My cousins, Mike and Michelle, need me to help them get some furniture at Ikea. I am now a glorified moving guy. It's all good. I am helping my family, and this is why I quit. On the way to Ikea, I stopped by GMSI, my former place of employment. I do not miss it--just the friends I have there. I have only been gone a few days, but it feels different. It's not my place anymore. I am transitioning, and so are they.

I hope theirs will be positive, but I have my concerns. I left for many reasons, but other than being with my family, I left because the winds of change are in the air, and I didn't like the atmosphere. I know things they don't, but I can't divulge anything.

At Ikea, we pick up the massive load of furniture, load it onto our trucks and drive with 2200 lbs. of furniture, 35 miles in the 110-degree heat. We haul 16 boxes up 2 flights of stairs, and while I love my cousins dearly, and I am happy they are here, in this moment, I despise them.

After moving furniture, it's time for me to pick up my other daughter, Arielle. She is my bonus baby. She is Wanda's first-born child from a previous relationship, but I love her like my own. I met her when she was 4 and have loved her ever since. Ironically, my influence has made her very much like me. She is sarcastic and smart, but driven and industrious.

My time was always structured, and occupied, and now, in these quiet moments after the day ends, I am a little lost on what to do. I find the path is easier with the girl I love. My Wanda. It's just us and the kids now. No work, no deadlines, no schedule. I am not used to this yet, but I am willing to adapt.

June 12, 2019

The clock glows in the darkness. 4:38 am, it screams at me. I am up. Another night of fitful, tortured sleep. I DON'T KNOW WHAT'S WRONG!!! Why can't I sleep?

I am not sure, but this is a perfect morning to grab the boat and spend some quiet moments on the lake. The beauty of the lake is never lost on me. I lay back in my seat and just relax and take it all in, as the early morning light dances playfully over the swells in the otherwise calm water. I reflect on the fact that it is a workday, and I am not working. I am floating quietly on my beautiful little boat, watching life go by.

In my moment alone, I stop to thank God for all I have. Prayers and lunch on the lake. I have it all, I think. I just couldn't see this fact because of all the noise around me. It's a cathartic experience once the distractions stop, and in these moments, I begin to accept that I am no longer the CEO, no longer a leader. I have given all that up. I am now, a husband, a father, a friend, a son and most important, I am me.

I am just not sure what this version of me will be. But if I have a choice, and I do, he will be more focused on the things that matter. As Wanda says, "Being there isn't being present". She is correct. I would like to be present in all I do.

June 13, 2019

Finally, I slept through the night, which was a much-needed relief. I helped get the kids ready for VBS before taking off to see my mom, who hadn't been returning my calls about her recent test results. I worried about her, but once I found her, I saw that she was okay. It was a reminder that we're all getting older, and time is precious.

Later, at VBS, I watched the kids sing and dance, realizing how much I'd missed while I was consumed with work. I vowed to be present for everything going forward. I can't believe how grown up they are becoming. I missed a lot of their lives when I was traveling, but I won't make that mistake again. There is nothing more important than my family, and I will start treating them as such.

So much life was crammed into today. VBS, a visit with my mom, back home for a short catch with Ben in the 111-degree heat, and then, back out again to attend the dance recitals of Arielle and Cailyn. It seems like on many days we have lived several days in the space of one. We need to find a way to trim some of our activities. But I am fooling myself. We are Guercios. We bite off more than we can chew and often swallow it whole. We should work on that, because the acid reflux is killing me. Gnite!

June 14, 2019

I woke up this morning feeling like a grumpy bear with a cactus in his ass. Why? Because last night, once again, Wanda showed no interest in any romance. I mean, she wore a pretty nightgown, but it's like she was saying, "Hey look, I wore something nice to remind you what you can't have." Talk about mixed signals!

My mother-in-law, Marlene, who we affectionately call "Abuema", is staying with us for a month or so. This morning, she was up and making noise. I asked her to be quiet and not slam doors, but she retorted with, "Everyone should be up already." Excuse me? This is my house, my rules. Sometimes I feel like I'm nothing but a paycheck around here.

How many other guys feel this way? I'm sure I'm not alone. I decided to redirect some of my frustration into doing some manual labor around the house to distract myself from my emotional turmoil. Maybe some physical work will make me feel less frustrated. I drive up to Home Depot for supplies.

I came home and Wanda was awake. I hugged her tightly and squeezed her, telling her how much I loved her. But she got mad at me for something. Why do I even try? It's deflating to love her so much and have those feelings go unreciprocated. Does she not understand that I'm dealing with a lot of emotions since I resigned?

I know I sound bitter, and I am. It's been a long time for me and Wanda, and early in our marriage, we were the couple everyone was jealous of. I felt her love in everything she did, but then I started traveling all the time, and I know that created a wedge in our relationship. It will be a difficult transition for both of us, but my hope is in the coming months, we will find our pace again. I have given her everything she ever dreamed of, but it is never enough.

I decide the best way to my woman's heart is through authentic Mexican cuisine. So tonight, I make one of her favorites, Carne Asada, which literally translates from Spanish as "Grilled Meat". The food is awesome, and we dine like royalty. It is also family movie night and Wanda chooses a movie she grew up with called, *The Journey of Natty Gann.* Simply put, this is the worst movie I've ever seen. It was so bad that I will end up making fun of it for months to come, which hurts Wanda because I found out this movie meant a lot to her and her brothers.

None of this helps my current dilemma with my relationship with her. I can't shake the feeling that something is off with us. I left my job to be with her full time, but it feels more like she is annoyed at my presence. I wish there were more give and take in our relationship. I need her to reciprocate the attention I give her.

In the end, I said goodnight to the kids, feeling grateful for our time together. We prayed and gave thanks for all our blessings, especially the blessing of time. It's something we all cherish, and it's the reason I quit my job – to have more time with my family. The fact that my spouse and I are disconnected doesn't help, but we will have plenty of time now to work on things.

June 15, 2019

As part of our new agreement, I'm helping with the grocery shopping and taxiing the kids around. It's a bit of an adjustment, but I'm enjoying this domesticated side of myself. I am just one day short of getting a choker with a bell on it. Maybe Wanda will stop at the pet store and pick one up for me. Make it a black one, with some studs. I want to look cool.

I took Arielle to the Apple store. I personally don't understand the draw of the Apple brand. I think they make a great product, but I think other platforms offer similar if not better performance and options. But Arielle wants an iPhone.

I am always impressed with the power of branding and the lucrative revenue streams that are created by the ability to market your products to a loyal fan base. I catch myself thinking like a CEO for a minute. I understand the value of creating a great brand and I will do this with my new venture, but for now, I am taking a break. Man, I miss working.

Today, we hosted a Father's Day party with the family, and it was great to spend time with loved ones. As the night wound down, we said our goodbyes in our traditional family way. We kiss and hug and have our Italian/Mexican/Jewish goodbyes. First in the house, then at the door, once more on the patio and then of course, standing at the curb, waving goodbye to the cars as they leave.

This ritual has gone on in our family since we were kids. I can remember leaving my grandparents' home in Yonkers, NY, in the rain and snow, with them standing in the doorway waving to us as we left. I smile with this memory, remembering leaving in a particularly violent snowstorm, but knowing we were going to be ok, because Grandma and Grandpa waved us off, which in my young mind, was equivalent to an invisible protective shield that would carry us safely to the next dimension. In this case, that dimension was the Long Island Expressway, via the Throgs Neck Bridge, and home to our little Village in East Northport.

June 16, 2019, Father's Day

Woke up the third and final time. It's been a fitful night of aches and pains and restless sleep.

I lay in bed and read my Father's Day cards from Wanda and the kids. Wanda gave me $50, but I would gladly trade the cash in exchange for some alone time with her.

Ladies, the greatest gifts husbands give wives, and vice versa, is the gift of each other. But here I am, $50 richer. Money doesn't buy happiness, but in Asia, $50 can buy you a massage and a happy ending. I have been told this many times by locals and colleagues alike. I will pass.

At Sunday Mass. I pray for guidance, health, healing for others and peace. I really need the peace and comfort my faith brings because in these early days of restment, I need all the help I can get.

After mass, we go to my sister Krissy's house. This is the first Father's Day with all the family in 30 years. It is a special day, and it has been a real treat to have the whole family together again. For the first time in a long time, I feel like we are all "Home."

On the way home, even though we had an enjoyable time with family, Wanda and I fought. Father's Day is heading to an unhappy ending. There has been a quiet and uncomfortable tension between us since I quit. I am trying to be patient, but in all honesty, I am worried. I quit to be with her, but she doesn't seem like she is excited about this new arrangement.

I hate it when we fight. A lot of it is me. I am so lost, anxious, moody, and horny. I feel like a hormonal teenager some days lately. My emotions are all over the place.

She finally came to bed but there were no happy endings. Goodnight, Wanda. Remember, I quit to be with you and the kids. I have a small hint of regret building, predominately because of your behavior lately. I will be patient, but I hope this feeling goes away soon.

June 17, 2019

I am up early to head to the lake. I am taking my niece's boyfriend out for a dawn patrol on the Jet Skis. Maybe a little high speed, early morning riding will take the edge off my disappointment.

We fished, swam, ate and laughed, along with riding a long way. I feel better today. The lake and the ocean are two places that can melt all my stress and frustration.

We said our goodbyes and headed home. I was starving, so I stopped and grabbed some supermarket sushi. A step up from rest stop sushi, but risky just the same. I am fairly convinced this is how I will die. From bad gas station sushi. It used to be Chinese rest stops, where vendors sold everything from pig's feet to duck beaks, and now, it will be a package of tainted sushi that will kill me. I take my chances and scarf the raw fish as if it were my last meal. It very well may be.

Back home with Wanda and the kids, I take a shower and helped Cailyn with a science experiment. Not at the same time. Lol! Did you know that household beans like lentils and pintos will germinate? Me neither, but we are going to find out how. Together.

Guercios love movies. We love the experience of going, but for a family of 6, it's an expensive proposition. But all that aside, we head to a matinee showing of *Secret life of Pets 2*. The theatre is mostly empty, and I am surprised. Then, I realized it is Monday. I love this restment thing!!

This is why I quit. To be with them. I need to stop worrying and start enjoying myself. So far, this transition has been difficult. Another side of me, the CEO side, the businessperson, "Peter Graphite" is a man without a purpose. I hope to find some consulting work soon. Or purpose. Or both.

June 18, 2019 (My Mom's Birthday)

I always wake up early now. I am tired from yesterday and fell asleep early. I don't think Wanda is that into me right now. I am not sure why, but things feel off for us, and it saddens me.

I grab some coffee and drive to my mom's house after a battle with morning traffic. Traffic sucks. How do people deal with this? Oh yeah, they have to. I did too, and I will have to again, but for now, I do not deal with traffic. I had not realized this until now. Score one for quitting your job. No more traffic issues!

I knock but my mom doesn't answer the door, so I call her on the phone. It is her birthday today and she is 75 years young. She answers the phone and hangs up. I called back and she sounded surprised.

Peter: "Mom, it's me. I am here."

Mom: "Where are you?"

Peter: "I am in front of your door. At your house. Remember? I was coming over?"

Mom: "Oh yeah!! I am in the shower. Be there in a sec."

(Me, now waiting, wonders how she answered the phone in the shower. I check the doors, they are open. The security gate is too. My mom opens the front door in a towel.)

Mom: "I wasn't kidding, I was in the shower. I am naked."

Peter: "Yes, I see that. You wore your birthday suit!"

She pauses and then we both laugh. She tells me to go fishing while she gets ready. My mom and my stepdad, Rod, live in the same house she and my dad bought. It is on a community lake in a suburb of Phoenix. It has great fishing and I have loved coming here for years. In many ways, it feels like home.

It is times like these that remind me of the simple joy of being in the moment. Not worrying about Revenue reports, Forecasts, Budgets, and Strategy Presentations. No, in this new world, your mom answers the door in a towel and tells you to go fishing.

To the Dr. we go! Mom does not stop talking for the entire 35-minute ride through traffic. I missed her. She can talk all she wants. Hearing her voice makes me happy, as it always has.

After the Dr., I drop her off and drive through the neighborhood. It is an amazing drive, full of nostalgia. I spent a lot of time here growing up and the memories of my 20's are everywhere.

I drive across town to meet Wanda and the kids at a photo shoot for Arielle's senior pictures. Arielle looks so beautiful and grown up. The little ones and I play "True Surf" on my phone while we wait. I love this. I could never have done this when I was working.

I surprise Wanda and the kids by taking her to her favorite Indian food buffet. I am not a big fan of this food, and I will certainly be crapping the excrement of the Devil in 6-10 hours. The things we do for love.

Back home, I take the kids for a swim before bed. The cool water feels good on this hot night, even if the water temp is near 90 degrees. The outside temp is still 106. Ahh, thermal differential.

I put the kids to bed and then I try to put the moves on Wanda, but I have no moves apparently. I sit in my office, writing this, depressed that we have all this time and Wanda chooses to take it for granted.

Life is short. Don't waste moments, make them!

June 19, 2019

Wakey, Wakey, shake and bakey!!! I do not sleep past 6 anymore. I usually go to sleep between 10 PM and midnight. No matter what, I keep waking up at 6 AM, just like when I used to work.

I use this time to do some early morning shopping for landscape lights. Household projects will keep me sane.

Back home we ate breakfast and read a devotional. This story is about reaping what you sow. Plant bad seeds, grow bad plants. Plant good seeds, grow good plants. This applies in all aspects of life.

I spend some time writing, but my mind is wandering. I have an appointment at 2 PM with a financial advisor. I do not trust anyone, especially with my money. Growing up in NY taught me hard lessons. I learned a bunch more in Arizona. Trust is not given; it is earned. I am always cautious about giving others control of anything. It never ends well for me.

I met with the financial advisor. His heart is in the right place, but I wonder if he is as well versed in finance as he should be. I am considering just investing on my own. It would be helpful to have someone who could offer guidance, but I think I will just hold off for a while.

Later in the day our landscaper comes over to measure the side yard for a putting green. I have always wanted a backyard that has a putting green. We live in Arizona, so we can go out and use it all year long. This is one of those things I said I would do when I resigned, and I am going to make it a reality. Procrastination is dead!

June 20, 2019

This morning, I am picking my cousin Mike up for Golf with Grandpa Rod and friends. It is early, and I am tired. I am working on approximately 4 hours of sleep.

Driving to Mikes, I can see the Woodbury Fire out east is still burning strong, and the smoke rises ominously providing an eerie backdrop to the Superstition Mountains. I have never seen these forest fires so close, and I begin to worry they will spread into populated areas.

We greet everyone with hugs, and the hope of a good round, but as we all tee up and tee off, we say goodbye to hope. We are all miserable. There are 5 of us, sucking at a variety of levels. I have seen better golf being played by children.

As the hot, arid morning drudges on, I see moments of brilliance through the thick, lingering stench of suckitude. The moments are marginal at best. After a series of great putts for me, and a variety of almost golf-like shots from others, the round ends.

Or so I thought. We decided to go around a second time. Why? What did I do wrong? Apparently, we are gluttons for punishment. But then, something magical begins to happen.

I have found my lost golf swing. All I had to do was stop thinking! Full disclosure, it has been a year since I last played. I missed golf, and I used to be good. I plan to play more often, and my goal is to become a scratch golfer. I am currently a nineteen handicap.

At home, I peel off the clothes that stick in places they shouldn't and take a rejuvenating shower that brings me back to life. Afterwards, I go downstairs and make something to eat, and drink half a gallon of water. I think I will live.

Wanda is getting ready to take Arielle to the Dr. and she looks gorgeous. I try and get her alone to make out, but she wants nothing to do with me. She is rushed and not in the mood for my antics. Actions speak louder than words, though. Be available for your partner. If you say you love someone, you need to show them, not just say the words. 5 minutes is all it takes to make someone feel important.

Wanda leaves and I have some time to hang out with the kids and write some of this book, but that only lasts for an hour, as I am now feeling bad. I am sick, feverish and flu-ish. My stomach is loudly grumbling and gurgling, and I am sleepy. I don't know what is going on, but I am a mess.

It is an ugly scene in my bathroom, with bouts of pooping and vomiting. It is food poisoning or some type of stomach bug. It's two exits, no waiting and I just ran out of toilet paper. I am a disaster. Amid this chaos, I say terrible things to Wanda who continues to show no compassion towards me. I do not understand her sometimes. Zero empathy. A heart of stone. The good news is I pass out at some point, preventing me from having to deal with another second of this agony.

June 21, 2019

I woke up for the 9th time. I look over at Wanda who is sound asleep. We fought last night but I can't stay mad at her. I rolled over and put my arm around her. I love her but she makes me so mad sometimes. Later, we take showers, separate ones of course. The irony is that I quit my job to be with her, and I have never felt further apart.

I go to pick up Ben from his sleepover. I am feeling horrible and beaten up, but I promised I would pick him up, and I kept my word.

This is my mantra. Do what you say you will, and don't break your promises.

We came back home, and I rested. I need it. I cannot get up. I am so weak. While I lay in bed, Wanda is packing for a trip to Mexico with Arielle. I hope the time apart will help both of us. Ben and Cailyn will stay, and Abuema has been here with us, so it will be nice to have her here while Wanda is away.

After some rest, I dragged myself to Walmart to get the rest of the lights and a plant. This is what I do to myself. I ignore the fact I am sick and try to soldier forward. It is a foolish trait. One I learned from my father, who would never take time off when he was sick. The only time that man was down, is when he was in traction due to a significant issue with his bulging disk. The original Ironman, and the apple doesn't fall too far from the tree.

There is a famous story of when I broke my shin bone water skiing. I refused to admit I was hurt and powered through for another day until I went to the doctor. He told me I had fractured my tibia when I fell on the ski going 30 MPH. He was preparing to cast it, but I told him he couldn't, because I was a drummer, and I had a show that night. He looked at me with astonishment. "You understand your leg is fractured, correct?" I said, "Yes, but we have a show tonight. Just give me a soft cast and I will deal with this myself." And I did. Painfully, not heroically.

After a long day, Cailyn is relentlessly going on about how I promised her a bike ride. I tell her no, because I don't feel good, but she cries that I don't keep my promises, even though I said to, "Always keep your promise". I am being fed my own teaching, and it tastes as bad as the Sushi I ate a few days ago.

After much drama and arguing, I am riding a bike. The seat massages my tender butt in a way that makes me want to poop with every peddle. The things we do for our kids. We rode for 2 sweaty miles and afterwards, I needed a wet wipe and a "Tucks" medicated pad.

Everyone goes upstairs to get changed. I am going to rest and write. Our neighbor Terry mentions to me his mechanic may want to buy the

Lexxus Arielle wrecked after an unwise decision of texting and driving. I guess we will see what happens. I like that I am leaving myself open to letting things work out on their own. This is not my modus operandi. I am a guy that drives things to my will. Laying back has never been my strong suit, but here I am, laying.

June 22, 2019

I spent the day fixing things that were broken around the house. It was a productive day, and I enjoyed the satisfaction of checking off the boxes on my extensive list of tasks. I did some yard work and then headed to my cousin Mike's for a few drinks.

On the way home, I picked up our boat. I was excited for an early lake day tomorrow, a 5 AM dawn patrol, with my friend and former employee, Kirk Fisher. He's known as "Cubby" due to his likeness to a baby bear, but more so because of his tendency to come into a delicate situation and rip things apart like a bear cub who has been trapped in a campsite. Cubby is a former Marine, stout and strong. He is an awesome person, likeable and funny. I love hanging out with him because I can be myself. He knows the real me.

I know I must wake up early, but here I am, writing this book at 12:43 AM. I'll regret this decision in about 4 hours when it's time to wake up, but for now, I am just focused on putting my thoughts to paper. Writing this book has become a cornerstone of every day, and while it sometimes keeps me from my much-needed sleep, it has become a great therapeutic relief to the stress and anxiety I feel.

June 23, 2019

I woke up, but it's so early and I am so tired, I can't go to the bathroom. I am going to a lake that has exactly zero bathrooms. I am a little worried about this fact. I don't do well in strange places of defecation.

I met Cubby at the supermarket on the way to the lake. There is an eerie red glow in the air, as the Woodbury Fire continues to burn close by.

We drive towards the lake, and it is a crazy scene of smoky fire residue and plumes of smoke. Thick, billowing red smoke, which is still dropping red hot, embers. We drive quietly and with concern. We are driving into a forest fire to go boating. Let that sink in for a second.

We arrive at the Laguna Boat Launch at Canyon Lake. It is a beautiful and picturesque cove at the east end of the lake. It has a 3-lane boat ramp and parking for about one hundred cars. It sits in between two large mountains and overlooks the southeast end of the lake.

We arrive to find a scene from the Apocalypse. We park and get out of the truck, but as we do, we are met with hot ash falling all around us. Rain would be a better description.

As we stand here to take in the scene, we realize it isn't just ash, it's burning embers. We discuss the possibility of leaving, but that's what cowards do, so we rig the boat and push off, heading deeper into the maelstrom that is Canyon Lake during the Woodbury fire. Let's go boating!!

This is why I like Cubby. He followed me into the firestorm many times when we were teammates at GMSI. Today, he would still follow me into the fire. You don't meet people like that very often. Cherish them and feed them beer and cheap, supermarket sushi.

We boat and fish in the clouds of a firestorm, the filtered and smoky sunlight casting a red glow and weird shadows. As the wind shifts, we find ourselves trapped here in the cove at the northernmost end of the lake, smoke and embers racing towards us down the steep canyon walls.

Burning ash fills our lungs, raining on the boat, and burning the hairs on our arms. It's time to go, and not a moment too soon as the wind picks up, making our precarious anchorage a deathtrap.

We count our blessings and drive swiftly to the safety of civilization. Fishing is over for today. (The Woodbury fire would end up burning over 123,000 acres over the course of 2 weeks.)

At home, resting after our fire boating session, Cailyn comes to me and tells me she doesn't feel good. Her neck and face are hot. She has a fever. Never a dull moment here at the Guercio Asylum.

Cailyn's fever doesn't break, so off I go to get her medicine. I hate it when the kids are sick; I feel helpless to make them feel better. I give her medicine, hug Abuema goodbye, and head back out to church with Ben. It's Sunday and church is our weekly appointment with God. We don't miss it, as we have a lot to be thankful for, and I need my weekly visit to give thanks, and to reflect. Most of all, to seek guidance and a path--the path I am supposed to be on, and the one I continually pray for.

Later, Cailyn's fever finally breaks. Thank God. I hate to see her not feel well. There is no more helpless feeling than not being able to help your kids when they are ill.

I tuck the kids in and say our prayers, Tomorrow is a new day of possibility.

Wanda calls from Mexico, and I am glad to hear her voice. I miss her, and even though we were fighting when she was leaving, I am over it, and I tell her I love her and miss her. Despite everything I may write about her, and our lives, I love her more than words can say. Wanda and the kids are the primary focus of my life.

June 24, 2019

I slept well last night. I must have been tired, and it was my first good sleep in a long time. The "Sleep of the dead", as my grandma used to call it.

I need to go to the Doctor today. I have developed some alarming spots on my head, arms, and legs. I am worried, but not overly concerned. I also wanted to talk about my moods, non-sleep, anxiety, and other stuff going on in my now resigned person.

He says I am normal, whatever that means. He burns some growths off, like warts, but more like skin tags. The liquid nitrogen stings and the smell of burning skin makes me nauseous. He insists I am in good shape and gives me a referral to a dermatologist and a foot Dr. for my ankle and Achilles, which haven't been right since I dislocated my ankle in October of 2018.

On the way home, Wanda called me to let me know our friends Kathy and Dan had another incident. This time, they arrested Kathy, a Mexican woman who is here without proper documentation, and take her to Florence Prison to be detained. Florence is a small city about 40 miles southeast of our house. There is a federal prison as well as an ICE detention center.

Immigration is involved now, and Wanda asks me to shelter Kathy. I don't want to, but I know she needs our help. I am upset because Wanda seems to jump to help other people, but sometimes forgets there is a guy named Peter who needs her compassion as well.

It makes me sad how little interest she shows in me these past few weeks. I am going through a major life change, to be with her, and it's as if she doesn't really care.

I want her to be happy, but she hasn't put any effort into our relationship lately, and then, blames me for everything wrong. I am hurt and disappointed she never sees my side of things. Now, she wants me to get involved in someone else's drama. Don't we have enough on our plate?

June 25, 2019

I had a difficult night feeling disconnected from Wanda. She wore a beautiful nightgown but showed no interest in any romance. I am confused and feel like I'm receiving mixed signals. It's like she's reminding me of what I can't have.

No matter, there is work to do. I finish a variety of chores, and afterwards, I take a shower and do some manscaping. It's bathing suit season and I don't want to be flaunting a "crotch afro," just in case I get lucky.

We eat dinner as a family and have a fun time chatting and laughing. After dinner, I let everyone know that I'll be in my office writing for a while. A while could be 20 minutes or 6 hours, depending on the day.

"My definition of wealth. Money buys things, love fills your soul. "

After three hours of writing, I headed to the bedroom. I am surprised, but Wanda and I connect with a little romance. It is amazing, as always. I don't think she will ever understand how much she means to me, or that our time together is the most important thing to me. More than anything money could buy. More than any accolade I will ever receive. I just want to love her and be loved. That is my definition of wealth. Money buys things, love fills your soul.

June 26, 2019

I wake up in a better place emotionally. Wanda and I had a good talk, and we are even discussing going away together, just the two of us, so I start looking at vacations for us. I want to go somewhere tropical, with a beach and adult beverages with umbrellas.

This morning, I was enlisted as a homeschool helper. Wanda is the real teacher; I am just here to observe and assist. It's all good, and I enjoy being together as a family. That is the real benefit of homeschooling. You set the tone for a child's educational environment.

The day is spent schooling, researching vacation ideas, and watching a movie.

As we lay in bed, I am talking with Wanda and the weight of my exhaustion is heavy. We are having a conversation, and I fall asleep on her in midsentence. There is a danger in this, as she is a night owl, and I fear when she is mad at me, I will be vulnerable in this state. I am sleeping with one eye open from now on! I am kidding of course, I think.

June 27, 2019

I woke up and started to work on travel plans for our vacation. I am excited to get away with Wanda, just the two of us. It's been a long time since we have been away, and I think this is just the kind of break we need to reconnect. Raising kids and homeschooling is a huge burden on a romantic marriage. By the end of the day, we are exhausted. Not the optimum climate for romance.

I always tell my single friends, if you ever want to evaluate your relationship prior to marriage, babysit a small child for the weekend. This is the true litmus test for couples and should be mandatory prior to marriage. A sick baby, replete with green diarrhea and vomiting should be the gold standard for relationship trials.

I am late for my health insurance appointment! I took a quick shower and ran out the door. After almost 30 years of company sponsored Insurance, we are on our own. I am nervous about the cost of being self-insured. For a family of 5, in this post Obamacare world, I expect to pay as much as $1500 a month for basic insurance. How is this affordable care, again? Our house payment is just a little more than that. The insurance meeting is an eye-opening experience. I was very lucky to have good insurance all these years, and now, I am going to find out firsthand how lucky I was. I shared the news with Wanda. In the end, we agree that insurance is risk mitigation, and we will shop for a more inclusive plan later in the year.

For the time being, we tell the kids to lay low and no activities that could involve an ER visit.

June 28, 2019

It's Lake Day, and I am going to see if I can catch a fish or two.

Any hopes of catching a fish are lost within the first hour, but this is better than being on a plane, or at the office. After an unsuccessful morning of fishing, I found a quiet cove and jumped into the water to cool off. I lay in the water, which according to my depth gauge, is 111 feet deep. I float quietly, thinking about life and what will come next. I hope it will not be the ever-elusive lake shark that lurks beneath me, even if it is a figment of my imagination.

Wanda calls and wants me to come home so she can run some errands, which is fine; I am done here anyway. I have caught nothing, but time alone has helped me unwind and calm my inner craziness. I still feel guilty about leaving my employees, but I am starting to make peace with the situation.

This whole transition is difficult. I lived a certain life for almost 30 years, dreaming of the morning I am having right now, but I still feel the pull of being the CEO, of being a caretaker. I need to get into a better mindset, but I know old habits are hard to break. I hope my team at GMSI remembers how much I care about them, and how much I miss them.

I finalize our vacation. I am excited about getting away together. Wanda needs a break as badly as I do, but the excitement doesn't last long, and Wanda and I are fighting again. Something is missing between us, but I can't put my finger on it. It feels like she is mad at me all the time. Maybe we are spending too much time together. I hear stories of how couples divorce after the man retires because they drive each other crazy. Too much time together sometimes exposes the personality traits we overlook in our mates. The traits that gnaw at us, that drive us insane.

We each go our separate ways. There are no good night kisses, no hugs, and no joy in Guercioville tonight.

June 29,2019

I don't sleep anymore, which drives both Wanda and I crazy. As an offering of peace, I offer to make her breakfast, but she doesn't want anything. I tried, babe. I always try. Wanda leaves and I go grab some things for breakfast at the store. I am feeling a little depressed. I gave up everything I worked for to be with my family, but my wife seems to lack any interest in me.

I am not sure how to deal with all this, so I will immerse myself in projects to fill my time. I will also throw myself into writing this book. I am sure she will read these entries and be mad at me all over again, but this is a book about massive change, and with change comes conflict. I hope we can get past all this animosity.

Wanda is on the phone. She is always on the phone now, trying to help Kathy and her horrible situation. I fear Kathy will be deported and Dan will do nothing. He wanted to be out of their relationship anyway. What a perfect scenario for him. I would never leave my wife to suffer, no matter what. Think about what this is doing to your kids, Dan.

"I need things that bring me a feeling of completion...I need a purpose."

I go back out to cut the lawn and Wanda takes her mom shopping. I am starting to really enjoy the yardwork and being outside. It's been a long time since I have had the time or freedom to dedicate my efforts towards my own house or my own family. I relish the afternoon heat, and the feeling of accomplishment as I drag the lawnmower back and forth on our lawn, creating linear patterns that resemble a bar chart from my former life. I realize that I need things that bring me a feeling of completion. I need to finish tasks. I need a purpose.

It's what I have done for the past 30 years and now, away from the role of business leader, I am carving out a new life, one where I find smaller tasks to complete. They are simpler ones, but the results are just the same for me psychologically. I am learning a lot about myself, and many things I am not sure I really wanted to know.

Wanda comes home with a roasted chicken, and I make an impromptu dinner while she stays on her phone trying to organize some way to help Kathy. I am going to be honest. I am starting to feel like our roles are reversing, and I am not sure I like it.

Once again, we fight, and I go to bed angry. This is a recurring theme in this new, "restment" world. I am frequently met with regret about my resignation. I think to myself, "This isn't how it was supposed to be!" But the sad reality is that this is exactly how it is.

There is no going back, so I will focus on looking forward, overcoming these adversities and look to better times, better days, and better feelings.

I am sure Wanda is stressed about Kathy, and homeschool planning and a myriad of other things, and I am sure my daily presence is something we are both getting used to. I really think we need to communicate our expectations better, or this is going to be a recurring theme in this strange new world of not working.

June 30, 2019

I hate the way things are. I am most disappointed that the one person I really want and need in my life right now is the one that is least present. She assured me the life we wanted was on the other side of retirement. It wasn't, and it made me feel betrayed.

She painted a picture of me being liberated from the stress and anxiety of my work life, but instead, I traded that stress in for disappointment at home, and a wife who was anything but present when I needed her. She promised me heaven and I got Bayonne, NJ. And so, ends this first month out of the cage and off the hamster wheel.

We cast our expectations to others around us, but they do not always accept our expectations as their reality.

Maybe I made a mistake in leaving my career? But it's too late to turn back. I made my bed, and now I am lying in it.

2

July, 2019

July 1, 2019

I slept horribly. I hate going to sleep hurt and mad. I am swallowing my heart daily. Wanda is unsupportive and focused on the drama of Kathy, oblivious to my own strife.

I am taking Arielle to Canyon Lake for some Jet skiing. My solace these days is on the water with people I love. The peace and tranquility of nature replaces the acidic bitterness that now resides in my heart. I have realized that taking people to the lake brings them joy, and in turn, replenishes my own.

I want to adopt Arielle. She has been my "step" daughter for the past 11 years, but I think she should have the choice of being a Guercio if she wants to be. I asked Arielle if she was interested in me adopting her. She hesitates and says nothing. I tell her to think about it. I am sure after all these years, she knows I consider her my own, but if it is important to her, I want her to know I want to make it official. Blended families deal with a different set of circumstances, and I want her to know she is not my "step" anything. She is my kid, whether she has the same last name or not.

The day is a blur, but later, I feel horrible. Between not sleeping last night, an early start to the lake, 5 hours of Jet Skiing, the meds I am taking, the sadness from the disconnect in my marriage, or just total mental and physical exhaustion, I am shutting down. My neck and back hurt. My head is swimming. I am bloated and gassy from a medium "Cotton Candy Blizzard" from DQ, momentarily forgetting I am severely lactose intolerant. Who wouldn't want some of that? Maybe I need to reconsider why Wanda isn't more amorous towards me. It could be because...I am an aging fartbox.

July 2, 2019

I am up and listening to Wanda softly snore. I need her warmth, her heart, and her body. I roll over and scoop her into my arms, my hands working around her body to pull her close to me. Her warmth envelopes me like a warm blanket on a cold night. I love her every curve like a fat kid loves cake. I pull her close and match her breathing, feeling her heartbeat and rhythmic breath, I fall deep asleep.

I wake up startled, with Wanda still pressed against me, our bodies intertwined and molded perfectly into each other. She fits me like no one ever has. I run my hands over her hips and legs, back up to rest in the small of her back. I breathe deep and fall back to sleep.

An hour later, our dog, a 110lb. Shepherd mix rescue named "Wally the Wonder Dog", starts barking. Wanda screams for him to shut up in her calmest voice. I smile. She rolls over into me and we return to our regularly scheduled snuggle. Welcome back Wanda!

I kiss her cheek and go downstairs to make coffee. Please God, make today a better day for us.

While sitting on the toilet, I answer emails. I am not sure why I do this, but there is great clarity in working while pooping. It is very cleansing in more ways than one. I am extremely focused and present in these moments.

When I was working, I would write messages from the throne at 5:45 AM. My teammates knew after many years, and by my own admittance, that I was writing them whilst enjoying my morning constitutional. I had immediate focus on the tasks we needed to complete, and I would write thoughts about a project, or instructions on a topic. They laughed and said, "We always know when you write us from the can".

I am writing today, but I am also watching Wanda school with the kids. She is patient, smart and amazing. I have always seen her as the most beautiful girl in the world, and I hate it when we are not connected. It throws everything else in my life off. She may be my "pH." She keeps me balanced.

I believe authoring a book is about capturing your moments of clarity. I set aside time to write, but sometimes it doesn't feel genuine. It feels forced, so I have learned in these moments to just walk away. It keeps me from trying to write things I must, rather than what I feel organically.

We are trying to get the kids to go to sleep, but they have other ideas. I don't get mad because there were many years I was in a foreign country and our bedtime kisses were done via Skype. I remind myself how lucky I am right now, but I still want to give them Benadryl and Melatonin with a sidecar of Dramamine.

Prayers are said, and I tuck them in and tell them how much I love them. I remind them how lucky we are to have this time together. Tomorrow we are going to the lake. We thank God for the blessing of each other, and the time to share every day together.

July 3, 2019

Ben greets me as I head downstairs. He is up and dressed and fed the dog. I guess they really want to go to the lake. In no time, we are on the water and on our way. It is a beautiful morning, even if it is a little hot. Ok, it is very hot, but no matter, we are here, the kids are happy, and we are used to the intense heat of the desert.

Many of my friends and clients from around the world have asked me, "How do you live in a place that is so hot all summer long?" My answer is always the same, "Pretty darn good! We just invest in good sunscreen and air conditioning."

The kids and I took a long ride to the back of the lake. They kept begging me to "Blow up the tube!" "The Tube" is a 2-person, inflated vehicle of death when tied to a speeding boat. We are at Saguaro Lake today, and this is a perfect place for dragging your children around, tied to a speeding boat. What could go wrong? I whip them relentlessly as they cackle wildly, spilling them occasionally from the speeding tube for added drama. Mission accomplished.

Back at the beach, they swim and explore and laugh constantly. I am just watching the kids, as they don their goggles and dive under the murky green water to chase Bluegill and shad. "This is why I left my job", I keep thinking to myself. This is exactly why I left my job, to be here, with them, doing something other than worrying about making the next million dollars for others.

All this turning and jostling has made my neck hurt so badly, but my wife is not a caretaker. While I am quick to massage her aches and pains, it's a bit of a one-way street. I am reminded of a story that best explains this element of interpersonal relationships in a way that resonates with me to this day.

I was on a plane over the Aleutian Islands on my way to China in 2015. There was a movie trailer playing on the entertainment screen in my seat. I wasn't really paying attention until one of the actresses said, "In love, there is the loved and the lover. The loved always has the upper hand." I can't find the movie that the quote is from, but it sounds very Shakespearean to me.

It is true and can be applied to many situations other than a love relationship. This quote has stayed with me since the day I heard it many years ago. And I guarantee, many of you can relate. It's always best to be the "Loved".

July 4, 2019

Big surprise, I am up early. I always wake up at 5 or 6 now. I hate that I have all this time now, and I can't sleep. Old habits die hard. The positive takeaway? I watch a lot of sunrises.

I make coffee and feed the dogs. This is my new ritual, like the old one, just without me having to jump in my vehicle and drive to work. I drove to Walgreens for some Icy Hot. My neck still hurts, and I need something more than a massage. I also want to smell as old as I feel, so it's a win-win.

I dive back into bed to snuggle with the kids and Wanda. I am going to make us all breakfast being it is July 4th, and it is a day to celebrate freedom! The freedom of the country, and in some sense, my own.

After breakfast, I change into my board shorts and head to the backyard for some swimming and exercise. I have gotten so fat over the years, sitting in planes and desks. I have vowed to get back into "surfing" shape, like I was in the mid 2000's, when I was surfing regularly. It is a tough road back. I am much older, and much more broken, but my commitment to feeling better drives me to keep going. And, if I am in better shape, maybe Wanda will take a deeper interest in our sex life. Or not. Either way, I will be in better shape, and that can't be all bad.

After a swim and workout, I sit down to write. I get a good 2 hours of work prior to dinner. I find that my work ethic hasn't changed, just my title and my location.

Later that night we raced up the street to watch fireworks. I look around to see my family smiling and watching the show, their happy faces illuminated by the brilliant lights of the fireworks. This is why I left my job. I will make this statement 14000 times over the next 12 months.

When we finally got home after battling the traffic from the show, everyone headed for bed. We are exhausted and I feel like I have no energy. I admit to myself that the pace of the past 11 years has damaged my stamina, but I am happy. It's Independence Day, and this year that statement means more to me than it ever has in the past. I am independently unemployed. Off the Hamster Wheel and running free!

July 5, 2019

Today is what some might call a "lazy" day, but in our newfound state of restment, we like to think of it as a well-deserved break. We decided to hit the lake with the kids, once again. Hey, why not? We don't have any other pressing engagements to attend to, do we?

But, as usual, the day is not without its challenges. Wanda and I seem to be fighting more and more lately, and the tension in the house is palpable. I left everything behind to be with her, but sometimes it feels like she doesn't want me here. We need to figure this out because, as of today, I've only been home for 28 days, which also happens to be the same length of time as a women's menstrual cycle. Coincidence? Nope. Her periods end sentences, not menstrual cycles, so I assume the problem is me. I am her cramping and bloating.

July 6, 2019

Today I cut lawns, front and back. It is a hefty undertaking, a job for a professional, not some guy who is recently unemployed. After the yardwork was finished, I stopped by my niece's house to buy her inflatable Kayak. This is the precursor to terror as I plan on taking it out on the sea at our house in Kino Bay, Mexico. Pray for my safe return. All I can envision is the scene from Hemingway's *Old Man and the Sea*, where the fisherman is dragged to sea by the giant fish. This fits perfectly for my dramatic death at sea. I am kidding, I think...

After my niece's, I stopped at my cousin Mike's house. He is a great man, and I am proud of him. He is a former NYPD officer and a 9-11 first responder. He also became the captain of his volunteer fire unit. He is that guy. To me, a real hero. He looks like me, bald and beautiful with the big Italian eyes, but he is a special person. The kind that runs in when everyone is running out. I take that part from him, but he is steps above me in the valor department.

Michelle is his wife, but his girlfriend since they were teenagers. She is smart, funny, kind and sensitive with a great and wise outlook on life. She idolizes Mike and that makes me love her more. I am glad they are happy in their new Arizona home.

After some daytime cocktails, I left my cousins and headed home. Once there, Wanda suggests we go to a movie and dinner. We just fought, so this will be challenging for both of us. I know she wants to stab me in the throat but is refraining. That's true love, when you want to kill your spouse, but refrain because you are hungry and want to see a movie. Wanda and I are both headstrong, and the fact remains, neither of us is willing to give an inch when we think we are right.

We fought at dinner, so much so that we had the waiter wrap up sushi to-go. Keep in mind, it's summer in the desert, and we are taking sushi to go, so it can sit in a hot car while we watch a movie. Some lessons are harder to learn than others.

"Love is complicated, and so is bipolar disorder. I am confused some days which one of those we suffer from. "

We continue to fight all the way to the movies, to the point where once we park, we are almost screaming at each other. We are going to miss the movie. Honestly, I just want to grab her right now and strangle her, but at the same time, I want to grab her and kiss her hard.

Love is complicated, and so is bipolar disorder. I am confused some days which one of those we suffer from.

We both argue our points vehemently, but nothing seems to be resolved. I hold her hand as we walk, part of my psychological warfare. I am not sure if she wants to, but I am the peacemaker. She comments often that I can be over something in 5 minutes whereas she can take from a few hours to a few weeks. I do not hold that kind of grudge. It is unhealthy and it creates other issues, but mostly it is boring and childish. Bottom line, life is short; don't hold resentment.

After the movie, we went home, got in bed and kissed goodnight. I was surprised. We have not really liked each other lately, but she rolled over and said I should kiss her. I am really concerned about our relationship. Can it stand this test of togetherness? So far, we are not very good at this togetherness thing. I am quietly looking at trips to Uranus.

July 7, 2019

This morning, I am helping a friend in need. Her husband died unexpectedly and left their estate in probate. His family members are fighting her, and the court is freezing all assets. I feel so bad for her. It is hard enough to lose your mate, but even harder when you must mourn the loss, and fight for your own marital assets. I pray for a speedy resolution. She is desperate for help, so I offer my assistance, financially. She needs it, and I am happy to help her.

God teaches us to give, and to help those who need it. I have been burned many times helping people who asked, but I still do it. My dad used to give money to people on the street when we lived in NY, and I would ask him, "Why?" He answered, "Who am I to judge? If he has to ask for help, then he must need it." That message never left me.

It's church day and I am not motivated to do anything today. I swim with the kids several times through the day, and I spend hours looking at stock trends and writing random thoughts. I need to figure out a way to make some passive income for us or we will surely run out of money in a few years. The problem for me is simple. I don't have confidence in the markets, which makes investment planning difficult.

We're always running late in this house, and it's no different on this Sunday morning. Showers are a mad scramble as we rush to get ready for church. I hate being late, but it seems to be a recurring theme for us. Despite the rush, I love going to church. It's a chance to connect with God and reflect on the week.

Later, Wanda and I talked in bed. The tension is still palpable, but I try to ease it by giving her a massage. Unfortunately, it seems like she's still distant, and it's a real bummer. We were always so rock-solid in the romance department, and the thought of losing that connection gets more depressing by the night.

July 8, 2019

Wanda leaves with her mom for a doctor's appointment and I decide to call my mom to say a "quick" hello. A 5-minute conversation is finished in an hour and 45 minutes. I love my mother, Cory. She never has a lack of words, and she likes to use all of them.

I wake the kids and get them breakfast. It is school time! We have been homeschooling our kids since 2018. There is good and bad in all this, but the best part is being able to shed the confines of a rigorous and rigid public-school schedule, as well as teaching our ideals, not those of the modern public-school regime. We school when and where we want. Flexibility is an amazing learning tool. I wish more parents would consider the benefits of homeschooling.

Public schools are outdated, designed to create factory workers for an industrial society that doesn't exist anymore. I firmly believe we need to take a hard look at our education system and provide students with learning tools that will help them succeed in real life, not just academics. What good is a kid that can do algebra, but doesn't know how to manage their own finances?

We start school using the schedule that is meticulously organized by Wanda. The kids know exactly what to do, and I will admit, Wanda is great at this home-schooling thing. I am just the substitute teacher.

Abuema and Wanda come back from the Doctor and Abuema seems no worse for the wear. I hugged her and let her know I love her. I ask the most important question you can ask after an exploratory procedure like a colonoscopy. "Can you still cook, Mama?" Laughter ensues.

Wanda and I kiss, and I leave to pick up the last remaining personal item from GMSI, my drums. My dad bought them for me in 1984, and I played them professionally until 2000. These drums are my last connection to him, other than his golf clubs. I am not sure why these things matter. He isn't in them, but to me, they are my last physical tie to him.

I drove the route to work for the first time since I left work. The route I had taken so many times seems familiar, but foreign as well. I am going without a real purpose, just to pick something up. How many times have I driven this road to get to work to invent something, or have a big meeting, or sell the company. So many times, I drove stressed about a work situation, and now, on a gloriously sunny Monday at 1:15 PM, I am just a guy who used to own the company, driving to my former workplace to get my drums. The feeling is surreal yet calming.

I arrived at my former place of employment, and I am greeted warmly. As I look around, I am shocked to find they have not made any of the improvements we budgeted for since I left. Sadly, I feel like they will fail. They lack something I know they need. Heart and commitment.

"Culture eats strategy for breakfast!" is what Peter Drucker says. I agree. They do not know how to fix the problems they have. I do, but I relinquished my position as CEO, and it's not my place to offer guidance anymore. Some of the problems are related directly to the people in charge. They do not understand what we do, and they do not understand what we created. They don't understand the employees or the culture I built. They don't get it because they do not understand the importance of these elements, and ultimately, they will fail because of it.

I loved my clients in a very sincere way. As well, my employees, vendors, bankers, lawyers, investors (Some days, usually on an exit) and CPA's. The current management does not understand that we created something dedicated to our industry and our clients. It succeeded even when it failed because it learned and believed it could be better. And then we made it better.

"The most important thing you can develop in a business is strong relationships."

We cared about each other, about our products and most of all, about the best interests of the clients. The new culture? Metrics, strategy, and a cold relationship with the industry. The most important thing you can develop in a business is strong relationships. And here, at the place that was built by relationships, they are dying, and they don't even know their heart stopped beating. Yet.

Later in the day, we saw the movie *Toy Story 4* and it made me cry. It made me think of all the things we let go of that we can't go back to, including our childhood. I cried partially because it represented a weird change in my life too. Woody left the kids in favor of love and adventure with a new girl in a new place. I left a job for a new girl, my wife, in favor of love and adventure. They never talk about the need for residual income in animated films. They all end happily ever after, and it is assumed everything will be taken care of. I wish real life worked like that.

July 9, 2019

I wake up to the sound of my alarm blaring, but I am quickly silenced by Wanda's gentle nudge. I wrap my arms around her and take a deep breath, relishing the feeling of her warm body next to mine. But alas, it's time to get ready for golf.

I grabbed my trusty cup of Kauai Coffee Company's Koloa Plantation blend and headed out to meet my cousin Mike. We're playing at Augusta Ranch today, supposedly the best 18-hole Executive course in the valley.

We paid up and hit a few balls on the range. It does not look as ugly as I have seen us hit before, but it is not pretty, either. It is like a passed out, drunk cheerleader. She still looks ok, but you do not want to kiss her for fear she will throw up in your mouth.

We are a twosome and they put us behind a threesome of ladies over 65. Maybe over 75. They are playing slowly. One is barefoot and she stops in the fairway adjacent to ours to tell me the story of Sam Snead playing barefoot and winning the PGA championship. She also smells of last night's Vodka and sex toys.

It is 10am and it is 108 degrees. It is going to be a long day.

We are playing fast and not that bad. We catch up to Bea Arthur and her Golden Girls again. This time they waved us onto the green from the tee box. Cool! They are letting us play through. This should open things up. I swear that one of them told Mike he had a nice ass, those saucy dames!

We finished eighteen holes of hot and sweaty golf. It is a nice course, great greens, but too short for me. I need to play a Championship course. Mike shot 74 and I shot an 86. Par is not 72 though, I found out it is 60. Scratch golf is going to take a lot of practice.

Back at home, Wanda is schooling the kids while I write. Dinner is uneventful, except for the fact that Panini is here! It is great to catch up with my brother-in-law and share some laughs.

As we say goodnight to the kids and head to bed, I hold onto hope that the romance between Wanda and I will reignite soon. She falls asleep on me again, but I don't mind, and I can't help but feel grateful for this quiet moment together. Clothing and all. Goodnight, babe.

July 10, 2019

I wake up to another morning filled with weird dreams. It's like trying to sleep on a local train in Japan - you're constantly stopping and starting. I make coffee for me and Jesús, and we head to Canyon Lake for some Jet Skiing.

The drive up is gorgeous, with the Superstition Mountains providing a stunning backdrop. Jesús and I sing along to classic rock, the volume much too loud for this hour of the morning, but we don't care. We're happy to be alive.

We had breakfast and beers on the beach, enjoying the stunning Tonto National Forest scenery. The water is a chilly 65 degrees, but we don't let that stop us from splashing around like a couple of 6-year-olds.

After breakfast, we take a long ride around the lake, exhausted by the time we make it back to the docks. But before we head back, I take Jesús to be baptized, lake-style. It's a tradition I made up - new riders must jump in the 105-foot-deep water near the head of the dam. Jesús takes the plunge, and I do the same. It's a little spooky but refreshing.

My own anxieties fueling my comedic outburst, I pretend I am pulled under water by something, and burst out of the water, gasping for air like a man on the verge of drowning. "Jesús!! Get out of the water!! It's a Lake Shark!" I scream at the top of my lungs. The words are absurd even as they spill from my mouth, but I can't shake the feeling that there's something lurking beneath the surface, something massive and hungry and very, very real.

As we get back on our skis, terrified and cackling, my phone starts chiming repeatedly, and I realize it's bad news. My employee, Eddie Arroyo, has died of a heart attack. I'm floored. Eddie was a good soul, and I immediately regret leaving the company. I feel guilty for leaving my people, leaving Eddie. I'm sorry, bro. I love you and thank you for your warmth and your helpful nature. Knowing you made me a better person.

The rest of the day is a blur, filled with texts and phone calls about Eddie's death. I try to write my feelings down, but it's tough. I deeply cared about everyone I interacted with during my 30-year career, and now they're dying, and I'm not there for them or their families and the guilt is overwhelming. This argument has happened often since I left. I fight with myself and my guilt. I am not sure how to stop. I couldn't do anything to prevent Eddies death, but the guilt I feel in not being there for my team is an immensely heavy burden. I am landscaping while they are suffering.

After dinner, I take a drive to clear my head and pick up groceries. I grab Wanda some flowers, just to show her I love her. We settled in to watch a movie, but my heart isn't into it. My real-life drama is still playing out in my head.

Goodnight, world. Goodnight, family. Goodnight, Eddie. You will be missed. I am sorry I left you.

July 11, 2019

I rose early, as usual, but today feels different. A sense of anxiety permeates through me as soon as my eyes open. The feeling of impending doom that I just can't shake. However, my stomach grumbles and my appetite takes over, so I head downstairs in search of food.

After drinking my morning caffeine, I focus my attention on my latest project: financial planning. As someone who understands the markets, I know how they operate, and the emotions involved in investing. But in today's uncertain world, I can't help but feel that investing is risky. The financial industry is full of greed and lacks ethics, and I don't entirely trust it.

Despite this, I spend hours researching various strategies, reading articles from CNBC, Cramer, "The Wall Street Journal", and Bloomberg, as well as private investors who swear by their methods of making millions on just a few thousand dollars. I decided to invest in a mix of mutual funds, Fortune 500 index funds, and pot stocks, feeling confident that marijuana will soon be legalized in Arizona and other states.

Dinnertime comes and goes, and I can't even recall what we ate. I'm writing this on a Sunday, and the events of Thursday seem like a distant memory. Ever since I left my job, I've been living a life free of alarm clocks, schedules, and meetings. It's a drastic change from my previously well-organized and structured life, but I'm embracing the chaos.

I realize now that my previous life was making me ill and unhappy. I had been living with so much stress for so long that it had aged me beyond my years. But after a month of being free from those burdens, I'm starting to feel happy again. I still have moments of fear and uncertainty, but overall, I'm enjoying life without the constant stress.

And as I drift off to sleep, I thank God for the peace he is bringing, and to take care of Eddie's soul.

July 12, 2019

I wake up from a deep sleep, feeling like I'm experiencing it for the first time in years. Back when I had a job, I woke up at 6am every day without fail, even on weekends. But now, without that routine, my body has been able to relax and truly rest. I've been having some vivid dreams lately, including some about my wife Wanda, and even my old friend Eddie Arroyo who passed away. It's strange how our minds process things when we're finally able to give them the space to do so.

With Wanda homeschooling and me not working, we've fallen into a comfortable routine where we can spend the day in our pajamas if we want to. It's a refreshing change from the daily grind of corporate life, where even something as simple as getting dressed feels like a chore.

I feel like a drug addict who is on methadone or some type of treatment to overcome addiction. I am convinced some days I feel bad because I am "coming down" from a life of stress and anxiety. Between financial analysis, raising capital, inventorship, leadership, responsibility, global travel, technical discussions, stringent client requirements and the fear for the safety of my team, I was a wreck. And now, I am a dad. I am a husband. I am...becoming something else. I just don't know what. I am transitioning.

Sometimes I feel as if we are living outside "The Matrix". We are home, not rushing, for the most part, not stressed, and we do things during the day that I used to dream about. When I used to travel a lot, I would wish to be on the lake on my Jet Ski or boat. Today, I often am. By myself. We see early matinees, with just a few other people. We eat at odd times. We shop during the day, on a weekday, and we enjoy the whole store to ourselves. I would often wonder about this life I have embarked on. Could I do it? I think I can. I need to write though. I need to speak to others. I need to share what I have learned and offer guidance on how to be impactful, but also to take care of yourself in the process.

I didn't understand this before. This feeling of living outside the rat race. There, I said it. We are all rats, and I don't want to race anymore.

I used to eat $1000 dinners. Stuffed lobsters in Shanghai or Sushi in Toyama, Japan. Now, I am sitting in the parking lot of a public park in Mesa, Arizona, with my wife, eating Taco Bell as the sun sets. And do you know what? I am happy. This is all I need. Experiences aren't measured in dollars; they are measured in feelings.

Speaking of feelings, tonight I am accompanying Wanda to speak at a homeschool panel, one that is moderated by a woman who is a homeschooling veteran. The premise of this panel is that each person will respond to a series of predetermined questions that were submitted by non-homeschoolers, those wanting to homeschool, or other home-schoolers that have overlapping questions. I know she is nervous as she is somewhat new to homeschooling.

They hand the microphone to Wanda, and there we are, our family pictured on the big screen. We are a good-looking crew if I may say so myself. She explains who she is and what she has done, and why she homeschools. As I listen, I am filled with pride I haven't had before. Not just for my wife, but for what she does as a homeschool mom. She is amazing, she has taken the role of teacher, mother, school nurse, nutritionist, tutor, and guidance counselor. She works hard at this, and I am very appreciative that she is giving our kids the best she can give.

After almost 2 hrs. of questions and answers, it is over. Wanda was fantastic! She comes off stage and I tell her how proud I am. We kiss and we talk to other participants about homeschool topics, and non-homeschool topics.

These are the things I used to teach others that worked with me. Pride, accountability, and focus. These are my pillars, yet here Wanda employs the same tactics in her everyday life, but I just haven't realized this until now. I should not have been so reluctant to come here with her. I need to support her more. Her happiness will ultimately lead to mine, and I want her to know I appreciate her, and that I am proud of her.

July 13, 2019

I wake up to make coffee and get the day going. It is Saturday, yardwork day. I love working outside like this. I love going to the lake and I really like being outdoors. I think this is partly because for the past 28 years, I have spent the bulk of my days inside. Inside an office, a warehouse, a manufacturing facility, a plane, a car, or our house, and I have missed being in the fresh air. I revel in the freedom of hearing the noises of birds, wind, and neighbors.

Wanda is going down to the ICE detention center with some friends, to visit her friend, Kathy today. We kiss goodbye and I tell her I will see her later.

Finished with all the yardwork and my chores. It is about 111 degrees today, and I am spent. Too much sun for one day, and I go inside and rest.

I go to my computer to write, but the kids want to play games. We all decided to be lazy and have a couple of hours of game time. They play and I read about penny stocks, liquidity, volatility, and general investing overviews.

Wanda comes home. Once again, her Iron Bra has thwarted evil. She could not get past the metal detectors at the site she went to because the metal in her bra set off the detectors, so she sat in the car for 2 hours while the other ladies visited. They will not let you in an ICE detention center once you set off the metal alarm. People have smuggled God knows what in various orifices of their body. Metal objects. I shudder at the thought. "Is that a file in your vagina, or are you just happy to see me?"

Poor Wanda. She is hungry and mentions how much she wants a whopper. I am just making the kids lunch, but I offer to get her one. She says "Yes!!", much to my surprise. She is on a diet because she thinks she is too heavy. I like her this way. She is delicious and full, like a woman should be. Her want of a whopper Jr. was very out of character for her. So, off to BK we go!

Ladies, we see you differently than you see yourself. Most guys you are with could care less about any of the imperfections you dwell on. We don't care about your stretch marks, wrinkles, extra pounds, or the fact you haven't taken a shower. We love you just the way you are.

And if you are a guy reading this, I must ask you; would you sleep with you? Think about that the next time you criticize your woman.

I am once again checking emails and reading. Wanda never thinks I read books, but I spend most of my days these days educating myself. I am figuring out a new life strategy and it requires immense research. Also, I am studying how to be an effective author. This is all new to me, but being I have 3-4 books I want to write; I should probably figure out an effective way of presenting my material.

I was oblivious to this when I was working, but we spent a lot of money on eating out. Making food at home is one of the keys to sustaining our wealth. Managing money will be one of my primary focuses moving forward. Managing how to grow our "wealth" will be the key to maintaining this way of life. "God, please be with us. Bless us and provide for us." I say this prayer often in these early days of the unknown. We went from a steady six figure income to zero when I resigned. I worry most about whether we have enough money. We will see what happens, but for now, we are fine.

We all head upstairs to bed. Wanda and I just talk and play on our phones for an hour. We are both exhausted and after an hour, we turn the lights out. We snuggle in the darkness, and I gently rub Wanda's back. She says, "I really love you, you know". I tell her that I do. She repeats this to confirm I understand, "Babe, I really love you." I feel it. I tell her I love her too. I do not know how it happens, but we gently touch each other, and one thing leads to another and.... well....XXX!!

July 14, 2019

I am sleeping more soundly now. It took over 35 days to happen. I even have dreams now, something that hasn't happened in years.

I have been writing for 2 hours this morning, but I need to stop because it's time for church. At church I thank God for the gift of my family, and this time he has granted us. I also thank him for Wanda. I do love her so.

Afterwards, we went to Cousin Mike's for a family BBQ. It is great to have the entire family together again. In the old days, when Mike and I were kids, every other Sunday was family dinner at Grandma and Grandpa's in Yonkers. When we left NY, all that ended. In this moment, I feel nostalgic, as I reflect on a similar scene, 35 years ago in Yonkers, when my dad, grandparents, Mike's dad and our extended family were all in the dining room, eating a traditional Italian Sunday dinner. All those people have since passed, and sitting with Mike, watching our kids play and the rest of our family talking and laughing, I feel a great sense of peace.

Back home, Wanda and I watched another movie called *Widows*, which I promptly fell asleep on. I am falling asleep earlier and earlier. This will not bode well with Wanda, but I can't help it. I am so exhausted. I haven't recovered from the past 28 years yet, and honestly, global travel for an extended period will really mess with your circadian rhythm. I am confident I have suffered from perpetual jet lag for the past 10 years.

Sleep is one of the most underrated things we can do to stay healthy. I am just starting to understand the value of a sound sleep. Of rejuvenation. I have really punished myself over the past 10 years, and it is going to take some time to heal.

July 15, 2019

It is Monday again. And this morning I stayed in bed with Wanda until 8:30 or so. I just love to be close to her. There have been so many Mondays in my career I have awakened early, only wishing I could spend a few more minutes next to my wife. Today, as I wrap my arms around her to feel her warmth, I am grateful for this simple pleasure. Not getting up for work and snuggling with my girl.

As we get up and move about, I read the notifications on my phone to find that another friend has died. My childhood teammate from baseball, Randy Alvieri has died of a heart attack at 54. He was the greatest athlete I ever played with. I am incredibly sad. He had a profound influence on me at a young age, because of the type of person he was, and because he did things other players couldn't do, and made it look easy.

Randy inspired me to reach beyond the limits of what we think is possible. He told me once when we were in the dugout, "Don't think too much, just trust yourself, just like in practice!" He was way ahead of his time, and his family were some of the nicest people I met. My childhood continues to degrade into distant memories. I can't help but wonder, "How much time do I have left?"

It's Prime day, and I am finished shopping, but my heart isn't into it. I end up with grief and an iPad. I think Prime day and Black Friday are both psychological warfare, designed to trick us into buying things we don't need because we are afraid of missing out on the bargains.

I work around the house to clear my head. Randy's death is a shock. "Eddie, Randy, who else?" I spend most of the day in a reflective and somewhat numb state. I repair anything I can find that is broken, as if it is the metaphor to the current range of emotions I am experiencing. I can fix a sprinkler line, but people are different. Too many moving parts.

As I slide into bed, Wanda meets me wearing the "Instigator", which is what I call her pink nightgown. It appears she has a plan for healing my aching soul, and in truth, nothing would be more medicinal.

July 16, 2019

I wake up after only a few hours of sleep. I feel ill. Disoriented. I go downstairs to make coffee and try and poop. As I may have discussed previously, there are no real bathrooms on the lake, and this morning I am taking Cubby fishing. I have tried to go to the bathroom in the Arizona Wilderness, but I am always concerned that once I squat down, a rattlesnake will bite my ass, a scorpion will sting my testicle, or worse, a Prairie dog will scurry up my exposed anus. I really do think I should consider seeking some professional help.

On the lake, it's an amazing morning and we are quickly getting underway. We are on the water and fishing by 6:15 AM. It's not a good day for fishing however, and by 8am, It's 101 degrees. I am not sure how much of this I am going to be able to endure on fewer than 4 hours sleep, but I am grateful we are here, and I try and relax and enjoy the scenery. I have a problem relaxing, and this is one of the things I need to work on. What good is all this time if I can't relax and enjoy it? It is a leftover ailment from many years in the pressure cooker, but some habits are harder to break than others. We fish halfheartedly for a few hours, take a swim at 10am and decide to call it a day at 11am.

At home, we finalize our vacation plans! We will go to Puerto Rico. I am usually excited about vacations together, but this one does not feel the same. I am not overly excited. I am on vacation with her everyday now. And silently, I still worry about money.

July 17, 2019

Early wake up for us today. Wanda and I are taking Dan and Kathy's kids to school for their first day. I feel bad for these girls. They are such great kids, and they miss their mom. I feel great empathy for their predicament. I fear they may not see their mother again for a long time. I am crying inside, but I keep my emotions bottled up tight, so they just see the smile.

I remember what it is like to be little and have your mom not there. When I was younger, my mom was in and out of hospitals, and I know what it feels like to be the only kid that didn't have their parents show up at school for something. It's a heavy emotional burden for an

8-year-old to deal with. I pray that they will have a good day and that their mom will be home soon.

Wanda and I go to breakfast together, a rarity these days. We go to one of my favorite spots here near our house. It is small, not fancy, and delicious. I love it here. It is simple food, cooked by people that care. I support small businesses because I refuse to continue to feed multinational conglomerates. The small guys need us. Now, more than ever.

The kids work with Wanda while I finalize the design for our putting green. It is going to be nice to just hang out and putt and think. Or Putt and drink.

Wanda takes the kids to painting class and I go shopping for dinner. I do this a lot now. I shop, I cook, I fix, and I generally do things I couldn't do when I was working. I am happy to do this, as I am grateful for this time, and to help where I can.

I jump in the pool to cool down before I BBQ. I love the feeling of splashing into the cool water when the temperature outside is over 110. I bask in the feeling of weightlessness and float on my back, looking up to the Heavens. I pray sincerely, giving thanks for this life I have been given. I have come a long way over the past 35 years, and I look forward to sharing my whole story in the upcoming books I will write, but today, I just pray with thanks for my life.

Gratitude is an emotion that many entitled young people don't understand. Be thankful for what you have; no one owes anyone anything.

I prepare a dinner of homemade burgers, fries, and hot dogs. I finished cooking but no one is home. Looks like a cold dinner for everyone. I know how Wanda used to feel when she would make me a nice dinner, only to have me not show up because I had to work late. Sorry babe! Payback is a female dog. Xo.

Wanda and I talk for a while about the current situation with Dan and Kathy. We are aligned that she needs to help Kathy, because no one else will, especially not her husband. I am still feeling a little bitter about the time this is consuming, but I understand. Kathy needs Wanda, and so in the interest of helping others, I will do what I can to make sure Wanda gets the time and space she needs to help Kathy and her girls.

July 18, 2019

I have no reason to get up early, but my digestive system is so programmed to wake me up at 6 AM, it doesn't understand I don't have to go to the office anymore. I need to get my digestion in order, or I fear I may never sleep again.

I have adopted another ritual. I wake up early, get my coffee, and go to the bathroom. I feed the dogs, let them out and then head upstairs to my office, where I read the news and start writing. I do this like clockwork.

I take calls from former clients and friends while the kids school. I am relieved to speak to those from my industry. They miss me, and I miss them. They let me know how impactful I was, and I am deeply appreciative to hear these things. I needed it, as I have been struggling with many emotions lately, but none stronger than the guilt I feel in leaving my clients, many of whom I have had the privilege of working with for over 25 years.

I explain to many why I left, and sometimes, I feel like a broken record, but they all want to understand the story, so I tell it. After I explain the situation, the environment I left, and my need for a break, they all get it and wish me well.

They also understand I miss them, and my role as a leader. I assure them I will be back sometime, although it may be in a different role. I feel appreciated, like what I did mattered, and that helps me calm my overwhelming feelings of guilt. I didn't leave them; I left a situation I could no longer be a part of. Many tell me they wish they could do the same, and in that type of response, I understand that my path is the right one. I also understand that my philosophy that relationships are the key to business, not metrics, is supported by the outpouring of support I receive from my former colleagues and clients, many who will be friends for life.

We finish eating and I go back upstairs to work on some projects. I am being offered several consultancies, but I am not sure what I will do next. I am not finished with my "Restment", and so rather than jump back into the fray, I let the offers sit for now.

In all honesty, I have been away from my industry for fewer than 45 days, and I am not ready to go back yet. Besides, I have a non-compete in place for the next year, so working in my field will be impossible. I think I am just going to stay put for now. I am going to stay true to the reasons I left, and I am going to write this book. I am going to explore other options and I am going to catch my breath.

I finish my work and notice the kids are out in the pool. I throw on my swimsuit and go swim for a few. I have not been here for most of their childhood. I left my career to be with them, and so, in the middle of the day, when I should be at work, I am home. And now, I am going to swim with them, much to their astonishment. The kids are giddy. Daddy's home!

After dinner Wanda and I are arguing about something. I don't want to argue, in fact, I don't even care about what we are arguing about. I am tired, and so is she, so we should just go to sleep, but we don't. Wanda puts in a movie, and I drift off to sleep. Never go to sleep angry. You never know when your mate may not wake up again. Like poor Eddie.

July 19, 2019

I wake up ahead of the alarm. I was sleeping so well for a week, but we went to bed at midnight and here I am at 6 AM, up since 5:43 AM, watching Wanda sleep soundly. I have sleep envy.

I pack my things to leave for a 2 day homeschool conference with Wanda, all within a 20-minute span. Traveling globally for so many years has taught me how to be efficient and expedient when packing. As well,

I also drew from my experience as a drug dealer and counterintelligence officer, in making quick exits. Ok, I made the last part up. I was never a counterintelligence agent.

We are going to the Homeschool Conference in Phoenix, but before we head to the city, we stop at the local gas station for gas and lottery tickets. I still buy lottery tickets. You can't win if you don't play! I am a guy that took the chances. Luck is simply the meeting of opportunity and preparation.

At the conference, we are seated for the opening remarks. After a few prayers, a few songs and some updates, a man named Woody Robertson speaks. The guy is me in lots of ways. I really love his speaking style, very engaging, and his story is almost like mine. A self-made man. I liked him so much I agree with Wanda to attend his talk on "Affording College".

We attended various lectures on Homeschooling, and in the middle of one of them, my phone rang. I know this number. They tried to call me several times, so I stepped out. The call is from a local semi-conductor company who is interested in what I know about a certain technology. It turns out I know a lot. We talk and agree to a meeting for consultancy and possible collaboration. Awesome. The offers are coming. I am not that motivated to do any of this, but it's nice to be wanted again. Moreover, it is good to be recognized for the sizable and heartfelt contribution I have made to my industry.

I miss Heinz and Heraeus, but more than that, I miss driving a successful business that provided value to our clients and offered a hand in bringing Next Gen technology to fruition. These days, the only value I am bringing is to my backyard, where I spend my days picking up dog poop and repairing leaky sprinklers. It is different from being CEO, but there are obvious similarities.

We are late for the "Brain Training" seminar, something both Wanda and I were excited about. It's about how smart people think, and Wanda and I often compete for the title of "Know-it-all," so this is right up our alley. We arrive late and it is packed. There are only 2 seats left. One in the very back, in a row littered with babies and homeschool moms. The other is the front row. Before I can ask Wanda what to do, she beelines for the front, looking back and mouthing, "Sorry!"

She isn't.

I take my place among the other homeschool moms in the back. This is my identity now. No longer am I the powerful decision maker, driving excellence and creating value. No, I am now Wanda's handmaiden and Uber driver, and I am banished to the back of the castle, to dwell amongst the breast-feeding mommies and fidgety babies.

In a way, I feel like I belong here, with the "People". And you know what? It is ok. These ARE my people. We run through a series of exercises designed to test our mind. I kill it. "Still sharp as ever!", I think to myself. The other homeschool moms are floored. "How did you do it so fast?", they ask. I tell them, "I don't think about the complexity, I just focus on the instruction and don't overthink it. Plus, no one is currently suckling at my breast", referencing the mother behind me who has a baby attached to her nipple. They all laugh at the irony in my truth.

"I am still smart. I still have value and I am still strong!" I repeat this to myself a few times, reminding myself that just because I left my career, it doesn't mean I have lost my worth. I hope not anyway. Time will tell. When I left work, I lost my identity, and I hope to find a new one. One that doesn't involve breast feeding if I have a choice.

Success is just about overcoming all the pain and frustration you face on the way to your goal. Many can't make it to the finish line, but I have learned a secret technique. Lie to yourself. If you listen to your doubts and pains, you will always fail, because it is far easier to quit than to persevere. Don't quit. Dig deep, keep fighting, keep moving forwards. No one can stop you, but you!

Later that evening, as we head out to dinner, we meet Woody, the keynote speaker from earlier in the morning. I tell him the story of my professional journey, as well as my recent departure. He and a friend are both listening intensely. We agree to have this discussion another day, and we trade numbers. It was a good day today. Though, I can't admit that to Wanda; she will make me come back next year!

While I am not a fan of chains, I take Wanda to her favorite theme restaurant, The Hard Rock Café, in downtown Phoenix. I am hungry and we eat like kings, laughing and slurping, all under the backdrop of famous guitars and the jacket John Bon Jovi wore during the *"You give love a bad name"* video. After dinner, we walk hand in hand through the streets of Downtown Phoenix, talking and reflecting on the day.

Back to the room for some writing and hopefully, romance. Neither of us brought pajamas, so there is a strong chance that we may end the day on a happy, if not naked note!

I write for a couple of hours while Wanda plans the day for tomorrow. She has a belly ache. I blame it on the BBQ pork sandwich from Hard Rock, but it is clear my hopes for romance are slowly diminishing with every complaint she makes.

I rub Wanda's back for a little while, but I know she isn't into any romance. I am tired anyway and fell asleep rubbing her. I think I said something weird when I fell asleep. Oh God, I hope it wasn't something about her, or worse, another woman.

July 20, 2019

Uh oh, we overslept. We hurry to get ready, but Wanda is laboring and still complaining about her stomachache. I am dealing with my own internal issues. The trouble is that Wanda has already claimed the bathroom. I am convinced I will have to poop out the window. We are on the 16th floor and the windows only open a little, leaving me a challenging position of defecation.

As I sit in the "Compass Room", of the Hyatt Regency, waiting for breakfast, I pull my phone out and read on my LinkedIn account that my good friend and client, Dana Eipper has died. I feel so bad. I cry right there in the restaurant. Dana and I had a longstanding friendship that reached beyond our work as vendor and client. He was a caring soul who really helped me and the company back in the mid 90's when we really needed help. He was a good friend too.

Life is so short. Don't put off anything that is important to you. You never know when you won't have the luxury of tomorrow. I feel very strongly about this, and it further supports the fact that my leaving the company was the right decision.

I take the bags down to the truck and say a prayer for Dana. I am floored. 3 friends have died in the span of 3 weeks or less. I am more convinced I need to figure out what my next path will be, before my number is called. I know that seems like a morbid statement, but based on recent events, it is what it is. I need to find my way. To where, I have no clue.

After checking out of the hotel, I walked to the convention center. My heart isn't in it. Dana died. Randy died. Eddie died. Why am I still here? I feel bad for all of them. Our lives are but a blip in the fabric of time. Use it wisely. There are no re-dos.

Back at the conference, we attend a myriad of talks and exhibits, curriculum, and shopping. My heart is not really into any of it. I am on autopilot, as I have done many times before in my life, especially on long trips. I feel bad because I want to support Wanda, but my heart is hurting from the loss of 3 close friends.

We are supposed to leave on vacation tomorrow, a romantic one, to Puerto Rico, but I am not excited. I feel the anxiety I used to feel before a big trip for work. Odd that I am now able to travel for fun and I get the same anxiety I got from business travel. I have been traveling for more than 25 years. Maybe...I am just traveled out for now?

Later, the keynote speaker, a vibrant woman named Heidi St. John, gives a great closing talk on remembering why we home school. I loved the talk and I love my Wanda. This has been an eye-opening experience, and I am committed to doing what I can to help her be successful. For the sake of our kids, her, and our marriage.

July 21, 2019

We are leaving for Puerto Rico tomorrow. I still feel stressed about leaving the kids and traveling. I think it has more to do with flying, but I have grown accustomed to being home with the kids, and I will miss them.

I like being home. We live in a nice house in a great neighborhood, and we have so many things we want to do, and never have time to do them, even though we are "retired". That is the irony of quitting my job. I did this to be with my family and the days are so filled with activity for Wanda, the kids and I, we still feel busy.

I start cutting the lawn. I like to do the yardwork. It lets me be with my thoughts, and today, I have plenty. Anxiety set in yesterday but today it has blossomed into full blown panic. I have not been on a plane since my last trip around the world in May. I cut, sweat, and think. These are all good things. It means I am alive and operational. The other option is death. I think of Dana, Eddie, and Randy. What were their thoughts in the days preceding their death? I wonder. I hope they are in heaven.

Enough of this yard work. I want to go inside and spend time with the kids before I go. Wanda needs me to run errands, so I go grab a few things and then the kids and I game upstairs. I realize they do not feel the same anxiety I feel; therefore, they are calm, while I am a basket case.

We head to church, and I pray deeply for our safety and the safety of the kids while we are gone.

I could never share the intense stress and anxiety I felt before trips with anyone other than Wanda. In some cases, the anxiety was crippling, but I forced myself onto planes around the world. It is a true testament to my fortitude. I had anxiety because I was constantly leaving, and I didn't want to. I was constantly worrying about flight connections, weather, angry clients, being far away from my life, and mostly, because I didn't want to do it anymore. I hated flying and was even developing a case of vertigo that was exacerbated by flying.

My stress is heightened after we endure a 3-hour delay for our flight. We are taking a red-eye and it's late. We finally took off, but I have a middle seat. I am going to lose my mind. I NEVER sit in a middle seat due to my claustrophobia and need to stretch my legs. Always an aisle. Tonight, there is no aisle, no upgrade to first, just a middle seat next to a large, snoring woman on my left, and a sleeping and oblivious Wanda on my right. I pray and fold my arms and go deep into my happy place in the hopes all this will be over soon.

Bon Voyage!

July 22, 2019

Our overnight journey takes us to Miami, where we will connect to Puerto Rico. I haven't slept and it's 8:30am. We are both exhausted and angry when we board our connecting flight. I sit next to a little girl on the flight, and she makes me think about my own little girl, Cailyn, and our first trip on a plane together. We took her to NY for my 35th High School Reunion and family time with Mike and the kids. She was so excited to be on a plane, and her smiling little face still stays with me. It's been less than 24 hours and I already miss my kids.

We finally land in San Juan, and it is pouring as we land. It has been raining on and off, and I can see as the plane lands, the streets are beginning to flood.

We decided to rent a car. I thought it would be cheap, but it turns out the "discounted rate" is a mere $730 for the week. $730 is a lot of money for an unemployed guy, but I pay anyway, telling myself I am on vacation and shouldn't be so frugal.

We leave the airport and are immediately lost in a storm, in the middle of San Juan. The rain subsides, and we finally find our way back to the highway that will take us to our destination, the lovely Rio Grande, but I took the wrong exit and now we are seeing ALL the local flavor of PR.

We make it to the hotel a little after 5pm. I have been awake for almost 36 hours, and I shower, trying to rinse the sins of life off me.

When I come out, Wanda is snoring loudly, and I am tired too, so I lay down for a little nap before dinner. We fall asleep together and wake up too tired to move. Screw it. Room service and a movie. We stay up until 2am watching movies on my tablet and eating overpriced room service. I still feel blessed to be here.

Be thankful for what you have, where you are and who you are with.

July 23, 2019

I can't believe we are waking up at 10 am. I woke earlier but was still tired, so I went back to sleep. We justify our late sleeping to the time difference and exhaustion, and order great food seaside while enjoying tropical drinks, watching the teal-colored water, and enjoying the strong sea breeze.

It is getting late, and windy, so we discard any plans of doing anything of significance. The tension is high because Wanda is insistent we go to San Juan, despite the fact hundreds of thousands of people have blocked the city and are demanding the expulsion of "Ricky", the corrupt Governor. It is short of a coup d'état, but pretty close, and she wants to "be close to history?"

We agree that exploring the local jungle and some time by the pool to relax would be a better idea. We hung out and walked around the jungle near our hotel and found a river. The "Rio Grande". It is a bit of an ambitious title, as it looks more like the "Rio Pequeño".

We watch tv and movies and just chill. It is quite nice. We even have a loose plan of what to do and where we want to go, but tomorrow is golf, so we are taking it easy. For clarity, I golf, she drives the cart.

Sex is apparently something dogs do on vacations, not married couples. I am a little surprised. We have always had a wonderful sex life, and vacations were always a smorgasbord of love. Not this time. These are new days, and in these new times, sex is apparently only for procreation.

July 24, 2019

I am awake after 6 hours of sleep, but I feel ok. I look out the window and it looks cloudy with breaks of sun. We are golfing today, and I am hopeful the weather holds. It is 85 degrees with 40000% humidity. That is not an exaggeration.

It is very windy, very muggy, and ridiculously hard to hit the ball the way I am used to. In Arizona, there is no wind, so you grip it and rip it, but here, it's windy, muggy and miserable. We are golfing with a father and son from Houston, Steve and Caleb. Caleb, who seems to be about 14, has never golfed, so we are coaching and going slowly. Steve and I are frustrated mainly at the fact the humidity is up in the 100k's and the drink girl is AWOL. It is so humid; my nose hairs are curling like a bad perm from 1986.

We are constantly being watched and chased by Iguanas. They scamper away when I get close, but being descendants of dinosaurs, I am going to keep an eye on them. My golf wasn't bad, and the scenery was amazing. I don't really care about my score; I was happy to have this experience.

We are tired and drunk as we meander over to the grill. We decide on a light dinner and more planning on what we will do in the coming days. One thing is for damn sure; we are going to San Juan, whether there is a revolution or not! Wanda demands she see San Juan during a government overthrow, and by God, we are going! Please help me.

We go back to the hotel and plan on watching a movie on pay per view but find the Pay Per view is no longer working in our room. We are paying about $300 a night for this room. I would have expected that the TV would work. Oh no, now we will have to talk to each other. That isn't wise, so I pull up my laptop and we watch a movie on Netflix. Crisis averted!

July 25, 2019

I wake up with a backache, a shoulder ache and an everything ache.

As I shower, I feel something on my anus. I think it may be a hemorrhoid or an anal fissure. It is a grape of some sort. I am terrified. What could this be? I can't be sick now, my insurance sucks!

We had a big breakfast at the buffet in the hotel and decided to take a ride to the town down the road called Luquillo. We get to Luquillo and find a row of "Kioskos", like small spaces where you have a counter to order and some seats to sit down and eat. The music is played at a level of 165 decibels, shattering ear drums and unclogging drains, and while it is loud, the food is great, and the drinks are cheap.

We take advantage of this opportunity to do a little shopping for the people at home. I hate buying souvenirs anymore, as I brought them from all over the world, but Wanda likes to shop, so I indulge her.

After Luquillo, we head to Fajardo to find out where the ferry takes off from so we can visit other islands, but find the Ferry no longer launches here due to the horrific hurricane damage. Bummer.

Luckily, we use Google Maps to find a nearby Marina. We figure at least there will be a restaurant and some place to get a drink. We find a wonderful little place overlooking the Marina called "El Yate", which means, "We won't fight if we are drinking". This is how we travel. We try the places the locals go to. We like to explore.

We are early for dinner, but it is perfect because we'll get to watch the sunset. We take a table right on the edge overlooking the water in the harbor. It is great because we can watch boats coming in and out of the Marina and enjoy our drinks. We had a really good time. I know Wanda doesn't realize this but most of the time I look at her I'm just amazed at how beautiful and precious she is. I wish she appreciated how much I love her.

After dinner, we look for a Walgreens so I can find some Preparation H in case my anal raisin is a "roid". I don't know why, but while she shops and goes to the bathroom, I head to the counter and buy a pack of cigarettes. I feel horrible about myself because it has been about 5 years since I smoked, and this is one of the few things I'm proud of quitting other than my job.

We go back to the "5 o'clock somewhere" bar, which is where we spent most of our nights drinking, laughing, and figuring out what to do tomorrow. I step away from the table to have a cigarette, but after 3 drags in the rain, I throw it away. It tastes disgusting and I am reminded of why I quit. I will smoke about 6 more before I finally get the message and throw the pack away.

We tried to watch a movie, but once again the pay per view is out so we stay on our phones for an hour and then fall asleep. In case you wondered, it is day four of our sexless vacation. We have been together for 12 years, and we have never had a dry spell like the one we have been experiencing since I left work. I am not mad anymore, but I am concerned. If this is the new normal, I am going to be a very unhappy guy.

July 26, 2019

We wake up early-ish so we can get a jump start on San Juan. We go back down to the breakfast buffet to fuel up for a long day in this island's Capital. We are strategic in our execution. We need to stay lean and mean, you know, in case we need to flee the civil war that is imminent in Old San Juan.

After a few stops in the local stores, we find the sights and sounds of Old San Juan. There is no unrest I see--just coffee shops, restaurants, bars, and many historical sites that line the narrow streets. We stop at the Gate to Puerto Rico, which is a gate to the old city of San Juan. There is a lot of history here, and I am enjoying it. There are forts, statues, and the most beautiful cobblestone streets, lined with blooming bushes and trees. What was I so worried about?

I did witness a drug deal, right here on the street in broad daylight. I am reminded of my days in New York, where you could see this anywhere in the city, but I am older, and this transaction leaves me unsettled. I asked Wanda if we can leave. She says no. I plead with her, angrily letting her know we are in harm's way, but she just ignores me and keeps on shooting her pictures.

I am infuriated. How can she put us at risk this way? Why doesn't she think about our kids? Why isn't she bothered like I am? The answer is much clearer than I thought. I realize it is because I am a maniac. Sorry for overreacting, Wanda.

We find the place where the Piña Colada was invented, and it seems to be legit. We sit down in the nicely furnished restaurant and order a couple of Piña Coladas, as well as some dinner. The food is incredible, and we are excited to have found yet another gem in our travels on the path less traveled.

Next stop, the bar where they filmed "Despasito". I am nervous. I am a horrible dancer and if you ever saw Puerto Rican dancing, you would know that they take their dancing seriously. I dance as if I am convulsing due to electrocution. Should be a fun night.

We walk through the doorway, into a dark hallway and then, through another door. As we open the door, the sound of salsa music and laughter envelopes our ears. The music is pumping so loud you can feel it in your chest. The small dance floor is packed with people dancing as only Latin people can dance. The room is alive with music, drinks, testosterone, and the smell of... wood? I look around and can see that the whole place is made of heavy timber, like from a ship. We meander through the labyrinth of rooms for hours.

It is 12:30 AM when we leave San Juan. There was never a worry, other than me. Mr. Anxiety.

July 27, 2019

It's Saturday, our last day on vacation and we missed the ferry to the island we have been waiting to go to all week. I am so bummed, and tempers are flaring because our plans are ruined. I also have a grape residing in my ass. The struggle is real.

The one thing that has always bound Wanda and I is our appreciation for food, and we are hungry. We drive aimlessly until Wanda finds a place for authentic Puerto Rican food, served just off the road in a small shack-like restaurant. Once again, we found a gem. Great food, good people and through the magic of food, we stop fighting. We have done nothing we planned while we were here, other than golf and San Juan. While the trip wasn't what we expected, it was still a treat to be alone together on this beautiful Island. We agreed to come back, next time with the kids.

July 28, 2019

It's going to be a long way home. We have a 6 AM wake up call for a 9 AM flight. Our first leg is from Puerto Rico to Dallas, and unlike the flight here, this one is calm and relaxed. I am saddened by our lack of romance on the trip, but happy to be going home. I am grateful for the time we had to spend together, but I am really worried we have reached a point in our marriage where she is willing to settle into a non-romantic kind of relationship.

We take our seats in the boarding area and begin to read when I hear our names being called over the loudspeaker. I think to myself, "Oh no, they are going to bust me for smuggling an anal grape onboard!"

I walk to the podium and let them know who I am. The agent looks at me and asks for ID, and I obliged. She smiles, and says, "Thank you for being an Executive Platinum Member with us for many years, Mr. Guercio. Please accept this upgrade to First Class as our way of saying thanks!" Things are looking up already!

We land in Phoenix, clear customs and instead of going home, we are racing to downtown, to the old Orpheum Theater to see a one woman show about women, for women. This is how things go in my house. It doesn't matter that we just travelled for 9 hours, we are going to a show! I really miss the kids!

It is comical and entertaining, but I am tired and in need of a cold pack for my swollen anal stowaway. I am one of the few men dragged by their wives, but it doesn't bother me. It's ok, because the secret to a happy marriage is saying yes, even when your heart says no.

As soon as we get home and hug our kids, I can breathe again, the stress of travel and being away behind us. I traveled the world, and now the only place I want to go...is home.

July 29, 2019

It's the first day back home and we are having a relaxing day to catch up on life around the casa. I am convinced there is something that has changed in Wanda. She spends all her time on Kathy and other things but gives zero attention to me. I don't think she understands that once you push someone away enough times, they don't come back.

July 30, 2019

I spent the morning with Arielle on our Jet Skis. I showed her how I can tell when we are going to get rain, simply by identifying the pattern of the clouds and the direction of the wind.

Later that evening, we get the rainstorm I predicted; Arielle is mildly impressed, but I am over the moon with excitement. It rarely rains here in the desert, so when it does, it is a big deal to me.

I sit in the backyard, gin and tonic in hand, watching the rain and relaxing. As I sit and sip my drink, I thank God for getting us home safe, for giving us a nice day on the lake, and for the rain. I sit for an hour just listening to the pitter-pattering of raindrops on the patio and surrounding bushes. I should have recorded it, as the sound is soothing and relaxing, lulling me into a state of relaxation I haven't felt in a long time.

July 31, 2019

This morning, Randy from the putting green place is here to install our new putting green, but it is pouring. They want to put in the putting green anyway. I am stunned, but at 7:30 am, and much to my surprise, the team shows. They are going to dig in the mud. I can't wait. I have always wanted a quiet place to practice my putting, and now, we will have one.

I am also going to edit our vacation video from PR. There is some really cool footage, and I am excited at our photographic and videographic handiwork.

I am starting to enjoy staying home, but I look at my bank account often and feel genuine concern about how long I can do this. My sincere hope is that this book will do well, and I can continue doing this and speaking to others about my experiences. Or I may get a job. Right now, I am starting to feel happy, despite my disappointment with Wanda, and that is a feeling I have not felt in a long time.

I went to Walmart and grabbed some things for the putting green, but now I need to rush back home to prepare for a 1 PM consulting call. I am speaking to the founder of a great program designed to tailor a path to an affordable college degree. Woody Robertson is his name; the guy who spoke at the Homeschool conference. He turns out to be a great person, a good human with a good heart and I know he gets the premise of my other book, *Drink my Kool-Aid*. He is a culture guy. Me too, and culture building is the reason I sit here today, writing this book.

Woody and I have a long talk about him, his family, his past and present. He tells me of things that ail him and that bring him joy. He is at a place, emotionally, I have been many times. It is the emotional crosswinds of the balance between the direction you are in, and the one you should be headed to. They are never on the same trajectory.

Dan calls me to talk about Kathy. We reach a solution that may help her. Communication is so important, but many times we don't communicate the right messages. I hope things will work out for them, and this saga will end happily.

After a fantastic dinner of eggplant parmesan and mashed potatoes, I go up to write my entries for the day. I am not motivated to write today, but I remind myself I committed to this, and by God, I am going to finish it, "so sit your now healing anus down and write!" As I sit and write, I feel better. Writing has become a much-needed therapy for me, and my mind is healing, and the grape in my ass has diminished to raisin status. All is well in the world for now.

July is over. I have been away from work for a little less than 2 months. Not everything has gone according to plan. My relationship with Wanda is strained, we lost our life insurance and I have not made a dollar since June 7th. But you know what? It's ok.

I have been able to rejuvenate my soul, I was able to spend time with my family and my friends, I am playing golf, going to the lake, and doing things around the house. I am not working at my old job, but I have one. I am a dad, a husband, a friend, and a son. My worth is measured by others now, not by my achievements as a CEO. It has taken me about 45 days to understand something important.

Our worth is not measured by what we do for a living, but by the life we live.

3

August, 2019

August 1, 2019

I woke up around 6 AM this morning. It is the first day of School for Arielle. Her Senior year of High School. That thought stuns me. How time flies. How many things did I miss, that I do not realize, because I was always working, always travelling, always...absent?

Apparently, 7:15 AM is slang for 7:25 AM. We are late, but here in 2019, that's how things work. You are a winner, even if you just show up. That's nonsense though; the real world does not work like that. The real world is measuring our every success and failure. The real world is using complex metrics and statistics to quantify whether we are worthy of the next stage of initiation, or if we are weak and useless. Life has a way of ordering out the weak, just like nature does, and some of them end up in management.

Wanda leaves for breakfast with the "girls" and I am going to home-school today. We are going on weeks of sexless, loveless days. I continue to love her, but I am losing faith that we are going to make it. At night, I massage her, and she falls asleep. I fall asleep while she is on her phone. We are sleeping on our relationship, and we just went through the entire vacation with no romance, and no sex. I am incredibly sad about this aspect of our life. I am having serious concerns about the direction of our relationship, and I hope we find a way back. I don't want to be in a marriage without sex or intimacy. I have been there, and it deflated me in more ways than one.

The kids and I work from 9 AM until about 1 PM. They do most of the work without supervision, and I am there to answer questions and explain techniques. This is how I wish I learned. Take the structure of public school away and focus on the kids' learning styles, and it is amazing what they will accomplish. I am extremely proud of them, and more so, of Wanda for doing all this.

During school, I take a call from my cousin Anthony about a business opportunity, and I write some emails. It's nice to be able to schedule my own day, instead of the way it was when I was CEO. My assistant would schedule my calendar, and it was always jam packed. Morning to night. I never got a break. Now, I make my own schedule and I am much kinder to myself than my assistant ever was. (It's ok Stephanie. You were a great help and I appreciate all you did to keep me on task!)

Around 2 PM, the kids finish school. It is still blazing hot here in Arizona. Daytime temps exceed 115 degrees most days. The kids and I decided that despite the intense heat, we were going swimming. We hang out in the pool for a few hours, laughing and splashing and generally enjoying our time together.

Once again, I would never have been able to do this as CEO. Swim at 2 PM on a Thursday? Never! Why though? Why don't we make more time in our lives for moments so simple as these? I don't have an answer, but we are trained that taking off from work to be home with family is bad. We have been fed the guilt of management past. If I have another chance to lead, it will be focused on work/ life balance.

Take time to regenerate and reconnect. It is so important for your personal well-being and promotes a stronger and happier work environment.

After dinner, I headed out to the garage to prep the Jet Skis for some time on the lake. When we bought these, we already had a boat, but I wanted to use them to rent them out to others. I ended up using them for our family and friends a lot more than renting them. They bring joy to my family and the others that use them. In that, I am ok that they are not generating revenue. They are generating smiles, laughs and excitement. That is an acceptable ROI to me.

Of all the great things I have been learning about not working, the single greatest joy comes from being with our kids on a daily basis. I am immensely grateful.

I take a shower and inspect my anal raisin. Is it hemorrhoids? Is it a butt zit? Is it cancer? Oh God, please don't let me get cancer, we have such bad insurance now. This is my thought as I drift to sleep.

August 2, 2019

Today, I am going to the lake with my sister. It is on these kinds of mornings I most appreciate my decision to leave the C-Suite. I am relaxed, excited, and happy. Most of all, I am grateful for the time I spend with my family.

I make sandwiches and snacks for the lake, and as I pack the cooler, I think about the many days I would have liked to be right where I am now. We end up working a lifetime to build a life we may never have wanted in the first place. Worse, some of us may never see the fruits of our labor. Many have died much too young. They worked for a tomorrow they would never see. I reflect on the many years I spent making excuses for not doing what I am doing today. "I am too busy", was the common theme.

Joey is my middle sister, and one of my best friends. She survived breast cancer a couple of years ago, and her recovery served as one of the inspirations for me being able to leave my career in favor of a slower pace. She is funny, smart, and creative, and I love her with all my heart. I feel extremely fortunate that she is here, and now, in the middle of a work week, we are going to ride some Jet Skis together.

As we drive to the lake, we laugh and talk about everything going on in our lives. We are in different places on our journey, but I find so many things we have in common. Life is life; we all deal with our own stress, anxiety, sadness, and joy, but the sources are remarkably similar. It makes me feel less disconnected from reality.

I think to myself as I push off from the dock, *"If you let things come to you, and have a little faith, everything you worry about will work itself out"*.

One of the most important lessons I have learned in life is to be forthright and honest. Why? Well, for the obvious reasons, because you don't want to be a person who isn't trustworthy, but equally as important, is because Karma is an angry bitch, and she most likes to wreak her havoc on you when you feel as if you had a plan well figured out.

Be honest. No one likes a liar.

Back home, the putting green crew has finished. I tipped them Ice cream and cash, and they joked to me that the cash tip was a nice gesture, but in the hot and arid afternoon, the ice cream was equally appreciated. I think about how simple it is to take someone's bad day and make it a little better. In this case, it was $60 and some ice cream, but I feel as if we could apply this lesson to anyone we meet. Be nice to people.

Do the unexpected. Make others feel appreciated and important. It takes so little effort to make someone's day.

My sister-in-law, Marlene, and her family are in town for our nephew's birthday, and tonight, we are going to have his party at Chuck E. Cheese to celebrate his second birthday. We arrive at the crowded kids place around 7 PM. As I scan my surroundings, I am met with what I see as a breeding ground for germs. Ball pits and runny noses. Dirty diapers and pizza. Nothing good can come of this, other than a case of hoof and mouth disease, or in the worst scenarios, ringworm, lice, or streptococcus. I shudder at the scene, and decide I will stay vigilant, keep my hands in my pockets and wash frequently.

I will do the same for my kids, but as I explain to them my concerns, they just dismiss me and tell me loudly, "Dad, stop being so overprotective!"

Old habits die hard, and protection is what I have been doing for the past 30 years.

August 3, 2019

Today is the 36th anniversary of our move to Arizona. It was on this day in 1983, I arrived here, in the stormy and beautiful desert of Phoenix. It has been an amazing Journey. I am happy I live here, and I am happy to have had a business here. If you would have asked me to envision what my life would look like today in 1983, I would not have foreseen where I am today. I reminisce for a few moments, thinking about friends I left in NY, and those that are no longer with us. I am melancholic, yet grateful.

Wanda leaves for the Mexican consulate. I wish this Kathy saga would end. It has been so draining for Wanda, Kathy, and her kids. I continue to pray for her, and for Wanda, that there will be some way to find a happy ending, but the reality is much grimmer. Deportation is likely.

Mike and Michelle come over and we cook, swim, putt, and drink for hours. It is a perfect beginning to the new life of the putting green, and more so, it is a perfect evening of family fun and laughter.

As we putt, Mike and I share a cigar together and a strong IPA. In the air, I smell the dust and unmistakable aroma of rain. I tell Mike my prediction and he dismisses it. "It's just a bunch of wind!", he replies, as the gusts become stronger, and the lingering stench of precipitation fills the air like the smells of an open-air market. In the end, we will say our goodbyes around 9 PM, just as the rain starts, just like I told everyone it would.

August 4, 2019

The heavy rain from last night has flooded the new putting green. I am convinced we can't have nice things. When I got my Audi, the first night I had it, I parked it in our driveway. A process server knocked on our front door late at night. He was serving a ticket to my son Adam, who had been caught running a yellow light on a traffic camera. Our dog Wally, who is capable of opening doors like the raptors of *Jurassic Park,* ran to the door and opened it, leaving the process server running for his life. As Wally pursued him, he jumped on the hood of my brand-new car, leaving a crater in the hood.

The putting green will survive, just like the Audi did. Just because it isn't perfect, doesn't mean it doesn't work well. People are like this too. *They have their own "dents and scratches", but are still valuable, productive, and worthwhile.* I know; I am one of them, and many others worked for me.

Today is a church day, but first, I am driving Wanda to see Kathy at the detention center here about an hour south of where we live. I agreed to do this to make peace with what has become a volatile situation with Wanda. I want peace between us. This Kathy situation is adding layers of undue stress on Wanda and our marriage. I am trying to find ways to quell the animosity.

I drop her off at the center and fly my drone at a now dried up lake nearby. I finish my drone footage and go back to get Wanda. She is happy. She got in to see her friend and seems in good spirits, even though it is becoming more likely Kathy will be deported.

As we drive back to our house, we pass a little Mexican food stand I saw on the way in. I look over to Wanda who is quietly looking at the sites and ask her if she is hungry. Wanda loves Mexican food and surprises. I stop and we have a great lunch of authentic Mexican cuisine.

As we pulled back on to the freeway to head back to our house, bellies full and spirits alive, Wanda takes my hand and looks at me and says, "I love you very much, do you know that?" I say yes, but in my heart, I wonder, based on the events of the last few months. I don't dwell on the past, I just tell her I love her too, and let her know I need more than what we have been experiencing lately. We agree to try and connect more on an intimate level.

People say, "Behind every great man is a great woman". I like to use, "beside" instead of behind.

As we end our day, later that night, we kiss our kids goodnight and close the house. I find my way upstairs and slide into bed. I am exhausted. Wanda is reading on her phone, but as I pull the covers up and roll on my side, she rolls over to meet my face. She touches me and tells me she loves me, and thanks me for everything in our life. As we kiss, I pull her closer to me, and as the glow of our lava lamps casts orangish and red shadows in our dark bedroom, we make love.
It has been a long time since we connected like this, and I savor every moment.

I hope and pray this won't be the last of this kind of evening together. I really miss the kind of relationship we used to have. The one with frequent time together, focused on each other, whether it was in the bedroom or just in our day to day lives. I miss you Wanda, and I need you. I am lost right now, and your love and compassion serve as a beacon to me in a sea of darkness and uncertainty. Please remember that I need you too. You are my world, and lately I have been feeling like we are experiencing a total "Marital Eclipse". My tide is high, wade into my ocean. There are no sharks, and the water is warm and clear. I love you.

August 5, 2019

Another early morning after an incredible late-night rendezvous with Wanda. I am tired, but life doesn't stop because we stayed up late. It's 6 AM and my internal clock is up and ready for the day. I take Arielle to school and head to Chompies to meet my former CFO, Omer, for breakfast. I have chosen Omer to be the CFO of our new company, "InfinityGo", and we have agreed to get some good food and discuss the formation of our pitch deck and financials. It is hard for me to believe that he and I started as adversaries when he first came on as the site controller for our business. He didn't understand my culture, and we clashed often in our early days together. But here we are, a few months removed from our duties at our old company and enjoying a delicious breakfast at the best Jewish Deli in all of Arizona as we plan on how we will make our new venture a success. He gets me, and I, him.

His friendship reminds me that some of the best relationships start off as adversarial. There is great satisfaction in working through issues and finding common ground. It is not an easy undertaking to face conflict and resolve it. It requires understanding and patience, and these are two elements that take time. I am happy we took the time to develop a better relationship. I feel strongly his alliance will allow us to be successful in our new ventures.

I finish breakfast and head back to pick up Arielle. She is starting work today. Her first real job at *Watch me Grow*", the very daycare our children went to. She is excited and nervous, but I am so proud of her. She is a great kid, industrious and kind, and I love her more than she knows.

I think I am going to take the rest of the day off. I am tired, my hands are cramping from all this writing and I want to take advantage of the fact I am home with my wife and kids. I have no schedule, nowhere to go and nowhere to be. I am just going to languish in the fact that I am not traveling, not stressing about a situation at the office, and not gone all day.

I find we put much undue burden on ourselves, myself included. I am finding there are treasures to be had in just silently thinking and living in the moments we often take for granted. I have time now, and I am going to focus on myself for a change, and hopefully find my new path, and ultimately, new purpose.

August 6, 2019

Today I helped my mom and Rod with some errands and house chores. Afterwards, we hung out in the backyard and talked while I fished.

As we talked, I got a strong bite, a big catfish. As luck would have it, we caught the whole thing on video!! I am excited. This was the kind of day I left my job for. One where I can be with my family, focusing on the things that I have put off for so many years. It brings me joy. A joy I have long forgotten. I love you mom! Thank you for a happy day of existence!

August 7, 2019

I spend most of the day running errands in the 400-degree heat. I am tired and hot, but I press on. I am redoing the backyard lighting, and as usual, nothing goes right the first time. In the past, these types of setbacks would drive me crazy, as I was working with limited time, but today, I am not stressed. I take things in stride, and as my projects run into hurdles, I overcome all of them with a little patience.

I can thank my friend, Jorg, and other good Germans I worked with for that. They taught me the value of systematically solving problems using common sense and order. Also, I am not pressed for time anymore. I know now why retired people always seem so happy. There is great peace in not living by someone else's schedule.

Make time for yourself. You need it and you deserve it.

I stop by the supermarket late in the day for some chicken breasts. I cook every day for my family, and I love it. The food is amazing, and I beam with pride as my family enjoys the fruits of my labor. I am strongly considering writing a cookbook after this.

After dinner, fat and happy, I take a walk around our neighborhood to watch the sunset. The clouds are rolling in, the dark clouds turn shades of pink and red as the sun slowly fades. I sit on a bench in a park near our house and take in the tapestry of colors on this warm August evening. I am calm, I am happy, and I am content. All feelings I have not had the pleasure of experiencing for 20+ years. I am deeply grateful for this time. For the first time since I left my career, 2 months ago, I feel more at peace with my decision. I miss being the leader of GMSI, but I don't miss what it did to me emotionally.

Don't let your job become your boss. You hold the ultimate control in how you use your time.

August 8, 2019

Another beautiful morning here in Arizona. I drove Arielle to school and then stopped and got the family breakfast sandwiches at Sonic. There is not much going on today, I am just finishing my lighting project and writing.

I finish my work around the house and decide to take Ben to hit some golf balls at the Trilogy Golf course across the street from our house. The heat is stifling! 116 Degrees. We only last 20 minutes until the heat forces us to go home. On the way, Ben suggests a swim before dinner. I am happy to oblige.

We swim for an hour, just talking and laughing and generally goofing around. These moments are not lost on me anymore. I cherish every single one of them. One day soon, all this carefree fun will end, and I will have to go back to work, but for now, I rarely say no when my kids ask me to do something. I consider it my obligation to them for having put work and my business responsibilities ahead of their wants and needs.

Tomorrow is a new day and filled with new possibilities. I am going to wake up early and play golf. I have no tee time, but I am not worried.

I have time, and in that, I can be flexible. This is a gift. Time is an amazing asset. I am going to pay closer attention to the time I have and remember that it is not infinite. Not for humankind anyway.

Time is a gift. Health is a form of wealth and love is a treasure of immeasurable value.

August 9, 2019

As promised, I woke up at 6am and headed to the golf course. It is a wonderful morning of serene beauty and good golfing. It has been hard not being at the office, driving our business and caring for the health and safety of those who work there. I am a little lost, and I feel like I lost my purpose to some degree. But I am finding my way, and I thank God for the opportunity to be here.

I finish golf around 11am, and the heat of the day envelopes me like a warm blanket, fresh from the dryer. I am starving, but first I need to go back home and get Arielle and give her a ride to work. I decide to surprise her with a little lunch before she goes to work. She is elated. We rarely do things just the two of us, but my offer of lunch and some time together brings a big smile to her face. It's the little things in life that make others happy. And as coincidence would have it, I read a post that encapsulates my thoughts for this day. It says:

Tip your server. Return your shopping cart. Pick up a piece of trash. Hold the door for the person behind you. Let someone into your lane. Small acts can have a ripple effect. That's how we change the world.

I agree. I have learned that selfless acts are the simplest way to show someone else you care, but also, these same acts are how you change the world around you. These are easy things to do and require little to no effort. Just some humility and care. As Ghandi said, *"Be the change you want to see in the world".*

August 10, 2019

Today is Saturday. I am moving some furniture from Mike's house to Adam's apartment. I can now include moving guy to my ever-growing list of new personas.

It's no big deal, it's for my family and I am happy to help. Do for others; there is no greater gift than being the solution to problems other people have.

August 11, 2019

The past few days have been uneventful. We are just enjoying summer here in Arizona. I know this is a book about a year of my life, but let's face it, some days are boring. And that's ok. My life was a 3-ring circus for many years, and I am happy for the quiet normality that these past few days have brought. I adore this time, as it has been 30 years since I have been able to sit back and just exist.

Tomorrow is a new day, and a new week, and all I can think of right now is snuggling up with Wanda and falling asleep on her while we watch a movie. And this is how the evening goes. No regrets.

I am starting to appreciate each day for the gift it is. In my old life, weeks would turn into months, then to years, in the blink of an eye. Now, I am finding that time is slowing down, and in that, I can find the peace I have been seeking. It is still surreal, not working, but I am settling into a rhythm, and embracing the possibilities that lay before us.

August 12, 2019

This morning, KK and I went to Saguaro Lake for a little daddy/daughter time.

On the way, we stopped by Subway for sandwiches and drinks. KK was so excited to order her sandwich. She was...Joyful, I would say.

I asked her, "KK, why are you so happy?", to which she responded, "Because you are here, and we are going to the lake…WITH SAND-WICHES!!"

It doesn't take much to make her happy. A boat and a sandwich from Subway. Her joy comes from within. I am taking notes, as I forgot how to be joyful over the many years I led GMSI. She doesn't worry about anything. Her joy comes from a much simpler place. She is simply happy to be with me, and to have a turkey sandwich. I need to better understand this concept. It will help me in finding my own lost joy.

It's Monday, and most people are living their work lives. I was them, and I never take that for granted, that I can be here on a weekday with my little girl.

We stopped off at a little beach on the east end of the lake. It is littered with shells and KK loves to hang out and collect them. As I watch her play in the water, collecting shells and talking to the bluegills, I begin to understand that the joy she feels is what I have been looking for. For many years, I was her. Carefree and full of wonderment, like when I was little, playing at the beach or in the snow. My joy came from simply being in the moment. I need to remember this.

The key to joy is not in buying things; it is in your heart and embracing your inner child.

We sat on the shore and ate our Subway sandwiches. As we watched the bluegill play, a pair of smallmouth bass came out of nowhere and ate a bluegill. We are stunned. It happened so fast! We sat in silence and then, feeling the need to quantify what we just witnessed, I explained the food chain to her. She gets it but doesn't like the harsh reality of survival of the fittest. She asks me, "Was your work like that?" I tell her that in some ways, life imitates nature, and yes, my work was sometimes very much like the scene we just witnessed. She asks me, "How did you not get eaten?"

I pause for a second, thinking about her question. I answer her as honestly as possible, with the following explanation. *"In life, be the big fish. But always be on the lookout, because there are always bigger fish than you or me, and they attack without warning."* She listens and then goes back to eating her sandwich. After a few moments she says, "Dad, can we go fishing for the big fish?" And I smile. She gets it, even at 9 years old. She doesn't want to catch the big fish for any other reason than to stop them from eating the small fish. And I was like that too. She is a protector and I smile with pride at her thought process, particularly in her willingness to solve this complex biological problem with a rubber worm and some 10 lb. test.

After many hours of baking in the 110-degree heat, we agree it's time to head home. As we cruise the lake, she puts her hands up and revels in the rush of wind and spray, happy to be out here, happy to be with her dad. It reminds me of how I felt when my dad took us sailing. Same elation, different generation.

When I arrived back home, our housekeeper and friend, Paty, was there. I love Paty. She is a hard-working single mom who has overcome much adversity herself. I am always happy to see her, as she reminds me often that the greatest joy in life is just being alive. I remind myself that I am indeed alive, and home with my family, and I am slowly finding the joy in what she already knows.

Happiness comes from within. You choose whether to be happy or sad. Choose happy!

August 13, 2019

It's Tuesday, a workday for most, but for me, it's just Tuesday. As I sit in my office writing, one of my former colleagues sends me a meme. He says it is appropriate for my new life. It says, "If you see me talking to myself just move along...I am self-employed, and we are having a staff meeting".

I smile at the relevance of this. It's true. I have morphed from a once dynamic leader, a guy who took on the challenges of industry, to a guy who sits in his underwear, drinking coffee and writing books. I am ok with this newfound role, and I write him back to let him know all is well.

Today I am taking Ben to the "Main Event" to bowl and play. A daddy/son day. We arrived to an almost empty parking lot. Ben and I pick our bowling balls and head to our lane. Ben is stoked. He says, "Dad, can you believe we are here by ourselves?" I smiled and high five him, reminding him this is why I chose to leave my career, to be with him, to do things like this.

As we begin to bowl, I am reminded of why finger foods and bowling don't mix. Actually, I am reminded of scenes from the movie, *The Big Lebowski.* I realize I am slowly embracing my inner "dude". Turns out that I am becoming "the dude", in more ways than one. I knew I should have come here in my bathrobe. As a consolation, I order a White Russian.

We finished our game and returned our rental shoes. Ben plays games in the arcade for an hour while I reminisce about my grandpa John. He was an amazing bowler, always carrying a high average. He bowled several 300 games in his lifetime, and I think of the many times I tagged along to the alleys with him, where he would feed me Sprite and French fries and hand me quarters for the arcade machines, like Pong and pinball. And here I sit, 40+ years later, with my own boy, doing the same thing I did when I was a kid. Times have changed, and technology has changed, but the joy of a day at the bowling alley with your kid hasn't. I miss you grandpa. I hope you are throwing nothing but strikes in heaven.

August 14, 2019

I wake up early to get ready for the day. I am taking my mom to her Dr. appointment in Phoenix, and I want to write some thoughts for this book prior to leaving to get her. My thoughts are diverse, some for this book, some for my future books and still others, just about life. My thought process continues to revolve around two key elements. Death and joy.

I realize I am not going to live forever, but how much time do I have left? I ask myself a simple question. "If you knew you only had a month left to live, what would you do?" I can't answer that question honestly. I can only think of how sad I would be if I had no more time with my family and friends. And then I realized, the weight of the revelation like getting smacked in the mouth with a dead fish; *I lost my joy when I lost my dad.* How did I not see this before? When he died, my joy died. I have never realized that until just now. My joy wasn't contingent on my dad being here, but without him, I had let his death steal something incredibly valuable to me. I lost my ability to feel the joy associated with living my life. Now I need to figure out how to recapture my spirit, and in doing so, find my inner peace and the feeling of joy I so desperately crave.

I drive with this thought in mind to pick my mom up for her Dr. appointment. She tells me how grateful she is for taking her, but the truth is, I am grateful for being able to be here for her. I want to talk to her about my earlier thoughts, about joy. Did she feel joy anymore? I want to ask her, but she gets emotional talking about my dad, so I decided some thoughts are better kept to myself. But I wonder; *Did she too lose the joy she used to feel when my dad was alive?*

After we finish at the Dr., my mom suggests we have lunch at Macayo's, a great Mexican food restaurant near her house. I called Wanda and asked her if she wanted to meet us for lunch. She agrees. And an hour later, my mom, Rod, my family, and I are all happily chatting, eating lunch, and enjoying our time together. And guess what? I felt it. I felt...joy.

The joy we seek resides with the people we love the most. Align to them, and joy follows.

August 15, 2019

I wake up today with a renewed sense of what it feels like to be joyful. I remember a scene in the movie, *Footprints*, an independent film starring members of my parish at St. Annes, including my Pastor, Father Sergio Fita. The movie chronicles the story of the way of St. James. It is shot on location and details the experience that each of the pilgrims endures during the 500 mile walk from Saint Jean Pied de Port, France, through four of Spain's 15 regions, ending at the Cathedral of Santiago de Compostela in Galicia. I have had the pleasure of speaking to many of the film's participants. For most, it was a life-changing experience. The one common denominator, other than pain, was the joy they felt in embracing their struggles, while immersing themselves in their faith. Their explanation of the many emotions they felt during the walk all culminated with that one common feeling. Joy.

I am up early to meet Brad at the lake. I am taking him on the boat to discuss our new venture, InfinityGo. He will serve as COO. But today, he and I are just out to enjoy time and nature. And we do. And in these moments, I recognize a common theme when I take people out on the lake. They experience joy. This is fitting, as our new venture focuses on redefining travel and social interactions. I understand more clearly that the key to our success is in sharing the joy that people feel when they are connected with each other, doing things they wouldn't normally do. This will become the cornerstone of our new business, to find ways to bring joy to those who use our services. I realized something simple.

If you let yourself say yes more, you will find more opportunities to be happy.

Today taught me a valuable lesson about how we choose to use our time, and whether these choices bring us happiness. And I find that we all have the power to determine our own happiness. It lies in the choices we make. Choose wisely.

August 16, 2019

It's another day of Groundhogs. Wake up, take Arielle to school, blah, blah, blah, blah!

It's Friday, and today we are starting a new trend. All kids have school on Friday, leaving Wanda and I alone for 6 hours. Rather than waste this opportunity, we dedicate ourselves to "Fridates". This is the term Wanda coins to describe our Fridays moving forward. A day for us to date each other. This morning, I surprised her by taking her to her favorite breakfast restaurant, First Watch. I am not as big a fan of this place as she is, but to see her happy and upbeat makes me happy. And in keeping with my own desire to rekindle my relationship with joy, I am willing to make sacrifices. "Say yes more, Peter".

We finished a great breakfast and I decided we should go to her favorite mall and just hang out. She is floored. We NEVER do this. When we first started dating, we would spend countless hours just walking around malls, eating mall food, and exploring the bargain racks.

She suggests the Arizona Mills Mall. We peruse the many stores and walk hand in hand. We share some treats and snacks and generally just relax together. We are at ease, and this feeling is something new for both of us.

It has been a hard road for Wanda as well. She supported me through my insane work and travel schedule, always holding down the fort and raising our kids, while I was out trying to change the world. Now, in our new reality, I think she is finding a rhythm as well. The stress of doing everything by herself is diminishing with me being home, and I try and make sure that if there is something I can do to alleviate some of her burden, I will do it. I am where I am partly because she was there for me.

We enjoy a quiet afternoon shopping, and if she is happy, so am I. Just being together, alone, and without the constant interruptions of my business calls, or misbehaving kids, is a treat all in itself. There will be more days like this. I promised her.

Later in the day, we surprise Arielle with a car. A 2005 Ford Taurus. It will replace the one she wrecked, and while it isn't fancy, it will take her around town, and to school and work. Wanda and I surprised her at work. Wanda went inside and asked Arielle to come out to the parking lot. She is stern, so Arielle thinks she is in trouble. As Arielle exits the door of her work, she gets in my truck, but I tell her she should take her own car. She is dumbfounded. She doesn't have a car. Or does she?

I tell her to get out of the truck and Wanda hands her the keys and tells her to drive her own car, pointing to the Taurus in front of her. Arielle starts to cry. She is so excited. I am excited. Her joy is ours, and this further supports my earlier statements that we can derive joy through helping others.

It was a good day. A day that offered me the opportunity to bring happiness to others, and in that, I find my own happiness as well. Not just happiness, but Joy. They are very different. While I should expound on that thought, I will just let you ponder.

Before I fall asleep, I pray, asking God to help me to have the opportunity to continue to find ways to help others, and inversely, help myself.

The most valuable form of payment we receive has no monetary significance; its worth is measured in the gratitude of others we help.

August 17, 2019

I find great joy on the water, as I have stated many times before. The greater joy I feel isn't in my own experience, but in sharing it with others. Today, I am meeting my friend Cubby for a rousing morning of warm beer and Jet Skis. Cubby and I are kindred spirits, and I could not have asked for a better friend. We have braved the wilds and dangers of forest fires together, as well as the many trials and tribulations of our years at GMSI. He is one of a kind.

He shares that all is not well at GMSI anymore. Since I left there have been numerous issues, and he fears that the current ownership is going to make drastic changes. I knew this prior to leaving the company, but I could never say anything.

As he shares some of his own frustrations, I realize that the company is in trouble. He will most likely be ok, but I fear many others will eventually be subject to the reality of a failing business. Layoffs, terminations, and shutdowns are all possible. In the meantime, I will keep them in my prayers. There is no sense in me alarming him, but I feel great angst when I think about the welfare of many others that are in harm's way. And now, there is nothing I can do to stop it.

When you take the spirit and culture away from a company, there is nothing left to hold it up. Like a balloon with a slow leak, eventually, all the air will escape, leaving a deflated shell of what was once something valuable. The most valuable thing? The people...the culture.

August 18, 2019

After church is over, we head back home to see my oldest son, Adam, and our grandson, Jordan. We had a nice day, but we were all exhausted, so we say our goodbyes and I convince Wanda to go upstairs with me and watch TV. She is tired too, and happily agrees. It is 7:34 PM. We are officially an old married couple.

August 19, 2019

I spend the morning bouncing between Home Depot, Lowes, the UPS store, and a few other essential stops as I continue to work on checking the boxes on my now lengthy list of tasks I want to complete. I am finding a rhythm to my daily schedule, and this brings me some much-needed focus.

I finish my errands around noon and head back home. I spend a few hours writing, as tomorrow, Ben will be playing with me on his first real golf course. Ben and I set out to the driving range. He has been asking for a golf glove since he started playing, and on the way to the range we stop at Dick's Sporting Goods for a glove and some balls.

He is meticulous in his selection, even though there are only 2 kinds of gloves available for kids. He is more like Wanda. Calculated, precise and structured. I am more loose, able to make decisions quickly and require much less structure. I work in the abstract; he is in the details. This balance bodes well in business partnerships but in the selection of gloves, I find it to be a waste of time.

We headed to the driving range and hit balls in the balmy, August evening. It's after 8 when we finish. We have a big day tomorrow, so we pack up and head home. I tuck Ben in, and we say our prayers, as he drifts off easily to a restful sleep. I wish I could sleep like that. I have not slept properly in months, and it is really starting to take a toll on me.

August 20, 2019

It's 5 AM. An early wake up for us. It is Ben's first time on a real golf course, and I want to make sure he is ready. We drive about half an hour to the course known as Shalimar. It is a special treat to be able to have Ben play his first real round of golf with his grandpa and myself.

We meet up with Grandpa Rod and find that he has invited some of his friends to golf with us. 3 of them. We are a "Sixsome", which on most courses is an absolute no-no, but this is Shalimar, and here, anything goes!

To beat the intense heat of the Arizona summer, we tee off at 6:46 AM. The sun is strong, even at this early hour and I am anxious to get going, as we still have school and a variety of other activities to finish today.

We all tee off and it is a brutal collection of short hits, sculls, shanks, and slices, including my own. If hole #1, at Shalimar Golf Course in

Tempe, AZ were a battlefield, it would be littered with corpses, weapons and the dead and dying. Hole #2 was only slightly better!!!

Ben, however, plays great! I don't care about my score. I care that my kid, my Benny, is playing golf with me, driving the cart, and having fun. It is a dream come true to have one of my kids like to play golf with me. SUCCESS!!!

Later in the day, I have business calls to make, and I am also prepping dinner. I need to remind Wanda what a catch I am. I am sure other women would appreciate who I am as a man--if not at the very least, for my cooking and handyman skills. My prowess as a lover may be overstated.

I head upstairs around 8 PM to pay some bills and write some pages. By 9:30 I am completely spent. I go through these phases where I can stay up all night and then wake up at 5 AM to go to the lake, or the other extreme; I fall asleep during a movie on the couch at 8:30 PM.

Wanda comes to bed around 11:30. We attempt a romantic interlude, but we are both exhausted, so we kiss goodnight and fall asleep instantly.

August 21, 2019

I must be honest. It's 6 AM and I wake up very "stimulated". It has been a couple of weeks since Wanda and I have been together. I have always been a person with an active libido, but lately, it has been in overdrive. I know she will kill me, but I need to feel Wanda close to me. I put my leg over her butt and rub her back. I know she hates being awakened but as soon as I start, I stop because my colon understands that It's "poop thirty", and I must make my way from the warm bed with the hot girl, to the cold and lonely confines of the guest bathroom. I am a prisoner of my own digestive system, a sure deterrent for any early morning sexcapades.

In the cold, quiet of the guest bathroom, I read some emails and answered several more. I do my best work here.

I make some coffee and head to my office to begin writing and finishing emails. Today I am going to meet Chuck Moretti, head of a software company here in town. His group was instrumental in designing and building the RCM's (Reactor control Modules) for our CVD reactors at GMSI. I like him a lot. We have known each other for many years, and this is the first time we are seeing each other outside of work. I am not sure what he has in mind, but my guess is he wants to talk about a work opportunity.

That is the thing about my resignation, I am surprised at the types of offers I am getting. I guess I was more respected than my own co-workers gave me credit for. In love and business, the dynamic seems to be the same. You may find love in the strangest places and in the most unexpected situations. Business is remarkably similar. Love and business are intertwined in their similarities because they both revolve around relationships.

Chuck wants to golf, so I drive the 40 miles to the beautiful Legacy Golf Resort here in Phoenix. We talked about the state of semiconductors, his company's progress with one of my longtime mutual clients, inventions, and technology. It feels good to talk shop with grown-ups again.

He asks me what I have been doing and I tell him the truth. Nothing. I have done nothing but hang out, write, and field some employment offers. I told him I built a putting green and that I go to the lake often, which made him smile enviously.

We talked about the future, mine, and his. We finally get to discussing how to work together and I just ask him point blank, "What am I doing here and what do you want/need from me?" It turns out that he sees an opportunity in the semiconductor equipment space, and he knows how to capitalize on it. He wants me to consult and if needed, raise capital, and lead the company. I am interested and we talk through a myriad of scenarios and how to move ahead.

It is a very productive day, in the 117-degree heat, playing golf and drinking. This is the way business should be done. Chuck is the one who says it best. "We work 60-80 hours a week to run our businesses. The least we can do is take half a day here and there to work on the course. It's where the best ideas and deals come from."

He is right. What good is working all the time if you don't make any time for yourself? There is not enough emphasis in the corporate world on employee PTO. As I have said, happy employees make for productive ones. This is a dialogue I would like to dive deeper into in the future, once this book is written and I can consult or speak publicly. I feel many of us burn out due to lack of self-maintenance. I would like to see this change.

People need to step away from the workplace periodically to stay fresh. I miss this aspect of my former life, the part where I could influence these types of scenarios. I miss helping people achieve goals. There is great satisfaction in seeing others succeed.

As an aside, I played one of the best golf rounds of my life. I used to be a 6 handicap, but then life got in the way. My first marriage crumbled, the recession hit, friends changed and just like that, no more golf. Now, I plan on playing every week. Golf will save me in many ways. It will reconnect me back to that thing I lost. Joy. I never let myself feel it after my dad died, and now, I was experiencing these moments of joy, many on the golf course. Golf helped me clear my head, align my thoughts, make plans, heal, and reinvent myself.

Later in the evening, I am sunburned and tired, and I fall asleep on the couch. Wanda tries to wake me repeatedly, finally announcing she is going upstairs without me. After giving myself a second to get my bearings, I head upstairs and get changed. As I pour myself into bed, sunburned and hungover, I make a futile attempt at trying to seduce Wanda, but she just laughs at me.

"Dude, you were just fast asleep on the couch, and now you want to fool around?" I pause and answer her with the best rebuttal I can offer. "Well, I did get a nap."

We both laugh and I hug her and fall asleep. Tomorrow is another day that ends in "Y". See you there!

August 22, 2019

No matter what I do, I am stuck in work mode as far as sleep goes. My body and mind have been conditioned to wake up no later than 6 AM. It's a carryover from my career, but I use this time wisely. I wake up early and have time to collect my thoughts and write, or at the very least, to sit outside and watch the birds as the day comes to life.

At 10 AM I have a call with Brad and Cort Bucholtz. Cort is the CEO of the consulting and software group, Singlemind, who will be developing our new App platform for InfinityGo. I have this call in the parking lot of a Walmart. No longer do I have a fancy office with the latest technology. And I don't need it. Just a phone and a vision. That's all.

After the call, and some groceries, I raced home to prepare for a call with Omer on our financial plan. We discuss everything we need to build a cohesive financial model, which is required when you start up a new business. Investors want to see that you understand your cash flow and expenses, and for a new business, understanding this intimately is the only way to ensure you don't run out of cash before you find your success. It feels good to work again, even if I am not getting paid.

The rest of the afternoon is spent trying to find a colleague who has disappeared. He owns a company that has defaulted on its payments, and I am trying to find him to offer some solutions. He called me frantically a week ago looking for advice, but I haven't heard from him since. I have lost 3 friends this year, I don't want to lose another.

I have not written a word of this book today and I find that I miss my daily writing session. I am becoming a writer, something I have dreamed of since I was a young kid, when I would sit and write fictional stories just for fun. Like my life as a CEO, I have had no formal writing training, but have been writing most of my life. No matter, I don't let the fear of inexperience stand in the way of doing something. I just dive in and figure things out as I go.

After a movie with Wanda, I go upstairs and tuck the kids in and pray. I thank God for the blessings of life, my family and friends, the love He brings us and for the many wonderful opportunities. I do love putting my kids to bed. I have traveled so much in the past 11 years; I have missed at least 40-50% of all the good nights my kids have ever had. I am making up for lost time.

We turn the lights off around 11:30. It's been another long day, but to my surprise, we found a moment for romance. I am never too tired for her, and the day ends happily.

Afterwards, I couldn't sleep, and I lay in the dark and breathed. It is quiet and peaceful. I love the night. Sometimes it's good not to see EVERYTHING. The darkness tends to hide what is unimportant, like a filter of clarity. I think about the direction things are going, our finances, our love life, our kids, house, cars, bills, opportunities, lesions, and bruises and pretty much everything that is on my mind. Then, I filter down, in the darkness, to the things that matter most. One of them is happily snoring next to me. The others are down the hall. I love my family. I am incredibly grateful for the time this resignation has given to me. When David Cassidy of the Partridge Family died, his last words were, *"So much wasted time".* I don't want to waste a moment.

His words stayed with me. How many days and nights, hours, and minutes have I devoted to building my business? To clients and vendors, investors, and employees. On trips and endless meetings. So much time; time I will never have back. So many moments I missed with my family. I may not have enough money to retire, and I may not have the title of CEO anymore, but I have what is most important. The love of those I care about the most. I get to spend every day with them. I prayed for this, and God listened.

I traded wealth and status for love and time. Time and love are the greatest assets you can have. They always bear fruit. Always pay dividends. Money doesn't buy love; well, maybe on an hourly basis, but it does not get you unconditional acceptance and support. You cannot buy time. Once it is gone, so are we. I am glad I left Heraeus, it was time. I am open and hopeful to whatever new path comes my way. I pray daily that God may guide me onto the path He wants me on.

August 23, 2019

I have a 9 AM conference call in the parking lot of Dunkin Donuts. The call went well, and I grab some breakfast treats for Wanda and I and head home. I arrived home to find Wanda has decided to rearrange her office. I am extremely impressed with her, as always. She planned it out, on paper, to scale no less, and then executed exactly as she planned it. I can appreciate good planning and execution. She would have made a great Operations Manager.

We spend hours working on her new office, but we need to go. It's a little after 3 and we need to go get the kids from school. We leave on time. We arrive early and hang in the car and go through messages and calls while we wait for the kids. Because we are early, we have this time.

Always plan to be early. Being late shows others that they are not important.

It's after 7 PM now, and the grind of the past few days is really wearing on me. I am tired, but not in a bad way. I feel like we are accomplishing a lot these days. We hung shelves, did the laundry, worked on books, taught our kids, and spent some quality time together. I am dedicating my days to my family and their needs.

It was a good day and one that reminded me of the reason I resigned. I am still concerned with our long-term finances, and I think about three things. Cash flow, health insurance and life insurance. These are the most important aspects of this new life without a job. The simple way to resolve these worries is to get a job and work for a big company that will eat my spirit in exchange for a 401K, health and dental and a promise that if all the stars align, I will be able to leave and live the rest of my life in peace and harmony. It's a fallacy though.

That dream does not exist for many, as I see it. We work ourselves to death. From CEOs to those making minimum wage. We all run on the same hamster wheel, the only difference is how long and how hard we run. I left because I was tired. I was the minimum wage guy in 1983, and the CEO in 2019. I spent a lot of time chasing the dream. I realized after many "almosts" and "next times", that it was time for me to stop chasing and start living, for my greatest fear is dying before I have a chance to live.

Speaking of which, I lost my life Insurance today. The Insurance company screwed me on a portability loophole. They have tried to screw everyone I have seen them deal with in our company. Now if I die, I have no death benefit for Wanda and the kids. It hurts bad. I don't want to die and have them worry about money. I have had life Insurance since the 90s. I paid and paid. Now, it is wasted money if I cannot convince them to give me my portability. I will try. If not, I will find new Insurance.

I need to stop worrying about dying and who gets what when I go. I need to choose life; to live and be here for Wanda and the kids. I choose to go a different way than most, because I think I understand now, through faith and love, that time is my greatest asset. I am going to spend that time with my greatest treasures, my family and friends and the experiences of life I will share with them.

In the end, I will accept death, and I will continue to pray that the Lord will take me in and let me join the party in Heaven. I would like to see many people again. Especially, my dad, my grandparents and my best friend, Stephen. It has been a lonely existence without them in my life. See you guys; hopefully, just not too soon. I still have things to accomplish. Like this book, another business, and a retirement on the ocean, somewhere warm, where I can watch sunsets glisten over the golden water, holding Wanda's hand and watching our kids play with their kids.

That is my dream now.

August 24, 2019

I wake up with some anxiety that we are living without a safety net, in the sense that we are living on our savings, paying for our own insurances and now, without a death benefit policy. I try not to worry about these things, but as soon as I open my eyes, these worries fill my thoughts. I need to find a way to create some long-term stability for us.

It is a beautiful and clear morning, and I am never without appreciation for the life I am living, or the sunrises and sunsets I see daily. I drive over to a park close by to fish in their little public lake. I sip my coffee and cast my line while I collect my many thoughts and try and center myself. I am worried, but unlike my past life, I will not have to dwell on this long. I will make some calls and fix what I can, and what I can't, I will stop worrying about.

Worry is a disease that attacks our lives like cancer. Don't smoke, and don't worry about things that are out of your control. Worrying and stress will kill you just as easily as carcinoma.

I am slowly adapting to this new life. It hasn't been easy, and there are certainly many things I struggle with emotionally, but I am open to change, and willing to live outside my comfort zone.

It is Cailyn's birthday on the 28th and we are having a party for her today. In the past, Wanda was the CEO of the house, and I was the CEO of the business. In this new role, she is still in charge here at the house, and I am the Vice President, and I don't like it. I want to be in charge, but "happy wife, happy life", as the saying goes. She "asks" me to get the cake and party favors squared away, so off to Walmart I go, to get the birthday cake and buy balloons and candy rings. I can almost feel my estrogen levels rising. I am confident I am just a few weeks away from full blown "Manopause".

I am kidding of course, but I am confused by our roles sometimes. I don't mind helping her, but it feels weird and not masculine. But I wonder, is it a problem? Is it not manly to buy your daughter a cake and party favors? Or to help your wife? I think society convinces us that our roles are clearly defined when the only one that should define our roles is...us.

When I arrived home, Wanda made me lunch. I am floored. Wanda never makes me lunch. I am the cook now, but she wanted to do something nice. Her love language is acts of service. I am physical touch, as we discovered reading the book, *The 5 love languages*. Somehow, we make it all work. Paula Abdul was right. Opposites DO attract.

Cailyn has a great party at *Main Event*. There are games, attractions, laser tag, an obstacle course and...ADULT BEVERAGES!!! Wanda and I grab a drink and toast each other as chaos ensues all around us. I think this is how Nero felt watching Rome burn.

I am tipsy from our libation, and I am not sure what I say to anyone as I run around herding children and electronic game cards. It is mayhem. The kids had fun and there were smiles all around. Mission accomplished!

As we leave, I see on one of the many TV sets mounted around this gargantuan fun palace, that Andrew Luck, quarterback of the Colts, has resigned. His body battered, he decided to focus on family, even though he wanted to keep playing. I feel for him. I was good at what I did too. I didn't want to leave, but I couldn't do it anymore. It was killing me. I relate to him. I hope he finds his path and that in retrospect, he realizes he did the right thing.

We finally got back to the house around 8 PM. I go out back and marvel at the stars, sitting in the dark and thanking God for all we have. We don't have Andrew Luck money, but we have our faith, and each other, and in that we have everything we need.

August 25, 2019

I woke up a second time, filled with the fresh emotion of weird dreams, pee and last night's pizza. I need to visit the guest bathroom. I am happy to be regular; it's part of my schedule now. Schedules are important as they provide direction and clarity. They offer a view of control in one's crazy life. A schedule provides a way to manage the complexity of time and offers better life efficiency. I am a big fan of the digital calendar on my phone.

It is Sunday and I tackle some yardwork. I checked the chemistry in the pool. Everything looks good now. I used my chemistry skills to create an algaecide. The guy at the pool store wanted to charge me over $200 for chemicals and I told him I was going to make my own. He laughed at me. It doesn't matter what he thinks, I do things my way. It reminds me of a meme I saw a few weeks ago. It said, *"They laugh at me because I am different, but I laugh at them because they are all the same."* Embrace your uniqueness. There is only one you. Stand out!

I feel motivated this morning. I have written for hours, and I am filled with gratitude for this time I have been able to enjoy since I left my career. I sit and pray. I pray the IRS sends my overpayment, that the stock market corrects, and that we find our way to be together each day, just as I had prayed from 2017 to June of 2019.

I will always remember the sleepy, satisfied look in Cailyn's eyes, on the night of June 7th, as I prayed our nightly prayers. I thanked God for the opportunity for me to be able to have the strength and faith to leave my job and be with my family. A family that for decades supported me as I raced around the world to drive our company to a place of success. Cailyn smiled and said, "Daddy, now you don't have to go to work anymore?". I answered her, letting her know that I was finished. "Today was my last day of work. Starting tomorrow, Daddy will be with you and the family, every day, just like we prayed."

In that moment I realized the power of faith and prayer. My faith provided me with a competitive edge. It gave me strength because in prayer, I left my doubts and insecurities with God, and was able to go out and rise above my own expectations. I give God praise on a daily basis because he gave me the gift of this amazing life, and the promise of life everlasting. I know many of you don't believe in God, or the presence of any deity, or the afterlife. I don't push my faith on you, and I was doubtful once too. My dad's death soured me to the faith, and his memory brought me back to it. I hope my words and actions will help guide you as well.

August 26, 2019

A new week dawns and I am up to greet it early. I watch the sunrise and then head inside to get things going. I agree to a consulting call this morning with Woody regarding his company's acquisition. They will never pay me, but Woody keeps calling. He is a nice guy. I don't care if they pay for my expertise. I give it willingly to him because I know he needs a sounding board. I did too at many points in my career. My normal hourly rate is $500/ hr., but for him, I am willing to discount my time. The final cost? Free.

I am not ready to go back to work, but there are opportunities, and I cannot turn a shoulder to a good opportunity. So, I make myself available to "discussions".

In bed later tonight, I am hoping for some romance with Wanda, but she comes to bed wearing her, "not tonight" pants, along with a "sexual deterrent" T- shirt. It's ok. I love her and understand that not every night can be a romance novel, but my libido begs to differ. This is marriage, for better or worse.

Marriage is not about the ceremony, but about a relationship that nurtures the love of two people. Nurture each other. The ceremony ends but the honeymoon should always remain.

August 27, 2019

I think about the day ahead. It's going to be another packed day. I have 2 appointments today. One downtown with my accountants and the other a lunch in Scottsdale with the head of a PR firm here in town. I am going to wear professional clothes for the first time in months. I am excited to have some professional meetings. It has been a while since I felt like a CEO. I still don't feel like one, but the activity of putting things together is a nice change from my existence of the past few months, where the most I put together was a dinner order.

I have to leave for my appointments and Wanda and the kids take off for breakfast and a movie. It was the plan all along, and I am delighted they can get out during the day. Again, the benefits of home schooling and my break are synonymous. We get to do what we want at times when others are in school or work, so we get to do things without the crowds.

I drive to my appointments the same way I did for the last 8 years on my way to work. I am now driving by as a man without a direction, or a title. I am many things to many people, but I am not the CEO anymore. As I drive by where I would have turned off all these years prior, I am reminded of what I have now, and how I got here, and I thank God for all these great blessings and the opportunity to exit the fast lane in favor of spending time with my kids and my wife. It is ironic that this one road had so much influence on my emotions over the past 10 years. Now, it is just another exit on the freeway--one I will pass by this time, on a new path, living a new life.

At my accountants, we sit and discuss tax and formation for my new entity, InfinityGo. It is an Uber-like crowd sharing model for international travel destinations. I will also start a private company called "AZ Lake Adventures" which will serve to offer travelers and visitors the opportunity to go out on the lake, on our private boat and Jet Skis, to see the lakes, eat food and hang out with locals that provide the tours.

After a hot lap across town, I arrive at the *Grassroots Kitchen* to meet with David Weissman, PR Guru, and an all-around cool guy!! We had a great lunch and David takes great interest in my new direction. He did my testimonials for Cox Business, as part of a marketing campaign I was involved in, and I always appreciated his demeanor and candor. We discuss how he and his firm can better help us position the new business, and he offers many helpful suggestions. I think he will be an integral part of my future.

I am finished here in the city and as I drive the 40 minutes back to our house, I receive a recruiting call from the world's largest Semiconductor Equipment company, Applied Materials, also known as AMAT. They offer me an interesting proposition to assist as a consultant for their group. I let them know I am open to discussions, and we agree to circle back at a later date.

Later in the evening, I am perturbed. I am trying to cook dinner, write this book and start a new business and Wanda is lying on the couch watching a movie, falling asleep. I am not happy. I am feeling bitter. It is never lost on me that Wanda is quick to help others around us, but for me, not so much. I give her massages, she doesn't reciprocate. I cook her food, but she doesn't offer to cook for me anymore. She wakes up every day after me, to make Arielle breakfast, but she never did this for me or my other kids. She wonders why I seem agitated sometimes.

If you keep disregarding a person's importance, they will show you how much you mean to them. Treat people as you want to be treated.

August 28, 2019

It's KK's BDAY! I love this kid. My little girl. She is 9 years old today. It is going to be a great day. I have calls today for InfinityGo and my offer with Applied Materials, but I want to dedicate my attention to Cailyn. Once breakfast is finished, I raced upstairs to take my calls. It bothers me a little that everyone else is downstairs playing and working. I would like to play but all play and no work makes Peter a broke boy.

Cailyn wants to go to Olive Garden for her birthday dinner. As I have said before, I don't like chains, but Olive Garden is a family favorite. Not mine, but Wanda and the kids love it, so happy wife, happy life. I like "happy spouse, happy house". It puts me in the mix, somewhere. The other way, it is all about the woman. Guys, we matter.

We have a nice dinner and come home and tuck everyone in bed. Wanda and I lay in bed to finish a movie we started. She joins me in a sexy nightgown, after wearing a tight mini skirt all day. It is torturous to see her in all these sexy clothes, only to be rejected for any kind of coital activity.

The movie ends and Wanda is complaining that her neck and back hurt. I offer to rub her back and neck, and she rolls on her side. I massage her for 45 minutes, but she wants nothing to do with me. Classic. She gets hers; I get none. I am getting really fed up.

August 29, 2019

My wife has lost interest in me, and it is driving me crazy. I miss the way we used to be. I said this would be a book about the good, the bad and the ugly. It bothers me that she isn't more attentive, but I accepted her and all her imperfections, as she did to me, a long time ago. We need to find a better balance together. Lately, I am feeling quite unimportant.

I need a break, so I put the boat back together and take it back to the boatyard. I really need to write, as this book won't write itself.

I arrive home and decide to hang out with Ben. We play games and watch videos on YouTube. TV is strange. It offers so much content, especially with expanded cable packages, the internet, YouTube, Hulu, Netflix, Amazon Video and more. Our kids are inundated and barraged with a myriad of choices and triggers and content; it is no wonder they have some of the hardest times with adjusting to the "real" world.

Unlike the past 28 years of my life, I do not have a host of stressful conduits running through my brain, 24-7. Now, I think freely. I am relaxed, for the most part. I worry about money running out, but now I see that I have value outside my longtime role as CEO of GMSI. I have worth to others and more importantly, to myself.

As I left my 28-year career as the face of GMSI, my biggest challenge was to understand my identity and my purpose. I did most of what I set out to do in business, but now, I needed to understand who I would become post-GMSI. I have some great ideas, but it is all talk until you do it.

For the past 2 months I have spent the time I needed to heal. To unwind a very tight clock, as Stephen Millman wrote on my Facebook page the day I left. *"You are like a tightly wound clock. Everything is ready to spring out, splaying pieces everywhere".* He is very descriptive. And accurate.

I realize just how many things we don't deal with as people. Emotionally, mainly. All of us. We get stuck in life's wake and overlook our own mental health. We aren't machines, but just like a piece of heavy equipment, we all need a preventative maintenance cycle to keep us running at peak performance. Many of us haven't seen the service center in years. I am one of those, and I fear that my repairs are going to be costly. Golf is therapy, and therapy is expensive. Lol!

August 30, 2019

I slept poorly last night. I woke up at 2:30 AM, 4:30 and then at 5:34. I don't understand this lack of sleep. I have a feeling the problem lies partly in my frustration with our current sex life. Maybe I just need to stop fixating on things I can't fix. Maybe I just need some melatonin and fellatio. A massage would be nice too.

No time for whining, we need to go. Wanda will go to Pinal County, to see Kathy as she goes to court. I will take the kids to Eagleridge and drop them off. I am towing Jet Skis this morning, as today is Cubby's birthday and his present is a day on the skis.

He got his nickname, "Cubby", from the way he could come into a room and destroy all the delicate parts he was working on, like a baby bear demolishing a campsite. I love him. He is my buddy. He gives me his trust completely. "Where you go, I go", he has always said to me. He was one who came a long way and followed me through hell. He is a real friend.

This is another dream realized. It is Friday at 11am. I am in the water, staring at the most gorgeous canyon you will ever see. I have 2 Jet Skis, a great friend, who is celebrating his birthday, and I am not in an office, or a meeting, I am at the lake, "Dogfish Head 60 Minute IPA" in hand, chatting and taking in the beauty of nature. It is in these moments I am most grateful for the blessings I have been given. I offer thanks to God, as I have many times before. The life I am living is the life I prayed for. Believe what you want, I believe that my prayers are being answered daily. I hope yours will be too.

We finished our long morning of riding and drive back to town. On the way back, we decided to stop for prickly pear Margaritas. After 2 of them, I realized, "I have had a 20 oz. IPA and two margaritas, and now I have to drive through city traffic and freeways to get the 30 miles back home.

I am" Bunk" or "Druzzed". These are my definitions for those states of intoxication that leave you between buzzed and drunk. One more drink, and you could be topless. No more drinks and maybe you can manage your way home, with a breath mint and a prayer. "Please God, help me to get home safely. Help me to do the speed limit and for once, stay in the lines on the freeway". I have a horrible tendency to drift on the freeway. I am a drifter. I hugged Cubby and drive off, heading for home. I am feeling the effects of the second margarita. "I wonder how obvious it looks if I drive with one hand over my eye". I make it home safe and I vow to make better choices.

How quickly time passes now. Day turns to night and Monday to Friday. All in an instant. I need to get a better hold of time. I just don't know how. It was easier when I worked because my days were structured to respond to the needs of the company and others. Meetings, lunches, and trips were all scheduled by my assistant, Stephanie. Now, days pass without me even realizing it. "It's Wednesday? It was just Sunday" is a popular phrase at our dinner table. I need to better manage my time, for this is a finite commodity, and lately I fear mine is running out.

It's after 9 PM when we say goodnight to the kids. Wanda has some calls and I need to write these words. The mood has changed, and I am sure we are both exhausted now. As we meet in our bed, we play and laugh and then fall asleep spooning. I love my woman. I speak harshly about her sometimes, mostly out of frustration. I sincerely hope she finds her path in life, as I look for mine. She is a great homeschool teacher and mom, but I wonder if it is enough for her. The kids will get older, and I wonder what she will want to do. A new career? Maybe she will travel with me. Maybe, she will write a book too. I fall asleep in the comfort that only she can bring me. Intertwined in each other's arms, my thoughts fade to dreams.

August 31, 2019

Speaking of dreams, it is 4:53 AM. I am awakened from a fitful slumber, filled with vivid and bizarre dreams. I tell myself it is exhaustion, sunburn, and the aftereffects of prickly pear margaritas, but my logical side thinks it may have something to do with stress. Why would I be stressed? I don't work; I go to the lake and play golf, and I am generally happy most days. I don't understand myself anymore. I settle on the conclusion. I am a man without a purpose in life. I need to find mine.

I finish my morning routine and go upstairs to play a game. I want to just relax and drink my coffee. I usually read the latest financial or technology news, but this morning I decided I want to play a game. I love video games and have since I was a young kid in the 70's.

As I sit to game, I see the icon for this book staring at me through a littered screen of icons for notes, games, and PDF files. I click the Microsoft Word Icon for this book and start reading. I am mildly impressed.

In truth, I am my harshest critic. Some of this is funny, but more so, I find that I am writing an honest portrayal of my experience.

I hope people take something from this, as I have hoped they would take something from my leadership. I don't have a deadline, a publisher, or a book deal, yet I am compelled to write. Games can wait.

Wanda peeks into my office and comes in to say good morning. She sits on my lap, squirming on my legs to get comfortable. We sit and chat, and it feels good, until she insists, I am writing her in a negative light after reading a paragraph. She says I am making her the villain and me the martyr. There is probably some truth to this, but I will write about our experience honestly. She is defensive, as if I would expose her shortcomings to others. Oh wait, I am! But I am sharing mine too. All of them, openly and with veracity. I tell her if she wants me to write her in a different light, she should put out more. (I will sleep on the couch tonight.)

I wanted to end this chapter with something compelling. I draw from a lot of different sources for my own inspiration, be it business leaders, religious figures or otherwise. I reflect on a post I read from someone named Ashley Elizabeth Lynne. She wrote a story about leaving your comfort zone. I read it on a train while travelling up to Cambridge, England from London. I wasn't in a good headspace, and her words resonated with me, as if she were talking to me, reading my mind. The takeaway was simple.

Don't get caught in your comfort zone because mediocrity will kill your creativity and drive.

I totally agree. I was successful because I went where others refused to go. Why? They were scared. Me? I was scared not to. And therein lies the difference between those that lead, and those that follow. Leaders don't get comfortable, and we certainly aren't afraid to take chances and live outside our own comfort zones.

Be bold; there is nothing brave about mediocrity.

4

September, 2019

September 1, 2019

A new month of possibilities. I am up early after another night of restless sleep and weird dreams. I go downstairs for coffee and a bagel. I miss waking up from a deep sleep and rolling over and snuggling Wanda. I wake up early now, so I just let her sleep.

I have a few things to do today, and at the top of my list is fixing the boat. I have committed to servicing the *Red Barchetta* myself, a task that I usually leave to the professionals. But I am handy, and I want to understand how to do these things myself.

I drive to the boatyard and hitch up the boat. On my way home, I decide I am going to make the family breakfast. Waffles and eggs, because, well, I can. We have an awesome family breakfast, something we don't do enough. We laugh and share the details of our week, over fresh waffles and warm syrup. I am satisfied in these moments.

I go out to the driveway and sit in the boat reading the service manuals that will allow me to perform the expert repairs I am about to undertake. I am someone who reads the directions on anything I am going to build. I do this same thing in business. I read whatever information I can to better help me be successful. Too many people disregard instructions that are designed to help them. I am from a different school of thought. Work smart, not hard.

The greatest education we receive doesn't come from speaking; it comes from listening. Close your mouth and open your ears. People will teach you everything you need to know if you let them.

Educated by the pages of the service manual, I set off with a new-found confidence. I begin to repair the many things that I have neglected since I bought this beautiful vessel in 2014. I have struggled to remove many parts, including the jet ports that are covered with caked-on debris. As I rinse the ports out, I accidentally spray high pressure water on the kill switches that line the engine housing, and one of the vital switches becomes dislodged and falls into the engine. I stand in silent disbelief for what seems like an eternity, surveying the damage. Then I stand back and yell that four-letter word that rhymes with "stuck". A hint, it's not "DUCK".

Maybe this WAS a job for professionals, but I am here now, bleeding and drenched in sweat, and I am not about to give up. My OCD won't let me leave this project without finding the switch, but defeated, I leave the mess and go upstairs to take a shower because it's almost time for Church. Maybe a prayer in church will help me find the switch. Without it, the boat won't start.

In church the sermon is about humility. The message is simple. *Don't gloat, don't brag and be humble. No one likes a self-absorbed ass-hole.* Not exactly how it was presented, but this is my takeaway.

On the way home we stop at Ono Hawaiian BBQ. I scarf the food in minutes, as I realize that while I struggled with the boat, I forgot to eat lunch. It reminds me of the many times in my career I would be immersed in a project, and I would forget to eat. Some things never change, regardless of the setting.

Once home, I try to get the switch out of the engine, but to no avail. It looks hopeless. I am deflated. My boat is so important to me and the family. It is our escape from the oppressive heat of summer, and it is a vehicle of joy for the many who accompany me. I am concerned it will be a costly repair. If I had only taken a little more time to assess what I was doing, maybe I wouldn't have destroyed it. But tomorrow is another day, and I will remain hopeful I can find a way to fix it. Some days, it's better to walk away and leave things for the next day.

If a problem seems unsurmountable, walk away. The best attack on a complex issue is sometimes best resolved with distance and time.

September 2, 2019

I slept well. Not a solid 8 hours, but at least I feel somewhat rested. I am still bothered by the incident with the boat yesterday, and it is starting to consume me. I get like this when I need to fix something. Whether it be at home or in my business life. I learned long ago; problems will not fix themselves unless a solution is offered.

The risk here is serious. If I start the engines and the switch is lodged in the impeller, it will ruin the jet drive. If I don't figure something out, the boat will require service. Expensive service. The acronym for BOAT is "break out another thousand!" I commit to a speedy resolution.

These issues mirror many trials and tribulations I have faced in my professional life. I am not a quitter, and I am convinced there is a solution, but I need to think through the situation and do some research to ensure I cover all my options.

After an hour of research, I find I am on my own. If I were lost on the water, how would I resolve this issue? Then it comes to me. I will try and bypass the switch completely, which will allow me to start the engines and hopefully free whatever remnants of the switch remain.

As luck would have it, I find an obscure article that supports that in an emergency, the kill switch can be bypassed, by cutting the sensor, and then hot wiring the wires back together. Sounds dangerous. I like it! The replacement switch is $248, splicing is free, which fits nicely in my budget.

I work all day on the repairs. If I ever sold the boat, I would want to make sure the new owner had a vessel with the fail safes installed, so even though I will hotwire the engine as a short-term fix, the long-term fix is new switches. It is the right thing to do. The ethical solution.

I breathe deep, cut the wires, tape off the ones that I do not use and twist the two wires I want to jump together like a surgeon reattaching an amputated limb. A little electrical tape to finish and then I fire up the engines and BAM!! It starts right up. I stand back and admire my handiwork. I finished all the things I had procrastinated for the past 3 years and overcame a seemingly insurmountable problem. The most important takeaway? I didn't quit!

Never give up. Quit once, and you will find quitting to be a regular part of your toolbox. Find solutions, persevere, and rise above adversity. The only limitations in life are the ones we put upon ourselves. Behind every great success story is a trail of failures.

I finish all my tasks a little after 5 PM. It has been a brutal and triumphant day. I am reminded of the importance of a clear head and critical thinking in the face of difficult situations, and above all else, I am filled with pride. I didn't give up, and I learned something new. This mantra has existed within my psyche for many years, and it is never lost on me that the only way to overcome strife is to face it head on.

Jesús, my brother-in-law, not my lord and savior, has come to stay for a few days. Over dinner, he asks me if I can drive him to an appointment in Tucson tomorrow morning. I say yes. I say yes often these days, and the value in that is in the joy and assistance I can offer to others.

Be the solution, not the problem.

September 3, 2019

It's 4:45 AM and my alarm is going off. I am disoriented, but in the darkness of this early morning, I collect myself and drag my aching body out of the warm comfort of my bed, grab my laptop bag and head downstairs. There are no lights on, and it is pitch black. As I reach the bottom of the stairs, I step off, and to my surprise, there are no stairs where I thought they would be. I freefall a few feet and land on my bad leg, the one that I dislocated my ankle on last year. I am in pain. As I collect my belongings and my thoughts, I take a second to thank God for not letting this be more serious. It should have been, I should have broken my leg, but by the grace of God, I am intact. Gracias a Dios!! (Thanks be to God!)

Abuema looks concerned and continues to ask me if I am ok. I am not, but I am stubborn and proud, so I tell her I am fine. While I make coffee, she tells me about a dream she had. Her friend Sylvia recently died, and she said Sylvia has come to her in her dreams several times. I am spooked. I wonder if when you die, you can communicate with the living. I hope so. I would like to haunt a few people that have wronged me in my life.

I recently figured out a way to take my SiriusXM Radio in the car and the boat, so Jesús hits play, we turn it up loud and crank the hits of Metallica. It is 5:41 AM. The sun is rising, and we must be in Tucson by 7 AM. I feel like Belushi and Ackroyd in *The Blues Brothers*. It is indeed dark, and we are wearing sunglasses. Hit it!!

We drive and talk and sing loudly as we drive from my house to Tucson, the early morning light kissing the mountains and valleys. It is much too early, and my leg is throbbing, but as the miles go by at 85 mph, I can't help but smile. I am alive!

We arrived in Tucson just in time. Guercio time. I am out of coffee and my body aches from my fall earlier in the morning. My plan is to sit here and write while Jesús has his meeting. I turn my laptop on and while waiting for it to boot up, I check the messages on my phone. As I scroll through the posts on Facebook, I find that my friend and fellow drummer, Andy "Double Bass" Passaretti has passed away unexpectedly.

Andy was born with mild Down Syndrome and some type of congenital spine or leg disease. He still maintained a happy and positive existence. From the day I met him when we were 14, to his death he was always excited and happy, positive, and never focused on what many of us would call disabilities. He lived his life the way he wanted to. I am crushed. That is 4 people in my life that have passed away since mid-July. I am wrought with a mix of sorrow and worry for my wellbeing and that of many others my age. We are dropping like flies, which supports one of the reasons I wanted to leave my job.

Getting old sucks. I feel like I did when I was 16, but my body feels like it is 80 some days. Many years of abuse, physically and mentally, have taken their toll. I look in the mirror and cannot believe the face looking back at me. I remember 25-year-old me, Giant afro, suspenders, and ripped jeans. I was in great shape and weighed 165 pounds. Today? I am a dishonest 212 pounds and on any given day, my "moobs" (man boobs) are bigger than Wanda's.

Getting old is better than being dead, I guess, but I am deeply reflective and feel no urge to write. I just sit and think about how swiftly life moves. I often waffle between regret over leaving my position as CEO, and elation over the newfound freedom I am afforded now. In this moment, I just count my blessings, just thankful to be alive.

I am still stunned about Andy. Andy touched a lot of lives in a positive way, and he will be missed. He lived life his way, and for that, I am grateful I was able to call him my friend. His life was inspiring to me, and I will use his life and death to motivate me to reach beyond my current situation. I need to find my way. I am worried. Will I find it before God calls me back?

The melba toast and coffee I had at 5 am have done nothing to quell my hunger, so I suggest we stop for breakfast. I know a place. The Waffle House. We have a history, me, and the Waffle House. When we first started out, I sat here eating breakfast as a young man building a business. I had many "scattered, smothered or covered" items from this place over the past 25 years.

Today, I was sitting down for the same breakfast I had in 1994, only as a "free" man. 25 years later. I drive a nicer car now, and I have had more success, heartbreak, and disappointment than I care to admit, but I have also achieved my goals with regards to work. I accomplished my vision.

I think of what people will think of me when I am gone. Did I leave a positive legacy like Andy? I hope so. I have always tried to be a friend to those around me, even when many would take advantage of my generosity. I think to myself, "Will anyone come to my funeral?" I wonder if others think the same thing I am. This has been a recurring thought for me since I left my job.

How will people remember you? Will they see you in a positive light, or have a dim view?

Back home I lay in bed reading posts about Andy and Hurricane Dorian. The damage is immense, in both cases. Andy will be missed, and Dorian has messed up a lot of lives in the Grand Bahamas. It is a sad day all around. I am filled with a deep sense of remorse. Why am I here, while so many others have been taken from this world? I am not special. Why them and not me?

Abuema and Jesús are watching the end of *Sole Survivor*, the story of the Seal Teams lost in Afghanistan. I sit down and eat my snack while watching these fantastically brave soldiers give their all. I am filled with pride, hate and sorrow. War is hell, and so is everyday life, with death being the common denominator.

Writing is the last thing I want to do right now, but I need to get these thoughts down on paper, or in binary code, as the case may be. I haven't been writing long, but these have been some of the easiest pages to write. The emotion flows from my brain, through my heart, into my fingers and on to this page.

Later that evening, I go out to the putting green for a little quiet time. In the silent darkness of the evening, I think of Andy, Eddie, Randy, and Dana. I look to the heavens, letting them know they all had a great influence on my life, and that I wish them peace, and that God will grant them entrance to heaven. I ask God for help, that I may do something worthwhile with whatever time I have left on this earth. Something more than managing a successful P&L.

September 4, 2019

I am taking Jesús to the lake today. I need to clear my head and Jesús has been looking forward to the trip. After yesterday's news, and the deaths of others this year, I am not really into it, but a promise is a promise and the time on the water always settles my active mind. I am grateful he is here, and I am happy to share the beauty of the lake with him.

I hotwired the boat, and this is the maiden voyage with my surgically modified watercraft. As we launch the boat from the trailer, I step onto the bunk boards, the boards the boat sits on when it is on the trailer and feel a mushy sensation underneath my feet. The bunk board is made of wood, and through years of being waterlogged, it has rotted and is now falling off. I don't care. I just park the boat, assess the damage and in a very uncharacteristic moment, decide I am not going to let this spoil the day. I smile and tell Jesús I think we are screwed, so we might as well go enjoy the day. And we do. I am learning to put worry behind me when I can. I am quite proud of my demeanor, considering if I can't figure out how to fix it, we will be stranded.

After a full day of fun, I approached the trailer and found the bunk board is much worse than I first thought. It is completely rotted in the center. I look at the damage and I put my "German" brain to work. I realize I can possibly fill the rotten section with my wadded-up T-shirt. The only issue is I have no screws. But I do have duct tape, and duct tape fixes everything but a broken heart!

I make the repair, but the true test is whether it holds when I take the boat out of the water. We set the boat on the trailer by hand and then slowly inched up the boat ramp, allowing the full weight of the boat to rest on the bunk boards. Holy crap! It worked! We got it out of the water; now let's see if it will hold for the next 40 miles, along the steep canyons and winding roads of the Apache trail. There is nothing worse than having your boat fall off the trailer at 55 MPH.

We drove slowly on the way home. God was with me. Through the bumps and turns, through all the adversity in my life, God has guided me and watched over me. And today, he was there again. We make it to the boatyard and we both breathe a sigh of relief.

The smiles and joviality don't last long. While I am still basking in the glory of my repair, I look at my phone and it is blowing up. The many notifications inform me that my old company laid off more than 30% of the workforce, including most of the key people I hired. I do not understand the choices in who they let go, but I am confident these are people that were loyal to me. This signals the end of the company to me. I left less than 90 days ago, and we were positioned well. 90 days later, they cannot make a part, get an order, let alone ship one on time. They have alienated every one of our clients, and after 27 years, I see the company I built crumbling before my eyes.

Paul, Andrew, and Neil were my executive team. I trusted them to do the right thing and carry the company forward. I put my trust in the wrong places. Paul especially--I brought him to the position of second in command and protected him many times. In the end, he bad-mouthed me and minimized my importance. Um, I founded the company, remember?

They forget that before them, we built GMSI by doing the impossible. By caring for our clients. I credit Rex, Mike, Phil, Aimee, Cubby, Johnny, Brian, and many more. I credit the customers, most of all, for keeping us in business. Without them, we were nothing, as I explained to everyone that worked for me many times. Paul never understood that, and this is what happens when you stop servicing your client base.

This will cost them their jobs too, and most likely the jobs of everyone else. I want to do something to stop the carnage, but I am no longer in charge, and I am powerless to help.

When things got bad, I rolled my sleeves up and fixed problems. You guys point fingers. You are protecting each other, but I assure you, your day is coming, and I am not sure you realize that.

I will work hard to make sure everyone you laid off today gets a job, somewhere, because I love those people. But honestly, you should all be ashamed of yourselves. You learned nothing I tried to teach because you are egotistical. You don't know better than me. I built that company.

Gents, I know that YOU matter the most to yourself. That is not how leaders act. Leadership requires you to always put the needs of others ahead of your own. That is how we stayed in business all these years! People do not follow self-absorbed people for very long. You have all failed. Most of all, you all failed me as friends, and that hurts, because I trusted all of you with the lives of others.

I am physically ill as I begin to make calls to all the people who lost their jobs. I called every one of them personally. Not because I had to, but because I wanted to. They didn't deserve what happened, and while I am guilt-ridden for leaving them, they are all surprisingly grateful for my call. And they all say the same thing. Paul, Andrew, and Neil were the ones that made the choices in the layoffs. They kept the new people, the ones that weren't loyal to me.

I feel like I failed all those people, and I am incredibly sad. I know how this story ends, and it isn't pretty. This, as I see it, is the beginning of the end of my legacy. 28 years we were in business, and 90 days after I left, almost to the day, I can see the carnage that will ultimately doom the company and end the vision Rex and I so desperately worked to create.

September 5, 2019

I can't sleep. I wake up early, before 5 AM and try and figure out how to help the people that lost their job yesterday. I am supposed to play golf with Mike this morning, but my heart isn't into it, and more so, my guilt is riddling me with remorse for leaving my team and my clients.

It is too late to cancel, so I halfheartedly get dressed for a golf game I feel I don't deserve. I have never felt like more of a failure than right now. My mantra is "Guercios never quit", but that is exactly what I did, and all these people who were so near and dear to me, lost their jobs, their security and in the case of my long-time client base, one of its best supply chain partners.

I made a promise to Mike as well, and I certainly don't want to ruin his day with the weight of my personal issues. I tell him what happened yesterday and how It made me feel, and he reminds me of something I forgot. He says, "Well, I wouldn't blame yourself. What did the new owners do to ensure things would change if you stayed? You told me you left partially because you saw a future, a future you didn't want to be a part of, or one that may not include you, Heinz or the Leadership team."

He is right. I didn't just leave because I needed a break. I also resigned because I didn't like the direction Corporate was moving, and how it would affect our business, and probably the entire group I worked in. I don't find peace in this thought, but in a more direct way, Mike has reminded me that I left because I wasn't happy, healthy, or appreciated.

The only way to change your future is to learn from the past and let it go. If you dwell on your past, you will never be able to create the future you want to see. Always look forward.

As with every round of golf I play, it is over too soon. The truth is, I could play golf and swim in the ocean every day and die happy. These are two activities that allow me to think more clearly, to remove the focus on certain problems in my life and to better align my thoughts.

The weight of the people who lost their job is heavy on my conscience. I am not the CEO anymore, but they were my people. My friends. The drinks and golf only cloud my guilt. I wish there was something I could have done to help the company stay strong.

Truth is, my former management team made sure I was not involved after my exit, even though that was my agreement with my former employer. In that, and other careless decisions they made, lies the real failure of the company, but my leaving was the catalyst, and I knew that. I left anyway. I left because I had to. I was depleted.

I arrive home and Wanda tells me she must go run errands in support of Kathy, who got deported, as we thought she would. Wanda needs to grab some money for her, as well as get her a suitcase and other essentials. Wanda starts saying something to me, and in a drunken manner, I exclaim, "I am not schooling because I have had a few drinks!" As I say this, I see her face change. She knew I was going out today, but not that I would be drinking as much as I did. But because Kathy called, and the plans changed, she expects me to take over for what she was doing. I don't, instead telling her I will go with her on her errands.

We drive over to Kathy and Dan's house in silence. I do not like Dan. All this landed on us, and he has done little if anything to help his wife's situation. Why should he? This is exactly how he wanted things to go. Divorce by deportation.

This has been such a burden on Wanda and Kathy, and Dan has pretty much sidestepped any responsibility, leaving Wanda to do whatever she can to help her friend. He doesn't realize this situation has also put an enormous strain on our marriage, not that he would care. Selfish people only care about themselves.

I sit on the couch talking to their kids. I am sad for them. One day their mom was there, the next, she was gone for good. I feel for them, as I have lived that experience. I don't talk about my childhood, but I understand their pain, and I let them know everything will be ok in time.

I hope I am right. Some scars are hidden deep beneath the hypodermis. No band-aid can help those wounds. Just some late-life, intensive counseling, a boat, and some golf.

September 6, 2019

The kids have school outside our home today and Wanda wants to drive down to Mexico to meet Kathy when she is deported. She is hesitant in asking me, but to her surprise, I am not mad. I tell her to go. Kathy needs a friend, and I am sure Wanda wants to make sure she is ok.

This morning, I got a call from Brian and Charlie, my sales team at GMSI. They were handpicked by me, and now they are unemployed. Brian has been my friend for 20+ years, and he is old like me. I worry how he will fare in his waning years of work. I listen to them explain their feelings and I console them as much as I can. They both did a fantastic job. The overarching theme here is not that they did a bad job; they were loyal to me, so they were terminated. I will keep them and all the others who lost their jobs in my prayers, as well as pray for all that remain. Even those that went against me. Love thy enemy…

After a morning of calls, I head upstairs to my office to try and forget about all these things for a few moments. I play a few games, but my heart isn't into it, so I decide to write instead. Nothing good is coming of that either. I am not focused, my heart and mind with those at my former company. "I failed everyone" is the recurring jingle in my head.

I look for a diversion and notice a copy of the book *The Art of War* by Sun Tzu. Aimee gave me this book during a particularly difficult time in my life, and I refer to it often. She also gave me *The Alchemist* by Paulo Coelho. Aimee was one of my closest friends at GMSI. My confidant and my sister in many ways. We came a long way together, and I miss her more than anyone. She is now aligned to the adversarial managers that remain at GMSI and they have told her not to communicate with me.

I hope she will be ok. She went through a difficult time when I was CEO. She had a breakdown and left the company shortly after we sold to Heraeus. I understood. She was under so much pressure and told me that she felt way over her head in the new culture. She left and took a mental health break. I respected that, and when she was better, she came back. Ironically, I left for the same reason; the only difference is, I can never go back. Her books and friendship will always remain priceless gifts to me. I love you Aimee, you were the closest thing to an adopted sister I ever had.

As I cook dinner, I think about GMSI. I wish there was a way to have stopped what happened to my team yesterday. It is my 3-month anniversary of leaving today, and in 90 days, the staff I left to carry the business forward have effectively run the company into the ground. I do not like my former management team. They failed me, and everyone else at the company. I guess my inspirational speeches didn't reach everyone.

You would think after 28 years they would have heard me. The ones that heard, that really listened and lived my guidance, are the ones that are still in it to win it. Sadly, I believe the company will shut down. A victim of greed, stupidity, inexperience, poor management, and a change in direction from the acquiring party. The perfect storm of death.

I wish it were the old way. I could have saved the company from itself, and as I drifted off to sleep, these thoughts leave me distraught and filled with guilt.

September 7, 2019

It is early when I sneak back into bed to snuggle Wanda. She is exhausted from her long day yesterday. We snuggle and talk in our bed while the kids play. I needed her comfort, and I shared some of my thoughts from the past few days. She consoles me and lets me know that I left the company in good hands, and that while I may have been able to do something if I stayed, I didn't, and the others should have been able to carry forward. "That's what you paid them for, Peter". She is right. It doesn't make the sting of the layoffs any easier to digest, but her words provide me with some peace.

I spent the day toiling about in the yard. The warmth of the summer sun relaxes me, and while I am perspiring profusely, I feel good. The activity cleanses me emotionally and physically. As the kids and I enjoy the pool, Wanda comes out in a bathing suit. Wanda NEVER swims in the pool, but here she is, for the first time since we bought our house, coming for a swim with me and the kids.

We spent an hour in the pool with our kids, laughing and splashing. At one point, Wanda climbs on me, wraps her legs around me like she wants to make out, instead giving me hickeys on my cheeks. I am mad for a second, and then smile at the comedic value in her playfulness.

We go inside for an evening of family movies, snacks, and togetherness.

Later that night, we even managed to have a little late-night romance. I got lucky today, in more ways than one. I am lucky to be here, alive and with a family I love more than life.

September 8, 2019

I wake up after 8 AM. A rare occasion for me. I don't know if it was the stress of many sleepless nights, the late night with Wanda or the stress of the past few days relinquishing as I begin to accept the situation, but I am rested.

Wanda and I just sit on the couch and snuggle with each other. It feels good to be connected again. Ben is up and he wants to play some 3-Up on the putting green. 3-up is a putting game we made up, and it turns out to be a fan favorite. We are basically the only two fans.

We play a few games, but I need to work on the book. I told him I am inspired. He laughed and said it's ok, that he wants me to finish it so we can play more. I like the way he thinks.

I spent a couple of hours working on this book, as well as my outlines for my next book. This book details the story of what happened after I left the company; the next book is called, *Drink my Kool-aid*, and it details the journey I took to get here. I am excited to be writing and I am motivated to find that new path in my life. I still pray for guidance daily.

As I finish getting ready, Father David, our priest and friend from Ghana, comes over. We met him when he was first assigned to our parish a few years ago, but now, he is family. He lives in Ghana now, and we miss him daily. He is a warm and intelligent man, but more than that, Father David is my friend. He guided me through the transaction with Heraeus, giving me strength when I had doubt. He reminded me that my faith is not a straight line, and God has his own plan, and sometimes, you need to let things play out his way for your prayers to be answered.

I have needed someone to talk to, especially after the recent layoff at GMSI. The timing of his visit couldn't be better, and his presence is steadying. He helps me align my focus and consoles me that my leaving was only part of the reason the layoffs occurred. He is soft spoken and wise, and I appreciate his friendship.

"*Money is necessary, but love is mandatory.*"

We go to church later in the day, and I am comforted by the surroundings and my closeness to God. I need this in my life right now. Actually, I have always needed God in my life, but there were many times I chose not to include him. I was wrong. The inner peace I have sought for so long comes in part from my faith. It grounds me and reminds me that love is the key to all we strive for in life. Money is necessary, but love is mandatory. And in these quiet moments, listening to the word of God, I find great healing.

I have been missing my mom, and as soon as we are in the car, I call her and tell her I love her. She is by far the strongest woman I have ever known. She overcame the greatest of adversity with a sense of humor and an easy confidence that made me love her even more as I began to understand her journey. I watched her as my dad withered and died from cancer. She was the caretaker, as always. She is my rock and I have been thinking of her a lot lately. She has been struggling with her health for the past few years, and part of my willingness to leave my career was to be here for her if she needs me. And she has. But I can do more, and I let her know if she needs me, I am here for her, just as she has been here for me since I landed in her fallopian tubes on the way to her uterus.

A Mother's love is the closest we will get to understanding what Heaven must feel like.

September 9, 2019

Today, I am taking Father David on errands, driving Ben to his activities and then back and forth to the house. I also need to return some golf clubs I don't like. I find that even though I don't work, I often have days that are non-stop and hectic. The only difference is I am not driving a business, I am driving my truck.

I shaved my beard yesterday. I need to prepare for meetings, and quite honestly, I had begun to look like a guy who lives in a carboard box near the underpass of a freeway. I am not sure I even want to work yet, but at least I should look the part if I am meeting prospective employers.

It is still hard for me to be so domesticated. I often think back to just a few months ago, where I was responsible for hundreds of people and millions of dollars. Now, I cook and clean, and text myself recipes from the internet. My, how far I have fallen--or risen, depending on your perspective.

I head upstairs to work on the business plan and pitch decks for InfinityGo. There is a lot of work to be done, and as they say in show business, first impressions are everything. I intend to take the many lessons learned over my past 25 years and apply them to this new venture.

I am committed to making it wildly successful, and it all starts with a good plan.

With dinner complete, we head home to watch movies and hang out. I should be writing or working on the InfinityGo business plan, but I don't have the energy or the motivation. As the movie rolls, I fall asleep on the couch.

September 10, 2019

I don't think Wanda was too thrilled that I fell asleep on the couch last night. I woke up in the dark and on the couch, and when I went upstairs to bed, she was already asleep. She is not a morning person, but I am throwing caution to the wind, and I slide next to her like a Blue Angel fighter moving into a tight formation. I am shot down immediately, and I eject. Dogfighting can be a dangerous affair.

It doesn't matter because I have a morning meeting for a consulting job, and I need to get ready soon. I make my way downstairs and brew some coffee while I read the latest trends in semiconductors.

9 AM and I am dressed like the CEO I used to be. It feels foreign to dress in a suit and to put on a tie. Dress shoes? I haven't worn them since I left work. Before my meeting, I am taking Fr. David to the Dentist, and on the way, we have an engaging conversation about all the things going on in the world. I love to hear him explain to me how life and politics are in Africa. Long story short, the government sucks. The people in power take money and there is little to no infrastructure. Stop me if you have heard this story before. There should be more people like Father David. Selfless and easy going, he focuses on making the lives of others better.

At my consulting gig, I am greeted by a lovely woman named Sloan. She is pretty and personable and makes me feel right at home. She informs me that the CEO of the company, Gerald, will miss the meeting due to illness. I stay and listen to her anyway, and she shares her life story, as well as that of the company. I am always amazed how open people are with me. I do not know if this is something special, but I have always been able to create strong trust and most people have been very giving and open with me. I feel very blessed to have that effect on people, and I am genuinely interested in what they have to say.

Just as I am about to leave, the CEO, Gerald, walks in. He apologizes for his tardiness, explaining he is undergoing kidney treatments in the late hours of the evening, and he is tired. He is a genuinely sincere person and I go back to the conference room so he can present his company and their direction to me. Also, in attendance is their Director of Operations and the COO.

They seem like good people with good tech, but like many start-ups, have money issues and marketing challenges. They ask me to help them with their positioning and offer guidance on how best to generate investment interest. I let them know I see potential, but we will have to take a deeper dive to understand what I can do.

All in all, the meeting went well, and we shake hands and I leave. My purpose has been cloudy lately, and I am certainly a man without direction, but today reminded me that I do have something valuable to offer, I just need to find my path. I pray for this daily, that God will help me find my path.

As I drive home, I call Wanda to let her know how things went. She is encouraged but is honest and reminds me that I left my career to rest. Going right back to work defeats that purpose. I really don't want to work, but I feel guilty that I am not working. I can't explain it, but I have been in a funk lately. I attribute this to watching my company implode, and to my lack of purpose.

My good friend and mentor, Guy, gave me very sage advice when I left. He said, "Peter, make sure you don't lose your purpose. It was the hardest part for me after I sold my company, and I struggled with it for 18 months afterward." His words resonate with me now. I am a bit lost, saddened by the recent events of my company, and disappointed in my current relationship with Wanda. I want to enjoy this time, not worry, and feel depressed, but I struggle with these emotions daily.

September 11, 2019

I wake up early and pray for the souls lost in the attacks of 9-11. I lay in bed watching videos from that sunny September morning, and I end up crying, as I relive the moments of that horrific day. I remember it as if it were yesterday, and it will stay with me forever, as it will with most.

I am focused on writing this book, but I take a moment to bring some important points to those that follow me on Facebook and other social media outlets. I post a few simple paragraphs and a picture that best represents my feelings on this solemn anniversary.

On this day, I ask you all to remember this simple message. Once, we were united, One nation under God. We weren't Democrats or Republicans, right wing or left. We were people. We were Americans. We stood beside each other and consoled each other and wept together. I would never want a return of 9/11, but how I miss the pride and patriotism we once shared as a nation. Remember that feeling today.

God bless all those lost on 9-11, and the many battles fought thereafter in faraway places that claimed the lives of so many more. God bless all those service people, soldiers and first responder's, cops, and firemen. You are all the true heroes, today, tomorrow, and forever.

Never forget but find a place for forgiveness. The path to peace is complex. A dialogue of forgiveness and understanding is the path to peace and salvation.

PG 2019

This morning, I took multiple calls from people from my past, and I also made time for a meeting with Chuck over lunch. I am often too busy to understand how many great people I have had around me in my life. I lost my dad, but there have been many other people in my life that taught me so much, and as I drive home from my meeting, I realize maybe he sent them. I smile at the thought.

Back home after a busy morning, I find everyone is ready to ride bikes. We took a long ride and I found it was just what I needed to clear my head. I cannot stop looking at Wanda. Some guy's tire of their wives, often talking about how attractive other women are. I have never lost my appreciation or attraction to her. If anything, it has grown considerably through the years. She is still everything I have ever wanted, and I love her so much. This makes her constant rejection extremely frustrating and deflating. I have never cheated on her and never really looked at another woman the way I look at her. The past few months have left me unhappy, unsatisfied, and bitter.

I cannot change people. I must accept the traits I do not like, as she has as well. It is called marriage. If you don't like it, I suggest getting a dog and some water-based lubricant. Not for the dog, but for you.

Now, I am here every day, and while I try to spend more time with her in every other sense, there never seems to be a good time for romance. It seems like there is always a reason she does not have time for me.

If you love someone, show them. Words can be interpreted in many different ways by different people, but actions will always support the sincerity of the words you speak.

I make an amazing dinner of Grilled tri-tip, Santa Maria style, with roasted red potatoes and green beans. I feel great satisfaction and dare I say, pleasure, playing the part of chef to my family. I agreed to cook our dinners when I left my job. I did so begrudgingly. But now, it is a labor of love, and I enjoy being able to create delicious dishes for those I love.

Each day that passes, I find myself getting a little more depressed. I need to snap out of it. I just don't know how. I pray that I will find my way and that things will improve between Wanda and me. If anyone can work a miracle for me, God can.

September 12, 2019

I woke up angry. Angry at Wanda for not being more attentive to me. Angry that my former employer laid off my staff. Angry that things are not going like I envisioned them. I admit to myself I am not only frustrated and angry, but discontent and a little depressed. I get like this sometimes. The stress of life coupled with my dissatisfaction with my love life makes me feel, "Hormonal". It is the ongoing direction of my life, and I am just pissed.

I leave the house and go to the store for some Prilosec. I have been taking it since I had a breakdown in China in July of 2018. After an endoscopy and several other tests, doctors found I have an acute case of esophagitis and a hiatal hernia. I often suffer from stomach pains and acid reflux, and I am forced to take Omeprazole, and most likely will for the rest of my life. The doctors suggested I lose weight and keep my stress levels to a minimum. I laughed at the surgeon at the time, reminding him what I do for a living. He smiled and rebutted that his job can also be a source of great stress, but the trick is in how we manage it. I took his advice, and as part of my healing process, changed my attitude, and my place of employment.

I go back home and make breakfast for everyone. While cooking, I received a phone call from Chris, who was our equity investor after we took the company back from 3M. Chris and I discuss his possible involvement in my new venture, and we agree to stay in touch. There was a time when Chris made my life hell, but in the end, I earned his respect and trust. Providing investors with a significant return on their investment is one sure way to change their attitude towards you.

As soon as I hang up, Adam, my oldest son, calls me. I feel bad for my son. He is in a difficult situation. He is only 24, but he got his girlfriend pregnant, and now he is struggling with the harsh realities of raising children and trying to maintain a relationship with his girlfriend. They have little money, and, in all honesty, they make their own misery most days. I tell him to make better choices and to think about his direction in life, promising him we will catch up over the next couple of days.

I meet back with Wanda at the house, and we discuss plans for the rest of the day. Wanda is leaving for a party tonight sponsored by her Mexican women's group, and they are using the party to help raise money for Kathy, who has been deported. Kathy doesn't have financial resources yet, and these women are providing support from the U.S. An admirable cause.

I head to my office to try and work on this book and the many other projects I have been tasked with. Between forming InfinityGo, agreeing to do some consulting work, and writing this book, my days are as busy as when I worked a full-time job.

With the kids fed and happily snuggled in their beds, I sit down with a glass of wine and decide to do something I haven't done in quite a while. I game my face off. I don't usually take this time for myself, filling my hours with a litany of other tasks, but tonight, I am just going to sit down, relax, and enjoy some wine and a quiet game of PC Golf. I finish the bottle of wine and play games for hours.

It's getting late and I go to bed. I am hopeful Wanda will come home in the mood for me like she used to, but I have lost my exuberant hope. I feel pathetic lately. I am a guy who traveled the world and turned down many advances from women in favor of my fidelity and commitment to Wanda, and my thanks is rejection from the person I want most.

I hate myself lately.

September 13, 2019

Father David and I talked yesterday, and I confided in him that my dream is not this life. My dream is to cash out, liquidate everything and move to the beach in a beautiful place like Mexico or Aruba. I want a little place with a boat so that I can fish, swim, and write. My long-term goal is to be watching sunsets and working around our house, living a life that made me happy and fulfilled. Wanda doesn't want this kind of life, at least not now. I don't want to work the rest of my life to try and provide her with the life she wants. I am grateful for what we have now. Why can't she see that I don't want anything else? I just want to be.

We drop the kids off at school and an enormous wave of love for them comes over me. I am sure that they would benefit from the life I described in the paragraph above. They don't need fancy cars, big houses, or every gadget to be happy. They would appreciate a life near the water, taking them away from electronics and into the beauty of nature. The reality is, we could indeed cash out and move away, but Wanda is not ready. The real issue is Wanda's love for this house, and the area where we live. I get it. She waited a long time for this house, and the many luxuries we have attained over the years. Her dreams are not my dreams, and herein lies a valuable lesson I learned.

If you are willing to give up what you think makes you happy, you may find the things that do make you happy. The things that bring you Joy are unmistakable.

Father David is leaving for Ghana soon, so we take him to breakfast, and afterwards, we shop. We buy him a battery pack for travel charging, a travel plug adapter, a large suitcase for his return trip, and some blankets for him and his fellow priests. I pay for everything because he is a sound investment, and I want to help.

When I was in the midst of uncertainty during 2016, he was instrumental in keeping me focused. He knew of my struggles to get the company to where we were, and understood the demands and stress associated with my travel and the growth of the company. He is also one of the few that understood my greatest wish was not wealth, but security for my family and all those within the GMSI network, the vendors, customers, and most important, my employees. He said that my altruism would be blessed by God if I stayed the course. And it was.

Now many may mock my insinuation of Divine Intervention, but as for me, I give credit where credit is due.

We arrive home and I go upstairs to work. I am sending things for InfinityGo and planning meetings in support of the development aspects with Cort Bucholtz and his team at *"SimpleMinds"*. I say this tongue in cheek, as his real company is called Singlemind Consulting. He is a good dude, and I am excited to be working together. I am still torn on structure, ownership and other details related to the venture, but time works all these details out. That, and a slew of expensive invoices from legal counsel.

I have to relinquish my duties as writer, entrepreneur, and consultant because it's time to make dinner. I am the chef of the house now, and dinner doesn't cook itself.

September 14, 2019

I say I am writing, but lately I feel like I am venting. I often write out my angry feelings towards Wanda, and then erase them. It doesn't make for productive writing, but this exercise is cleansing and useful to my current mental state.

Mike and Michelle come over around 3 PM. The tension between Wanda and me has subsided for the most part. We mend fences by staying out of each other's pastures. A few drinks and some food, and by bedtime things will be fine. I hope.

We spend our time with Mike and Michelle mixing cocktails, cooking, swimming, chatting and later, cigars and scotch while we putt on the putting green. All is not perfect, but for now, it's pretty damn close.

The party wraps up at 10 PM with sloppy hugs and long goodbyes. I lock the doors and head upstairs, hoping the atmosphere is friendly. We manage our way to civility and watch a movie and fall asleep. Another crisis averted through patience and understanding. I say this with a bit of sarcasm, but in these uncertain times, we take what we can get.

September 15, 2019

It is Sunday. I am moody, but all that emotion is not necessarily a byproduct of my relationship with Wanda. It comes from watching GMSI fall apart. It comes from the fact that we have no money coming in and I am realizing the biggest source of angst comes from things I don't understand. There is a lack of joy lately.

I spend most of the day cleaning and doing research for the InfinityGo workshop I am attending in Portland, Oregon. I booked the tickets today, and I am eager to start this new venture. I think it will be remarkably successful, and in that, I hope to find the purpose and joy I am currently lacking.

I said I wanted to do nothing today, but I am not built like that. I am always thinking, always moving, and always looking for something to do, like a Great White Shark, who will perish if he stops swimming. If I am supposed to be relaxed with this hiatus; it hasn't happened much so far. Maybe you are supposed to act maniacally for the first 3 or 4 months before you settle into the relaxation phase. I am reprogramming; rebooting is a better word, and I think my operating system is hung on the bootup sequence. I may need to flash my bios.

Wanda and I are in a better place tonight. Maybe Father David talked to her. I don't know, but the mood is different, and we chat and snuggle while we watch videos on her phone. I wish every night were like this. I really need Wanda to be a bigger part of my life right now. I feel like I am drowning some days, and she is the only person that knows where the life jackets are.

She is wearing something pretty and I want to unwrap her like the present she is to me. And to my surprise, later that night, I did just that. I don't care that it is late, or that I have an early wake up call. I live for these special moments with my wife, and I am not letting time manage me anymore; it's the other way around now.

September 16, 2019

It's so early. The alarm sounds at 5:15 AM. Father David says goodbye to Wanda and I, and his parting words are something we can build on. He tells us to be patient with each other. I expected something more profound but often the simplest statements leave the greatest impact.

Father David and I make small talk while I drive him to the airport. I can tell he is a little melancholy, and I am sure he is not eager to make the 30-hour journey home. I pray that he travels safely and that he comes back to see us soon. Ghana is a long way from Arizona. I will hope that God will bring us together again soon. While you thank me for my generosity, it is you that deserves all the thanks, Father. Thank you for your love and guidance.

It is still early morning when I arrive back to the house. There are shopping lists and laundry that needs to go to the cleaners. I am taking my first business trip for our new company, InfinityGo. I am mildly excited, but I would much rather stay home every day. Life has a different plan for me, or so I think it does. I could be wrong.

I also realize that my flight is leaving in a couple of days, and I failed to book accommodations. I manage a last-minute reservation in a place reserved for hookers and homeless people. I used to stay in 5-star hotels, and now I am starting over. No matter, a bed is a place to sleep, and home is where your heart is.

It is time to take the kids to chess and then back home so Wanda can take them to Atrium, a religious class. It is going to be another long day. The kids finish class and I drive them home. Wanda will take them elsewhere, and I am going to finish prepping for meetings while I make some calls, write some emails, and grab my laundry from the cleaners so I can pack for my trip.

After the movie we lay in bed and watched videos and surf the net. I fall asleep repeatedly, ultimately relinquishing my technology devices for the warmth of Wanda and a sound sleep.

September 17, 2019

I wake up aroused and I really want to grab Wanda, but I am too tired, and she would kill me. The days often have a feeling of "rinse, lather, repeat" in their monotony. While I am grateful for this time of rest, many days feel like the day before. I am sure if I were working, I could say the same thing, but at least my 401K would grow with every passing payday.

I need to shower and pack. I am leaving for my first trip since I left the hallowed halls of Heraeus GMSI. It has been a little over 3 months since I left. It is a daily struggle, and the more I see my former colleagues struggle, the more depressed I become. I let my people down. I have narrowed my issue with all this into that one sentence. I feel like I deserted people that counted on me for guidance and leadership, and the feeling of guilt is a burden that hangs heavy over me.

They suffer, I golf. They are terminated and I go on vacation. The dynamic is one that leaves me unable to genuinely enjoy this time off. I have considered calling my former boss back and going back to work. If the company is struggling now, I feel a strong pull to fix it, as I always have. The only issue is, it's not my company anymore. It's theirs, and they are equally responsible for the current situation. I have never felt more helpless or useless in my life.

My targeted departure time arrives. As I load my truck with my luggage, I remind myself of the good things in my life. I love my wife and kids. I have 5 valid offers of employment or consulting, and I am preparing to leave, to see if I can validate the largest venture of my life. Not bad for a retired guy who left the highest levels of employment, with one of the largest companies in the world, to take a break and regroup. I silently pray, *"Oh lord, God in heaven, Jesus Christ, please bless me always. And my family and friends. And all those around me. Amen."*

I fly to Portland to meet Brad and Cort to discuss InfinityGo. We are participating in a workshop with developers and App Designers. We are creating an App for InfinityGo that will support use on Android, PC and iOS. I intend to connect the world through an infinite number of activities. That is tomorrow. Tonight, we sampled the finest beers Portland has to offer. All of them!

I am not going to be able to write during this trip and in truth, I am not sure I even want to finish this book. I am concerned that it is boring and lifeless. That my life is so mundane, no one will care about the real message I am trying to convey and the real struggle of leaving my position. I am not thinking clearly lately, as I am struggling with my own emotions. This time off offered me the reset that I desperately needed, but it triggered other emotions, ones that I wasn't prepared to address, nor eagerly willing to deal with. I need a break from my break.

September 18, 2019

Brad picks me up and we drive down to Lake Oswego where we will meet Cort and the Singlemind team. I am feeling lethargic, and it is important I can effectively communicate our vision for InfinityGo to the development team. I have been here before, many other times in many other countries, and I worry I am too hungover to perform.

The meeting lasts over 6 hours. My worries were unfounded as I presented the InfinityGo vision with passion and clarity. The development team is impressed, and we are able to accomplish the goals of the workshop. They will take a few weeks to do the necessary market research and brainstorming, and we will meet again to discuss the next phases based on their feedback.

We celebrate by continuing our tour of the Portland beer scene. I will surely regret this tomorrow. I have never spent time with Brad in Portland without vomiting. Tonight will be no different.

September 19, 2019

The morning light peaks through the blackout curtains, hitting me squarely in the hangover. I am up, but the thought of raising my head from this pillow seems like a task that will require too much exertion on my part, so I lay low for now, allowing the waves of nausea, depression, and dehydration to wash over me. I made the stupid mistake of hanging out with Brad in Portland. This is his town, and I am merely a rookie to his legend as a beer aficionado.

Brad is going to pick me up to take me to the airport in an hour. I need to get myself together. He suggests breakfast at this little café his friends own on the way to the airport, The Cricket Café in Portland. I agree. A Bloody Mary will take the edge off my unsteadiness, and some eggs benedict will fill the void left by last night's evacuation of my digestive tract.

Brad and I recap the events of the trip. It has been a productive journey and I look forward to the launch of this new venture. With a little luck, we will be in the App Store and Google Play by March of 2020.

The flight back to Phoenix was uneventful and gave me time to ponder my thoughts. In many ways, I feel like I am a man without a country. A vagabond, traveling from town to town in search of a place I can call home. I have given up everything that defined me as a professional and in that, I fear I may be stuck in this state of flux for more time than I considered. I am going to take things day by day for now, and I will continue to pray that I find myself again.

I arrive home after 6 to the hugs and kisses of my loving family. Wanda and I chatted about the events of the trip, and she seems relieved it went well. She is happier to see me in the driver's seat once again, and I know she understands I am a little out of sorts lately. I liken it to the feeling of being disoriented in a dark cave. I need to find my inner "Wheat lamp".

September 20, 2019

I am going to visit my cousin Mike so he can show me the renovations he has done at his new house. I am happy for him and Michelle. He worked as an NYPD officer for 20-plus years, through 9/11 and the turmoil that followed. He deserves this and I am elated to see them making a home here in Arizona with the rest of the family.

We grab a few beers and head to the driving range. I share some of my thoughts with Mike and his advice is sound. "Bro, you need to stop worrying about things that haven't happened. Change what you can, and the rest will figure itself out". His words are my own thoughts, but it is nice to have some kind of affirmation that I am on the right path. I appreciate my cousin and his sage advice. It's nothing I don't already know, and in order for the advice to be effective, I need to implement the strategy. I will try.

There is nothing notable to mention for the rest of the evening. It was another night in a string of nights of cooking, watching a movie, or writing. I am struggling with my direction, but I am staying true to my advice of letting things come to me and having faith that everything will work out.

September 21, 2019

I am taking a mental health day today, and my intent is to do nothing. I am going to focus on my kids, Wanda, and our ever-expanding bellies. I need time to think, and the best way to keep my focus is to stay busy. And today's busy doesn't involve work. Just me, some fresh ingredients, and a hot pan. The food is delicious, and it is a day well spent pampering my family and myself.

September 22, 2019

Yesterday I decided that I am taking the family on a vacation. We haven't ever been on a real family vacation that requires international travel or airplanes. I decided I am going to spend our kid's inheritance, and the first order of business is an all-inclusive resort for the family, and I intend on pulling out all the stops.

This morning, I am meeting Cubby for a little lake time. He greets me in the parking lot of our meeting spot and gives me a big hug. I needed that. He and I discuss the latest happenings at work, and it is clear to me that he is unhappy, as is everyone else. I don't blame them. They are being held hostage in a combative environment. I know better but I can't say anything to him as my role is not as CEO anymore. I am just his friend.

I give him some of my own wisdom, and it is truthful and direct. "You are one of the most valuable people there and other than me, you are the only one who knows how to make our technology work. Use that leverage to your advantage, and I assure you, you will be one of the last men standing." He digests my words and his face and mood lighten. I miss being able to provide guidance and leadership to others.

Cubby and I spend a few hours cruising the lake, talking, and fishing. We share our fears and hopes for the coming months, and I find that he and I share the same worries, and the same need to find our path. I am confident that in time, that path will be revealed for both of us, but for now, we focus on the waning days of summer in the most beautiful place in the world.

The long shadows of fall are starting to replace the bright lights of summer and soon, we will be wearing jackets and sweaters as a new season begins. This same analogy applies to my life. Soon this season of summer will end, making way for the next phase in my journey.

September 23, 2019

I spend the morning writing and researching destinations for our family vacation. We have considered the Dominican Republic, Aruba, Jamaica, the Bahamas, and Hawaii. All of them offer a wide variety of options and different levels of service, but in the end, I am drawn back to Mexico. Unless you have had the chance to see the diverse beauty of Mexico, you wouldn't understand the draw. It is one of my favorite countries in the world and has been since my early trips in the mid 80's. Wanda and I took our honeymoon in Cancun, and I have always wanted to take the kids back to see the ruins of Tulum, and the clear waters of the Caribbean Sea. I haven't been overly excited about anything lately, but this trip sparks my adventurous spirit and the anticipation of departing from our norm.

In the end, we chose Akumal, a tiny seaside town an hour south of Cancun, and 20 minutes from Playa Del Carmen on the beautiful Riviera Maya. I can't wait!

September 24, 2019

Today is a day of little to write about. Tomorrow is Ben's 11th birthday, and I am more focused on giving him a happy birthday than any of the other things going on in my life now. And for the first time since he was born, I will be here before and after his special day.

I am thankful for many gifts in my life, but none more so than the second chance I got when I married Wanda. She gave me love, kids, and hope.

September 25, 2019

11 years ago, today, on a warm summer night, our Benny was born. He caught us by surprise, in the middle of the night. Wanda was screaming and I had to wake up little, 6-year-old Arielle, because no one was awake to babysit her. I was terrified. A dad again at 43, no one to watch Arielle and my beautiful wife in pain. Benny always liked to make an entrance and he still does.

I was so proud of Wanda, of Arielle and of Benny. He was perfect, a love baby. And so began our adventure together, as new parents, and old parents. As a family. We already had Deveny, Adam, and Arielle, but now, we had a baby we made together as a couple. We loved each other's kids, and now, we were blessed with one of our own.

Your birth inspired me, Benny. To be better. To provide, to love. Thanks for being born, kiddo. You continue to bring us great joy, as you have since you were born.

I write these words and post them to my social media accounts. I want the world to know what a gift my family is, and while I talk a lot of crap, my love and appreciation for my family is second to nothing.

I remember the stress I felt at being a dad again at 43. Was I too old to be a good dad? The answer was no. All a dad needs is to be present and loving. I am both. Most days, anyway.

Today is a day that reminds me to count my blessings and inventory what is important to me. As always, my family is at the top of a long list of things I am thankful for. Ben is elated with the day and as I tuck his newly turned 11-year-old self in bed, he hugs me tight and says, "Dad, today was a great day. Thanks for being here". I let him know it was my pleasure, and as I stepped away from his room, I shed a few tears. I am emotional lately, and his words serve as a reminder that I am not so far from my path that I am lost, just disoriented with my direction.

My goal in resigning was to be here for my family, and I am. My current life direction is clouded with uncertainty, but the one thing that is on track is my commitment to family and friends. I am there for them and in that, I find a level of contentment that eclipses my confusion as to the direction of my future. Goodnight Ben. Thanks for keeping this old man young, and for knowing the right things to say, even if you don't realize it.

September 26, 2019

I often wake up early and read the news on my computer. This morning, I read that Ginger Baker, the co-founder and drummer of the band "Cream" is critically ill. So many of my childhood idols have been passing away over the past year. By my estimates, in 10 years, there will be no more "Monsters of Rock." No more "Heroes of WW2". One of the greatest generations will be lost to the memories of those that still remember. When we are gone, our generation, I wonder what history will say about the generation born between 1945 to 1975. I hope they will remember the life-altering changes this generation provided. I am sure that like many before us, history will remember the influences of this great generation, and hopefully, the contributions of my own.

Getting old sucks. Live your life on your terms. It is a short ride before you reach your final exit.

September 27, 2019

Today, we went shopping for Halloween costumes, had lunch and generally just spent the day together as a family. These are the days I quit my job to have. We took a picture of us in our costumes, and while I am smiling, on the inside I am still struggling with some challenges related to my lack of purpose and my relationship with Wanda.

You could never tell by looking at my face. Many people have become experts at sheltering their feelings under a veil of smiles and laughs. The fact remains we need to be mindful that not everything we see is reality, not every smile resides on the inside, and not every picture tells the real story.

I am in a funk, and I am not sure how to get out of it. I don't even understand it. I have everything you could ask for, yet I am still feeling deflated and unworthy of these gifts. I felt unworthy because I was depressed. My wife and I were a mess, I was unhappy, lost and while I seemingly had everything, I felt like I was worthless. I left my company and good people lost their jobs. I was a mess.

I try to put on a happy face, but inside, there is a battle between good and evil. I should be ecstatic about the direction of my life, but as I have plenty of time to reflect on the past, I am saddened by the degradation of my former company and my inability to shepherd those in harm's way. I am concerned that I haven't made any money and that we have crappy, expensive insurance.

Feeling like I need to get out of my head, I drive over to Trilogy Golf with two golf clubs; A driver and a driver. I buy 70 balls and proceed to hit hard, long, arching drives for an hour. There is something very soothing in this exercise. I feel more settled. I am anxious these days. I need to find ways to relax. I am always in my head, a place that can be a veritable house of mirrors.

September 28, 2019

My anxiety level is lower today. I am taking Ben and his cousin Greg to a VR place at the mall prior to Ben's birthday party. It is interesting to me to see how technology continues to push the boundaries of what we can achieve. VR is one of those that will most likely take a while to be fully adopted, but I can see it becoming a great training tool for those in school, the armed forces or just as a means of escaping the realities of the real world.

We finish our lunch and head home for the party. I hate backyard kids' parties. I used to love them when Wanda and I were first married, but now I end up running around like crazy, cooking and refereeing, and generally keeping peace.

The party was as chaotic as I feared. All in all, things are going well, and most importantly, Ben is having a good day. That's what matters to me in the end, and it is the reason I subject myself to this torturous event. A gin and tonic disguised as a sprite will get me through this carnage.

The kids start filtering out, jacked up on sugar and adrenaline, and I greet parents, telling them, "Wait 'til you get them in the car, Mrs. Iforgotyourname. They had 2 cans of Pepsi and I think I saw your boy snorting the cotton candy mix on the side of the house. Good luck!"

September 29, 2019

Today is Sunday. I sit at my desk trying to formulate witty thoughts to share for this book, but my heart isn't in it. I decided to put aside today's writing in favor of a trip down memory lane. I am missing my professional status as a CEO and leader of an up-and-coming technical materials provider. I miss leading people. So, as a way of recapturing some of the past magic, I thumb through photos, pictures, technical papers, and emails from my former life. They are all being categorized for my next book, *Drink my Kool-Aid*, which I have begun to outline. I am looking forward to telling that story as well.

It is surreal to see young me, and the people I worked with for 25 years. I am taken aback by the amount of time that has passed, as well as the amazing growth we experienced over the past decade. I am filled with pride, but the one element I miss the most is the leadership aspect. I miss helping teams to be successful in their endeavors. I miss goal setting, and more so, goal achieving.

I had said recently that I wasn't sure I wanted to finish this book, but now I realize, I want to tell this story. Not every story is a fairy tale, and not all end happily. I want this one to, but only time will tell where we end up. It's only day 122 or so.

The past is simply the shadow of your future. Cast a large shadow by shining brightly!

September 30, 2019

A new week has dawned, and it feels a lot like every other week since I left work. I never had the patience to sit for long periods. Reading is the one thing I can do that requires being in one place and focusing for long periods. It turns out, writing is the other.

Today, my calendar is empty. I am not sure if that is a good thing or not, but being I have the time, I will do something I enjoy. After all, the driving range is 5 minutes from the church, and as luck would have it, I am dropping kids off at church!

Golf has become more than a hobby to me; it is my therapy and my way to relax. I always loved the sport and come from a long line of good golfers. I gave it up for many years in favor of work, and now, I want to work on my game to see how much better I can become. I am seriously thinking about building a golf simulator at the house.

The month ends today, and it has been much more emotional than previous ones, leaving me in a state of anxious frustration. Maybe even a little depressed. I should be happy and relaxed, but I am usually tense and moody.

This is not how I envisioned things for Wanda and I when we discussed me leaving my position in favor of a slower pace and a happier life. I am not complaining about the life we are living, as I am deeply grateful to have this opportunity, but on the other hand, I thought I would have felt different. Free? But the thing about wishing I were free is that freedom from work and stress does not necessarily equate to being free of your own emotions, and in that, I find that I am forced to face my feelings more than I care to admit.

Many days, I refuse to address my feelings of failure, insecurity, guilt, lack of self-worth and direction or many of the other negatives that self-reflection reveals. The fact remains, that I do feel all these things, and I will need to face my feelings to find a new path.

I have no one to blame, although it would be easy to point a finger at Wanda, my work, or any other source of stress, but the truth is, it is I who chooses how to deal with these things, not any of the sources. And that is going to take some work on my part. I am up to the task.

To find your center, you need to understand your boundaries. Only then can balance occur.

5

October, 2019

October 1, 2019

It is a new month, but the only thing that seems to change these days is the date on the calendar. Most days live the same as the one before.

Mike and I are going to Lone Tree Golf Club. He is also retired, but the difference between his situation and mine is that he receives a pension from the city of New York for the rest of his life, and when I left my job after 28 years, I got 4 cans of sauerkraut and a couple of cases of German beer. I am not bitter, but his stress and my stress will be quite different as time marches forward.

October 2, 2019

This morning, Jesús is back in town and asks me to take him to Tucson for another appointment and to pick some things up from his storage unit. We take the long drive to Tucson together and talk about our lives. Jesús is looking for work in Mexico, but the economy there doesn't offer many opportunities for him. He is an attorney by training, but he can't break into the field now that he moved away from the bigger city he lived in. He is not worried though. I tell him all my concerns and the feelings of inadequacy I have been struggling with and he offers some great advice. He says, "Don't worry about it". His response seems so simplistic, but he is offering my own advice back to me, and I find the coincidence amusing.

I am starting to try and adopt a new mindset, one where I don't try too hard to fix things out of my control, and to focus on the positives of the day. This helps me not to get lost in my own sea of anxiety while still being a productive member of society.

I have also been contacted by Applied Materials to do some consulting work for them. It will require that I get released from my non-compete early, but I am looking forward to the chance to contribute to something in my field. I remain hopeful that based on the recent events at the company, they are no longer going to hold me to my non-compete clause.

October 3, 2019

I am meeting my former head of legal from my old company, Kim, for dinner in Scottsdale tonight. I am bringing Wanda as well, and I am excited to see Kim. She is one of my favorite colleagues from Heraeus. Not only is she one of the best IP and corporate lawyers I ever worked with, but she is also a good friend.

When I was CEO, I was asked to sponsor and mentor a group of colleagues on a program of my choosing, that would bring improvements to the culture of Heraeus. I chose a controversial subject because it was important to me. The subject was empowering women in a culture predominately managed by men. Don't get me wrong, Heraeus offers opportunity to all, and they foster a great culture, but what I noticed early on, is that there was still an air of male dominance and chauvinism in the top ranks, as most women served male managers. Almost all the managers were men, with the exception of a few upper-level women in Research and HR.

The program I sponsored was not popular among my colleagues in management, and I was asked several times to reconsider my position. I did not. I moved forward with a wonderful group of women from around the world to identify how to better position women for their place within the company at leadership levels. I wanted to offer an honest perspective to the leadership within the company to better illustrate what I saw as an old-fashioned way of thinking. But I left the company before they finished, and I always wondered how they did.

I asked Kim how my project went. She smiled and said it was presented at the annual presidents' meeting, and that my team did an amazing job. She did confide in me that not every president was enamored with the subject matter, but it did what I had intended, which was to bring awareness to the direction the company was taking with regards to the role of our female colleagues, especially at the management levels. I smiled as she told me that they thanked me for my willingness to sponsor the program, and that I was missed among many of the colleagues, man, and woman alike. I felt a deep sense of pride, because in my eyes, all men are created equal. Even Wo-men.

The only difference between men and women lies in our reproductive organs and our opportunities.

October 4, 2019

We are leaving for our family vacation in 2 days, but I can't shake this feeling of emptiness. Nothing feels right anymore, and I don't understand how to get my head right. It's hard to walk away from everything you've known at the top of your game, but I did.

I walked away with nothing but the want to be with my family, and the hope that I would find a new path for myself, one that would bring me joy and not kill me.

So far, I haven't found either. The path or the joy. Sure, I don't have to go to work, but I realize that I am not experiencing the joy I thought I would, and many days I feel like I have no real purpose. I cook, I drive, I golf, and I write.

Feelings and reality are often not aligned, and I know this, yet I continue to wallow in my own dissatisfaction with my direction in life. Feelings we can control; reality is another story. I continue to pray for guidance, but I know in my heart, I am the only one that can control my feelings and emotions. Right now, emotion is at the top of the leaderboard.

I tried to talk to Wanda about this, but I think she feels I am just stuck. And I am, but there is more to this than just being stuck. Wanda suggests we go see a movie to take my mind off these thoughts and I reluctantly agree. After all, it's "Fridate", and we are supposed to be enjoying our day together.

I guess the first step to recovery is admitting there is a problem. My problem is simple. I have lost my way, and no number of movies or golf games is going to correct this. Only I can. And while we are on vacation, I am going to figure out what to do next.

October 6, 2019

This morning, we flew to Cancun for our family vacation. The kids are excited and the energy in the house is chaotic.

We drive to the airport and check-in for the flight. As we approached the security gate, I found that the gate agent gave me TSA Precheck, but not the rest of the family. The line is not too long, so I take the little kids with me, and we get through security in 5 minutes. 20 minutes later, I see an angry Wanda about to get strip searched. I feel bad, but there is nothing I can do. She takes it in stride. I bought her an adult beverage to provide a soft landing.

We board the plane and find our seats, and once we are all situated, I say a prayer, just as I have on every flight I have ever taken--only this time, I am not alone, the whole family is here.

The flight was smooth and on time, and we arrived in Cancun during a rain shower. It rains all the way to the hotel, and once we arrive, we are asked to wait in line to check-in. It took 45 minutes to get our keys and we were muggy, wet, and now being devoured by mosquitoes. Vacation is fun, right? Food is our only priority at this point.

The resort has a beautiful buffet, and we eat and talk about our plans for the week. The buffet is an amazing mix of foods from around the world. We finish dinner and head back to the room for much-needed sleep. We agree that tomorrow, we will hang out here and get our bearings and enjoy the resort. In the meantime, we will sleep and dream of happy days and tropical drinks.

October 7, 2019

After breakfast, we walk around the grounds to get a feel for what to do. We spend the day swimming in the sea and playing with fish. The kids are delighted to be here, with us. The recent depression I have been feeling is muted by the laughs of my kids and the endless flow of tropical drinks Wanda keeps getting us. I am happy-ish, and I sit and take in the scenery with gratitude. I don't take what we have for granted; I feel incredibly blessed--actually, I just wish my attitude matched my gratitude.

We are all exhausted. We have an 8 PM dinner reservation at one of the restaurants. The night is humid, and the mosquitoes are out in force after the rain. We will spend the next 10 days nursing a menagerie of bites and bumps. Viva Mexico!

October 8, 2019

One of the reasons we chose this area for vacation was to be close to Tulum, a famous historical landmark on the azure seas of the Caribbean, that was once home to Ancient Mayans. Wanda and I spent our honeymoon here in Cancun and Tulum, and we wanted to share this with our kids.

The problem is, we are in the jungle and the kids are getting eaten alive by mosquitoes and poor Wanda is spending most of her time waving her arms around the kids and herself while they devour her flesh. Once at the entrance, we purchase our tickets and immediately head to the kiosk where bug spray is being sold.

Once the bug spray is applied, we walk up the path to finally get a glimpse of the ruins, all the while coughing and spitting the copious amount of bug spray we have in our eyes, nose and throat. Are we having fun yet? The rest of the afternoon is filled with oohs, and aaahs, whining and tears, bleeding and arguing. I don't remember it being this way when Wanda and I came last, but then I remember, "WE WERE ALONE!"

After 3 hours of listening to the kids whine, we agreed to walk to the beach and wash the sweat, blood, and disease of the jungle from our bodies.

We arrive at the beach, and there is no hesitation, and we all dive into the warm and cleansing waters of the sea. We splash and frolic in the small surf and sandy bottom of Tulum beach.

By some miracle, we make it back to the parking lot, drenched in sweat, bleeding, and thirsty. I fumble for the key and try to unlock the rental car, but nothing is happening. Upon further inspection, I find the engine is running. I start freaking out.

"Someone tried to steal the car, Wanda", I scream with exasperation. She looks stunned and is silent for a few moments so I can finish my childish ranting. With an easy calm, she opens the back hatch, and the rest of the locks open. She is the Ying to my neurotic Yang. I may have been the CEO of GMSI, but Wanda is the CEO of Guercio Inc., and she knows how to manage the staff with grace and fury.

The car ignition is keyless, and we apparently got out of the car, locked it, and walked away with the engine running. The car has been idling in the parking lot, in the jungle for a little under 7 hours. Good thing it had a full tank of gas.

We drive back to the hotel in the dark; our only plans are medical attention and intravenous fluids, interspersed with Piña Coladas. Wanda and Cailyn caught the worst of it and their bodies were covered with welts and bites. We administer first aid and hydrate while we pull our-selves together in time to make our reservation at the Brazilian Steak-house. We are battle-worn and hungry, and tonight, we dine like kings.

October 9, 2019

After the challenges of yesterday and the fact that there are numerous storms around the area, we decided that today, we will give our children a reprieve from the tortures of family vacation and stay at the resort. We will relax poolside, swim in the sea, take rides on the lazy river, and eat at several different buffets that the hotel offers. It is a wonderful day of relaxation and fun.

The kids will be ready for our next adventure at Xcaret, a waterpark and historical site located on the ocean, where we will swim through caves and canyons in freshwater cenotes, explore the jungle and the surrounding aquarium, and snorkel in private lagoons, teeming with colorful fish and other sea creatures. My sincere hope is that none of them will eat us.

October 10, 2019

Ben and I will leave by shuttle to the Bahia Principe, about 20 minutes away, to play the Riviera Maya golf course. Wanda and the girls will leave for their excursion to a famous church, and we will all meet up later to have dinner.

After breakfast, the shuttle picks us up, and Ben, who is fluent in Spanish, sparks a conversation with our driver. They make fun of me, which is perfect because self-deprecation is my comedy style!

We arrive at the course, settle in, and pay the exorbitant green fees and rental charges. The course and facilities are meticulously kept and the condition of everything, from the clubs, range balls, and landscape is perfect. We are quite literally in the jungle.

We hurry to the first tee where the starter stops us. In English, he tells us to expect rain for the first half of our round. He is particularly careful to explain the hazards of the course. Not the water and sand, as you would expect, but the danger related to the creatures of the course. Snakes, crocodiles, and jaguars are among the things to watch for. I am not sure if he is joking, but he looks serious and there are signs behind him warning of the same.

As soon as we tee off, the sky opens again. I don't care. At $300 for the round, I am playing in a hurricane if need be. And so it was, Ben and I taking turns, standing in the rainy fairway hitting our balls on what can only be described as jungle perfection. I have played many of the great courses in the world, but there is nothing that compares to this course.

As we play, we are treated to iguanas playing in emerald, green lagoons, cenotes, right on the course, and lakes, complete with crocodiles and the occasional snake. I can't remember a more enjoyable day of golf. I am sure Ben will never forget it. The real joy is not in how we play, or the fact that the course is in incredible shape--it is in the fact we are playing alone. There is no one else on the course.

Wanda and the girls meet us as agreed, and we all share a beautiful dinner. It is the perfect ending to the perfect day, and I am more committed than ever to finding ways to come back and enjoy the spectacular beauty of this incredible place.

October 11, 2019

The drive to Xcaret is only 20 minutes, and once inside the park entrance, we find our parking spot. We open our adventure with a swim through an underground river, through caves and marshes that line the shores. The water is frigid, and while it is 90 degrees outside, the river flows from underground and rarely warms above 60 degrees. The swim ends at a set of stairs that opens to the sprawling beach, and the turquoise waters of the Caribbean Sea.

After getting our bearings, we walked the path into the jungle to find the aquarium. There is everything from exotic fish to dolphins and the layout of the exhibits is ingenious, as the tanks and pools have been perfectly integrated into the landscape.

As we meander through the paths of the aquarium, we reach the snorkel beach, a protected lagoon. It is here that I realize my dream of watching my kids swim with tropical fish, on reefs teeming with life. It isn't the open ocean, as I have done many times in Jamaica, Aruba, Mexico, or Hawaii, but for them, they experience the same magic I feel when swimming with sea life.

After an hour and a half the little kids want to explore the water park. We round a trail and below me, down a steep path, lies a large cenote, a waterfall, and a gigantic jungle gym incorporated into the rocks and waterfalls, complete with slides, ropes, and nets. The kids go crazy, sliding and climbing, as I sit in the cool shade, just watching them and smiling.

Later, we find Arielle and Wanda looking for something to eat. They stumbled upon a Mexican Buffet, but we need to hurry, as we are going to see a show about the history of Mexico. We feast on a plethora of Mexico's finest dishes.

This trip is just what we needed as a family. The past years have taken a toll on everyone, and I sometimes forget I wasn't the only one who struggled during my tenure as CEO. They lived every stressful event, and endured the long days of travel as well, just in a different sense. I am filled with love as they stuff their faces with the finest comida Mexico has to offer.

We finish dinner and race over to the theatre. It is cavernous and is decorated like an ancient Mayan playing field. The lighting and sheer opulence of every prop, costume, and stage setting is phenomenal. The show takes viewers through a performance of every stage of Mexico's history, from Ancient Mayans and Aztecs to the modern day. I am lost in a world of wonder and immersed in the rich history of the country I call my second home. Mexico, te amo mucho! We walked out of the theatre at 9:30 PM. We are sunburned, tired, soggy, and full, but there is not a single frown on any of our faces.

October 12, 2019

Today we went to Playa del Carmen to visit Jorge, Wanda's cousin. My stomach has been cramping a little since this morning, and I think I may have contracted a bit of Montezuma's revenge. It's true what they say about Mexico. It's a nice place to visit, but don't drink the water. I threw caution to the wind, immersing myself in rivers, oceans, lagoons, and pools and now, I fear the wind is going to blow back hard.

We met Jorge and had lunch and then started walking the streets of Playa del Carmen. My stomach begins to gurgle, and I tell Wanda of my dilemma, but she doesn't take me seriously and keeps on walking and talking. In an instant, it hits me, and I must find a bathroom.

Without uttering a word, I turn towards a small taco shop on the corner. I waddle over, like a geisha girl, to find the small bathroom, dirty, but unoccupied. I lock the door and as soon as I sit down, my insides growl with the sounds of aggressive evacuation. The noises emanating from the small bathroom resonate through the thin walls and into the dining room. I am mortified, but my shame doesn't last long. It gets worse, as the manager is now banging on the bathroom door, yelling in Spanish, "If you aren't a paying customer, it will cost you 10 pesos to use the bathroom!" I ignore him, but the knocking continues.

"Señor, Señor, diez pesos por el bano!"

The manager keeps screaming, and banging loudly on the door. Where does he think I am going?! Wanda realizes I am gone and calls me on my cell phone. I let her know, "I am locked in the bathroom at Taco's R' Us and the manager is banging on the door asking for money!"

Within minutes, I hear Wanda's Spanish voice scolding the manager, as she explains to him that I was about to shit in the street and that asking for money to use a bathroom is petty. She lets him know that we won't be eating here, as she hands him the 10 pesos. Not that we would want to eat here anyway, after what I did to the bathroom. I love my girl. She is fierce, like a lioness. Don't mess with her cubs or the head of the pride. She will rip your face off.

Later in the evening, we head back to Jorge's place to see his house. It is a beautiful, 3-story compound, complete with jungle gardens, work-shops, and a real cenote. As Jorge explains where the cenote is, Ben runs ahead, into the darkness. Within seconds, we hear a splash, and fish Ben out of the cenote. He is scared, but he is ok. We learn two lessons. One, don't run in the dark. Two, cenotes are cold.

It's getting late and we need to get ready to go home tomorrow. Wanda holds my hand. She seems happy and that makes me happy. I ask everyone, "Hey, other than survival mode at Tulum, was this a good va-cation?" Everyone answers simultaneously, "The best trip EVER!" My work here is finished.

October 13, 2019

We headed home. It's been a great time together, and I am reminded on this trip how important these people are to me, and how lucky I am to have them. I haven't found clarity for my direction, but I did relax, and I soaked in every moment of family time, and in that, I found peace.

October 14, 2019

We arrived home late last night, and everyone was still sleeping as I quietly went downstairs to make coffee. As I reflect on the adventure of the past week, I am reminded of a quote by Hunter S. Thompson, one of my all-time favorite authors. His quote reflects my thoughts, as I sit on my toilet for the 4th time in 2 hours.

"Life should not be a journey to the grave with the intention of arriving safely in a pretty and well-preserved body, but rather to skid in broadside

in a cloud of smoke, thoroughly used up, totally worn out, and loudly proclaiming "Wow! What a Ride!"

He is right. One of the reasons I left my career was to live, and no one can accuse me of not using this time to experience the life I was missing. Real life beckons us daily. The trick is to figure out how to balance the demands of our everyday life with the needs of our soul. This balance eluded me, and still does, but I am convinced that the perfect existence lies between a productive career and a full and stable home life. I know that my journey has had more work than home life, but I am at least making the effort to make up for lost time before it's too late.

With that being said, we did nothing today. It's Monday, and this is exactly the kind of day I used to fantasize about when I was working, and now, I am living it.

October 15th, 2019

Another fitful night of sleep. Been getting over Montezuma's revenge and this time it's lingering. I am slowly feeling better, but I also have a cold and a sore throat, and most annoying is my dry cough. I wake up to pee and can't go back to sleep. This is my new norm.

I really need a medical marijuana card. I need relief from all this, and I know some edible THC will do that. My sincere hope is that Arizona legalizes marijuana. I would much rather eat a gummy filled with THC than take an opioid or drink liquor.

Tonight, I am supposed to go to a concert with Mike. In the morning, I need to be up early to take my mom to the Doctor, but I never go out anymore with the guys. After I retired, I was tired, and just stopped going out socially. Even Wanda tries to get me to go out, but after I left my career, life moved on without me. I have time, but no one else does.

This time away from work is supposed to be about renewal, but I still feel the same, only now I am a man without a purpose. However, I am finding that there is great peace in writing. I feel less full of anxiety, and more stable in the words of these pages. So maybe my purpose is to be a wordsmith, as I have been told I should many times before.

Abuema is leaving today. She has been here for weeks, and I will be sad to see her go. We drop her off at the bus station and decide we are going to catch a matinee. We are going to the theatre at 1:58 PM for a 2:05 PM showing of *Abominable*. Guercio time is in full effect!

The movie is touching and beautiful. It's a fictional tale about a Yeti and a girl whose father died. I felt a lot of the pain the girl did, as I have always carried the loss of my father as a chain of sorrow. I cry at the littlest things that remind me of him, or a fond memory I have of him. I have missed him most of my adult life.

He did not see what I made of myself, and I missed having someone who knew me front and back. I pray for him daily and draw from our time together every day. He is the blueprint for me. I miss our talks and his smile, his intelligence and wit. I hope he knows how much he inspired me, and that I love him very much.

I need to change and go to the concert. Wanda is happy I am going too. Wanda holds my cheeks in her hands and tells me, "Have fun!" She says it with a stern undertone, meaning, "Don't be such a grouch".

I can't believe it is the middle of October already. I was just in the jungles of the Riviera Maya, and next month it's Thanksgiving. And then, 2020! Slow ya' roll, 2019, I haven't even bought Halloween candy yet!

I pick Mike up to go to the show, but I haven't said a word to him, as I am driving recklessly, phone on speaker, discussing the mechanics behind structuring a deal on something with a business colleague. I haven't stopped talking since I picked him up. This is the "Old me", the CEO. 100 miles an hour, 24/7. I like the new me, but I still have some old habits to break. I need to slow down and communicate better. I fear Mike thought I had abducted him and was taking him to the desert to meet his doom. Nope, just Phoenix!

We get into the city early and have a beer. The drive to the concert is only 5 miles away in downtown Phoenix and while I am not slobbery drunk, I don't think I could pass a breathalyzer test. Caution will be exercised.

As we round the corner to the venue, we are met with a long line of incredibly old people--at least 3-400 old people; people MY age and older, standing in line in Blue Oyster Cult, UFO, Schenker, and Dio concert shirts. Original versions!

You think with all these geriatrics here, they would park a few porta potties near the line. My prostate is the size of a cantaloupe and my bladder the size of a walnut. I must pee so bad it hurts. I really do need to get this checked out.

I am taken aback by the demographic for the concert. A bunch of mid-50 to late 60's people, interspersed with 20-somethings and the occasional wheelchair-bound senior. I wonder if this is what Noah's Ark would look like if it were loaded into a trailer park in Florida or Apache Junction, Arizona. Or, at a UFO concert, apparently.

The doors open and they finally let us in. Like herd animals running for a watering hole in a parched desert landscape, other weak bladdered men such as myself race like gazelles to the row of urinals waiting around the corner from the entrance. The sounds of splashing were so loud, you would have thought you were at the fountains of the Bellagio.

Tonight, we drink, we laugh, we rock, and we pee. I am reminded that I quit my job to find happiness and peace. I gave up a promising musical career for a life in business. Some dreams die to make room for others. Today though, all through the day, I found smatterings of joy and hints of what my life should look like. In this weird moment, in an old hall in Phoenix, I am smiling, happily buzzed, and at peace.

October 16, 2019

I woke up to take my mom to the doctor. We have a great talk, and she reminisces about my time in the limelight as a musician. She and my dad used to come to my shows, and she recounts the crazy experiences they had watching me play--many I had completely forgotten about.

She tells me she is worried about me. I told her I was fine. She doesn't believe me and is worried that we will run out of money and that I am depressed. I reassure her I am fine, that I am just finding a new path and taking a break.

I drop her off and go home. I am just trying to figure out what to do for work. "Nothing" is my preferred vocation at this point. After the past few months since I left my job, I have mastered nothing, so it would seem I am highly qualified for the position.

October 17, 2019

I've been sick all week. A head cold and the remnants of Montezuma and his digestive revenge. Today I have a series of calls related to my business and career options. I am also taking Cailyn to choir practice.

The rest of the day is a blur. Sometimes, I have nothing to say, so I go outside and putt on the green and then back upstairs to write. I feel like I am a caged lion, pacing back and forth in my cage, wondering when someone will leave the door open so I can run out and eat the tourists.

It is deflating to see a caged animal longing for the hunt. Nothing more wasteful than incarcerating the instincts of wild animals. This also applies to entrepreneurs.

October 18, 2019

It's Fridate. Over breakfast, Wanda and I started fighting. We sit together bickering when we should be laughing. I don't like this aspect of our relationship. She frequently blames me, but I am not the one that starts fights and I try not to stay mad when we do fight. Wanda holds a grudge, and that is not how I like to live.

Tennis and love have a lot in common. You bounce things back and forth until someone scores. The irony is that when you are scoreless, the lack of a point is called, "Love".

October 19, 2019

It's Saturday and I feel a little better. I get things done around the house. Later in the afternoon, Mike and Michelle have their annual Octoberfest, but being I just finished spending the last 2 years in Germany, I am not as enthusiastic as I could be.

It turns out to be a wonderful family affair, and I enjoy the beer and food of Germany for the first time since my last trip to Europe in April of this year. I miss my colleagues from Germany, and this event reminds of my many days and nights, roaming around Europe, looking for a beer and some food. I would usually find both in the most unconventional places. Europe as a whole is an amazing place. I feel very blessed to have experienced so much of it for so long. Bad news is, I will most likely be asleep by 8 PM. I say this in jest, but the reality is I fell asleep on Wanda by 8:30pm. It's ok, my Schnitzel needs to rest anyway.

October 20, 2019

This is going to be the Sunday we rest. I spent most of the day with Ben, trying to figure out how to build a golf simulator. This is something to fill my time and creating something from scratch fits well with my need to create. I need to fix Wanda's Jeep, and later in the day we will go to church. There are some days that have no funny anecdotes--just the boring reality of everyday life.

October 21, 2019

I wake up at 5 AM with an uncontrollable urge to go to the bathroom. I am dealing with an emergency, and as I stumble down the stairs to the confines of the guest bathroom, I fart, leaving me with an unwelcome guest in my underwear. This is a book about honesty, and regrettably, these are the details of my life after the C-Suite. I hate getting old. When did I become an 80-year-old incontinent man?

After feeding the masses a healthy lunch, I write for more than 3 hours, and things are starting to flow when I sit to write now. I have a better idea of how to be effective when I have time to write, and when I read my own work, I can see the improvements in my presentation and style. It's hard to do this because I have no formal training to write a book, but inexperience has never stopped me before.

I am starting to think clearly again. I am regaining my focus. I am looking at the future with hope, instead of despair. It is a vastly different dynamic from where I was a few short months ago; hell, even a few short weeks ago. It is October, and in the span of 4 months, I have changed my direction, my reality and hopefully, my mental well-being.

I stopped thinking about GMSI daily, and how they are faring. I wish them well, but I am spending my minutes cultivating some joy, some rest, and some fresh ideas. I am scared, but I have faith in myself, in God and in the mysterious fact that I am destined on a path that will lead me to the next phase of my life. I keep reminding myself, "*We learn from our failures, not from our victories.*"

I am still building the golf simulator, but it's slow going. I am disappointed, but the concept is coming together.

Later in the evening, Wanda and I watched a movie. I fall asleep as usual and any chance that Wanda would have sex with me is gone. I wake up almost at the end of the movie and try and pretend I was not sleeping. She is not buying it. I can hear the shackles of her libido locking down for the evening.

October 22, 2019

It's 5 AM and I am up. Why do I keep waking up night after night? One good night's sleep is all I am asking for. One night where I do not wake up 5 times through the night.

This morning, I am dropping the Jeep off for service at the dealership and they offer to drive me back to the house, which will save me $11.38, the cost of an Uber. I am on a fixed income of Zero. Every little bit helps.

I spend the day writing, taking business calls and doing research for InfinityGo. After lunch I go back to writing, but my mind isn't in it, so I take an hour and play some golf on the PC.

After dinner everyone goes their separate ways in the house. I write and work on some consulting questions and berate myself internally for not having a job. I shouldn't be so hard on myself, as this was the plan, but my guilt for leaving my employees and not taking care of them, as well as my fear of poverty override my sense of enjoyment.

By 10 PM, I am already falling asleep. It still hurts that we are not taking advantage of this time to catch up on lost moments, but I am not going to beat a dead horse. We all end up as glue anyway.

October 23, 2019

Not to sound like a broken record, but I am awake at 5 AM again. I am angry and to spite myself, I force myself to lay in bed and fall back to sleep. It doesn't work, and after an hour or more, I concede and get out of bed. The rest of the day follows in a similar fashion.

October 24, 2019

I am still waking up several times through the night. I am sure it is a mix of nervous anxiety and uncertainty. The two do not mix well and are only to be taken as prescribed by your doctor.

I cook breakfast and get ready for a meeting with one of my former clients from a large semiconductor company here in town. Before I leave, I say goodbye to Wanda who has recently awakened. She looks so good. I took a couple of pictures. I like to have her pictures with me always. She is my girl, for better or worse.

Around 10 AM, I meet with my former client, Mitch. He is more my friend than a client, and I find he and I are in a similar situation. Mitch will leave the semiconductor industry as well to venture forth in the woods in a small town in Minnesota. He and his wife will build a log cabin themselves. I like the idea. I want that, but my overhead is about $6-8K per month lately. I must find a way to stop the burn. I will have to get a job, or InfinityGo, or something. Male dancer is out. I have no dance skills and the body of a manatee.

At 2:30 PM, my cellphone rang. It's Ben using Wanda's phone. Ben sullenly informs me that he left his retainer at the park, and that he and Wanda are going back to get it. I listen to Ben tell me how sorry he is, and that mom is upset. I tell him it's ok, but to be more careful. He tells me he loves me and hangs up and I go back to my emails.

3 minutes later the phone rings. It's Wanda. She angrily asks me, "Why didn't you yell at Ben? Why are you not mad at him? Aren't you mad at him? He left the damn retainer, in the park. I cannot be responsible for everything here, Peter!!! You take him!!! I am done!"

After yelling at me, she hangs up. I sit in stunned silence. What just happened, and why is it my fault? I am perplexed, but I don't want to fight. It's exhausting.

They arrive home and Ben and I go back to the park, 30 minutes away. This is the second retainer he has lost. I let him know that his irresponsibility will now come with a consequence, a financial one. He is bartering and trying to understand the fiduciary responsibility he must now incur, and I appreciate his insightful questions and his logical approach to cutting a deal. I have great faith in Ben; he is a master negotiator/manipulator.

Ben is trying to deflect responsibility, and here, in the blustery spaces of the park, I explain that he needs to stop blaming others for every bad thing that happened. Own your actions. I am accountable. And I want that for our kids.

As we rummage through the garbage pails, swarming with flies and overflowing with the dirty and repugnant remnants of a picnic smorgasbord, I feel nauseous. This is the bowels of hell, and unless I come home with the retainer, I will have to face an angry Wanda. I would rather meet Satan, herself.

We search and dig in the filth for an hour. We find nothing. I look at Ben who is genuinely dejected. He has failed the family and now, he is going to be out the cost of a new retainer. Pretty much a gut punch for an 11-year-old. I know we are not going to find the retainer, but the fact we are putting effort into the search makes me feel good that he is learning a lesson.

I drop Ben off and tell him that everything will be ok. I told him to own his mistake, and let Wanda know he will make things right. As I hugged him goodbye, Cailyn bounds out the front door and scurries into the truck. We are going to be late. "Dad, you need to hurry!!", she tells me as I back slowly out of the driveway. Hurry? That's all I have done for the past 28 years. I don't want to hurry anymore, but here we are, hurrying through traffic to get her to choir practice.

We arrived late. The teacher is already making children cry, and I reluctantly send Cailyn into the maelstrom. Cailyn doesn't care. She is fierce. She is Cailyn. She walks right up and stands next to the teacher, waiting for her opening, almost daring the teacher to stop class, and let Cailyn walk on stage. You got to love this kid. She is most like me in heart and spirit. She doesn't break the rules, she makes them.

I am starting to find a rhythm I had lost many years ago. Less stressful. More patient. More laid back and "see what happens" rather than worrying about what could.

I need this change of mindset. I need to slow it down for my mental wellbeing and for the good of my family. I am not sure I can be a CEO again. I would rather be a dad and husband, and fish and golf and boat in our spare time. But the pay for that job comes in hugs and kisses, not dollars and cents. I will need to find a balance of making money and holding on to this lifestyle. If the kisses and hugs my kids give me were currency, I would be a billionaire.

On the way home, I tell Cailyn that we are stopping at the car wash because we are both a little angry for a variety of reasons. I tell her we will go through the wash, and when we exit, we will be all clean of our anger. She loves this idea, and we turn in to rinse ourselves of the dirty, negativity that lingers.

This is why I quit my job. To have these moments. I traded in the security, high pay, benefits, and perks of the C-Suite, for a life of kids' laughter. I know in the end, I will not regret this decision, even though my old boss, Heinz, told me he thought I might. He was right in some respects. I miss driving a business. I miss the culture and the magic that occurred sometimes. God knows if I will ever sit in the C-Suite again. It was a lot of hours, a lot of work, and a lot of responsibility and stress. Tonight, I will go out, and I will play 18 holes at Pebble Beach on a cheap simulator I built myself. And I will be happy.

Heinz, I don't regret what you thought I would. I miss you and the Heraeus executives I used to work with. I miss driving the business. I miss the leadership aspects of my career, and the joy of lifting people up, creating culture and driving innovation. I miss seeing the results of our teamwork. I will do something again, but I think a part of me died when I stepped down.

I reached the top of my field with my dream company, Heraeus, but I left on my terms. I will be ok, and I hope you are too, but I don't regret my decision. I embrace the possibilities.

I did not quit on you, I quit on a corporate culture that directed you and I to make decisions and carry out tasks I didn't believe in. I will miss you, and our talks, and will always value our time together. I will miss the paychecks and good insurance for my family, but mostly, I find myself missing the people I worked with around the world. The people. They were always the reason I kept going, even when I should have stopped.

A few key takeaways from the past 4 months. I miss flying Business Class around the world, but I am ok without Platinum Executive status. I have something better. I have marital status, and to her, I am Elite. I am happily married to a beautiful woman who gave me a family. She inspired me to be better than I even thought I could be. My kids are amazing. I see their happiness in the many things we do together, and the many activities I attend that I would not have been able to, had I stayed on the executive path we were on.

I gave up security for the unknown. I gave up the money for peace of mind, and I am ok with that as well. I am investing in a commodity much richer than the ROI on our 401K. My dividend is time with my family, and a peace for which I have been searching for many years.

I don't regret anything. I have faith in God, myself, and my family. I miss you though, and I am always wishing you and the team at Heraeus the best of everything in life and business. Thank you for the wonderful opportunity and I will always be grateful for our time together. Now, we can be friends, and in our line of work, a friend is a priceless commodity. Danke Schön, Herr Fabian. Danke.

October 25, 2019

After yesterday's events, today is much more relaxing and calmer. Mike and I enjoy a beautiful morning of golf and afterward, I spend time with the kids while Wanda scouts locations for her upcoming photo shoot. She is shooting her first wedding, alone. I know she is nervous and wants everything perfect for the couple. I support her efforts because she supports mine.

I make great hamburgers for dinner, and we continue our quest to be the best sexless couple in the modern age. I find that I fixate on our sex life more than I should, but when you have something so special and then lose it, you tend to dwell on finding it, much like the retainer at the park. I would look in dirty garbage pails if I knew Wanda's libido was in there, but it isn't that easy. The fact remains, I am so in love with you, Wanda, and I miss that aspect of our lives. But I am happy to be with you each day. No matter what.

October 26, 2019

This morning, I got a call from my mom that she is sick and going to the emergency room. I am frantic and I race from the house and drive like a maniac to the hospital. Once inside, I find that she is not there. I call and find that she and Rod are still at the house, waiting for me to drive them. She did not communicate clearly that she needed ME to take them.

This supports my insistence that former colleagues repeat their intentions. Many were annoyed when I asked them to recap a direction, but this situation is exactly why. The details are important, and if you are not clearly communicating, it leads to misunderstandings and mistakes.

I raced back to her house and took them to the hospital. After 5 hours, many tests and assumptions, no one knows what is wrong with her. I think there is another cause for her recent health issues, and no one has found it. I couldn't bear to lose another parent, so I told her I am going to be more involved in her medical treatment.

Wanda gets home after an exceedingly long day, and we fall asleep. I pull her close and tell her I love her. I don't have the heart to tell her that I was denied my request to work because Heraeus won't let me out of my non-compete. I will save that for tomorrow, and in the dark and still night, I match her breathing and fall asleep.

October 27, 2019

I had a vivid dream about Wanda, and it woke me up. I am also concerned about my mom, my recent denial of my request to work from my former employer and my mounting emotional burdens. I am not depressed, but I will say that I have a lot going on between my temples.

I get a call from Adam, but I missed it because I was working on something. Wanda came out to let me know he was calling her. His girlfriend is sick and needs to go to the hospital and her mom will not take them. He sounds frantic. I tell him I am on my way.

I drive over to their house and find that the emergency is no longer as pressing as it was an hour ago. I am furious, but I don't say what is really on my mind. They are broke and I offer them $150 for an Uber and food and remind them that one day I won't be around to call for help. I remind Adam of how it was for me when I was younger. My parents were awesome, but they were strict. When I "REALLY" needed help, like I was in jail, they were there to rescue me. But mostly, they let me make stupid decisions and then, in the words of my beautiful mother, "Suffer!"

We spend a quiet evening at home, and later that night, we find ourselves wrapped up in each other, just like in my dream. I didn't tell her what I dreamt, but somehow, she knew, and we spend time as lovers instead of Mommy and Daddy. I have missed her and savor the stolen moments we share.

October 28, 2019

I am going to write back to Heraeus to formally request they reconsider letting me work with Applied Materials. I don't see this as a threat to their business, but I am bound by the terms of my non-compete and I will honor my word. It doesn't hurt to try.

I have plans to work on InfinityGo's pitch deck today, as well as writing for this book. I don't look further than lunchtime today, mainly because I want to not do anything. Many people want many things from me, between consulting and advisory work, but in truth, I am more focused on watching an 80's movie and eating something delicious. I just want to be.

October 29, 2019

Today is spent supporting our efforts at forming InfinityGo. We meet with several attorneys to better position ourselves with the right team to help our growth and funding. Also, we will spend a couple of hours with the accountants and other financial people that will help us manage the business of tax and compliance.

It is a busy day, but I am happy to be pushing the business to fruition with Brad and Omer. It feels like work, and it is, but when you are a start-up, work is often performed on a sweat equity basis, meaning you work without a paycheck. I have been here before, but for my partners, they are in new territory, and I offer some advice on how best to deal with this phase. My advice? *Suffer.* Nothing worth having is easy.

October 30, 2019

After yesterday's long day in support of InfinityGo, Brad and I decided to make some corporate decisions, and we unanimously agree in favor of golfing instead of spending the day in front of computers. The highlight of the round was a masculine woman hitting on Brad, trying to entice him with snacks of "Kahlua, wheat thins and oral sex". I can't make this stuff up.

October 31, 2019

Halloween, and the end of another month of "Restment". It hasn't been as easy as I thought to step away from my career, but as the days go by, my direction seems to become clearer. I will be the CEO of InfinityGo, I will write this book and the others that will follow. I will look to work with others as a consultant, and with a little luck, I will find my path to happiness.

I am going to spend the day with my wife and kids today, and as an added treat, we are going to take them to the Children's Museum of

Phoenix. I joke with Wanda that I am excited to see a place where they display children. She doesn't laugh, but I think it's hysterical.

In truth, the museum is a fantastic place of discovery and activity for children. It was started by artists who focused on providing kids a place that was tailored to them, and I love coming here. My kids still appreciate me being here. I thought they would be sick of me, but if anything, I am convinced they never want me to go back to work again.

We have a great time, and the kids are delighted to be here, with us, as a family. As we sit in the crowded cafeteria enjoying a light lunch, I ask Wanda if she is still happy having me home. She pauses and then says, "Sometimes". She is kidding and puts her arms around me and hugs me. "I love you and I am really happy you are home. Now if you could be happy, that would make it all worthwhile." Her words stay with me. Does she know how I have been feeling lately? I will work on this happiness thing she speaks of, but clearly, I have some work to do.

Find something you love to do, and people to share it with. In this, you will find joy, purpose, and peace, and if you are lucky, you will discover yourself.

6 |

November, 2019

November 1, 2019

Last night was Halloween and for the first time in my life, I spent the whole day with my family. In this new month, I am committed to finding a clear direction for my future and hope that I can shed these feelings of depression that linger.

Yesterday was Halloween, and today, in my wife's culture, it is "Dia de los Muertos", "The day of the dead." In Mexico, today is the day they remember loved ones that have passed away. We display pictures of those we remember on homemade altars. Along with pictures, we place articles of clothing or items that belonged to the deceased. I don't believe the dead return to visit us, but I love my wife, and I am supportive of the culture. I am also terrified of zombies and ghosts, in that order.

Today being the day of the dead, I reflect on the many people I have lost along the way. My dad, grandparents, and other family members, but also friends and people I didn't know. The reason I decided to leave my career was in part because of my mortality. I wanted to take my chips off the table and sit in the lounge for a little while. That analogy still stays with me, and I am trying to be true to myself and live before I die.

It may seem insignificant to many what I am doing right now, but trust me, its significance will stay with me for the rest of my life, and even more so, it will stay with my wife and kids. The investment of time

I am making with them now will not bear fruit until much later in life, most likely when I am not here. They will remember this time, and in turn, me.

After the kids finish chess, we drive down the street to "SoCal Fish Taco Company". Instead of spending my afternoon in a conference room, looking out the window and wondering what my family is doing, I am outside the window doing it. I can't describe the freedom I feel in being able to do this, but I am also fearful that if we aren't careful, we will lose everything we worked for. It doesn't matter now; *I am in the moment, and I cherish every last minute of this time.*

November 2, 2019

My longtime friend and bandmate, Sean, is getting married today. We became friends, and then bandmates in the late 80's. We played music together professionally for most of the 90's and part of the early 2000s. I miss playing music together, but life flows, and sometimes people are in your life for a purpose, and then we drift away. Sean, however, has always remained in screaming distance. We are honored to share in this celebration of love.

When I find something I like, I stick with it. Careers, interests, clothing, food, and women all fall into this category. I am loyal to a fault.

I found out that my other longtime friend, Jeffie Q is going to be there too. Jeff and I had been best friends and bandmates for as long or longer than Sean and I have. After more than 30 years of friendship, we had a falling out and he hasn't talked to me in a few years.

I had to fire him, my best friend, in favor of doing what was best for the company. It is one of the hardest decisions I have ever made, in business or my personal life. I did what I thought was right, and in the end, I stood by my decision. I have tried to make peace with him since that day, but he will never forgive me.

Here is the real burn. In 2014, Jeff lost his job and was running into really difficult times. He asked me if there was something he could do at my business to earn money. He was talented, and we hired him. I helped my friend. When things got better, Jeffie came to me and sincerely thanked me for helping him and his family when they really needed it. He told me that I saved his life. I didn't feel that way at all. I just did what I hoped he would have done for me if the situation were reversed. True friends always want the best for you.

I stepped outside the reception for a cigar, and hopefully to find Jeff and make peace once and for all, but when he saw me, he just ignored me. I felt horrible, and there I stood, like a moron, smoking a cigar I didn't want, in the misty rain, alone. I stood looking through the large glass windows, framing all my old friends inside the venue, like a picture from an old scrapbook.

We had spent many years together as friends and bandmates, but now I realized, like an old coat that doesn't fit anymore, we had out-grown each other and moved on. This feeling settled with me in an uncomfortable fashion. These were my people once, but now; *I was the coat that didn't fit.*

I haven't heard from him again, and my guess is I never will. Not all stories have happy endings.

Say you are sorry and mean it, and then forgive and forget. It's the easiest way to foster strong relationships and a sure way to alleviate regrets.

November 3, 2019

Wanda could tell I was hurting, and she was compassionate and kind. We just lay in bed and watched a movie, and she hugged me and snuggled me until the pain of being rejected by my friends subsided. It doesn't really subside though. We push these emotions deep down, to a place we don't visit often. All the pain of our childhood lives here. The rejection and hurt, the bullying and the anger. All of us have a place in our psyche like this, where the bad things live. Try not to visit it too often; it's always best to learn from the past and move on. I am reminded of my own advice. *Don't let the past define your future.*

November 4, 2019

I am finalizing the pitch deck for InfinityGo. It has been a lot of work and research, and the vision is finally taking shape. I will spend the rest of the day working on our presentation. I am focused on making this next venture my last job, and I want to go out holding my head up high, and proud of what we create.

It is so hard to raise funding for an unproven start-up, but I feel like we have a great idea, a good team, and a great support system around us. I am excited about the prospect of leading a team to make our vision a reality and build a culture of excellence. It won't be easy, but if things go the way I think they will, we will leave a legacy greater than our own. We will leave something that will benefit users around the world with a platform that serves them. And in that, I find great motivation to deliver on our promises.

November 5, 2019

It's a slow day here in Guerciotown. I have been a little down since Saturday's wedding enlightenment, and I am just not feeling my normal, jovial self.

This has been a hard transition in many ways. Giving up my career, my title and the monetary benefits are obvious things to have to accept, but some of the other things I have had to deal with, including my changing relationship with Wanda, my loss of purpose and the difficulty in finding a new path have left me frazzled some days. I fight this feeling and try and stay upbeat, but inside, I am always thinking about the past 28 years, and how much has changed in less than 28 weeks since I left.

Sometimes, the hardest person to learn to live with is yourself.

November 6, 2019

Today is a dream day. I am playing 36 holes of golf at Troon North and the TPC Stadium course in Scottsdale. To golfers worldwide, this is a good day. I am meeting a childhood friend, Mike, along with Chuck and Steve. The morning is dreary, but sometimes you must endure a little rain to see rainbows. This is a day I have dreamed of for most of my adult life.

I woke up at 5 AM this morning, which doesn't seem like anything out of the ordinary for me, but late last night, Wanda decided to get romantic. We stayed up until 2:30 am, and while I was exhausted, it was worth it to me. It's going to be a real test of stamina today.

Troon North is exceptional in every way. Neatly manicured fairways, million-dollar mansions, PGA level greens, and gorgeous mountain vistas make this an exceptional experience in every way. And to top it off, we played great!

After Troon, we make the 20-minute drive to TPC Scottsdale. We arrive and go inside for some lunch before we play. The food is delicious, and we all share our history. Mike and I grew up together, played baseball, and graduated from the same High School. Now, 40+ years later, we are here playing golf, old men, playing an old game.

TPC Stadium is amazing. Mike is concerned we aren't going to finish, but I assure him we will. "Have faith", I tell him. At 4:45 PM, we make it to the famous hole #16, the Colosseum. We stand silent for a few moments taking in the grandeur of the moment, the setting sun illuminating our shadows in long strokes. It has been an epic day. An amazing experience, and I feel a sort of vindication that only comes from living our dreams. And I have been. I just need to remind myself that I am the luckiest guy in the world.

Another important note of interest today is Adam's birthday. I love you, Adam. I know we don't always see eye to eye, but that's mainly because you are taller than me now. Happy Birthday, kiddo!

November 7, 2019

After a day like yesterday, I find it hard to get started today. I ran some household errands this morning before taking my mom and Rod to a surgeon for a consultation on a cancerous growth on her leg. They will do surgery later in the month to remove the small mass. I worry about my mom; she needs to take better care of herself if she wants to live. She is stubborn, like me. I just offer my love and support, so I can be there for her like she has been for me all my life.

Driving home, I recount the story of yesterday's golf adventure. I know Rod, who is a golfer himself, would love a day like that. I would like to take him someday soon. The only thing better than making your dreams come true is helping others make theirs a reality.

November 8, 2019

I am trying to get in better shape, so every other morning, I get on my bike and ride a few miles. Not a leisurely ride, but as hard and fast as I can. I find that my stress levels are much lower if I get out and spend an hour with my heart rate up and my brain focused on breathing.

This morning, I am writing, and working on the InfinityGo business, and later in the day, I am going to meet my cousin Mike at his house for some beers and some time on the driving range at his course. I have been feeling down for the past few days. Maybe it's just me dealing with this new reality of unemployment, or the lack of social interaction, but an afternoon with Mike hitting balls, smoking cigars, and drinking beer is as good a therapy as there is.

Having Mike here has been a Godsend. He is like a brother to me, and I really needed a friend today. He is talking about going back to work next year, but I try and talk him out of it. I am selfish; I don't want to be the only one without a job. I understand his mindset though; he has a pension for life from the NYPD, and he is only in his mid-forties. He is bored.

I drove around town after golf looking for a Schlotzky's. Wanda loves these unique sandwiches; she had mentioned she wanted one, and today, out of the blue, I am bringing them home. When I get home with the sandwiches, she is all smiles. And in her smile, lies mine.

It is better to give than receive, unless oral sex is involved; then receiving is always the better option.

November 9, 2019

It's Saturday and absolutely nothing of importance, other than church, is happening today. Film at 11.

November 10, 2019

Looks like Sunday will be a continuation of Saturday. All of us are tired, and we decide to have a "Sedentary Sunday". This fits me well, as I can't shake my latest bout with mild depression.

I spend the entire day seated at my computer, writing, and researching. I don't think my ass moved from this chair for more than 9 minutes total today.

We convince the kids that we should start a new trend called, "Sushi Sunday", and we get some Sushi Neko and head home to dine at our favorite restaurant, The "Casa de Guercio". The service is horrible, but the food is to die for! Sometimes, literally.

November 11, 2019

A new week dawns. I begin the week with some mood-altering exercise and pedal my face off for 45 minutes. I plan to bike myself to a level of fitness I haven't had since the mid-2000s when I was actively surfing and playing hockey regularly. I am only in competition with myself, and so far, I am losing.

It is Veterans Day. I hold veterans in the highest of regard. From World War II vets to the latest conflicts around the world. Anyone who willingly separates themselves from their families to put themselves in harm's way to protect our country is a hero to me.

I took to Facebook to thank the many vets I know in my circle.

Thank you to all the veterans who have served. I am in perpetual awe at those who would sacrifice so much for their country, running into conflict while others run away. I was asked once, on a trip through China, why the USA is always at war. The gentleman, who I did not know, had cornered me on an intercontinental flight, and being the diplomatic American I try to be, I answered him. "Your statement is without merit, sir. The USA doesn't start wars, we simply respond to those who ask our country to finish them." He turned around, flustered, and walked away.

I am deeply appreciative of the commitment of those who serve, and I wish all of you a wonderful, healthy, and safe holiday! More than anything, I offer you, my gratitude.

November 12, 2019

I woke up early again this morning. I can't sleep anymore. I think about my past few months, then my past few years, and once again, I take to Facebook to post my feelings.

I'm glad I resigned as CEO. It took me a while to get on my feet and to remember why I did this, but every day I am reminded of one or two special events that make it all worthwhile. I missed so many moments in my family's life and in these few months, we've more than made up for it.

I am incredibly grateful for the opportunities that were presented to me but I'm even more grateful for the time I have with my family. Grab life: you're not promised tomorrow.

Love to all.

A few hours later, I went back to read the responses. All are supportive, but the most important comments come from those who worked with me. They appreciate what I did, and in that, I feel better about some of my pent-up angst about leaving them. It doesn't erase my feelings of guilt for abandoning those who were loyal, but it helps me shed some of the cloudiness that has hung over my mood lately. I miss my team.

November 13, 2019

Wanda slept all over me last night. I am up early, partly because she is breathing up my nose, partially because she is pressed against my spleen and small bowel, and like a sausage casing being filled with meat, she is squeezing last night's dinner out.

November 14, 2019

I woke up and went downstairs to participate in my morning cleanse. I am not riding my bike today--not because I don't want to be in shape, but because I popped a tire running over something the other day. I may need to switch to steel belted radials and a road hazard warranty.

As I read through my messages, I find my mom has been posting pictures of me when I was a professional musician. She has found many articles that were written about my playing or my bands, and it is a welcome surprise visit to Memory Lane. I look at the pictures and I am taken back to those days when money was scarce, but hopes were high. I was so young and optimistic.

Back then, we only cared about the music. Creating long-term wealth wasn't even a discussion, as we didn't look down the road; we just took things day by day. I used to say, "Don't worry about tomorrow, focus on today. Tomorrow will come whether we want it to or not." I carried that into my business life. As I recollect my advice to others, I realize that lately, I haven't been following my own advice. I am flailing and if I just learn to focus on today, maybe my tomorrow will be a little clearer. I commit to listening to young me, instead of old me.

November 15, 2019

It's Friday and another week has come and gone. I am still unemployed, a little depressed, and still pushing forward anyway. I am reminded of an excerpt from the writings of Daniell Koepke. It was called "Breathe". It is especially comforting and relevant today. It applies to many different situations, whether it be divorce, a life change like mine, or anything else when we are faced with adversity.

"Breathe. You're going to be okay. Breathe and remember that you've been in this place before. You've been this uncomfortable and anxious and scared, and you've survived. Breathe and know that you can survive this too. These feelings can't break you. They're painful and debilitating, but you can sit with them and eventually, they will pass.

Maybe not immediately, but sometime soon, they are going to fade and when they do, you'll look back at this moment and laugh for having doubted your resilience. I know it feels unbearable right now, but keep breathing, again and again. This will pass. I promise it will pass."
— Daniell Koepke, Internal Acceptance Movement

These words serve to calm my anxious spirit. So many things are going on and so many things aren't going my way. I have lost an opportunity to work with Applied Materials, I turned down two offers to be the CEO for emerging companies and I am still without a clear direction. I realize much of what I am feeling lies in my self-doubt. I don't know why I feel this way, but I ascertain it stems from not being in charge of my destiny like when I was working. I have to remind myself that indeed, I am in control of my destiny, and while I don't have the backdrop of GMSI anymore, I am still writing my script.

November 16, 2019

Saturdays are slowly becoming days of great laziness with my family. Wanda encourages me to put my yardwork on hold until tomorrow and just sit and watch movies with her. I don't want to, but I agree because I know it will make her happy.

In the past, I would never have devoted 4 hours to just sitting and watching movies, especially on the weekend. My work schedule was always so busy that my weekends were my solace, and there was no way I was wasting that precious time sitting and watching movies for hours. But now, my time is mine, and my family's, so in this new world, where time is under my control, I sit and cuddle up to manage my time with a greater focus on a "family first" strategy.

Both movies are entertaining, and while the yard needs mowing, I am not focusing on the things I need to do, but the things I want to do. There is a significant difference between the two, and I am learning the value of managing "want" over "need".

November 17, 2019

After a high-calorie, high-sugar breakfast, we prepare ourselves to do what we do best on Sunday. Nothing. Other than going to church at 5 PM, we have exactly zero on the schedule for today. I could do many things, but today, I chose to do nothing, and I am surprisingly ok with that.

November 18, 2019

After a long weekend of doing nothing, I am stir-crazy. I am not going to waste the day today. In the past, I would be traveling around the world, pretty much every other week. Being out of the country took a lot of the holiday spirit away, especially last year, when I traveled most of November, and then most of the first part of December. The holidays were simply another task I needed to complete.

This year is different. It is the first time in over 20 years I will be home for the entirety of the holiday season. I am excited to share this with my family.

While I am looking forward to the holidays, I have things to do right now, and this will be another week of serving those I love. I will drive people places, cook dinners, be a friend, and support Wanda in any way I can. Time moves swiftly these days, and I am trying to get a better hold of how I spend my time, and what I am doing to move myself forward. Writing this book is only part of a long list of tasks and lately, it has been the thing I spend the least amount of time on. That will change soon.

Wanda and I agree that neither of us is cooking tonight, and we plan to meet at Zupa's Café, our healthy choice for light meals. The thought of making dinner tonight ranks up there with getting dental surgery or a vasectomy without anesthesia.

November 19, 2019

After a long day yesterday, I am looking forward to today. I am going on my first homeschool field trip with Wanda and the kids. We are going to the Arizona Commemorative Air Force Museum. I love planes and the history behind the great people who flew them, so this is a particularly special treat for me. The museum sits off the runway at Falcon Field, an airport where I happened to start my manufacturing career, working for my dad at a local composite company.

As I sat in the bomb bay of a B-17, I had an eerie feeling about what it must have been like to fly in this tin can, while being shot at by angry

German pilots. It was very sobering to hear how many of these planes were shot down, and how many crew members perished. This is why I constantly remind everyone around me that freedom is not free.

Ben and Cailyn are happy I am here with them, not working, and enjoying the sights and history that lay before us. Cailyn hugs me and tells me that she never wants me to work again. I wish that were the case, but I will work again, soon. I think...

November 20, 2019

I would like to say I was productive today, but the fact is, I was not. I did for others, and while I can't put a measure on the value of this to me, to others I know it meant a lot. If my efforts meant something to someone else, then my time was well spent.

November 21, 2019

For the past 3 days, it has been storming. This time of year, in the desert, the weather changes dramatically, seemingly overnight. The warm, sunny days of late October give way to cool and stormy days and chilly nights. Fall is in the air.

Today, Ben and Cailyn will be in their first real Spelling Bee. The kids are nervous, especially Ben. He tells me he doesn't want to go up on stage, but I tell him the same story I tell Cailyn when she gets scared. "People are afraid because they fear what might happen. Fear is a wasted emotion. It cripples you with doubt, keeping you from your goals. Don't fear the unknown, embrace the opportunity to grow, and jump into scary situations with abandon". He sits quietly listening and then, in his best Ben logic, looks at me and says, "Dad, if that was supposed to be inspiring, it didn't work", as he stands up and takes his place on stage.

Maybe I should reconsider this whole motivational speaking program I have been planning.

November 22, 2019

The day is irrelevant. I am starting to understand the value of this time away from work. I have been so worried about my former co-workers, my employees, money, my future, and other things that seem important, that I forgot the reason I left my job was to rest. To rejuvenate. So rather than worry about the future, I am going to start focusing more on the present, as in the end, this is all we have control of anyway.

November 23, 2019

It is going to be Thanksgiving soon, and I am starting to wind my year down too. I am working on the final details for InfinityGo, including legal formation and our financial plan. Things are starting to make sense and I see the vision becoming a reality.

We took the kids and their cousins to *Main Event* today, and they played arcade games, bowled a few games, and generally enjoyed our time together. The boys explore the vast expanse of *Main Event*, carefully planning their agenda. Cailyn and Natalie have no plans. They are free spirits and let the day take them where it may. I like their style. There is a time for planning and a time for letting things happen. I am starting to take my advice.

We all worry so much about things we can't even influence that we miss the good things happening right in front of us. I am guilty too, but I am now adopting my old philosophy from my 20's.

Live for the day, we aren't promised tomorrow. Make today the best day of your lives, for some, it may be their last.

November 24, 2019

I am feeling the pull of holiday festivity all around me. I typically put up the Christmas decorations the day after Thanksgiving, but this year, I can put them up whenever I want because I don't have to worry about the restrictions of work. So today, I am starting decorating for Christmas.

As I open the boxes of lights, I find the map and legend I made that tells me where all the lights are to be placed, where I plug them in, and how to arrange the power cables. Taped to the map is a note I wrote to my family in case I died. As I stood in the driveway, I read the note and my eyes well up with tears. I have written these notes since 2009 when I realized that if I died, I would want Wanda and the kids to find something from me during the holidays, a time when they would most likely appreciate a note from the beyond. Part of this obsession comes from the deaths of my contemporaries; the rest, from my dad's premature death at 53.

As a result, I had subconsciously created an early death scenario for myself. And today, I feel like I am on borrowed time. But I am getting better at living for the day and making sure if tomorrow doesn't come, that I will leave a tangible piece of me behind for my wife and kids. I am building a legacy.

I still do this to this day; each year the notes become more intimate, and heartfelt. Wanda and the kids didn't know I was even doing this until last year when I finally shared my secret. At least now they know where to look if something happens to me.

The note I wrote last year, in 2018, was during a particularly difficult period, and as I read my words to my family, I realized just how down in the dumps I was. It was a very emotional time. I was constantly fighting to grow our business, the Germans weren't happy with the speed at which we were doing it, I was fighting delays and customer issues, and in general, I was spent.

I had thought about quitting back then, but as you have heard me say before, Guercio's never quit. That was until I went to Germany in February of 2019 for our Leadership team and Business Review meetings, and I realized that the situation throughout the company was going to change, and I didn't want to be a part of it anymore. And now, I am not.

I have been fighting my emotions for the past few weeks and today, this note hit me hard. After reading my note, I want to be close to my family. I go inside and give them all the biggest, longest hugs I can. They have no idea why, or what is going on inside of me right now, they just know I love and appreciate them, and as far as I am concerned, that's all they need to know.

Never underestimate the power of a hug. We are all energy, and energy flows. Connect yourself to others. I was criticized by many colleagues for hugging my employees and co-workers. It became part of our culture, but my colleagues didn't understand it. "Not very corporate", was a frequent comment. If I care about you, I will hug you. That's how I am built.

"Managing people isn't about getting them to do what you want, but rather helping them do what we need to succeed."

I tried to explain to them that managing people isn't about getting them to do what you want, but rather helping them do what we need to succeed. We are all in it together, and I hug people to let them know I appreciate them. After all, we spend more time together at work than we do with our own families.

Don't be afraid to show your emotions to others, it is a sign of strength, not weakness, and you will find that in doing so, you allow others to share their emotions with you. This, in my opinion, is one of the purest forms of communication, when you can share your heart instead of your words. The world needs more hugs and less vocabulary.

November 25, 2019

Monday morning and I am feeling fine. Well, not really, but I am pushing myself to get out of the funk I have been in. I scheduled an appointment with my doctor today to discuss some of the things I have been feeling and to make sure that I am not dying.

The doctor is ready for me. He takes my vitals, does the normal procedures related to a physical exam, and tells me he wants me to take some tests. In the meantime, he suggested I stop worrying so much and gave me a prescription for Chantix, as I told him all this free time and stress was making me want to smoke again.

I leave the office with a renewed sense of good health, and the confidence that I am not dying yet. I head over to the PGA store. I don't really need anything, but I figure since it looks like I am going to live, I should at least have the latest golf equipment, and at a discount!

I have been worried about death for a couple of years since I turned 53. That was the age my father died. I am living on borrowed time as I see it, and now I have no life insurance. To shore up whatever assets I have left when I die, I am going to see a lawyer about having a trust and a will. More risk mitigation. I guess old habits are hard to break.

November 26, 2019

'Twas two days before Thanksgiving and all through the course, golfers aimed for tiny holes, and swung with great remorse!

I wrote that in the bathroom at Shalimar Golf Course. I started thinking about how to write a children's book about Thanksgiving, set to famous stories of Christmas. My mind needs exercise, and this is my mental treadmill.

We are playing a round of "Generations" golf today. Mike, Ben, Grandpa Rod, and I are playing 18 holes at Shalimar, the tiny public course near ASU.

We finish the first 9 and we grab some cocktails and Mike lights us a couple of cigars. The sun is shining, but it is still cool, and the Chantix I am taking is making me sick with every puff of the cigar. Nausea aside, this is a day of magic.

I realize something now, and I must understand this. No amount of money will make you happy if you are sick. No amount of sex will make you love someone you hate, and not making choices rooted in making you happy, will result in misery. I am going to make choices that bring me closer to the happiness I seek, and hopefully, the peace I long for.

November 27, 2019

It's Wednesday, the day before Thanksgiving. Historically, this was a week where I went on standby, leaving the troubles of my career behind in favor of recharging my soul before a final, year-end push. This year, however, I have nothing to push. I have zero things going on today, and I am a little lost on what to do.

After writing for a few hours, I go food shopping for the family while Wanda schools. I have become quite a Chef since I resigned, and today I am trying something new. I find cooking to be an effective tool to help me sort out the many thoughts that occupy my headspace.

Other than the food shopping and cooking, I do little else. To-morrow is Thanksgiving, and tonight, I have a lot to be thankful for. I am alive, I have not worked since June, I am with my family, and for the first time in a long time, I am free of the stress of running a company. The only thing I need to worry about is whether I changed my under-wear or took a shower. Days run into weeks and weeks into months, but for me, it is always Saturday. And for this, I am truly grateful. I am just counting my blessings and taking things day by day, and today was a good day.

Sometimes, nothing is something.

November 28, 2019

Thanksgiving arrives. We spend the morning doing chores and getting ready to go to my sister Krissy's house, where our large family will celebrate the day. I should tell a funny story or share a memory of Thanksgiving's past, but I am just soaking in the day, happy to be with family.

It's Thanksgiving, and like many households, we spend the day eating way more than we should, drinking way more than allows us to legally drive, and talking way more crap about each other than should be allowed. And it is perfect.

There will be a time when we won't have this chance, and some of us may not be here, and my awareness allows me to focus on this special day with open eyes, a full heart, and deep gratitude we are all here together, here, and now.

November 29, 2019

Black Friday. With the advent of online shopping, I don't care about Black Friday. I will stay inside and prepare for imminent death and destruction, passing on the opportunity to buy things I don't need with money I don't have, to impress people I don't like.

Wanda and I have been getting along, and while we have no sex life to speak of, we have a marriage, and I am learning how to survive in this new environment. The secret? "Don't spend too much time in one place. Keep moving!"

November 30, 2019

Wanda put up our Christmas tree. It is beautiful and the light of Christmas does wonders for my mood. I feel the Christmas spirit, and while I can't say I am cured of my lingering depressive state, I am in a better place. Christmas is my favorite time of year, and this year, I am here to celebrate with my family. I am going to make sure it is the best Christmas we ever had.

Manage your emotions like you would manage a business. Weed out the undesirables and promote the ones that bring value and foster a strong culture of success.

7

December, 2019

December 1, 2019

I am not sleeping past 6 AM anymore. It's anxiety, or Chantix, or stress. I need to get past this phase, this "worry" phase. We are ok, yet I still have this sinking feeling that everything is wrong. I worked so hard to have the opportunity to take this time off, and instead of being happy, I am often filled with concern. Will I ever work again? Will my new ventures and this book be successful? Have I wasted all my time and given up my career for nothing? Will we go broke?

I put these thoughts aside for a second and say a prayer, having faith that like every other time in life, God will carry us through.

It's 8 AM and I am sitting in my office doing some online shopping. I take breaks to read about the world. I love to read, and I credit my love of reading for helping me succeed in life. Read a book. It will teach you everything you need to know. Books are life's instruction manual.

I write very infrequently lately but I feel a writing spurt coming on. This is how it goes for me. I write in large blocks when I am motivated, and then nothing when I don't care. I have a lot to say now, and writing frees me of the anxiety I have felt over the past few weeks.

Wanda leaves with Arielle for a mother-daughter day. I am glad they have this time together. I will have my time with the kids today too. For now, I untangle light sets and place them in their designated spots.

I discovered a few years back, after stringing half the house only to find that the lights I had just put up didn't work, that I needed to check them before putting them up. This supports my postulate that *"If you aren't making mistakes, you aren't learning anything"*. According to my own philosophy, I should be a genius by now.

After setting the lights out, the kids and I played a game of Fortnite. I do a lot with them, from boating and fishing to being their personal concierge and driver. But these simple moments, laughing and playing, remind me how lucky I am to have these beautiful little people. My big ones too, Arielle, Adam, and Deveny.

Later, I committed the ultimate Cardinal sin of Parenting. I got the kids McDonalds for dinner. Wanda forbids me from feeding fast food to the kids, and this is one of the Seven Deadly Sins, the Capital Vice of all "Leave the kids with Dad" sins. After our sinful banquet, I tell the kids to shower any of the evidence from their person. They happily bound up the stairs like they were about to dispose of the body from a murder, bellies full of their forbidden fruit, to wash away the wrongs of our indiscretion.

I put them to bed and spent some time in my office, writing these pages, as well as some pages for my next book, *Drink My Kool-Aid*. It amazes me how there are so many parallels between parenting and management. In the end, we are all just our children's babysitters.

Wanda and Arielle come home later that night and while Wanda recaps her day, she asks me "What did you feed them for dinner?"

"Fruit and Whole Grain cereal", I answer without hesitation. She is wise though. She knows when I am full of shit, and I am clearly overflowing. She looks at me, smiling, and states smugly, "I found the Mcdonald's wrappers in the trash. You guys did a poor job of hiding the evidence." Foiled again by my pint-sized accomplices. This is why I never chose a life of crime or politics.

December 2, 2019

By 10 AM, everyone is up and starting their homeschool and I am heading outside, finishing the lights. I asked Ben to help me when he was finished with school.

He never does stuff like this with me, but I tell him it would be a good chore to earn some game time. He agrees, but I have an ulterior motive. I want him out there in case I fall off the ladder putting the lights up on the high roofs of our home. In my mind, Ben's presence will ensure my survival, in more ways than one.

Ben is very engaged, and I am happy he is taking this as a learning experience. I share my map with him, and he loves the detailed layout I have created. He starts to pull light sets out and calls out the corresponding number from the legend I made.

He never gets into Dad/Son home projects but today, his enthusiasm is at an all-time high. I will capitalize on this. I show him how to connect light sets and in no time is putting them on himself.

To install the highest sets of lights, I have to ascend to the first roof of our two-story house. The only way up is on a 20-foot ladder to the lower roof, and then a precarious section of walking on clay roof tiles and up the pitch to the highest level. It is about 25 feet up all totaled.

This is Mount Everest to an 11-year-old kid and being up here even spooks me occasionally. But today is a day the torch passes. He will need to learn how to do this if there is any chance I will see these lights after I am gone. He is happy and scared.

I explained to him what I had to do to get the lights strung at the highest eave and over the garage. As I explain what I do, he looks at me bewildered and says, "Dad, That's crazy!" He is correct. It is. One wrong move and I will fall to my death to the driveway below. Maybe I will just break a leg, but they shoot horses, don't they?

As we descend the ladder off the roof, he is shaking again. I tell him part of life is conquering your fears, even if you realize that failure could result in certain harm. "Don't fail; that is the key. Plan for success and believe you can do something, then execute."

He looks at me and says, "Dad, save the speech, I just don't want to fall off the ladder". His message is well received. There is a time and a place for life lessons and being suspended 20 feet up on a shaky ladder is apparently not the time.

Once on the ground, he looks up at me, grinning ear to ear, and says, "Don't die, Dad. You don't have life insurance anymore!" I laugh at the irony of the statement. I don't have life insurance anymore. I will leave my family in a good place, but more importantly, with good memories and experiences. The true wealth in life is love and time. Love to share with others and time to do the things that mean the most to you. And them. These are in abundance at the Guercio house.

As we stand together admiring our handiwork, a neighbor walks over and compliments us on the house. It makes me happy that others appreciate our work. I do it for the kids, but the kid in me likes it too. The CEO in me appreciates that we met our goal, on time, and to the pleasure of others.

As we admire the house, the lights twinkling in the afterglow of sunset, I look up in the sky, imagining the crew of the ISS radioing down to Mission Control, reporting they can see our house from space!

December 3, 2019

Wanda is downstairs schooling, and I am upstairs bringing back a laptop from death. This is my valium. I have been building and repairing computers and electronics since the early 90's. I love fixing broken things, and I apply this to people whenever I have the chance. Lately, I have been focusing on some self-maintenance as well.

I said a prayer as I started it up and...it worked. Electronics are like people. We throw them away in favor of new and shinier objects, even when the most broken devices can be fixed with a little patience, love, and tenderness. A Philips screwdriver and a steady hand also help.

After a long day of school and computer repairs, I took a break. My back is killing me. It has been for weeks. My wrist too. I think to myself,

"Getting old is for old people--not me, a young guy with energy." The fact remains, that I am now 54 years old, and like my broken computer, I may be due for an upgrade and a new operating system.

As I lay moaning in bed from the pain in my aching body, Wanda offers to massage me, but tonight she has the hands of a bird of prey, and her talons dig deep into my pained sciatica, flaring up my already aching body. I ask her to stop once she draws blood, fearing she will pick at my carcass as I lay sleeping. Dramatic? A little. Factual? Very!

December 4, 2019

I received a call from Heinz today. As I suspected, GMSI is most likely going to close. It has weighed heavily on me, and in some respects has been some of the source of my recent depression. I don't want anyone to lose their job, and I still feel the company has value. I know the customers around the world don't want GMSI to close. I let Heinz know I would like the opportunity to get it into another company's hands before they decide. He lets me know he is open to discussions.

Heraeus is a good company, and while I know they are making their own internal changes, I also know they are a compassionate group and will not make a move until after the employees of my former company can enjoy the Christmas holiday. Everyone at GMSI is already worried.

After the layoff, a lack of orders, and a disconnect from Germany, they see the writing on the wall. Uncertainty looms over them and where I was always direct with everyone, the new management is much tighter-lipped. If there was a troubling situation, I would address it with my team. I choke back the tears, thinking about my people, and the 28 years of relationships I have made.

"Business" is not an inanimate object; business is a living thing made up of people who have bills, families, and worries."

"It's just business", is the standard statement companies make in situations like this. I have heard it my entire career. My issue is that making that statement does not exonerate the offending party. It is a poor justification, as it isn't just business, it's about people. "Business" is not an inanimate object; business is a living thing made up of people. People who have bills, families, and worries.

I commit to doing whatever I can to stave off harm to my people, my former clients, and those associated with GMSI. It may all be too little too late, and in this, I am filled with an enormous amount of guilt for leaving the company and my people to this end. In my own words, I remind myself, "You aren't defeated until you give up", and I won't give up.

December 5, 2019

Since Ben has been playing golf regularly, and doing quite well, Wanda and I decided we are going to surprise him with his own set of Cobra King golf clubs. I go to Dick's Sporting Goods and purchase a set for him. I also found a slightly used HTC Vive Pro VR set, and this will be another surprise gift of Christmas for the kids. We never spend this much on Christmas, but this year is special. I am home, and we are going all out to celebrate together after my many years of not being home for the holidays.

December 6, 2019

Mike and I are playing Golf at Superstition Springs Golf Club today. It is still cold here, at the most in the high 30s in the mornings. When we first moved here, back in the early 80's, we had an unseasonably warm Christmas in 1984. My dad convinced all of us to take pictures in our bathing suits and send them back east to our family. We did, and as part of this ritual, he forced me to swim with him in the 54-degree pool on Christmas day. I have been cold before, having surfed the winter swells of California in January, but I had a wetsuit. Our Christmas swim can only be described as self-inflicted torture, and I wouldn't have traded it for anything else in the world.

December 7, 2019

Pearl Harbor Day. As this is an important day in history, I will not bore you with the fact that it has been exactly 6 months since I left my role as CEO of Heraeus GMSI. I am dealing with a myriad of feelings about many different subjects.

The very first thing I feel is that I am in a good place with my emotional state, except when I am not. The real issue is I miss leading a business. I miss my purpose. I miss the industry, my employees, the technology, and the people I have friended around the world.

I do not miss getting on planes and flying around the world constantly, or working 80+ hours a week, but I miss the people I connected with most of all.

The second thing I miss is money. A regular paycheck and the benefits that come with my former role. Watching our savings dwindle is a hard pill to swallow. Our insurance is more than most house payments and money is flowing from our accounts at an alarming pace.

The third thing is not something I miss; it's something I feel. Regret. Regret that 6 months have gone by. I feel I could have accomplished more, but this is me. I always feel like I could have done more, even when things are going well. I also regret leaving my team to the welfare of others. It is clear they are in danger of losing their jobs, and the company as a whole. I will do my best to right some wrongs, but after 6 months, I am still lost on this new path.

December 8, 2019

It's a lazy, rainy Sunday morning. I love these mornings. So peaceful and calm, reminds me of when I was a little kid looking out the window at school or at home. The highlight of the evening is dinner at Baci's Italian Ristorante. Frank is a good guy. He suggested I start a pizza place as my new career. At this rate, I may end up delivering them rather than owning the place that makes them.

December 9, 2019

Another rainy morning and to make matters worse, my truck is leaking. Can you hear the money swooshing?

I am grateful for all I have and for the time I have been enjoying since June. The truth is, I am realizing I let 6 months go by and I worried and acted like a crazy man for most of them. I was stressed, and to some degree, I still am, but a calm is coming over me now. More like a blanket. Things will be ok. My faith helps. I believe in God, and I will continue to pray for a good path, for continued blessings, and the safety and well-being of all those around me.

Today is Monday, and it is my day to shuttle children to and from chess club, church, and wherever we need to be after these events. I have not seen storms like this in Arizona in a long time.

We are back at church as a family. Today is a day of obligation, and church was a good place to be today, to help me with my thoughts and my inner restlessness.

Around 8:30 PM Wanda's family arrives. Long hugs follow, and laughter, loudness, a variety of alcoholic libations, and exuberant proclamations in Spanish ensue for two crazy hours. That's how long it takes to "settle" in a Latin house.

I go upstairs to read in bed. Everyone is still downstairs. I may have made the drinks too strong, and I am fighting the overwhelming urge to fall asleep. I stopped fighting and I let it carry me to Slumberville, that place right off the intersection of Drowsy Town and Yawntucky.

December 10, 2019

I wake up before 6 AM and I need to go to the bathroom badly. The guest room is my Batcave but it is currently occupied by Wanda's family. I use this bathroom in the morning to start my day. I need privacy. I would never make it in a jail setting or the military. I need walls and silence. In those settings, I would most likely die of bowel impaction. I manage a cat-like poop in the litterbox in our bedroom, aka, Wanda's bathroom. I chuckle as I write this.

After breakfast, I head upstairs to write and see what the day brings. I am a little lost these days. I need to commit to something soon. The pressure is mounting, and I have a company to save, a book to finish, and a business to start. This is how my life has gone. I take big bites and spit out the pits.

Sometimes to succeed, you have to try different things until something sticks. I am willing to try new things outside of my comfort zone of field of expertise. I am reinventing myself, and I have no set direction, just a plan to find something that makes me happy and something that provides us with company-sponsored health insurance and a 401k. These are my lofty goals--health insurance and happiness.

December 11, 2019

I am not sleeping anymore, and it is taking a toll on me physically and mentally. However, it's another day I don't have to wake up for work, so I am grateful. My money never came in from the IRS for our amended tax returns and I have not deposited to our bank accounts in 6 months. Money is flowing in one direction, out. It is a scary feeling, but I keep my faith close.

For many years, I have played the role of Santa, and tonight and tomorrow I will have 100's of kids sit on my lap and tell me their Christmas secrets. Too bad I can't get their moms to do the same. I enjoy this activity, knowing I am bringing joy to these youngsters, and in turn, myself.

December 12, 2019

Another day of writing, and another night of being Santa. The kids are growing up. They are smart and ask me funny questions like, "Did you get my note?", their parents waving at me, telling me what they asked for. It is several hours of mayhem, and honestly, I love every minute of it. There is nothing better than giving back to others, especially when they don't ask for anything in return, other than a hug and a candy cane.

December 13, 2019

This day is entitled, *"The night Jesús drank all my gin. A lesson in humility and thanks."*

When I was working, after a particularly long and arduous journey around the world, my VP of Sales sent me a thank-you gift. It was a bottle of extremely rare, small-batch gin from Oregon. I treasured this gift, partly because of the sentiment, and mostly because its taste and botanicals were unlike anything I had ever had. I sipped it sparingly, on special occasions, knowing I could not get it anymore.

I shared this special bottle with my special brother-in-law, Jesús. He and I have had many a gin and tonic together, but I had never shared this bottle with anyone before. On this night, however, while I slept, he drank the whole bottle. I was extremely angry. I was mad that I opened my heart, my home, and my bottle to him, and he drank it all.

Was I acting selfish? Wanda thought so. She just dismissed it, saying I was acting like a child. Selfish and spoiled. I stewed on this for the entire day. As I thought more about it, I realized it was just a bottle of gin.

He is my family, and it is Christmas time. A time for peace and goodwill toward men, even if that man drank your rare bottle of alcohol. In the end, I apologized to him, and he told me how sorry he was. We hugged and made up, and then I hid all the good stuff in the liquor cabinet just in case he was tempted to move on to Single Malt Scotch.

The moral of the story? *Don't put so much worth in things when people are a much more valuable commodity.*

December 14, 2019

Tonight, it's a Mexican Christmas with Wanda's family! I am taking Cailyn to her Christmas Choir practice at St. Annes, where she will sing at the Christmas Eve mass. This Choir is a much better-organized affair than the other one she was involved in. Paul, the music director, is a patient and talented man and knows how to get the best from his students. He doesn't yell; he teaches, and this allows the kids to shine. That's what a good leader does. He helps the people around him to excel.

December 15, 2019

I have been waking up religiously at 4:30 AM for weeks now, regardless of when I go to sleep. Not with an alarm, I just wake up. Sometimes from a bad dream, but mostly I wake up as if I am late for something. Therapy is in my near future.

Today is my best friend, Stephen Andriotty's birthday. He passed away in 2007 but he is forever my best friend. I met him when I was 4 years old, and we were friends ever since. His death created a void in my childhood that will never be replaced. If you ever have the gift of a friend like Stephen, make it a point to reach out often. Life moves fast, and not everyone makes it to the finish line at the same time.

December 16, 2019

Wanda and I are in a good place lately, and it helps me greatly with my moods. We had an enjoyable day and a romantic night together, and to me, she has never looked more beautiful. After the night we had, if there was a rest of the day, I forgot all about it.

Love will make you crazy; sex will give you amnesia.

December 17, 2019

Today is the anniversary of my dad's death in December of 1992. I was at his bedside for 6 months leading to his death. He died of lung cancer that went undetected until it was too late to treat it. He was a smoker and an executive at Boeing. I am not sure which one was worse, but both most likely killed him. He put all his time into his work and was a man of great purpose and drive. I get many of my traits from him. He was amazing and there isn't a day that goes by that I don't miss him.

Last year, I made a speech to all our employees at our company Christmas party. During my speech, I began telling a story of his dedication, and the love and lessons he brought me, but I was too emotional to finish. I realized at that moment, even some 25 years after his death, that I may never get over his passing.

He was the strongest and most well-centered person I ever met. He was a little unconventional, but he was a brilliant engineer, and he saw things that others did not. He was clever and smart, warm, and funny. We were that family, loud and crazy in a restaurant, but playfully and funnily. We did not know other people existed when we were together as a family.

Many people don't know that during my childhood, around the early 70s, my mom was diagnosed as mentally ill. Bipolar disorder and manic depression were the exact diagnoses. She would bounce from hospital to home and back again for most of my early childhood to my early teen years.

During this time, my dad carried all of us, including my mom, and his work. He never gave up. He loved my mom dearly and their love was an intense one. He taught me how to deal with the real hardcore issues of life, and how to be graceful and kind, even in the face of despair.

I learned many things from my father, Denis Guercio, but the most important things I learned were the character traits and sense of responsibility he gave me. He was a dedicated man to all those around him. He was selfless. He did the right thing all the time, and he would engrain in me the importance of doing the right thing, even when it was easier not to. I modeled most of my adult life on his teaching.

While I may not check all the boxes, I always try to be the best I can be and to be a model for others. The option to be a better person lies within you, within your choices.

I love you dad. You live on because of all you gave us of yourself. Thank you for the great gift of love you gave me. Happy anniversary in Heaven.

December 18, 2019

The end is near. I was notified that the former CFO of our business group, Marco, left Heraeus. He was a partner to Heinz, and my friend Marco was a big reason we were able to grow GMSI as fast as we did.

I am actually glad he left because, like me, the years of stress and long hours had taken a toll on his spirit. I hope he can rest and regroup. Everything I saw coming is happening. I left Heraeus because I felt they were making changes in the leadership structure, and I didn't fit the new look. It turns out, I was right all along. It eases my grief over leaving this great company, as I watch my other leadership colleagues being replaced with younger, more consultant types. I know they will all be ok, but it hurts to watch the old being replaced with the new.

I don't know if this news makes me feel better, just vindicated. Leaders make decisions every day. That is what we are paid to do. I decided to leave before these changes became part of the company's fabric, even at Heinz's insistence that I stay. I didn't want to leave my team, the clients, or the leadership group I was a part of, but I left because I saw the writing on the wall, and the message was clear. Out with the old, in with the new.

The most worrisome topic for me is what will happen with GMSI. My guess is they will close it. I want to help them move into another home that will pick up where Heraeus has left off, save jobs, and provide our clients with continuity, but that's not my decision anymore. My opinion means naught, even if I have the right answers. I will keep everyone in my prayers.

All this emotion leaves me unable to effectively write today. Wanda has suggested we go to a matinee to take my mind off all this activity. I don't want to, but my focus is not on my work. I need this diversion as if I get too trapped in my many thoughts, I end up in a loop of despair.

After the movie, I cook dinner. I find joy in cooking, as it has become a little piece of the day where I can do something that benefits everyone in my home and allows me some time to decompress and stretch my creative wings. I don't look like I missed a meal, and someone has to feed this fat kid; it might as well be me.

December 19, 2019

After a particularly eventful few days, I am off to play golf with Rod in the 37-degree weather. Much to my surprise, I figured out how to adjust my swing to allow for my abundance of outerwear, and I shot a 73, which is 7 over par. Not bad for a guy that is wearing so many clothes I could outfit a small family.

Later in the day, Wanda and I take off for some Christmas shopping. We are going to combine shopping with a dinner date. After a long, cold morning, it feels good to sit with Wanda, sipping a cocktail and talking. Her warmth doesn't just come from her body, it comes from her smile. I love her more than she will ever know; I just wish she was more responsive to my needs.

December 20, 2019

Wanda and I enjoy a wonderful breakfast at the Hoosier Café. It is a classic, Midwest type diner, and I love the ambience of this place. A throwback to simpler days. As Wanda and I eat, we go over our expenses from last night's shopping. It is a savage reminder that I am not working, not bringing in income, and we are bleeding cash. We spent a lot of money and agree this has to stop. Christmas is about the birth of Jesus and goodwill towards men. It should not be so stressful and expensive. We agree to make a change next year.

As we drive home, my mom calls me. She is not feeling good and wants me to take her to the Emergency Room. I had plans to spend the day with Wanda in various stages of undress, but instead, I am going to do what I said I would do when I resigned. I am going to be there for my family. I remind myself, "Peter, you made the right decision to leave work. You will be ok. Have faith that God has a plan for you and keep pushing towards your goals."

December 21, 2019

With Christmas shopping done and presents being wrapped, we settle into a quieter rhythm of holiday life. Late mornings in our jammies watching movies and lots of food, make for the lethargy of the season.

I am not planning on working on anything for the rest of the year, other than this book and my ever-improving outlook on things. I can't control certain aspects of life, but I remind myself often that I can control how I react to them. This will become an important part of my mantra moving forward, and for now, I am starting to practice what I preach.

Being Catholic, we need to go to confession every now and again to profess our sins to a priest. I like going to confession. It frees me of the guilt and shame of my wrongdoings, but more importantly, it cleans the slate with God, leaving me renewed with hope. I find that my resignation acted in a way that is similar to confession. I was given a new chance to start with a clean slate. I feel better. Not 100%, but I am getting there. Day by day.

December 22, 2019

I am disconnecting from everyday life and falling into the doldrums of the Christmas season.

I sat down to write this morning, but not for this book. I wrote a speech. A speech no one will hear. I was reflecting on last year when I was the CEO, and I stood in front of all the employees of my business unit at the Christmas party, trying to convey the spirit of Christmas, and the memory of my beautiful father.

So, in these early hours in the dim light of Sunday morning, I sat down and wrote my speech, the one I would give this year if I had a job, a team, or a Christmas party.

When I finish, I wipe the tears that are streaming from my face. I think I had a crygasm.

December 23, 2019

After reading my speech, I felt the need to present it to someone, to share the details of the past year, and to better capture the essence of what this year, and the people I care about, meant to me.

I decided to share my work, posting this on my LinkedIn profile and Facebook. The responses are all positive, warm, and encouraging. I found an audience. They are my friends and family, and no one better to share my deepest thoughts with than with the people I care about most.

"An unheard Christmas speech..."
By: Peter J. Guercio

It is the holidays, and I am used to making speeches about profound topics, like love, gratitude, and year-over-year-end profits. I have also made companywide speeches comparing my staff and I to famous Hollywood Madam, Heidi Fleiss, and our customers to "Johns". That is another story for another day.

Thank you, Jen, for being such a good HR influence and life guide for the time we were together. And Stephanie, thanks for making sure I always made it home from wherever in the world I was. Thanks, Kirk, Johnny, Eric, Phil, Aimee, Mike, Keith, and all my clients, employees, and friends who have always believed in me despite my less-than-unorthodox ways. I love you all. Different, is the new black. ☺

I do not apologize for who I am, I own it gleefully!

I am grateful. Incredibly grateful. As many of you know, I used to be a mildly big deal. Lol! I used to be the CEO of a great company, Heraeus GMSI. I co-founded it with one of my best friends, Rex Dillman. With the help of people like Owen Cummings, Mark Ohre, Brian Foster, Matt Reineke, and Guy Watrous, we grew it until we could touch the velvet lining.

We built our company on relationships and technical expertise, but mostly on friendship and trust. That's how life and business are. It's not hard. Friendship and trust are all you need to conquer mountains. Don't make it more complicated than it is.

Last year, the pressure of the job and illness forced Rex to quit. This year, exhaustion, a clear sense that my life was slipping away, and the fact that I could no longer ethically stay in the environment I was in, helped me decide to leave the place I built.

I chose love. I chose my integrity. I chose my family and my sanity over money and prestige. Was it a smart decision? I do not know. It has been a very emotional and life-changing 6 months. But I see a bright future.

I am grateful for the many opportunities before me and for the people I still have in my life. My wife, Wanda, and our kids, Deveny, Adam, Arielle, Ben, and KK. My sisters, Joey and Krissy, mom and Rod, my cousins,

Mike and Michelle, and Aunt Carol. The band is back together!!!! For the 1st time in 30 years, we are celebrating Christmas with the WHOLE family. It is a special time; this is an incredibly special Christmas! I love you all! I am grateful we have this time together.

And speaking of time, we lost a lot of good people this year. Eddie Arroyo, Andy Passaretti, Randy T Alveari, Georgan Watrous, Bill Coldwell, Trina Andriotty, Dana Eipper and many more I have missed. I pray for you daily.

We lost countless celebrities, influencers, and many people close to all of you, that I may not have known. So many great people. At this point in life, I am grateful to be here. Forget whether I am traveling around the world, or if I am closing a deal or inventing technology with great people. I am alive, and at Christmas time, I reflect on that gift most deeply.

My dad died on December 17th. My best friend, Stephen Andriotty's birthday is on the 15th. My gramma died on the 27th of December. I am surrounded by dates of people I loved who are no longer here, and so I am also inversely reminded that I am still here, and I am grateful.

I am glad I had time to golf with Mike Imbasciani in November. It was epic and it is one of those things that will always stay with me. See you next year!

I chose to change my life this year. It was in fact, the hardest decision I have ever made. It took many years, 30 plus, to get where I was when I resigned, and I left many good people behind.

In my younger days, I was a long-haired, pot-smoking, carefree rock musician, and in many eyes, a fuck up. Truth is, I loved those days. They had a great influence in making me who I am today. We (I) occasionally ate out of garbage pails, met many great people, and learned a lot. We played big shows and we played for 3 people on a Tuesday night. It did not matter.

It was the experience of writing music and playing shows with my boys that was most important, and when it came time for me to grow up and get a real job, it made me hungrier than everyone else. It motivated me to prove I was as good as anyone out there, despite my unconventional path to get there. Remember, you are not defined by who you were or where you came from; you are defined by your actions. I cannot stress that enough. Find your purpose and do not let anyone stand in the way of your dreams. The only one that can stop you is you!

For 30+ years, we have all rocked. I thank Sean LaPointe, Shane Scott, Chris DeFelice, Michael Brandt, Michael S. McGregor, George Robbins Jr, Brett Richey, Patrick Laferty, Michael J. Whitman, Jeff Garten, and the boys from Crushed, and my lifelong friend, Jeff Quinonez, who doesn't talk to me anymore. It is a shame. We are wasting so much time, Jeffie Q. Life is too short to be bitter.

For us religious folks, this is the season of the birth of our savior. Jesus is the reason for the season unless you are Jewish, of which I am half. "The good half", my mother would say. Talk about conflict!!! Oy vey!! But surely, I digress, let's go deeper.

I often reflect on the feelings of the spirit of Christmas we felt when we were kids. I remember the snow, the cold of Long Island winters, the smell of Christmas Trees at the Elwood Nursery, and the occasional drunk Santa at the mall who would listen to your Christmas dreams through the alcohol-veiled consciousness of his dreams.

I remember the joy and anticipation of the season. The smell of pine in everyone's house. The tugging excitement of Christmas presents wished for, and the sense of unity and good cheer that most people had this time of year. Christmas changed somewhere along the line. The smell of pine slowly faded. The excitement of Christmas gifts became the stress of GET-TING Christmas gifts for everyone. The cheer everyone felt was replaced by anxiety, exhaustion, and sometimes...sadness.

The thing I try and draw from, more than any other thing in the Christmas season, is the gift of forgiveness. It is the reason we celebrate the birth of Jesus. If we look at things that give us the "feels" it is usually something that evokes emotions in us that we can relate to. The "feels" come from a good episode of "This is Us", for example. Are you crying for them, or is it because the situation struck a chord in your own life, and you cry for yourself? This is my admission; I cry because I can relate to the situation and draw upon my struggles. We all do. It is the common thread for all of us. We are all fighting silent battles, most of them within our heads.

And so, the thing that I draw from this time of year, the thing that gets me all "feely", is to see reconciliation. It is a fancy way of saying I like to see people forgive and be forgiven. It warms my heart. So, this season, in these days of Christmas, of the birth of Jesus, who died to forgive us, reach out and try and make amends with someone you hurt, or are mad at, or someone that hurt you. I promise it is the best gift you're going to get this year. And one size fits all!!!

I am appreciative of everything and everyone in my life. I don't know what tomorrow will bring, and that is ok. I have a lot of cool things in the works, and maybe if I am lucky, all of them will pan out. We shall see. But in the meantime, I am not stuck in a European or Asian airport, not planning a budget, or forecast for financial planners and CFOs, and I am not stressing about missed revenue projections or employee production. I am just watching the twinkling, LED lights of Christmas and soaking in the season.

I am writing books too. This is the page for today. Not many know this, but I am writing 3 books in the next 3 years. If you know me, I have a lot to say, but we can talk more about shameless plugs next year. For now, I want to wish you all a Merry Christmas, a Happy Hanukkah, and Happy Holidays if you are celebrating something else.

And to all, a Prosperous, peaceful, healthy, and successful 2020.

(If this were a speech, this is the part where I would pause for dramatic effect and hope someone would start clapping. This is also the part where I would expect people to clap because the buffet was opening, and they had heard enough of my melancholy and reminiscent dribble. ☺ Lets Eat!!!!)

December 24, 2019

I had originally written a scathing account of the tension, stress, and fighting we experienced on Christmas Eve and Christmas Day, 2019. I realize my anger and frustration do not align with the true message

Christmas should convey, so I chose to share a true story about one of my favorite Christmas memories.

Don't let anger guide your actions. You will not find peaceful resolutions, only a bloody soul.

"The Spirit of Christmas"
A short story about the true gifts of the holiday season, by Peter J. Guercio

I jumped in the car in the rosy glow of the morning and drove to the store. As I passed the yellow and red leaves of the trees in my neighborhood, I began to reflect on Christmas past. The ones that included people who were dear to me. My dad, my grandparents, and friends that are no longer with us. I thought back to a time when Christmas wasn't so commercial. It was about a "feeling", one that in essence defined the whole holiday season. It was the "Spirit" of Christmas.

When we are younger, we don't get caught up in the stress of the holiday season; we just experience the joy, excitement, and wonder of the season. As a kid growing up in Long Island, it was the lights at the mall, the hustle and bustle of shopping, the songs, the smells of pine needles, and the anticipation of Christmas morning and the gifts that would surely arrive.

Sometimes, it was the serenity of a winter storm, that would blanket our house and neighborhood with feet of fresh, undisturbed snow. I would go out and watch the snow fall, listening to nothing but the quiet sound of snowflakes and wind, and the sound of my heartbeat, only interrupted by the occasional sniff of my runny nose. The common denominator of all this was the constant and overriding sense of peace. People were nicer, food was better, and the general tone of life was more joyous.

I parked my car and sat back and thought for a second about the things we needed to get done before tonight. As I sat trying to remember whatever it was I needed to do, I thought about my mom, Cory. When we were younger, in the early 70's, my mom was having health issues. She had a rough patch where she was in and out of hospitals when I was 7 or 8. My mom is an amazing person. One of a kind, and if you know her, you know that description is probably an understatement. She and my dad were the best parents you could ask for. They were stern, disciplined, crazy, funny, adventurous, and creative. They were amazing. They didn't have a lot of money when we grew up, but we didn't know that then because we had everything we ever needed. Not WANTED but needed. There is a difference, as I learned later in life.

That year, I had gotten a bunch of monetary gifts for my Communion. I was so excited to have some of my own money. I would lay in my bed through that summer and fall, thinking of what I would do with all that money. "A baseball glove, a Mattel Electronic Football, a new sled", I would think to myself, trying to narrow down my choices, knowing I needed to make a good decision because I didn't know when I would have that kind of money again.

Mom is not a materialistic person, but she had always wanted this beautiful rabbit fur and leather coat. It's cold in New York, and my mom always gave up what she wanted so that we kids had what we needed. Dad too. I had asked my dad one day in the fall, "What do you think mom would want for Christmas?" He answered, "Whatever you get her will be fine, but if she had her choice, she would love that jacket in Macy's". It was a beautiful jacket.

I remember the smell of it, the fresh tanned leather smelled like the inside of a new wallet, rich and aromatic, as good leather is. The fur was the softest, grayish-white fur I had ever felt, and I remember how my mom looked as she beamed, admiring herself in the full-length mirrors at the mall.

I asked my dad, "Are you going to get it for her?" He looked away for a second and then back to me and responded, "I don't think so. It's a lot of money". I know my dad would give my mom anything she wanted if he could. He was like that. I am like that with Wanda. When you love someone so deeply, your wants and needs are always secondary to theirs. He was in love with my mom like that.

I thought about all this as we passed Thanksgiving that year. I watched my mom daily, as she worked so hard to make sure all of us were taken care of. She is a caretaker, like me. We try and make sure we take care of our "people". It's our motivation and our dedication.

As we drove home one day in early December 1972, I thought about all the things that I wanted for Christmas. It was just me and my dad in the car, as I liked to go anywhere he was going. I dug my father. He was a man's man. He taught me so much, and I was about to get one of the more important lessons of my life. One that would define how I looked at Christmas and how I chose to live my life.

As we drove down Jericho Turnpike, I saw the sign for the mall. I thought about all the things that I could get, you know because I was loaded! As we drove, I looked at my dad, the early evening light streaming through the windows of his 1965 Mustang, and thought of my mom. I don't remember what it was in particular that made me ask my dad, but I turned to him and said, "Dad, how much IS that Jacket mom likes?" I remember his face. He knew why I was asking, but he was smart. He just fed me the info I needed to process my thoughts; he didn't give me the answers to anything.

He said, "I don't know exactly, why?" I told him that I had been thinking about Mom and that I wanted her to have something special this year. She deserved it. He listened and said, "Well, it's expensive. Probably more money than we can afford." I thought to myself, "Well, maybe WE can't afford it, but I bet I could". So, I asked him point blank, "Well, what if I gave you my money from my communion, then could we afford it?" I never saw my dad get emotional when I was younger, but I could see in his eyes he was choked up about my willingness to be selfless. To give to my mom because that is what she did for us.

"You realize if you do that, you won't have any money left?", he stated in his logical and leading manner.

"I know Dad, but I want to get it for Mom. I know how happy she would be. Can you help me?"

He smiled the smile only my dad had. I loved that smile. His big, beautiful grin was surrounded by his black beard. He suggested we go to the mall and see how much it was. He turned the car around and we headed back to the Walt Whitman Mall in Huntington, NY. When we arrived at the mall, we went through the entrance near the fountains. I loved it there. It happened to be right near the Radio Shack and a toy store. As I walked past Radio Shack, I looked at all the cool things I could have gotten. It didn't matter anymore. The thought of walkie-talkies or the latest toy didn't mean anything to me at this moment. All I cared about was that jacket. My dad put his arm around me as we walked. He was...beaming.

As we approached the counter at the fur department in Macy's, an older lady and man greeted us. My dad had explained that I wanted to buy my mom a particular jacket, and he told them how I intended to pay for it. The staff listened to my dad intently, and when he finished, they looked at me and asked, "Are you aware how much a jacket like that costs, young man?" I told them I did. They brought it out and I looked at the price tag. It was way more than what I had. I was deflated. I looked at my dad and the salesperson, and they could see my disappointment.

My dad asked if there were any discounts available, being it's Christmas and all. I don't know if there was a sale, and I am not sure who did what, but the salespeople looked at me and said, "Well, there just happens to be a Christmas sale coming up, and since you are doing such a nice thing, we will use our employee discounts, and you should have enough." I was elated.

I am sure I didn't have all the money needed, and I am sure my dad worked some of his magic, but all I know is half an hour later, I was driving home with a big, beautiful, and meticulously gift-wrapped box, filled with the Jacket my mom wanted. I felt good, better than any feeling that I would have gotten from buying myself a toy or game. It was the feeling of joy, and it didn't come from anything other than the simple act of giving something to someone so special.

Their happiness would be my happiness, and in that, I learned the true meaning of Christmas Spirit.

On Christmas Eve, we would go to church. I couldn't wait anymore and asked my dad if it was ok to give it to Mom early, so she could wear it to church. He smiled and said, "Yeah, I think that is a good idea". I grabbed the big box and brought it downstairs to the living room where my mom was doing something. I stood in front of her and showed her the big box.

"What's this? It's not Christmas until tomorrow", she said, not understanding it was for her, not me. "It's for you Mom, open it!", I said with gleeful excitement. "What? For me? Really?" She seemed so surprised. I thought maybe my dad had tipped her off, but now it seemed as if she had no clue what it was.

She admired the wrapping for a second, shook the box, looked at me, and said, "What is it?" I think she knew, but maybe the reality of what was happening didn't sink in. She worked the bow off with careful precision, pulled the 2' x 3' lid off the box and moved the artfully arranged tissue papers aside. She paused as she saw what lay inside. It was the jacket. Her jacket. She started crying and I hugged her, and she hugged me back hard. She seemed stunned.

She looked up at my dad in astonishment and just said, "How?"

He answered her, "He did it. He used all his Communion money".

She looked at me with the love only a mother has for a kid. A love that transcends any tangible item in the world. The love that emanates from a place beyond money or things, but from a place deep within a person's very being.

I asked her sheepishly, "Do you like it, Mom?"

She screamed, "Like it?? I LOVE IT!"

She hugged me tightly, lifting me off my feet. She put me down and tried it on. It looked amazing. She was so beautiful. No, she was radiant! She jumped up and down, screaming and crying, laughing, and smiling. My dad was smiling ear to ear as well. My mom shot out the front door and began screaming, "I got a fur coat, I got a fur coat!!", as she ran to the neighbors to show off her coat. It was probably one of the top 10 moments of my life. It still is.

What I learned that night was the true meaning of Christmas. It was simple. The true meaning of Christmas isn't about giving or receiving, it's about the "Spirit" of Christmas. It was about the feeling of the season. It was the smells, the sights, the love, the peace, the goodwill, and the food. It was all these things. It was about feeling this sense of renewal and peace, like the untouched tranquility of the newly fallen snow. It was about love and making others happy. It was about joy. Not just my joy, but the joy of others. "Joy to the World, the lord has come..." made much more sense to me after this, as this same joy I give my mother is the same joy we feel in celebrating the birth of Jesus.

My dad died many years ago, but his memory serves to remind me of that Christmas jacket, and the many times we celebrated Christmas together. This story will always remind me of him, the joy of the season, and the true gift of Christmas which is the peace and fulfillment that comes with celebrating the birth of Christ.

I wish you all peace, love, joy, and good health. And mom, I love you so much.

December 25, 2019

Last night, we had a big fight after church and Wanda decided she was not going to give the kids their presents because she said they were spoiled and ungrateful, therefore, they weren't getting presents. She did this without consulting me, and it ruined Christmas. It was a sad night for me. The kids were devastated, and it sucked all the joy away from this beautiful night. It also drove a stake between Wanda and me, even though we had been in such a good place.

In short, I blamed her for ruining Christmas, and I stand by my word. I had forgotten my advice, that we control how we react to a given situation. Wanda is angry that the kids don't appreciate what they have. She forgets that the kids are a reflection of our behavior, and it dawns on me that if she doesn't like how they act, we should consider where they learned this conduct. And to be clear, I am a very grateful and selfless person.

We halfheartedly exchange our gifts with each other, and while I know Wanda bought things that she thought I would like, what I wanted didn't come from the store. It came from her heart and her body. I gave her an abundance of good things, but maybe I didn't get her what she wanted either, even though the value of her gifts was in the thousands. Maybe she wanted something I didn't get from the bank or the store.

After what can only be described as a somber Christmas morning, we head to my sister Joey's to spend Christmas day with the family. The mood is light and happy.

Our children are not happy. Cailyn is sick, and Ben is upset he did not get his presents. I feel bad. but once again, I am trying to be supportive of Wanda's parenting ideas, even when I don't agree with them.

My mom is sick, so she is not here. This is the first Christmas without her in a long time. I miss her. I miss my dad. I miss my friends, and there is an empty spot where my oldest child, Deveny should be. Christmas loses some of its meaning when the people we love aren't there to share it with you. Joy is reduced by a factor of humanity.

I am happy to see my family, but the nagging distress of Wanda's decision to take the kids' presents away robs the joy away from the day, and this Christmas, the one that should have been the most special, becomes the most disappointing. I know she wanted to teach them a lesson, but Christmas is a time of peace, not conflict.

December 26, 2019

It is an early start to a cold morning of golf with Ben, Rod, and his friend Jim. The only joy comes from Ben playing golf with his new clubs. I had demanded Wanda let them have one present, and this was the one. Ben had fun and I can see the results of better clubs in his play.

Jesús and his wife Diana are heading to NYC to explore the city and watch the ball drop at Times Square on New Year's Eve. Wanda and I offer to drive them to the airport. My plan is to drop them off and then confront the lingering angst of the unopened presents. Once we drop Jesús and Diana off, we spend a lovely 45 minutes of arguing about whether to give the kids their presents.

In the end, we decide to give the kids their presents, ending an argument no one would win.

December 27, 2019

Wanda and I are finally resolving the conflict of unopened presents. I say resolving, but after last night's fight, we give the kids their presents. Good, it's done now. Officially, the gifting season is over.

Good news! We finally got our tax refund. It took over 6 months, but we are depositing money into our bank account for the first time in six months. Things are looking up!

December 28, 2019

It's Saturday morning, and now that the stress of Christmas is behind us, and presents have been opened, I get to set up all the things the kids got for Christmas. The big hit is the VR system we bought the kids. I even gave it a try, for about 10 minutes, until an overwhelming feeling of nausea forced me to take the headset off. Virtual reality is much more sickening than real reality. If only I could take a headset off to stop reality in real life.

December 29, 2019

The exhaustion of having house guests, shopping, cooking, and fighting has taken a toll on Wanda and me. We decide to have a mental health day, and we stay inside most of the day, happily watching movies and eating leftovers.

Nothing of any great importance occurs today. I used to have these days when I came home from a long trip, but I always had to face the dread of going to work the next day. This year the tone is very different. I won't be going to work on Monday, or any other day for that matter. At least not for the next few months.

December 30, 2019

This morning, I am playing golf at the beautiful Phoenician Golf Resort with my former partner in GMSI, Matt Reineke. I love Matt. He was the first person to step forward and tell me he would fund my vision of building GMSI. He gave me $1 million on a handshake. In the end, I would double his investment, but our relationship isn't about money, it's about respect. Mutual respect and I hold him in the highest of regards.

I am taking Wanda for an overnight date to Talking Stick Resort and Casino, one of our hideaways. We love to play some slots, have a few drinks and people-watch. Tonight, we will focus on us, and hopefully, we will find our way back to a happy place together.

December 31, 2019

Tonight, for the first time in years, we aren't hosting our annual New Year's gala. We won't have to worry about waking up to a house full of garbage, dishes, and occasional vomit. As we drive home from the hotel, I share some of the events of the past year with Wanda. Kind of a private recap of where we have been, and what lies in store for us in the coming year.

We talked openly about the difficulties we had at the beginning of the year with my stress levels and overall dissatisfaction with my life. She was instrumental in helping me make the move to resign and find some peace. We discuss the difficulties we have had in our marriage, and what each of us would like to see in our relationship. We share the many adventures we have been on together over the past few years and I ask her a series of questions related to our direction, but being Mensa smart, she cuts right to the heart of my questioning.

"Babe, I love you more than you will ever know, and I am so happy we are together and that you left your job", she says, almost reading my mind. She adds, "And for what it's worth, I think you can do anything you set your mind to. I believe in you; just do it!"

Those words mean more to me than any of the cards she could have written to me at Christmas time. She believes in me, as she always has, and even though not every day is perfect, we are together, and we have been for a glorious and sometimes emotional 6 months. No work, no business travel, just us.

We go home and rest for a few hours before heading over to Mike's for a long night of New Year's Eve festivities with our family and friends. It is an awesome night, shared with those I love. I have felt regret, anxiety, and sadness many times throughout the past year, but none of that can compare to the joy I regained in having my cousin and his family move here, spending every day with my wife and kids, and shedding myself of 28 years of unbearable stress and demands.

This chapter will end differently. No grand statements or narratives, only this simple message.

I was scared, and now I am brave. I was sad, now I am happy. I felt imprisoned, and now I am free. The only thing that can stop you from realizing your dreams is when you stop believing they can come true. Dreams don't come true unless you make them.

Happy New Year! I think 2020 is going to be something really special!!

8

January, 2020

January 1, 2020

It's New Year's Day. A new year and new possibilities. I have always loved this day. It represents the single best opportunity to change your direction. It's a new year, and you probably haven't screwed anything up yet!

But this year, for the first time since 1992, I am not returning to my company. Not returning to get things in order. Not returning to chaos. Not returning to a life that made me unhappy. Not returning to a travel schedule that began to consume me, physically and emotionally.

Wanda used to tell me, "Be careful what you wish for, you just may get it!" She was right, of course. Now I am taking a different approach, putting my faith in God, and making myself open for opportunities to lead.

Happy New Year. I pray it will be an amazing year.

As I read the morning news, I found they stopped making the Volks-wagen Beetle after 70 years. I had one; it was a hand-me-down from my mom, and the story stuck a chord with me. I took to Facebook to share my eulogy.

Truly a piece of our past. My mom got her orange '73 Super beetle new in Northport. She named him "Vincenzo". Krissy, Joey, and I spent many a cramped car trip from our house to the beach, singing and laughing and not caring so much about the smoke my mom exhaled from her Kool Menthol or the ashes that would surely blow back in your face as she flicked them out the window.

We survived blizzards, traffic, heat, cold and the occasional trip to Grandma Ada's in Yonkers, stuffed full of Christmas presents, toys or the slobbery Great Dane named "Thor".

For us, Vincenzo was our link to others. Our mode of travel. Our family. We went from childhood to adulthood in our car. I started off as a passenger and eventually, a driver, although illegally at first.

Vincenzo carried us to communions, family parties, roller rinks and first dates. He wasn't just a car; he was a member of the family. He was "The People's Car".

We sold him when we moved out west. It was a sad day, but like all things in life, you take from the experiences, hold onto the memories, and you move forward. I will always smile when I see one of your relatives on the road and remember fondly the joy and freedom you brought so many of us. Auf wiedersehen!

January 2, 2020

We are all spending a quiet day at home, just relaxing, and hanging out with family.

After dinner, and a few too many festive cocktails, we pile into the truck and drive to the Phoenix Zoo for hot chocolate, kettle corn, and *Zoo Lights*. We walk the cold zoo and take in the last sights of the holiday season, happy and content. I gaze across the lake filled with lights and think to myself, "This is going to be a great year!"

January 3, 2020

Not much is going on here today. It's a lazy day.

Later in the evening, I retreated to the confines of my office, alone. As I sat in the darkness, I read a news report that a United States drone strike killed Iranian major general Qasem Soleimani while he was on his way to meet Iraqi Prime Minister Adil Abdul-Mahdi in Baghdad. This act of violence by the US Military is viewed as an assassination by many of the world's leaders, but I have a differing view.

I will reserve my comments, as this is not a political book, but I certainly understand this was a dangerous position for the US to take in the region. My bigger concern is for our troops, the people who protect us from the political acts of those who aren't there.

January 4, 2020

Jesús and Diana are leaving today and Abuema tomorrow. I will miss them. It is hard to have all these people in the house, but it's what Wanda wanted when she said she wanted a big house.

The Hotel Guercio is a nice place to visit, but don't drink the Gin.

January 5, 2020

It's Sunday and a supposed day of rest. I don't feel like resting, so I am going to tackle some yardwork and write. I feel like I have a lot to say these days, and I need an outlet. Writing has become like an old friend, the kind you greet with a hug and a smile.

I spoke to my team in China today as well. It appears there is some kind of mystery illness that is beginning to spread in China. It started in Wuhan; in a lab we had been near in 2018. My friends in China are concerned, as they are being asked to stay indoors and quarantine. Quarantine from what, is the question.

January 6, 2020

The day of the Epiphany. This is the day that the 3 Wise Men found Jesus, and to some Catholics, it signals the end of the Christmas season. The 12 days of Christmas if you will. I am melancholy, as this has been a unique Christmas season for us. The first in many years where I wasn't traveling or buried in the year-end stress of my career.

I will pray that people remember the spirit of the holiday season, even if the holidays are over. It's wishful thinking at best, but I am an eternal optimist.

January 7, 2020

In the wake of the recent events overseas, with the death of Soleimani, I have seen many comments related to our role in the region. I ask that we remember that we are not Republicans or Democrats, we are Americans. Americans died last week, and many weeks before. We are watching from the comfort and safety of our homes. This freedom we enjoy isn't free. It came at a great cost. American lives. Blood.

I don't want war and for sure, I am a Republican who believes in diplomacy over firepower, but sometimes, our armed forces must do what is required to protect our collective freedom when it is threatened. Remember who is over there protecting that freedom right now. American troops. Men and women, boys and girls, civilians, contractors, and soldiers. Pray for them. I for one have always held armed forces members and service people in the highest regard.

Pray for a peaceful resolution but remember that we enjoy a level of freedom many in the world don't know, thanks to the brave men and women who have willingly put on the uniform of a US soldier and fought for Your/ Our freedom. Let's remember them and pray for their safety and success. God bless America.

January 8, 2020

It's back to the grind for the Guercio family. After a long winter break, school resumes and life returns to its normal hustle and bustle.

My partner in InfinityGo, Brad, is out from Oregon for a series of meetings and a few rounds of golf. I am really starting to golf well. The many days of practice and playing on the course are starting to pay dividends. My golf game isn't about shooting par; it's about being out on the course, enjoying my days with people I love, and that is way better than shooting a sub-par round.

I leave to meet my long-time friend and former lawyer, Brian Foster, for some dinner and drinks. We caught up on the past 6 months, and we shared the happenings in our lives. I intended to share the vision for InfinityGo with him, but I refrained, instead just soaking in the joy of being with my friend and sharing a good conversation.

Life isn't always about getting somewhere; sometimes it's just about the journey.

January 9, 2020

Today I am taking the kids to their homeschool co-op group. I needed to get out of the house and spending time with my kids and the other homeschool friends we have made is a nice diversion from the monotony of our day-to-day schedule.

Tonight, I am going to make some steamed clams in white wine, so on our way home from the co-op meeting, I stop by the supermarket to grab the clams and wine. A word of advice; never take hungry children to a supermarket. A stop for a few items turned into a full-blown war of attrition, replete with bartering for snack items and drinks. I finally defuse what is turning into a violent confrontation by leaving them in an aisle while loudly proclaiming, "I don't negotiate with terrorists".

I get home and make clams. They were delicious and reminded me of my childhood on Long Island, eating clams and dipping bread in the sauce. I reminisce about a simpler time, long gone but not forgotten.

Later in the evening I read more about the worrisome events in Wuhan, China. This doesn't look like pneumonia, as they are reporting, it looks like another SARS outbreak. I was there for bird flu and SARS, but according to my people in China, this is much worse. End of the world worse.

January 10, 2020

Fridate!! I am excited to spend the morning with Wanda. We enjoyed a wonderful breakfast together. I love these stolen moments we share, eating and laughing, like lovers do.

We agree that this is good for our relationship and overall sanity, and later tonight, when the kids are ready for bed, I am going to enlist Arielle to watch the little kids while Wanda and I go see an adult movie. Wait, not a porno, just a movie that isn't animated!

January 11, 2020

Neil Peart died today. I am crushed. Neil Peart, the drummer for the rock band "Rush", is one of the most influential musicians of my lifetime, and for me, the reason I play drums the way I do.

As always, and much like Neil, I take to writing to free myself of the incredible sense of loss I feel in learning of his death. He, unlike me, got off the bus too late. He finally retired, after 40 years in the limelight, and his retirement is much more permanent than I am sure he expected.

I am reminded of a story that best illustrates the immense influence Neil Peart had on my life, musically and otherwise. In February 1995, our band, Cartoon Violence, was chosen to play "ABKS". "Arizona's Best Kept Secret." These concerts were showcase events for the top bands in Arizona. Rumors abounded that industry people were going to be in attendance.

The night of ABKS arrived and it was an absolute disaster. Sean had his normal bout of "spastic colon" episodes, usually right as we were about to step on stage, or sometimes, while standing on stage. Chris, who was always first at the show, was nowhere to be found. It was literally 5 minutes to showtime when he barreled through the backstage area at Boston's Nightclub, cursing and screaming about getting pulled over on the way to the show. None of this mattered as we needed to be on stage and ready to play in 5 minutes.

I helped him throw his equipment onstage as the soundman hurried to get his rig all connected to the soundboard. While he set up, the sound man said, "No soundcheck, we are just checking levels and going live".

Those words are not the words you ever want to hear when there is the possibility that there may be record industry people in the audience, and you are playing in a crowded club, filled with your peers. Musicians are the biggest critics of ourselves. We know when we put on a great show, and we also know every mistake that we and others make. Bad sound is one of those things that we critique violently. It is the death of a good band and a bad one. No soundcheck was the worst scenario there could be, short of a power outage.

As the sound man walked offstage, Chris looked at me and smiled, and in his own carefree and awesome way, said, "Fuck it. Let's blow some minds!" As we hit that first power chord in unison, all the bad things that could have happened drifted away, and we gelled. It was one of those nights where we were all "On".

We ripped through our 45-minute set to a loud and packed house. We played all original compositions, except when the sound man announced we had one more song. I looked at Chris and Sean, and simply said, "La Villa". We high-fived each other, took a breath, and let loose on 9 minutes of one of the most interesting, dynamic, and technically demanding Rush songs.

Halfway through the song, on the slow breakdown, I broke down. I don't know if it was the emotion of the evening, the immense joy and accomplishment I felt, or simply the memory of my dad, smiling at me as we listened to this song on my boombox. It was as if time was still, and in this cathartic and introspective moment, I put my head down and the tears flowed as I played this song.

I have never shared this with anyone. By the end of the song, and the set, I was covered in sweat, the hot stage lights baking us and stewing us in our own juices. No one saw my tears. Just sweat, and a smile.

I asked one of the owners of the club to throw a VHS tape into the lone camcorder nailed to the ceiling. The video acted as a marker of a time long ago, when we were a band of outsiders, playing what we wanted, not what the industry suggested. I have since transferred the video to digital, and sometimes I go back and watch and cry, just as I did that night.

I always liked this about Rush, about Neil Peart in particular. He never compromised his values. Rush never worried about what anyone else thought of them. They just played what they wanted and did things their way. I took a lot from that ideal in my life thereafter. I focused on being unique, on not doing what others did, on marching to the beat of my drum. It made me happy, and in the end, it kept me grounded.

I love you, Neil. Thanks for the Memories.

The fact that my idol died overshadowed the fact that today was Wanda's birthday and our wedding anniversary. I think she understood my grief, and while it wasn't how we pictured the day, as always, we make the best of difficult situations. I love you, Mi Esposa. Para siempre!

January 12, 2020

I spent the morning cleaning and arranging my office. My Mom gave me 3 beautiful Invicta watches over the past few years. I don't wear a watch, ever, but these mean the world to me, because she gave them to me. I clean and wind them and put them in their cases for a day when I may actually wear a watch. I also say a prayer that my mom stays healthy and happy.

January 13, 2020

I saw Rex today. My best friend and long-time business partner. It has been almost a year since we last saw each other, a drastic change from spending the last 26 years together. He is doing much better and it's good to see him getting back to his old self. We used to spend our days running a business, and now, we spend our days at home, quietly going about our lives and remembering the past.

I miss Rex. He has been such an instrumental part of our success as a company. I promised the impossible and he made it happen. You don't meet many people in your life that can transform your identity or direction, and he did both. He is still my biggest fan and tells me, "Bro, whatever you do, I am sure it will be successful, because it's you".

He always believed in me, even when I was leading us to a place no one believed in. He knew I wouldn't let him down, and I never did. I miss having that camaraderie in my life, where it's "us against the world". I have that with Wanda to some degree, but it's different. She has more of a reason to stay with me as my wife with our kids; he chose to stay with me totally of his own free will, and for that, I will be forever grateful.

January 14, 2020

Today is a special day. I am going to see Heinz Fabian, my former boss at Heraeus. We haven't seen each other since October, and I am eager to see how he is doing and to share what I have been up to.

It is good to see his smiling face, and I immediately notice something different when we sit and talk. Like me, he is at ease, which is a strange look for him, being I had never seen him look relaxed unless we were out and about socially, enjoying a beer and food in some part of the world.

Heinz let me know that he has stepped down as CEO of Heraeus Quartz, the division he has successfully run for the past many years. I am shocked. 8 months ago, he was asking me if there was any way I would change my mind about leaving, and here we are today, and he has left himself.

As I listen to him talk, I realize that my predictions are coming true. The leadership team I was a part of under Heinz has been completely dismantled. I was first, and had I not seen the writing on the wall, I would probably still be there, not writing this book and most likely as stressed and tired as I always was.

He seems happy, and that makes me happy. He will work on other projects for the company, but for now, he references his new freedom as his "relaxed state". I like to see him this way, as I have before on our long trips through Germany, China, and beyond. He got off the hamster wheel too, and I like to think that whether he admits it or not, my leaving paved the way for others. Even if that isn't true, I feel great comfort in knowing my friends are all going to be ok.

I asked him about the rest of the company and the future of GMSI. We discuss the layoffs, and he confides in me that things are not going well. Once I left, so did the momentum, the clients, the revenue, and the interest from Germany. I sense the end is near. I am deeply concerned for my former company and the people that work there. Unlike the C-suite, they are unlikely to have any golden parachutes—just the ones full of lead.

We say our goodbyes and we promise to stay in touch. I know he will, he is that kind of man. Genuine and sincere. It was an honor to work together, Heinz. Be happy and stay relaxed!

January 15, 2020

Today is a family day of sorts. We spend the morning schooling and writing, and around 11 AM we drive over to a park for a science class for the kids. The focus of today's lesson is on building a device that will allow an egg to survive a drop from 15 feet.

The kids have made their own versions of what they think will work. All are ingenious and I wouldn't hesitate to hire any of these bright minds for a future role in my company.

After the science lesson in the park, we go to the Phoenix Zoo. Wanda enrolled the kids in a science camp, one held at the zoo.

While the kids are at camp, Wanda and I take the opportunity to walk around the zoo. It is quite romantic, and I try and put the moves on her in the reptilian exhibit, but like the prey of many of these animals, my advances are swiftly defeated. No matter, we are here together and in the late sunshine of this beautiful winter day, I am content.

Another day in the books, together, and without me having to go to work.

January 16, 2020

I am leaving for Mexico today. I am going to play in a golf tournament with Chuck and Steve in Rocky Point, Mexico. I haven't been down to Rocky Point since the late 80's. We are attending a 3-day music festival, also known as the "Circus Mexicus", a lively gathering of 5000. I am excited, tired, and overwhelmed, but here we come Mexico, and this time, I won't drink the water!

A short 4-hour ride, and we are on the golf course, playing a quick 9. I am happy to be out, as I haven't taken a boy's trip for 15 years. After dinner at Bandito's, we take off for a Mexican pub crawl, which is literally how I have experienced this part of Mexico in the past. I made a promise to myself that I wouldn't let history repeat itself.

After midnight, we drive the dirt road towards the famous bar, JJ's Cantina. As we drive down the dirt road, I am taken aback by how much has changed in the 20 years since I was last here. None of the high rises that line the shoreline were even there.

JJ's is where I spent most of my time in my younger years. As we walk in, the memories come flooding back. I tell Chuck and Steve of the many places I threw up, picked up girls, or fell over questionably constructed railings. We smile and toast the evening; happy I am still upright and coherent.

January 17, 2020

I am way over my head in terms of my ability to hang with these guys. I throw up after 6 beers; Chuck drank that before we even went out last night. I will make a mental note not to try and keep up, and when no one is looking, I will throw my drinks in planters, making it look like I am pounding them!

This morning, we are playing a warmup round ahead of the real tournament, which is tomorrow. We open with an 8:30 am Bloody Mary tee time. Our focus is to learn the course, prospecting the land, cocktails in hand! It is windy and chilly, as it is in January on the Mexican coast of Rocky Point.

We all agree to play target golf as if we can target anything other than a porta potty.

I don't feel comfortable yet, but I pick my aimpoint, stand in, and swing, firing a blast out over the hazards into the safety of the fairway. Steve looks at me and says, "Dude, that was a 300-yard bomb! Play that way tomorrow and we have a chance at this thing!". I agree.

By the second hole, the wind begins to die down, the drink lady comes and by the grace of God, we are playing some solid golf. We feel confident that we have a chance to win by the time we tee off on the 19th bonus hole.

That is, until we went out. We went to see *Roger Clyne and the Peacemakers* play at one of the resorts. We drank. A lot. Then we drank some more. Then we went to more bars and drank more. By the time we got back to the condo, we had been out and about, drinking and socializing for over 14 hours. Tomorrow will come soon enough, and I won't be ready. Now please, make the room stop spinning for a few minutes so I can go to sleep.

January 18, 2020

Tournament day is here, and I feel like I have been sleeping on a couch and drinking too much. I take a shower to try and bring relief to my aching body, but all it brings is wetness. It's going to be another brutally long day.

Steve and I chat about our lives. Steve is a great guy and a wonderful engineer. I have known of his work for many years, but only recently did we have a chance to get to know each other on a personal level. I like his logical way of thinking and we share some great stories of our lives in the semiconductor industry.

Wanda and the kids are coming down to stay with Kathy. I have been missing Wanda and the kids, so it will be nice to hug my wife and kids again. But first, we have a tournament to win.

We arrive at the crowded venue early, but there are already hundreds of people, carts, and cars in the parking lot. I look around at the competition, and there are some serious golfers here. But I have been practicing for 6 months and today is the day I break out.

The wind is blowing, and it is no more than 38 degrees. I had practiced for this earlier this year, so my confidence is soaring. That won't last long. I am first on the tee, the wind blowing directly in my face, and a lagoon in front of me. I address the ball, slowly take my club back, and Bam! I top the ball, sending it directly into the lagoon. Our game continued like this for the next 3 holes. After 3 or 4 dreadfully cold and humbling holes, we find our groove as a team. It's too little too late, but we enjoy our time together, and as the sun comes out, so does our sunny disposition.

I am in Mexico, playing golf and enjoying my time away from the stresses of my old career. I am doing what I set out to do when I resigned. I am taking advantage of the time I have on this earth, and what a time it has been!

After the tournament, Wanda, Kathy, and our kids met me in the parking lot. I am so happy to see them, and we drive off to have dinner, drinks, and hugs.

We had a relaxing dinner together. Alas, the time together is short-lived, and I go prepare for another night of drinking, revelry, and madness, that only comes from being in Mexico, unsupervised and unchained at the festival known as the "Circus Mexicus".

January 19, 2020

The plan was to stay here until tomorrow and play another golf course up the coast, but I am tired and hungover and I miss my family. I let Chuck and Steve know how I feel, and they understand. I will spend the day with them and then Wanda will pick me up and take me home.

Over breakfast, we rehash our adventures, past and present. Chuck's friends are all professional people, just like me, and we tell our stories of business, family, and life over strong Bloody Marys and Huevos Rancheros. I find it amusing that all of us, even though we are in different industries, have similar stories. It just goes to show that no matter what any of us do for work, we all deal with similar problems.

The place is packed with football fans, party people, and locals. It's the playoffs, and the room is an eclectic mix of humans. I spend most of the time watching people rather than the game. I watch couples fight, people fall, and fans scream. It is never lost on me how misbehaved Americans are in Mexico, and how tolerant the Mexican people are towards them. This is a symbiotic relationship, as without the tourists, the Mexican economy here will die. I still apologize to Mexico on behalf of all of us pinche gringos! Disculpas a todos!

Wanda arrives to pick me up and I am overjoyed to see her. I am happy to have had this opportunity with Chuck and Steve, but my old body and my old liver are ready to slow down a bit. A lot, actually.

January 20, 2020

It's time for the long drive home from Mexico. I can't wait to sleep in my bed, next to Wanda. I am looking forward to being home. I find that the more we travel, the less I want to leave. This is definitely a carryover from not being home for a better part of the past 10 years, and I am becoming happily complacent being a homebody in our beautiful state of Arizona. I comment to Wanda, "I wish we could be together every day!!" We laugh and she tells me how we would get sick of each other.

This theory will be tested in the next couple of months, whether we like it or not.

January 21, 2020

I am having a legal meeting with a new attorney today. I am hoping he can provide guidance for our InfinityGo venture, as my first choice in law firms is prohibitively expensive.

He is in Old Town Scottsdale, and I am tired of driving, but we do what we must. We keep going, even when we don't want to, we keep pushing ourselves. That is the secret to success. Don't quit, keep pushing when you are tired and soon you will be eating the fruits of your labor.

I meet with Jeff, and he turns out to be a really down-to-earth attorney. I like his attention to detail and his approach to formation and risk analysis. I am excited to have found someone who not only likes our ideas but seems very straightforward about what we need and don't need.

On the drive home, I get another call from China. It seems the Chinese Government is starting to impose mandatory shutdowns and quarantines in time for the Chinese New Year. As I listen to my friends tell me of the latest events, I thank God that this has not reached further than China. Yet. I hope their swift action can help maintain control of whatever this is, but I know China, and I understand how many people go to and from daily, let alone during Chinese New Year. This could get out of hand quickly if they aren't careful.

January 22, 2020

Another day of InfinityGo activity. Brad flew in for a couple of meetings, and we are going to meet with another group of attorneys, have breakfast with Omer, and then we will all drive into Phoenix to meet with our corporate accountants for advisement on formation strategies best suited to our venture.

It was a long day of strategy meetings, and forming a new company is very time-consuming. In my early days, I would forget important details in the formation process, but years of experience have helped me to avoid the common pitfalls that plague many a new company. I hope.

Despite the many miles of driving and the long meetings, today was a great day, and for the first time since I left my career, I felt like a CEO again. This time it's going to be different though. I am going to utilize the people around me to help carry the load, and by doing so, I will free myself to spend more time with my family, and I will be able to reduce my stress load by handing off many tasks.

"By asking others for help, you are not admitting weakness, you are gaining strength."

By asking others for help, you are not admitting weakness, you are gaining strength. Let others carry the load and help you when you need it. There is nothing more foolish than trying to shoulder heavy burdens alone when those around you are standing by, willing to lend a hand. I write these words from experience and continue to refine my talents in this area.

January 23, 2020

After a busy week of travel and meetings, I am going to take the day off and play golf. I am working very hard these days, and while I am sincerely thankful to be here, and to have the life I have, I must be very careful not to fall into old habits.

A hamster wheel is much easier to enter than to exit.

January 24, 2020

I received the news today that the company I founded, GMSI, was being closed.

Almost immediately after the announcement, the calls came flooding in, along with text messages and emails asking me what I knew. I did not know anything. I just had lunch with Heinz last week, and we talked about saving the company by bringing in another buyer.

My only thought is about the people. All the people who put their trust in me for so long are now going to be unemployed. It crushes me. I feel like I failed all of them. I have often reflected on whether the "captain" abandoned the ship. I realize now, that I did not. I could no longer impact the business under the rules of the new owners. I brought culture and innovation; they brought rules and structure, rigid standards, and lots of overhead. We always delivered on our promise of innovation, and we had the trust of our clients and the quality of our products.

The picture on my wall, the one with the ship in heavy seas, reminds me of a metaphor Rex and I used to discuss. "Maybe the ship is sinking", he used to say. I would remind myself of this Zen-like balance and tell him, "The boat is not sinking nor rising, it is weathering the storm".

And in that, is the history of GMSI.

I wrote everyone an email, and it hurt me deeply to have to pen this letter:

Yes, my friends, I have heard the news.

My phone has been ringing nonstop for the past 24 hours regarding the closure of our beloved GMSI. To all who participated, you were the reason we lasted 28 years. I love most of you dearly.

Some of you minimized the values and ethics I continually preached; this is what happens when you let metrics trump experience. When you choose corporate strategy over culture. The secret to longevity is not in the product you sell or the level of expertise, it's about the relationships you foster. In that, is the strength to overcome any obstacle. You must nurture relationships.

When you take the heart and spirit away from anything, you have a soulless robot. A shell. Empty and devoid of light.

I am not at liberty to discuss any details, as I do not know any. I resigned last year in June, so my info is only what you have been told. I feel terrible. A great loss for the Semiconductor and SiC community as well.

Thank you all for a tremendous 28 years. Thanks, Rex, Mike, Phil, Aimee, and Cubby, for being the core, the heart and soul of a dream. Dreams come true because of people like you.

"Pride, Accountability and Focus"
GMSI 1992-2020

For the rest of this month, and many of the upcoming weeks, I will dedicate all my efforts to finding a way to save GMSI, to convince Heraeus that I can find a buyer, or two, and that their best play would be to bring in a strategic buyer who could use this opportunity to create a vertical integration. I know many in our industry who can benefit from our core technology, and maybe I can put myself back in a position to help grow it back to where it once was.

January 25, 2020

After the horrific news of the closing of GMSI, I started making calls throughout the industry to sense the interest level of prospective buyers. I am correct in my assumption that several strategic buyers would be willing to step up.

Almost immediately, I began to receive calls from around the world asking me if I would be interested in coming back to help the company if they purchased it. I said yes to most. It is my duty, even though I am supposed to be retired. After all, we called it "restment", not "retirement" for a reason.

I convinced myself, and Wanda, that I would be willing to come back if the right partner were to purchase the company. So long as the buyer would allow me to run it the way it was, lean and mean, with an emphasis on customer service and quality. I know Wanda is concerned I will fall back into my old habits, but I am more convinced I don't need to. I will see if I can keep that promise.

January 26, 2020

I have a potential buyer already, and he is willing to come right now. He is a long-time industry leader who sold his company and technology many years ago. His name is Gary, and he has already aligned us with a foreign entity that has an immediate need for GMSI's technology platform. I am excited but cautious. His buyers are most likely Chinese, and getting a deal done quickly with any Chinese company is not likely.

He already has approval to purchase; he just needs to do a site visit to corroborate the size and scope of the operation we built. It has been over 6 months since I last stepped foot in my old building, and honestly, I am quite nervous to go back. I am sure it will be an interesting visit.

Gary and I discuss the details. I like the fact that he is ready to move, and I know he is more than capable of helping to raise the capital required to purchase the company. He also brings a lifetime of equipment experience that will benefit the company.

We go to church later in the evening, and I ask God to take care of those who are in danger of losing their jobs, and to bless me with good sense and patience, to help lead a transaction for the successful sale of GMSI. I know he is listening.

January 27, 2020

While there are restrictions, Heraeus M&A has agreed to allow me to bring prospective buyers to the facility. I am told I do not act as an agent for Heraeus, which is fine; any money that is being offered to me is being offered directly from the buyers. I don't need anything from Heraeus, just that they are open to the buyers I bring.

I already have others calling me, but I would like to see what happens with Gary first, and I have reached out to Matt Reineke, my former partner in GMSI, to see if he would like to partner again. Either would be a great fit, but I want Matt to buy this. I like Gary a lot, but having any type of foreign ownership, especially if it is Chinese, will be an exceedingly difficult acquisition, given the issues they are having with the latest virus, let alone any BIS or ITAR considerations.

No, this should be in American hands, owned by an American firm, employing American workers. That would be the perfect scenario, and one I believe the client base would most accept. This is going to be an extremely complicated deal because I am NOT the CEO anymore, it's someone else's company, and they make the rules. I am undeterred. Those are my people and customers at stake, and I will do whatever I need to do to make sure they are protected.

A leader is not defined by his or her title; he or she is defined by their actions and words. Lead from the heart.

January 28, 2020

I can't believe I am doing this. I left the company I founded to find peace, and here I am, a little more than 6 months later, working for free to try and save it from extinction. Life is an odd journey. Just when you think you have it all figured out; life shows you everything you missed.

January 29, 2020

I meet Gary at 2 PM and we have a long lunch and strategy session. Gary confirms that the situation in China is much worse than the American press is reporting, simply because China doesn't talk a lot.

This only makes my concern for the rest of the world deeper. And for the United States. Statistics show that almost 3 million people visited the U.S. from China last year. And total, 143 million people visited China last year. The math isn't hard to understand. Do some simple multiplication, and you will see that an outbreak in China has the potential to affect the entire world population. Because the daily influx is so high, people coming and going from China will reach destinations worldwide in a matter of days. This is much more serious than I understood.

I can't dwell on this right now, as I have to take Gary to tour GMSI, and my mind needs to be focused on that. As we make the short drive from the restaurant, I show Gary the different points of interest around our location. We are in a technical hub of Phoenix, and our neighbors read like a who's who of the semiconductor and electronics world. We are in good company.

The facility looks great. Many of the improvements that were in process when I left are finished. Some of my team hugged me as they saw me, even though the building was supposed to be empty. I am happy to see them too, but the place feels different now. It isn't as vibrant, which is

understandable being they were told the company was shutting down.

I am mindful of this as we walk the many areas of my former building. This time, I am walking not as the CEO, but as a potential buyer. I know many are hurting, and I am considerate of that. I can't tell them why I am here, which is to save the dream I made a reality so many years ago. The one that gave them all jobs. The one that fed families and supplied some of the biggest companies in the world with critical products.

After the tour, we have a quick recap and thank Christoph, the new President, for the tour. He is cordial and friendly, as always; the only difference is I am not his boss, nor is he mine. We are equals, and I wish him the best in all he does.

Gary was impressed, and we talked at his hotel for an hour or so before I headed home. Home, where I live, not where I worked. I mention this because when I owned GMSI, I would always walk into the office after a trip and say, "Honey, I'm home!" In retrospect, it wasn't funny. The sad truth is I spent much more time at work than at home, and I don't want to repeat that mistake ever again.

January 30, 2020

I spend most of the day working on the structure of a deal for my old company. I stand to make a good amount of money to complete the deal, but that isn't my motivation. My motivation is to save jobs, and I am willing to take less in any compensation to make sure a deal gets done.

I have been asked to write a business case for GMSI, amongst other preparatory documents buyers and interested parties are asking for. In the past, I could do this at my discretion, or with the review of my legal team, but I have to be careful. I still have a non-compete and a non-disclosure that I must honor, and I intend to. But those restrictions make it difficult to tell the story of the company. I am in untrodden territory, but I am finding my way.

Building a company is hard work. Selling a company is even harder. Buying a company is the hardest of all. You take the biggest risk, and usually, the most expensive one.

January 31, 2020

So far, 2020 has been quite a whirlwind of activity. I am not complaining, and I am excited to see where all these things take us. At this point in my life, I am just along for the ride. Today is no different.

As I have many times when I am pressed with a difficult situation or decision, I head to the quiet tranquility of the lake. The lake is more a diversion than a destination. During any of the transactions I have led over the past 10 years, I have visited the lake before, during, and after. It is my place to sort out the big picture. It's a place to catch my breath and figure out where to go next. I do my best thinking at 65 miles an hour, wearing no shoes in 48-degree weather.

There is not another single boat as me and a couple of friends cast off from the docks, and as we crack open our beers and toast the day, I can't help but count my blessings. I am here on the lake with my good friends, drinking a beer and enjoying nature. I have a great wife, awesome kids, a loving family, and a nice home. I am blessed beyond measure. No matter what happens over the next few weeks, I will hold my head up high and continue to be grateful for all I have and all those I share it with. I am the luckiest guy in the world as far as I am concerned.

The truest test of resolve isn't when a situation is difficult, but when it's hopeless.

9

February, 2020

February 1, 2020

It's Saturday and Ben has an early basketball game. He has yet to score a basket in his games, and we are into his second season. He is always playing against bigger and taller kids, and I keep telling him, "Don't worry about how big they are, find your spot and shoot when you can. They can't block everything".

I can relate to his fear. There will always be someone bigger, someone stronger, and someone smarter. If you want to succeed in life, you need to put all that out of your head and focus your energy on what you do best, not on the perceived advantages of your opponent.

Basketball and life share this philosophy. Spud Webb was one of the smallest guys in the league, and Muggsy Bogues too. Both found a way to overcome their perceived disadvantage by being fast and nimble, able to weave and drive the lane against the big guys. We all need to find our inner Spud.

February 2, 2020

Superbowl Sunday. While I have no money on the game, I would put my money on Patrick Mahomes. Hunger wins championships and he is starving. His mentality is "Let my play do the talking", and he is correct. Many times, you don't need to say a word to be powerful. You let your actions say everything you need to say.

I learned long ago, that he who talks first is lost. With that in mind, I write the following paragraphs as a post on LinkedIn and Facebook as a response to the people who have written expecting me to comment on the recent announcement of the closing of GMSI.

Silence doesn't mean someone doesn't care. Sometimes silence is merely a calm before action.

Silence is a valuable tool for business and personal situations. There is a saying by George Bernard Shaw that I have tucked away in my memory box to remind me that sometimes, it's ok to say nothing.

"Choose silence of all virtues, for by it you hear other men's imperfections, and conceal your own."

If you are quiet, you will hear the answers to all your questions, and the hearts and minds of those around you.

As Confucius said, "Silence is a true friend who never betrays."

In silence, there is strength, and I am mute for a reason.

Happy Sunday.

February 3, 2020

I am continuing to reach out to prospective buyers for GMSI. I am surprised at the level of interest there is, and I am confident several of the people who contact me would be a good fit for the company.

After spending most of the morning on the business case I have developed for GMSI, I take a break and drive the kids to the chess club at St. Anne's. After I drop them off, I go inside the church and pray for a happy resolution to the current situation at GMSI.

Prayer is a useful tool for me. It settles my mind, focusing my thoughts on what is important. I know God hears me, even if he doesn't answer me right away. I will bide my time and have faith that he will answer me when he is ready.

February 4, 2020

There have been many people who have helped me on my journey. Some have inspired me while others have offered their resources. Most important to me, are the ones that offer their time. Today I am meeting one of those people who offered all three, Dr. Ron Birkhahn.

Dr. Ron is a well-respected scientist in the semiconductor world, but more than that, he is my friend. He has often given me wonderful pieces of advice that many others missed. He has followed my path for many years, both as a friend and as a client. He believes in me, and I in him.

As we walk the many paths and trails that surround Canyon Lake, he asks me how I feel about the closing of GMSI and if I have any intention of returning. I tell him what I can, and that yes, I will return, if the opportunity presents itself. I can't tell him I am working on deals to purchase the company, but I can tell he knows I am working on something.

He asks me in his special way, "Are you sure you want to come back?", and I answer him honestly, "No, I am not sure, but they need me, and I feel responsible for the hardships many will face if I don't try".

He walks in silence for a few minutes and then looks at me and says, "You can't save everyone all the time. Sometimes, you need to save yourself". He is right of course, as he always is.

Dr. Ron is wise and honest, and our talk reaffirms what I already know. I impacted people's lives, and to me, that is the greatest accolade I will ever receive. Not just with leadership, or our products, but with my personality and sincerity. His talk is reassuring and further reinforces that I am doing the right thing.

In the face of great adversity, don't cower in the shadows, shine like the sun.

February 5, 2020

The Senate acquitted President Trump on both articles of impeachment against him today. It's been a wild ride for the country, and now that this event is behind us, I hope and pray we can get back to the business of taking care of the important matters at hand. One of which is what is happening in China with the escalation of their quarantine efforts.

For the record, Nancy Pelosi tearing up the President's speech during his State of the Union address was despicable. While Democrats have hated Trump since he took office, this was one of the most unprofessional and outright disrespectful displays I have ever witnessed. What is happening to our country? Such division and hatred.

I talked to my team in China last night. Everything is shut down. It is only a matter of time before it spreads outside of China, and to the rest of the world.

I am alarmed when I hang up the phone. My Chinese friends have been confined to their homes for a couple of weeks now. How serious is this disease? No one knows, but the report from inside China is that people are dying, and if the Chinese Government has sequestered the country it has to be serious; the WHO is involved. I hope it doesn't spread further, but my science mind understands, it will. The math favors it.

February 6, 2020

As I read the news this morning, I discovered the Wuhan virus has spread to 18 countries. I was in China during the bird flu epidemic in 2013, and ironically, our hotel was next door to Kentucky Fried Chicken. They didn't shut the country down. It didn't spread as far as I know. The CDC is worried, the World Health Organization is worried, and I am worried.

I stay home today and work on InfinityGo topics, but I realize, I need to focus on the work I need to do to support the transfer of GMSI into new hands.

After we ate dinner, I took Ben to basketball practice. I find I am not alone in my worry. Several other parents are following the developments in China, and they are concerned as well.

I don't have any animosity towards China; in fact, I worry about the many friends I have there. These are good people, despite the general tone of the American public. People are dying, and conspiracy theories are already starting. This isn't a China problem; it's a global problem and we need to find a way to fix this on a global basis.

Geez, we just got past the impeachment. What else can happen?

February 7, 2020

This morning, I dropped the kids off at school and headed to the Legacy Golf Resort for lunch and golf with Chuck. Over lunch, we discussed the latest news. I am hearing of factories shutting down in Asia due to the virus. He hears the same.

This is troublesome because our venture would rely on a healthy economy. Factories shutting production down is certainly not the definition of good health.

Chuck built the control systems for our equipment at GMSI. I have known him for over 20 years. He is meticulous and smart, and best of all, likable and personable. I appreciate all he has done, even though we paid him a lot of money. We could have paid anyone, but we chose him, and he is grateful. He is a friend and a business partner.

This is how business should work. You team up with someone and you take care of each other. All good relationships are give and take. More give than take in the especially good ones!

February 8, 2020

I have been working feverishly to assemble teams to help me take GMSI back to its rightful place. Just to be open kimono, I have talked to the world's largest semiconductor companies and many are interested. I am not sure what the hell I am thinking. Do I really want to go back to work? Like this? Guiding a transition? It is going to be a lot of work, a lot of time, and a lot of change management.

I should focus on InfinityGo, but that will have to wait, because selling GMSI will bring my family a payday, and will help refill our ever-depleting bank account. It will help people keep their jobs, and the clients will benefit from not having to search for a new vendor. It's a win-win on paper.

In my heart though, I have my doubts. I don't want to work like I did before. It is grueling and I already know how the story ends. I need to find a new home for the company, but I don't want to do so at the expense of my health or sanity.

There are 5 possible buyers right now. Two are large OEMs, two are manufacturers and one is a strategic investor. I know who I lean towards for the sake of the employees, but I know they will be the most demanding. I am hoping Matt Reineke will come to the table, my top choice. Others won't move fast enough. He can move quickly, and he knows the value of what he is getting.

We shall see how things work out. Right now, I need to deal with the fact that my guts are popping out of my stomach walls, due to an aggravated Hernia. Old age is for the elderly.

February 9, 2020

I am sleepy. I haven't been sleeping right for months. Maybe it's a mixture of too many gin and tonics, too much food, or the stress of uncertainty. This is the painful reality of closing a deal. It's always "One more thing" away from being closed.

The actual closing of a deal is more of a relief, kind of like drunkenly falling in the door after a night out. There is usually no fanfare, no big celebrations, and no rest. Once the deal closes, that is when the real work starts.

February 10, 2020

The weather has turned overcast and gloomy. The overcast skies resemble my mood this morning, and when I feel like this, I have learned to turn my attention towards cooking.

Today, I spent the day writing and taking calls about the GMSI deal. I still have this unsettled fear I will fall back into my old ways, so I remind myself that all work and no play make Peter a pain in the ass.

I need to make sure I keep a balance. Work a little, rest a little. It all sounds so easy when I write it down. Living it is another story.

February 11, 2020

Today I am meeting with a large company regarding the possibility of buying GMSI. This would be a great fit for several reasons. They had called me to ask my interest level and then offered me an opportunity to just "run the place" if they bought it. I would like that very much. They are a publicly traded company, one of the biggest semi-equipment providers in the world, and I like the management team. I am sure we could accomplish great things together.

After the meeting, I caught up with Wanda in downtown Phoenix at the historic Heritage House. This is a turn-of-the-century gem, and I recommend a visit if you are in town.

Following the Heritage House, I surprised Wanda and the kids with lunch at the Hard Rock Café. We had a great lunch as a family, and I am getting excited about possibly going back to work. I think I am excited. I know getting a paycheck sounds fantastic!

February 12, 2020

It's my dad's birthday today. He would have been 80 years old. It is hard to believe he has been gone for 27 years. I can't imagine my dad at 80, but my mom is a firecracker at 77. I bet if they were still together, I would find them in the pool, skinny dipping, just like I did when I was in my 20s. I had very progressive parents, and in turn, they had very progressive children. For me, it was just another day of being a Guercio.

Happy Birthday in heaven, dad.

February 13, 2020

Today is a family field trip day. We are heading to an event at the Mesa Public Library for a science class by the lake. I am not thrilled to be coming today; there is still so much to do. But I made a promise and I intend on keeping it. I go with Wanda; part of the adventure is not knowing all the details. This is how she got me to go for a vasectomy. Ok, I made that up, but I assure you, this is how it would happen.

I took several calls from people interested in the purchase of GMSI. There is a lot of activity now, and there are several possible buyers Heraeus has brought in on their own. Those transactions would not include me. Even though I have brought several buyers to the table, Heraeus may choose to sell GMSI to someone else. I hope if that happens, I will at least get a chance to play some part in a new iteration.

I am not sure why I feel this way though. I don't want to work for someone else after owning the company for 28 years. I keep reminding myself this isn't just about me. It's about the people that I am trying to help. My friends, employees, and clients.

The event at the park is a science class. I don't know what they talked about, as I never got off the phone. Wanda is not happy that I am reverting to my old ways. I explained to her why I was on the calls, but she didn't care. She has heard it for the past 10 years.

"Hey, you were supposed to resign to be more present for the kids. You are here, but you aren't present at all. If you aren't going to engage, then why even show up?", she scolds me, like the child I am. She is a bit selfish and self-centered, so my struggle is an inconvenience to her. Our need for money doesn't matter to her if it interferes with what she wants, and this infuriates me.

I realized another reason to go back to work. If I continue staying home all the time, I am positive Wanda will eventually start plotting my murder. Or vice versa.

February 14, 2020

I do not like Valentine's Day. I loathe the idea of this holiday, simply because it has no meaning to me. Why can't every day be like Valentine's Day? I have explained this to Wanda many times. I bring her flowers for no reason, and we go to romantic dinners at least once a month. I show her I love her pretty much every day in everything I do.

It's Fridate, and Valentine's Day, so we decide to do something out of the ordinary. We have an early lunch at our favorite Mexican food place, and we go shopping at Ross, the discount clothing store. But I didn't stop there, we headed to Barnes and Noble bookstore, a favorite for Wanda and the kids. That is how you do Valentine's Day. You give her whatever she wants. Happy Valentine's Day Wanda. I love you, babe!

February 15, 2020

This morning as I scroll through Facebook, a memory pops up from 2011. It talks about Ben being potty trained. I can't believe 9 years ago Ben was just learning to poop on the potty, and right now, I am getting ready to take him to his basketball game. This is the very premise of this book. 9 years have passed in the blink of an eye, and I missed a lot of it. No more. I am taking a stand. I am going to be a part of my kids' lives whether they want me to be or not!

Ben plays well this morning but gets mauled by a much larger girl throughout the game. He is discouraged and dejected. I feel bad for him. He is working so hard and has yet to score a basket. I know it is grating on him and his confidence has taken a beating. I told him he was going to be fine, but I am considering teaching him how to conceal brass knuckles, you know, as a defensive tool.

February 16, 2020

I need to get out of the house. I woke up early and wrote for a little while, but there is so much activity surrounding the GMSI acquisition, that I just need to get out and get some fresh air. Cailyn has been bugging me to go to the lake. The weather is nice today, so I grabbed the boat to surprise her with a daddy/daughter day on the lake.

Cailyn and I raced around the lake for hours, fishing and eating and marveling at the beauty of this fantastic place. It never gets old for her. She always wants to come to the lake with me, and that means so much to me. She loves the water, just like me. This reminds me of my love of water and the many times sailing with my father.

Back home, we are having Sushi for dinner. Being in love means doing things for others you don't want to, just to make them happy. This is one of those days for Wanda, and I appreciate her willingness to let us eat raw fish until we are pooping goldfish. Love is a many splendored thing.

February 17, 2020

This Coronavirus thing is getting serious. The first reported cases are starting to show up in many places around the world. China is on lockdown and Europe is starting to see significant escalations in cases. I am certain it will make it to the United States soon.

We are ill-prepared for any type of health disaster here in the USA or even at our house. I am going to get some things to tuck away in case of an emergency. I will feel better knowing that in case of something serious, we at least have some fresh water and nonperishable food.

February 18, 2020

Matt is coming out to see GMSI tomorrow. He didn't even hesitate; he jumped at the chance to be involved. He doesn't overthink opportunity; he jumps in, and that's how to make money.

In less than 2 weeks, I have brought at least 5 buyers to the table, and Matt makes 6. He is the one I would most like to see buy the place, simply because he knows I am more than capable of making it successful. I already did, and he benefited financially because of it.

That's tomorrow though. Today I am doing a daddy/son day, because of course Ben guilted me with his reasoning, "Cailyn had a daddy/daughter day, why can we have one?"

In the middle of all this activity related to GMSI, InfinityGo, and the book, I stop everything I am doing to take Ben out. I shouldn't be bitter, but his timing is not the best. I must remind myself I left work to spend time with the kids and Wanda, and my old ways should not be my new ones.

Ben chooses a morning on the driving range, followed by lunch and bowling at the Main Event. Smacking balls far is good therapy, and after a hundred golf balls, I am cured of my sour mood.

Gary and his group will not be able to purchase GMSI because of restrictions being placed on foreign investment. China is in crisis. With the growing cases of this Wuhan virus, there is no way they will be able to do any due diligence, and they will definitely not be able to move money.

Ben and I spend half an hour playing games together. We have a great day together, and that's all that matters to him. We headed home and I reminded him I wouldn't be home tomorrow because Matt and I are golfing before we go to the GMSI meeting. Ben, being the boy genius he is, reminds me, "Remember Dad, we aren't working now, so save your receipts so you can charge this off as a business expense."

February 19, 2020

Based on the massive amount of time I am spending on the potential acquisition of GMSI, we have stepped back a little from InfintyGo, especially after finding Airbnb is doing something called "experiences", which is similar to my idea. We will still move forward but change the approach. I have some really good ideas.

I haven't been sleeping. I keep waking up at 2 AM, 3, 5 and 6. I am having bad dreams about Wanda. Vivid dreams, where she is hooking up with others in front of me. My subconscious is working overtime, being fed on a constant diet of sexless nights and rejection.

I am dealing with some news Wanda shared with me last week. She does not want to have sex anymore. She said she feels bad about herself, and since her hysterectomy, has lost all interest in sex. She assures me this is not based on her feelings for me but on her mental and physical state post-surgery. She says she loves me, but all I hear is, "You are fat, ugly, unemployed, and undesirable". The kicker? I am still expected to deliver on my end of the marriage, perfectly, daily, and without fault. That is the expectation.

"Hey, I don't want to do my part as a wife, but please continue to provide me everything I want".

Women feel more amorous when they feel good about themselves, and many focus on their perceived imperfections. Ladies, I am going to give you an important perspective from the men who love you. We don't care as much about how you look as you do. We just want to be with you, and we want to be loved and appreciated. That's it. No fancy analysis is necessary.

When sex is gone, love follows. Maybe love is gone too. I do not know anymore. It is very depressing. I am working so hard to get our lives in order, and in return, Wanda has been more distant to me than ever, especially since I resigned last June.

Many days I feel like I am wasting time. Wanda is a taker. I am a giver. This scenario always ends badly for me. The thing I have realized over the past 6 or 7 months is that I care much more deeply about her than she does for me.

Yes, my happiness does matter, but if I am not getting what I need, and I continue to accept the direction of a relationship that makes me unhappy, then it is me who needs to make a change. But divorce is not the answer. Our rings even have an inscription that says, "No matter what". Moving on from Wanda is not an option, so I will do my best to find our way back to each other. When you take divorce off the table, you find a way.

Matt Reineke has arrived to tour GMSI and discuss the purchase of its assets. I am wondering if I am doing the right thing anymore. Whose job am I saving? There aren't many of my people left, but the ones that are, I care about deeply. Am I just hanging on to 28 years of my past?

Matt and I played a round of golf before the tour at GMSI. We discuss how to best facilitate a smooth transition should a deal take place. He asks me to run the company, but with someone on his side taking care of the business administration.

As we golf, Matt explains, "Peter, you are one of the best pitchmen and business development guys I have ever met. This is where you should be. You don't need to be the CEO; you just need to put yourself where you can bring the most impact!"

He is right. I don't need to be the CEO. I can probably carve a better work-life balance if I am not the CEO, and the thought of just focusing on client-centered activity, coupled with my work in product development will allow me the freedom I didn't have when I was the CEO.

We finished our golf and tour of GMSI. Matt is floored by the progress since he last saw our facility. I am extremely proud of what we built. This is a state-of-the-art facility, and it is the culmination of 28 years of effort. I am so proud of what we accomplished, and his early investments were the springboard for our growth. I will always be grateful for his confidence in me and the GMSI team.

He agrees that the investment is worthwhile, and we structure the skeleton of a deal that will save GMSI. All is not lost my friends; there is hope smoldering in the ashes of bad news.

"Take care of people as if they were as valuable as treasure. Most are worth more with a little effort, love, and elbow grease. "

This reminds me of the parallel between this situation and relationships between men and women. A relationship that doesn't work for one person may be someone else's dream come true. Remember this before you throw away the people in your life. Sometimes, we throw away treasure just because it's a little tarnished. Keep the polish handy and take care of people as if they were as valuable as treasure. Most are worth more with a little effort, love and elbow grease.

February 20, 2020

The disease or virus in China has a name. It is a novel coronavirus known as Covid-19. In recent days, many countries have imposed travel restrictions worldwide to and from China. But I believe it will be too little too late. The damage is done, as many millions of people have already been traveling to and from China, the USA, Europe, and other countries.

This looks to be a serious disease. The gestation period can be as long as 2 weeks, and this is problematic as most who are infected don't have symptoms, meaning they continue to interact with others as if nothing is wrong. They are transmitting the spread of this disease wherever they go, and they have most likely been in contact with hundreds, if not thousands of people, especially if they travel for a living, like I did. The numbers are staggering, and epidemiology suggests widespread contact by day 49. That means the globe will have been exposed to this in less than 60 days.

I was contacted today by two of the largest potential investors in InfinityGo that they will not invest in our venture because it is rooted in the world of travel. If no one travels, what good is a concept that relies on interactions between travelers and hosts? I have invested thousands of dollars of our own money in this business, and in hours, it is dead.

I am heartbroken. I have such a great idea, and now, due to a virus that kills, it may never see the light of day. My worry is more focused on how the rest of the world will fare, as cases continue to rise, and the spread of this virus seems imminent.

I stop everything with this realization and pray, deeply.

February 21, 2020

I woke up early today to do some of my own research on the Covid-19 virus, and what can be done to prevent it. None of the articles I read are positive. Most renowned science communities agree this is already spreading on a worldwide basis. Most countries are not prepared and there is no cure, so biomedical companies are racing to develop vaccines now. As it turns out, Pfizer has multiple patents related to Coronaviruses. Coincidence? I don't think so.

The one report that sticks out the most is written in the "Washington Post", and it mirrors an article I read in the *Harvard Gazette*. This isn't going to go away, and it not only threatens lives but the economic stability of the globe.

And here I am, trying to help buy a company that will most likely not be able to visit clients, ship products to certain Asian countries, and may be faced with the challenge of negotiating an ever-changing landscape in the wake of this killer disease.

Today is a day where I just want to go back to bed. But that's what cowards do, and I am no coward. I begin to create a risk analysis that details several different scenarios, and how our business will be able to overcome them. That's what good leaders do. They face adversity and offer solutions.

Today is Friday, the day Wanda and I share our "Fridate". I have so many things I am working on, that I ask her if we can just stay home this morning so I can work. She surprisingly agrees. She knows how I am when I am locked in on a project, so she is giving me the space I need to create.

February 22, 2020

This morning, we are up early for Ben's basketball game. He has been a little down in the dumps about his inability to score a basket and this season is almost over. Just 2 more games.

Wanda and I tell him to play aggressively. I put my hand on his shoulder and said, "No one gives you anything in life; you have to take it, Ben. That's your ball out there. Take it!" The game starts and he is being overpowered by much taller opponents. Ben may be shorter than the other kids, but he is a speed demon, and he begins to use it to his advantage. His teammates see this and as he races down the court, beating his defender, he calls for the ball. His teammate lobs a long pass to the far corner and Ben receives the pass, stops, stands on his mark, and shoots. It's a beautiful high, arcing shot, and...HE SCORES!!! The drought is over!!

Later in the quarter, Ben races down the court into position. He is in position on the low post again. And he delivers. Another beautiful shot, arcing high and through the hoop, with nothing but net. A scorer is born.

When we got home, I ran upstairs to my office and quickly edited a video of his baskets to share on Facebook for our family. In my edit, I write a message about determination.

No matter how difficult an obstacle seems, you haven't failed until you quit. Pride, accountability, and focus have always been my mantra, but after today, I will be adding perseverance and determination to the list.

Congratulations Benny. Thank you for remembering our family motto. "Guercio's never quit!"

February 23, 2020

With the recent visits to the GMSI facility over, and bids in place, now we wait. Matt has instructed his attorney to draft a formal offer for GMSI. Other buyers have called and spoken to me or visited the facility, and now there is nothing for me to do but see how things transpire.

The key to closing an acquisition is to be patient. You can't rush transactions like this. The seller will ultimately decide what the best offer is, and sometimes, it isn't the highest bidder. Sometimes, like in my case, I turned down more money from other bidders in favor of Heraeus and particularly, Heinz, a buyer that was a better fit for me and the company.

February 24, 2020

I read today that the WHO-China Joint mission, which included experts from around the world, spent time in Beijing and traveled to Wuhan and two other cities to speak with healthcare workers and to assess the severity of the current crisis.

If this is something that global experts are flying to China to observe, and China is willingly participating, I fear the worst is already happening. The virus is spreading and soon, we will be dealing with a life-threatening disease on our doorstep. That is a scary thought.

Some days are boring, and some days are enlightening, but at this point, I am simply happy to just have days. Any days.

February 25, 2020

It took a while, but we have found a cadence to our weekly schedule, I still have many daily activities around this baseline schedule, but I like the structure.

When I resigned, I was lost for a while. I had no purpose; limited direction and I was dealing with a deep emotional struggle that even I couldn't understand. I don't feel most of those things anymore.

Maybe it was facing the reality that GMSI was closing; maybe it was me coming to terms with the finality of my decision. I do know that having a schedule and a pattern gives me purpose. I am helping my family, which is exactly what was intended when I left my career.

I am feeling hopeful. Sure, we are dealing with a serious issue now related to the Coronavirus, but I feel confident this will pass, InfinityGo will move forward, and with a little luck, GMSI will go to the right buyer, and I will have a place at the table again. I am ready for whatever comes our way.

February 26, 2020

Today we are working at home in the morning. The kid's school and I am working on this book and some final details for potential buyers for GMSI. We are taking the kids to chess club at the church, and afterward we are having an early dinner of Fish Tacos at SoCal Taco in downtown Gilbert.

Days like this are not lost on me anymore. I cherish them. I appreciate them and I hold on to them. If things work out favorably, I won't be staying home anymore. I will be back at work, either with GMSI or with InfinityGo. Either way, I feel like we are transitioning from the doldrums of uncertainty to the sunny shores of employment.

February 27, 2020

California, right next door to Arizona, reported its first Coronavirus case from someone who had not been outside the state. This is getting very real, extremely fast, and it's alarmingly close. I am nervous. This could get out of control in a hurry. After a recent call with Germany, it appears they are preparing to deal with an epidemic. It is feeling more and more like it's the end of the world. I am wondering if there is foul play involved with this. These are very scary times indeed.

February 28, 2020

If the world is facing an epidemic, a killer virus, I am going to do my best to fill out my bucket list now. I will start by playing 18 holes at Superstition Springs Golf with my cousin Mike. I would like to check off some of my other bucket list items, but Salma Hayek won't call me back. I am just kidding Wanda. You know you are my Salma. (Salma, call me!)

February 29, 2020

Happy Leap Year!!! It's a special day today. It's the end of the month, a leap year, and I am taking my former employees, Cody and Cubby out to the lake for a boy's afternoon on the boat.

The weather is pristine, the air is crisp, and everyone is healthy. If 30-year-old Peter were to see 54-year-old Peter, he wouldn't believe we were the same person. It's a nice day, and it's noon on Saturday. People are out and about, despite the looming threat of the China virus.

At the dock, I have trouble starting the boat. The boat feels sluggish. Unresponsive would be a better description. I notice that the starboard engine is not responding. I look back at the engine compartment, and I see the smoke begin to billow from the hatch. This is a dangerous scenario. This trip is over.

What a way to end the month and the weekend. My boat is one of the few possessions I can honestly say I love, besides my drums. It brings me joy, but more so, it allows me to share that joy with others, and now, the boat is dead. Never go out on a leap day. It's a day that only comes around every 4 years, so you know it can't be trusted. I should have known better.

It is always darkest before the dawn, but much darker if the sun never rises. Life is about perspective. Learn to appreciate what you have before it's gone.

10

March, 2020

March 1, 2020

And just like that, February is gone. So much has been going on, I am losing track of days and nights. I don't like this feeling. It feels like I am watching someone else live their lives through the lens of a faraway camera.

It is hard to understand how I feel now. As we enter another new month of bills and responsibilities, I am worried. We are bleeding cash. I am on the edge of a precipice. One way or another, GMSI will move to a new life, under whatever ownership it may find. It may even be myself and an investor.

I will have to go back to work somewhere unless this book becomes a "New York Times" #1 Bestseller. I have dreamed of a life where I am able to share my life experiences in the form of written words. But as it stands, I am looking at some different decisions right now. Many will be made without much influence from me. Others will be made solely on the premise of my involvement. I am at a proverbial crossroads. I am...scared.

So much has gone on this past week, and I have written little of it down yet. The beauty of how I write this book is in the simplicity of being able to write when I feel it, and if I don't, I have Google Maps, emails, and Facebook to help me piece together the days I may have missed. I can be anywhere in the world and voice to text a slightly illiterate work to myself at 2 AM on my cellphone.

Even though life is going 100 MPH right now, I can slow it all down, catch my breath and reconstruct these days through the magic of technology. Technology I had a hand in making through our work with GMSI. I find an ironic solace, like finding a long-lost lover after many years.

It feels good to know we have helped shape a tomorrow we did not understand so many yesterday's ago. People like Bill Gates, Steve Jobs, and many others helped create a life we didn't have prior to the 90s, and while I don't compare myself to them, there are many similarities related to the technical offerings we brought to life.

We used to do things one way; now we have the world in our hands, 24/7. Technology is amazing. Everything I dreamed about as a little kid is real today. And so many things I did not imagine. Things no one could. I am excited to see what the next chapter of human evolution brings, assuming this new virus risk doesn't wipe out humanity.

An update on my relationship with Wanda. We are somewhat lost. We are still not having sex and I no longer feel it is helpful to talk about it. It is what it is. It is a constant and saddening feeling to be rejected by the person you love the most.

We have to find a way, but we must find common ground soon, because I am losing hope. I pray every day for Wanda and me to be connected, emotionally, spiritually, and physically. I am just really lonely, and I realize how selfish Wanda has been these past months. I put her on a pedestal, and it's my fault.

I was exuberant with our relationship, and I wanted her to be happy when we first met. Now, she has a sense of entitlement and lethargy that makes me regretful for having spoiled her. She has been very absorbed in what is important to her, and only her.

We may never be the way we used to be, but I don't regret our time together. I have loved Wanda deeper than anyone I have ever known, but in the end, we need to be in relationships that fill us up. I am empty.

I am lonely. I gave her everything I had. My time, money, heart, and soul. I gave her a big portion of my life and she gave me a slice of hers.

But maybe all this is just melodramatic. I am sure Wanda would see things differently, as we rarely see eye to eye when it comes to our relationship.

It's time to write a new chapter in life--one I hope Wanda will continue to co-star in, but maybe we will just play cameos in each other's lives moving forward. Either way, I will continue to push for better days and happier nights.

Today is Sunday, and tonight at church, I will bring all these things to God and ask for guidance. My faith grounds me, and I could use some terra firma right now.

March 2, 2020

I woke up super early this morning. My old friend, stress, is making an appearance. I am uneasy about the deals we have pending, my employees, whose lives are in flux, my marriage, and a broken boat that brings joy to others.

I deserve to be happy and loved too. I gave Wanda a life she only dreamed of. I sacrificed and worked myself almost to death, and I don't feel like she appreciates any of those sacrifices. I give and she takes, is how I simplify my quandary.

I understand she has her work with the responsibility of the home-school leader, and I respect that it takes a lot of her time, but she isn't the only one who has a full plate. Doesn't she see how much effort I have put into being present and helpful? God, I sound so bitter, and I hate it.

March 3, 2020

This morning, Derek and I are taking Ben to his first 18-hole Championship Golf course since his day in Mexico last October. He is golfing with his dad and his favorite cousin. He is simply happy to be here.

"I find the simple joy of watching my kid laugh and golf, and it reminds me that we all control our happiness."

I see his joy and it reminds me that I need to find my own. The joy in this day is simple to see, but in the past, I may have looked the other way. Instead of worrying about the business deals I have pending, or the killer virus sweeping across the globe, I find the simple joy of watching my kid laugh and golf, and it reminds me that we all control our happiness.

After a great morning, we come home, and I go upstairs to take a shower. I let the warm water run over my sore bones and muscles on the hottest setting I can stand. I am trying to calm my mind and body, but It appears Peter Jr. has come to life. There is no one here but me, the former CEO and self-professed do-it-yourselfer.

Out of the shower, I pick up my phone to find that another Chinese investor cannot close, so I am not sure what will happen with GMSI. have been contacted by one of the largest European equipment OEMs, and they would be a good fit l. I don't know what will happen now, especially with the spread of Coronavirus. There is so much uncertainty I decide to put it all in God's hands.

What will be, will be.

March 4, 2020

My happiness is an afterthought to you, whereas your happiness is my primary focus.

I wrote those words this morning. It sums up my recent frustration with the way Wanda treats me. For the first time in our marriage, I feel like we may not come out of this tailspin.

We ended last night on another bad note. I am not happy. She does not realize that and it's making me crazy. Maybe she does and she is ignoring it, or tired of hearing about it. Either way, our decaying relationship is driving me insane. Not figuratively anymore, literally. I need to resolve this, or it will end me.

March 5, 2020

Our animosity carries over to morning. I am so depressed about our relationship.

I can't dwell on this now; my phone hasn't stopped ringing. One of those calls was from Gerald, the CEO of a local Tech start-up. He needs my advice. He won't pay me anything, but he is a good person and I hope I can help him find his path, as I am still trying to figure out what mine will look like.

I also received a call from a former colleague. He worked with a large Japanese company, and he wants me to be involved in the design and manufacture of some new products.

There is other activity today, but none of it matters, because I am so depressed about Wanda. I sound pitiful when I write this, but this is a book about my experience. This is my real life and my real feelings, and I feel I would do a disservice to the reader if I didn't share all the elements of my life. It's not all rainbows and unicorns.

The truth is, I don't feel like writing. I don't feel like doing anything. Our issues as a couple are crippling my creativity. Her negative actions take away my positive ones. She is stealing my joy, a joy her very existence once manifested.

Later in the day, I received a phone call from the European OEM that expressed interest in GMSI. They decided that the questions they had for me were "obsolete."

They will not buy GMSI, or maybe they will, but I won't be included. As it sits, I only see Matt and AMAT as the only other options. I know AMAT has visited GMSI and other than Matt, there is no one at the table favorable to me.

I ask myself, "Why did I quit again?" I think about the fact we have spent a little under $100K since I left. We are paying for our health insurance, which is not cheap, among other expenses we have incurred.

"*There is a certain peace in the insanity of this situation... Faith is believing everything will be ok, even when it looks disastrous.*"

I am terrified, yet calm. I know that sounds contradictory, but it is my state of mind. I am worried we will run out of money, yet I have faith we won't. There is a certain peace in the insanity of this situation. It is the peace that God will guide me through it. Faith is believing everything will be ok, even when it looks disastrous. Aimee, my former Administrator at GMSI, used to share many statements with me related to faith, the most famous being, "Fear tolerated = faith contaminated".

I miss my people, my friends, and my team. I have done everything I could to put them in a place to succeed, but now I don't know what will happen to them, and it makes me feel sorry I left.

Later in the evening, Wanda and I try to make amends. I just love my wife. I need her. The hateful things I think and write are from a place of frustration and angst. I wish she would find her way back to me, and to that place in her heart that used to make me feel invincible.

I still think we may be spending too much time together. Being stuck in the house too long may be just the thing to kill a relationship. I feel bad for those people in China that are quarantined. I am sure many married couples are ready to kill each other.

March 6, 2020

Today is the deadline for offers on GMSI. I see it as closure. One way or another, the future of my former company, and those who work there will be decided.

There are an exceptional number of signals that a major market crash is coming, and no one is listening to me. I post the following status on social media to alert investor friends that the news I am reading indicates a major selloff or recession is inevitable.

Investors. Pay attention.

Deutsche Bank's Torsten Slok believes that markets are pricing in a global recession. The question at this point for rates is whether the likely rebound in the Chinese PMI in March will be offset by a significant decline in ISM in the US and PMI in Europe.

The stock market is going to tank!

Simply put, money is nervous, and when money is nervous, financial markets lose. I believe there is a major market correction coming, and only a small handful of people are talking about it. This is what I have done every morning since the mid 90's. I read. These days, I can just bring my phone in the bathroom and conduct business while "taking care of business", if you get my drift.

I am still having issues with Wanda. I have purposely not shown Wanda any affection this week. I think she is happier about it. I feel like what we had is gone forever. Maybe I broke it, or maybe she did. In the end, it is still broken, and it doesn't matter who is at fault.

It's Fridate, but there is nothing romantic about this date. I have officially lost hope.

There is packing to get ready for our trip to Mexico tomorrow. You may have heard, it's the end of the world! Travel light. Coronavirus is now threatening our way of life. Many are infected; some are dying.

And here we are, the Guercios, packing the boogie boards and heading to Mexico for a little beach time to settle our nerves.

When the going gets rough, the rough go to the beach!

In truth, this trip has been planned for a while. So, in the morning, we will wake up and go to a little beach house in a place I consider heaven. Bahia de Kino, Mexico. Kino Bay. If the world is ending, then we should at least be by the tranquil seas of Mexico.

March 7, 2020 (A trip to Mexico for the End of the World.)

We woke up early and I started packing the truck. Wanda takes the dogs to boarding but no one is ready on time, as usual. We are the Guercio's. We are late for everything. I am not late for everything, they are, but I wear the mark of lateness by association.

We cross the border into Mexico and the checkpoint is empty. There are no other cars, and honestly, it's eerie. We arrive as the sun is setting, creating its brilliant tapestry of reds, orange, and blues in the clouds. If this is the end of the world, then the warmup act is visually impressive.

We are here to celebrate Abuema's birthday with a surprise party. While Wanda and I have not been getting along, she has sat next to me in the truck for the entire 6-hour drive, her hand on my leg, and mine in hers. Maybe the end of the world is an aphrodisiac.

I want to be clear; I am not a drinker. I may be able to drink, but I am not someone who has to drink, and while I write about my escapades with a variety of cocktails and libations, most days, I am sober.

With that being said, tonight is one of those nights I am drinking socially. But I am in Mexico and drinking here is an art form. Drinking in Mexico is a socially accepted part of the culture, and they are good at it. I am not. I am a puker.

There is already a slew of preparations in progress when we arrive at my sister-in-law's house, where the party will take place. I am greeted by my Brother-in-law with a hug and a beer, as we drink and prepare for the guests. This will continue for the next hour and a half until we hear Abuema pull up outside.

Abuema comes through the door unsuspecting, and as she enters everyone jumps out and yells, "Surprise!" She is shocked, and when she realizes how many have come to celebrate her, she starts to cry. We drink and laugh for hours, and there are all kinds of party trays, all containing meat. Wanda and I gave up meat for Lent. All drink and no food do not a sober Peter make.

Jesús asks me to run to the store with him. We are talking about our marriages. He is learning that "I do" sometimes means, "You can't". We laugh at the irony.

We stop at an OXXO, which is the largest chain of convenience stores in Mexico. As we pull up, a man is asking for money. He is obviously drunk, and as he approaches us, I notice his tattered shoes are held together with plastic bags and duct tape. I offer him my shoes, but he doesn't want them.

I give him 50 pesos and a couple of Marlboro Reds, and he starts singing to Jesús and I. He sings quite well, and I am convinced all the best singing talent in Mexico may come from the parking lot of an OXXO. Keep in mind, that I have been drinking.

My current drunken state, the nicotine high from the few cigarettes I have already smoked, no food, and a 6-hour drive, and I am getting as sloppy as a spring breaker let loose in an all-you-can-drink buffet.

We go back to the party, and instead of getting food, or doing something responsible, like not drinking, I break out the bottle of gin I have smuggled across the border. We finish the entire fifth in an hour and a half, and then German (pronounced "Hair-Mann" for my fellow gringo's) breaks out a bottle of vodka. In 3 hours, I proceed to get hammered. The fireworks are being staged, and I am the main attraction.

Back out at the truck, the scene has turned tragic. I have been smoking like a meth addict, and drinking like a league bowler, and now, it is all about to turn ugly. Jesús and I are sitting on the edge of my tailgate in the rain, smoking, drinking, and talking.

I have no idea what he is saying, or what I may have been responding to, but I stand up as I feel the first convulsions hit my duodenum. I am spasming like a dog about to heave up the grass he has eaten outside.

I look at Jesús and announce I am going to puke. It feels as if my digestive system has turned inside out, from my stomach to my nostrils. I am retching and heaving violently in front of the house, as party guests leave to find their cars. I don't care, I am too wasted to move. Some walk over and Jesús runs interference for me. Jesús steps in and accepts hugs and handshakes, shielding me from the social interaction. I am basically a vomit machine, spewing reliably every 10-20 seconds.

It's too late to help me, I am too far gone. I didn't cross the line; I jumped over it as if it were the Snake River Canyon and I was Evil Knievel. All in all, I drank 5 beers, 2 glasses of red wine, a shot of something that may have been dishwashing liquid or tequila, 3 strong gin and tonics, 2 vodka tonics, and a seltzer drink I found in someone's car. At some point, a man on a motorcycle drove up and handed me a bag of chicken wings. I thought it was a dream, but it turned out to be true; I ordered Uber Eats at some point, only aware of this because my family told me later.

It's like everything toxic is coming out of me, including my bad feelings towards Wanda, my guilt at leaving my employees and friends, the many friends that have died, the stress of having to constantly succeed, my disappointment with trying to save GMSI, not being able to get InfinityGo funded due to the China virus, and the pain of not being the CEO anymore.

It's all spilling out here in the rain, in front of my family's house in Mexico, and everything I have been carrying inside me, all the bad feelings and frustration, are flowing out into the street, bushes, and sidewalks. I lay here in the rain in Mexico, puking the hatred and disappointment of the past 8 months onto the tailgate of my truck, while the rain washes away any remaining remnants of my self-respect.

After an hour, I passed out on the tailgate of my truck, unable to move, so they left me in the rain, where I should be. Passed out and lifeless, like a dead fish thrown in a garbage dumpster. That's what they do with guys like me, former CEO's that boasted they would "Change the world".

I think to myself, "Just let me die", as I pass out again, loathing myself for being this way and losing it at Abuema's party.

As the rain falls, I am awakened by the sounds of someone in the truck. I hope they don't drive away with me, but I don't really care anymore. I can't move anyway. I am paralyzed by the immense amount of alcohol coursing through my veins. In fact, if they drive away, I will just fall out of the back of the truck at high speed and conclude my existence on this watery sphere. I think to myself, "It's been a good ride".

But then, a familiar voice whispers to me through the veil of tears and rain that have pooled on my eyes and face. Wanda leans in and asks, "Are you ok babe? Let me take you home". I can't see her face, or anything else for that matter. The rain and salt from my tears have temporarily sewn my eyes shut.

As I see the silhouette of her face, I am immediately humiliated I am in this position. But she is sympathetic. I apologize and she says it is not a big deal. It is raining hard, and I feel so bad. The world is spinning as Wanda drives away. I need air, and I open the window and peer my head out, and lay it down on my folded arms. I am hanging out of the car in the rain, like a carsick Great Dane. Too nauseous to put my head up, but if it is outside the car, I am ok for the ride home.

As we pull up to Abuema's house, I open the truck door while it's still moving, and stumble forward onto the street, unable to balance, and end up across the road, finally tackling a telephone pole. I prop myself up and puke whatever is left inside of me.

I am barely able to stand as I realize someone is holding me up. It's my Arielle. I am mortified. Mr. "In Control" is totally out of control. I hope my little kids can't see me.

I can't stop what is happening. I am powerless. "I hope I don't stop breathing", is the last thought I have before I pass out, clothes, and all. As I black out, I pray I do not have to puke anymore, and that everyone will forgive me for failing them, here in Mexico, at GMSI, and around the world.

I quit, and Guercio's never quit.

March 8, 2020

It's a day of reckoning. It all starts to come back to me. Much of what I thought was a dream really happened, and now I will have to face the music. It was all real, including ordering chicken from Uber Eats during Lent. I even failed God.

As I lay on my side, struggling to pry my eyelids open, I reflect on the past years of my life. I often punish myself for not seeing the amazing success I have enjoyed over the years. I did what everyone told me couldn't be done. But it was never good enough for me. I perceived elements of my success as a failure, partially because I didn't get rich; everyone else did.

"Even in my moments of success, I have found failure. I could have done better."

Generally, I am a positive and passionate person. But even in my moments of success, I have found failure. I could have done better. I could have helped someone more. I always have a reason not to accept my accomplishments at face value. I find the tarnish in silver linings. In that lies a character flaw that both drives me to achieve my goals and punishes me for reaching them.

After rising from my coffin, I make my way slowly down the marble stairs of Abuema's house. Cailyn greets me on the stairs with a big hug. "Dad, are you ok?"

In the kitchen, Wanda stands up from her seat at the table and hugs me. I hug her back, holding her close as I tell her how sorry I am for everything that happened last night.

Wanda hugs me tightly and tells me, "It's ok. I am not mad; we were just worried about you. I am sorry you feel bad, is there anything I can do?"

This is the compassion of a human being that loves her spouse. Not one that doesn't care about me. I pull her closer to me, and tell her, "Nothing babe, this is all I need". And some coffee.

I spend the day recovering, and later we head to church. Church is a different experience in Mexico. Profoundly serious and very holy. The mass is in Spanish; the message is about forgiveness, and, I realize I haven't forgiven myself. For anything. And there is a lot I have been carrying within my Judeo-Christian interior.

Perception is an interesting sensory skill. We respond to stimuli and perceive them as good or bad. We can also create something good or bad based on our perception. I am finding that many things in my life I perceived as bad, may have been the opposite.

Take my relationship with Wanda. I complain about many elements of our marriage, but maybe my perception that sex equals love was misplaced. I am about physical touch, and she is about acts of service. We don't speak the same love language, but it doesn't mean we aren't in love.

This newfound clarity will be the building block for a new Peter Guercio. Stronger, faster, more able to look at life through polarized lenses, rather than those of a kaleidoscope.

We enjoy a wonderful meal as a family. A family that easily forgave me for my indiscretion. Now all I must do is learn to forgive myself. Food fills my belly, and church and forgiveness will fill my soul. Joy is the missing element, and I won't find it until I can forgive myself for my failures. This will be easier said than done.

March 9, 2020

To Kino Bay, and beyond...

My hangover has been remedied with a steady diet of Mexican food, water, and love. I have been very introspective over the past 24 hours, my self-imposed therapy instigated by alcohol poisoning. What I found is that I blamed myself for many things that weren't my fault.

I take responsibility for the actions of others, or for situations that I feel I somehow caused. I need to break this cycle of self-perpetuated blame. I am not a martyr, so I should stop acting like one.

To circle back on my financial predictions from many days ago, the Dow dropped 2000 points and the S&P dropped over 7%. In one day. That is an enormous amount of wealth that was shed. I dread it will get much worse. The market is being driven down by fear. When the stock market drops like this, there is a very serious event that is spooking financial leaders, and none of that bodes well for the rest of us.

There is nothing I can do to influence the global economic picture and nothing else I can do to save my teammates at GMSI. I am beginning to accept that I didn't fail to find funding for InfinityGo; we just ran into a situation that I would consider force majeure. I didn't fail Wanda and she didn't fail me. We just ran into a software update problem that can be corrected by rebooting our OS.

And with that analogy in my head, I pack the truck and drive my family for a few days on a desolate stretch of beach in a magical land known as Kino Bay.

We drive the old road, the one with many old trucks held together with bailing wire and a prayer, riding on balding tires and rusty frames. All are driving in a deadly ballet, on this road Wanda calls the "Death Highway". The sun warms my face and soul, as we speed through the desert on our way to warmth and respite only Kino Bay delivers.

We arrive at the family house, unpack, and immediately walk 1000 feet up the street to "El Pargo Rojo", a beautiful seaside seafood cafe we eat at regularly when we are here. This is just what we needed. All of us.

Wanda is happily sipping her Pina Colada and I am holding my goblet filled with Margarita with both hands. The kids are happily snacking on chips and soon, it will be dark, and I will sleep the sleep that only occurs with the sound of breaking waves and the call of seabirds.

If there is a heaven on earth, it lies here, on the southwestern coast of Mexico, on the Sea of Cortez in a place called Bahia de Kino. This is a place I will call home someday, to live out my remaining years, happily planted with my toes in the sand, watching sunsets and dolphins while the world goes on without me. Honestly, I can't wait.

March 10, 2020

The day the earth stood still.

We woke this morning to an uncharacteristically tranquil sea. There is no wind, no sun, and no people. Kino is a small town, but a popular one. Today, there is no one. The lack of humanity is not the element that brings an air of isolation to our abode. The real overwhelming factor is the stillness of the sea. On any given day, the winds of the Pacific cross over the Baja Peninsula, bringing a constant breeze to this seashore. This morning it is overcast, calm, and serene, creating a scene of finality, or the calm before the storm.

And indeed, there is a storm brewing. Coronavirus is spreading throughout the world, financial markets are collapsing, Crude oil is tanking and for the first time in my life, I am faced with the harsh reality that the world may actually be ending. It sure feels like it is, and if it does, there is nowhere else I would want to be, than here at the sea, with my wife and kids.

While the world collapses around us, I take an early morning walk along the deserted beach, followed by a brisk paddle in the calm sea on our Kayak. Rain begins to fall around 11 AM. I have never seen it rain at the beach house, and the scene is beautiful and calming.

I checked the news of the world to see the stock market opened 1700 points lower, then made several large swings of over 1000 points throughout the day, closing with gains of more than 1100 points. It doesn't matter to me, I believe the market will correct itself again in the coming days, and volatility will rule the market.

We don't dwell on the financial news, nor the impending doom of Covid-19 that slowly disperses across the landscape of the globe. We are just in the moment.

I don't need to go back to the US. We could sell the house, cash out our investments, and live quietly here on the coast, making marlin tacos and margaritas for the tourists. I am serious about this, but Wanda immediately shoots down the idea. She wants our house in Queen Creek, and the mall, and the convenience of the fast pace of city life. Me? I just want to wear board shorts and a T-shirt and talk to tourists while they sip their drinks and eat my food. Maybe one day.

For now, we are full and happy, safe and sound, and while the world crumbles around us, I can't help but thank God for giving us this experience and time together. I am concerned about the future of mankind, but a large plate of steamed clams and a couple of strong margaritas dulls my immediate worry.

Little do I know what will come tomorrow.

March 11, 2020

The Dow dropped 1457 points today. We are officially in a bear market, and I believe the worst is yet to come. The big story today is that global economic markets are continuing to take a beating. I took to social media to share videos and a descriptive story about the day.

I know it's the end of the world, but I have an interesting story to tell. So, for one second, let's put aside the fact I think the market will go down another 3000 points. Forget we are all going to die from the common cold and democratic media sensationalism. Forget we are in an election year, and I can't wipe my ass because people are hoarding toilet paper. Yes, these are real end-of-day scenarios...

Oh yeah, the story. Watch the videos for the whole story, but to consolidate the day's events, please read on.

The rain from yesterday has subsided for now, but my weather radar shows a serious band of storms coming our way. We take advantage of this window of good weather before the rain returns by playing in the sea that is our backyard.

I am standing waist-deep in the calm water of Mexico, fishing. The kids are playing on their boogie boards and flying kites. There are no people around. No one, anywhere. We are alone on the beach and for miles, there is not a soul. Or so I thought...

As I cast my line to the sea, I caught Ben skimboarding out of the corner of my eye. I watch as he glides over the edge of the tiny breaking waves and down the beach. As I look to my left, I see something in the water that startles me. There, sitting in the ocean, waist-deep in water, is what looks to be a jackal. It could be a dog or a coyote, but where did he come from? I was just looking that way and there was nothing in that direction for miles as I surveyed the emptiness of the beach. A dog? From where? I was just looking that way and there was nothing. Now, a dog. In the water. Right there!

With great caution, I walk closer to the mystery guest, and he gallops over to me through the water, tail wagging. The kids and Wanda see this scene and run over. The Jackal is a dog with deformed back legs that point in the wrong direction like he was crushed or hit by a car.

As we inspect him, he licks us, and we all take turns petting this mysterious beach creature. Where the hell did he come from? "He just appeared!!", Ben screams to Wanda, and Cailyn chimes in, "We were right there and there was nothing. Then, he just showed up!"

Wanda and the kids go into rescue mode, and in no time produce a small bag of dog food someone left at the house and a makeshift water bowl. The creature scarfs the food and water with alarming speed. He must be starving and thirsty, as he gulps down large drinks of water.

I am startled by his appearance. The kids are not exaggerating. We have been here alone for hours and with the desolation of the beach, we would have seen him walking from a great distance. He just appeared out of thin air, and that is unsettling. I am just waiting for a scene from Cujo to develop, but for now, the kids play with their newfound apparition in the sand.

"Can we keep him, can we keep him?", the kids relentlessly ask me for 2 hours straight. I tell them I don't know this animal, and he could be sick, or violent, as said animal continues to lick them playfully. "Maybe he is just tasting them", I think to myself.

"He could be Jesus, Dad!", the kids try and convince me. "Yeah, he could be a dog disguised as Jesus and he is coming to us to test us before the end of the world", the kids argue, being they have heard my discussions over the past few days. But then Wanda looks at me and says, "Well, miracles happen every day for those that are open to them".

What? Wanda too? Let me get this straight. The kids and Wanda think this abandoned beach dog who appeared out of nowhere, and who may be a jackal, is actually Jesus. They try and convince me that it's Jesus, and he has come down from heaven to test us.

My science mind kicks into full rebuttal mode, asking them why they think this mangy and mangled dog-like creature could be the savior of the world. To which Cailyn responds, "He is here because he wants to see how we treat others who are less fortunate than us."

How can I argue with that? Indeed, we are facing a scenario that I could have never imagined. The world may very well be ending, and between COVID running rampant, the financial markets crashing and the latest trend, the hoarding of paper goods, there may be some truth to this.

I can't take any chances in these days of Armageddon. So now, against my will and better judgment, there is a jackal, who may be Jesus, living downstairs at the beach house.

They want to keep him. Of course, they do. It's the end of the world, and we are going to smuggle a dog, whose legs are bending backward, across the border to the "safety" of the USA, and its deadly Coronavirus and collapsing stock market. I couldn't script this better if I tried.

Just then, the calm of the day is broken as the wind picks up quickly, and soon, it is pouring. The dark foreboding clouds envelop the beach and the mountains around us. I don't believe in paranormal activity, but I can't deny the coincidence that has just occurred.

We are alone in Mexico; it's the end of the world and we have a beach jackal that may be Jesus that they want to take home with us to Arizona. Just when I thought this trip couldn't get any more bizarre.

As I sit back on the stairs in the rain, looking at the creature now casually lounging under the patio, I realize there is only one logical solution. I am going down the street for some Margaritas and Marlin tacos. If this is the end of the world, and Jesus is paying me a visit in his dog form, then I am going to need a cocktail and some fish before we move forward.

I am not sure why I am coming back home anyway. It's not like I have a job.

March 12, 2020

Black Thursday. As predicted, and I am not happy about being correct, the markets tank. The Dow drops by almost 2400 points in one day, the largest single-day drop on record.

It is pouring and has been off and on since we found the beach dog, now known as "Kino", named after his place of origin, here in Kino Bay. I am sure I am now committed to taking him home with us. We are going to take him to a local vet to get an assessment before I am forced to smuggle this stray across the border. I joke to myself, "Well, now I can add international smuggler to my resume".

My cousin Mike has called and warned me to come home. Food and toilet paper are disappearing from the shelves back home and there is talk from his contacts within the police department that the US Government will close the border. I can think of worse things than being stuck on the ocean, with nothing to sustain us but margaritas and fresh fish.

I once again take to social media to share my thoughts on the developing crisis we face around the world. I posted the following diatribe to my Facebook page.

Ok, listen. I am "confined" to this little house on the beach due to rain and ailing jackals, but while I am here a few words.

The Coronavirus hysteria is bullshit. So is the stock market crash. It is manipulation. This is insanity. And I fully hold the liberal media and some angry politicians responsible for this. Pelosi. Schumer. Those guys, lest there be confusion in my statement.

This, to me, is a clear case of a knee-jerk reaction to something that can be readily handled in a much more relaxed and intelligent fashion. I have seen a lot of this lately. (GMSI?)

Torpedoing our investments and 401ks will not get Trump out of office, it will get him re-elected. And don't get me started on force majeure, Marshall law, or freezing trading on the market. Global quarantine? WTF are we talking about here? For the flu? Please. Please, people, we are better than this. Cancel the NBA, NCAA, or Hockey? Hockey is played on Ice. As I see it, this is the only safe place to combat this virus. In the cold or the hot. I suggest hockey games for everyone. Or beach time. If the world is ending, let's make it a pleasurable experience.

So, let's help each other through these difficult times. Let's be smart and committed to solutions. Closing the world down and hiding is for cowards. China isn't hiding. Neither is Russia. Count on it. Wake up people. We are being handed a bullshit sandwich and not a little one. A party sub. Stop eating it. It's not real. It's full of nonsense with a side of misinformation. Have the salad. It's healthy.

And if I am wrong, well then, we will all be dead and broke soon, so it won't matter what you think of my opinion, as if you ever did anyway.

Me? I am going to make some coffee and watch the rain on the ocean, while seabirds dive into the water to catch their morning meals. Life didn't stop here. It's another day of living for all. Take a cue from nature. Live. Live your life. Don't believe the hype. It's not real. You are in the Matrix, and I want to help you unplug. If we are all smart, we will watch the market degrade and be ready to buy. There will be billions made in the recovering markets. I am going all in on Amazon, Berkshire Hathaway, and Boeing. No head in the sand here. Just some Marlin tacos, sunshine, and stray animals.

I am at peace with all of this now. Thanks for listening. I have to go check on our pet jackal now.

Have a good end of the world. Xo

The rainy day ends with a setting sun that pushes its way through the canopy of storm clouds. The sun never quits. It shines through the darkest days, and from now on, I am going to take a cue from the sun and shine brilliantly, even through the blackest skies.

March 13, 2020

"Life will find a way". This is not my quote, but a line from *Jurassic Park*. Jeff Goldblum made this statement after facing the ludicrous assumption that the dinosaurs would not reproduce. I love this statement because it rings true. No matter how dark it looks, life finds a way.

I have to tend to a jackal that may be Jesus. I walk the little castaway down the beach and back again. He seems tame. I am getting used to him, and while I don't want to smuggle animals across an international border, that is exactly what we are planning to do.

The market has risen with the sun, and at the bell, the Dow closes up almost 2000 points. I didn't expect that, but this gives me renewed confidence that global markets have read my post and are taking their heads out of the sand. It is a good day to be alive, and the world is still here.

We have decided to pack up and head home at the suggestion of our family in the USA. There are widespread shortages of essentials, like meat, cleaning supplies, and toilet paper. Mexico still has all those things, and we are coming home stocked with toilet paper and cleaning wipes, and we intend on sharing with those we love.

Before we leave, the kids and I play in the surf. Life is returning to as normal as it can be with the events of the past week, and what is still to come. That's the thing about worry. It stops you from being in the moment.

We leave Kino Bay and my mind wanders. Will I ever be able to come back here? What if the virus spreads here? What if the world ends?

These thoughts are broken by the sound of the kids screaming that the beach dog who may be Jesus is carsick and throwing up in the backseat. You think if the dog were Jesus, he wouldn't get carsick. I am starting to have my doubts this animal is the messiah.

March 14, 2020

We are packed and ready to go home. I have been reading reports that President Trump is going to close the borders to the USA, so we have to hurry. Abuema seems melancholy as we wave goodbye. We told her we would see her soon, but I feel like that may not be true. I don't know what will happen over the coming weeks, but I pray that this panic will subside, the virus will not spread, and that we can get back to our regularly scheduled lives.

March 15, 2020

Holy crap on a cracker! Let the hunting and foraging begin. We returned home late last night and even though I was tired from the long drive, I went to our local supermarket to grab some milk. What a difference a week makes. When I left, there was meat, fish and vegetables, canned goods, and toilet paper. A week later, the shelves are barren. NOTHING!

I went out early again this morning to 3 different stores and it is pretty much the same all over. Forget disinfecting wipes or hand sanitizer, toilet paper, or paper towels. Even paper plates and napkins are gone.

I spend the morning piecing together whatever is available, and I plan to stock up on meats and roasts that can be frozen. If I can find them. I will just go out each morning, hoping the shelves are stocked at night. I didn't expect this kind of panic from Americans, but here we are, panicking.

It's Sunday and I am ready to go to church and talk to God. I have a lot to say. As we file in, we are told that there will be no handshaking amongst the congregation due to Covid concerns.

After mass, we go to Olive Garden. Once inside, we are surprised to see they have been seating people at every other table. It is something they call Social Distancing, and they are implementing the procedure in response to the recent declaration of a state of emergency by the US Health Office.

Maybe we will just get this to go...

March 16, 2020

This morning, I woke early for yet another venture to the wilds of Queen Creek to hunt for meat and cleaning supplies. It is early, before 7 AM, and the parking lot at my local supermarket is packed.

I notice a congregation of people huddled around the empty cases of meat. They just stand and rock, frozen by the harsh realization that there is no meat in the case. "Meat Zombies". While they stare in disbelief, I swoop in and leave quietly with a big bag of chicken wings and a tri-tip, never shaking them from their apocalyptic trance.

The scene is surreal as I turn down the aisle where paper goods are supposed to be. There is nothing but more zombies, paper zombies, and they too rock back and forth, staring at the empty shelves. This is real and I write it exactly as I live it.

I need to see my friend Rex. I have missed him a lot since he got sick. We spent every day together for the past 27 years, and then he left. I share the latest happenings with him. He once again gives me the words of encouragement he always has.

"Bro, you're you. You will find a way to be successful, and this InfinityGo idea is amazing. Just keep going!" He says this knowing we are facing a global epidemic, which has now been classified by the WHO as a pandemic. This is why I have always loved him. He didn't care about the negative aspects of what we faced; he just knew I would find a way. He believes in me more than anyone else ever has.

I leave Rex and meet with the CEO of the company I have been consulting. While I want to help him save his company, I deliver the news no business owner wants to hear. "I can't help you and I believe in light of recent events; you should shut your company down". He is thankful for my honesty, and I leave the meeting feeling horrible for him, his wife, and all the work he has put in.

Later in the day, as I cook on my grill, I watch as the stock market implodes. By the end of the day, the Dow will shed almost 3000 points.

On March 13th, I posted the following prediction on social media.

1. *The Dow will see a low of 18500 and then recover.*
2. *Commodities and Oil will see the widest swings.*
3. *Transport and Airlines will recover most losses by year-end.*
4. *Amazon, Walmart, and Costco will all outperform speculation.*
5. *Those who see the election as a watershed for the economy will be sorely disappointed. Either way, the run-up to the election will create a volatile mix of uncertainty and aggressive investment tactics. Hold on for a bumpy ride. If I were to draw a histogram,*

it would look like the heartbeat of a crack addict at 3 am after a 5-day binge.

All in all, everything will be ok. Billions will be made. We are going to be ok. My "Presidential" advice would be this. "Wash your hands and don't lick handrails". I think this is sage advice.

It turns out my predictions were not only correct but accurate within a small margin. I am now being called Nostradamus in my Social Media circles, and I kind of like it.

March 17, 2020

Happy St. Patrick's Day. There will be no celebrations though. The country is on the verge of shutting down. The Governor of Arizona is discussing closing schools, churches, and restaurants as a way of mitigating infection risk. How do you shut a country down and recover?

As I write these words, I receive an email from our pastor, Father Sergio, that the bishop has suspended masses indefinitely. I am deeply saddened. I need church and the calm and peace it brings me. We are allowed to go to the supermarket, but not church. We need God now more than ever.

March 18, 2020

The Dow dropped another 1300 points and Oil dropped to an 18-year low. It's a bloodbath and Coronavirus has taken hold around the globe. It sure feels like the end of the world.

The schools are going to close. The church is closed and now the talk is closing the country down. Factories, businesses, and non-essential workers are all going to be asked to stay home. This is alarming because it makes me believe this is more serious than anyone realizes, and the reason for shutting everything down is that the government has no way to stop this.

I am taking my mom to the vascular doctor. When we arrive, they ask me to wait outside, and they take our temperatures. I would never have imagined this would be the way we would live our lives. Separated and distanced, isolated, and segregated. This is America, not Russia!

Social distancing is the new buzzword for this year, and I don't like it. You might as well call it social isolation because that is what it is. I understand the need to distance ourselves from each other to stop the spread of disease, but this whole thing is starting to look like a power grab, but I don't know by whom.

March 19, 2020

I have been home for the better part of 9 months. I thought I would be alone, but now, in the wake of COVID-19, I am going to be joined by the entirety of humanity, and no one has toilet paper.

We are all staying home, together. I never would have predicted this, and the irony is not lost on me that I left work to redirect my life, and today, I will have plenty of company in restment. An entire country of my peers.

I am totally lost. InfinityGo is dead for now. There is no way to move forward in an environment where no one can leave the house. I can't get a job, companies are shutting down, furloughing workers and those that are open are mostly essential services--hospitals and doctors, food stores, and home improvement places.

I am certain Amazon, Walmart, Target, and other big retailers will make a lot of money on all this, as we are being forced to stay home; the only thing we can do is shop online or go to the open stores. But what about the businesses that close? How will they recover? And their employees? How are they going to live without a paycheck?

I wrote something to my CPA, partly about my tax return, partly to let her know I am ok. This email summarizes my thoughts on the past few days since we returned.

Dear Cathy,

We made it back from Mexico and were greeted to the chaos of the end of the world. :)

We spent the past few days hunting and foraging. I wrote about it in my new book, and I wanted to share a quick excerpt I hope will make you smile:

"I feel I have reverted to a modern-day caveman, solely intent on foraging early morning openings of Safeway and Walmart to find bare essentials like toilet paper, paper towels, meat, chicken, pasta, and rice. I am hunting for roasts, hot dogs, and eggs. Butter is a commodity reserved for society's elite--not a mere peasant like me.

In these ends of days, we are reminded of what is most important in life. Rich or poor, we all require the same essentials. It is like a car. Ferraris or Yugo, all need gas. I am at ease with this notion, the reality that we erect mass structures, flaunting our wealth, like the women of the red-light districts of Amsterdam selling their sex. We hold it out like an appendage of ourselves, but it is a facade. These are to distract from the fact that at the very core of our existence, all we really need is two-ply toilet paper, in the jumbo pack. And it is with this vision, firmly tethered to my subconsciousness, that I lean back in my seat and smile. We are defined by our needs to wipe our asses. My, how far we have fallen. :-)"

Take care and call me about my homeschool expenses, Expenses related to forming my new Company, 1095-C, and understated expenses for health Insurance.

Hope you are having a peaceful and healthy sequestering.

P

March 20, 2020

The Dow drops another 900 points. Boeing is wiped out. My mom's nest egg is gone, as well as my supposed inheritance. Our investments have all tanked.

The good news is President Trump is moving quickly to aid those affected most by these chains of events. He has passed legislation allowing for extended unemployment and paid sick leave, and there is discussion about a stimulus package that will aid businesses. Where is all this money going to come from? The short answer is simple, from you and me. The taxpayer. The slaves to our system.

It is a bad day for many, as they have lost everything they worked for. I am at a loss on how to help myself, or anyone around me, so I do what I can control. I cook.

I read the news and find the border between Mexico and the USA is now closed. Maybe I should have just stayed in Mexico. At least I could fish for dinner, and there was plenty of toilet paper.

This is our new normal. We wake up, listen to the bad news of the day, and try and get things done so as not to dwell on the craziness surrounding us. We go to bed early, hoping this madness will end when we wake up, but it doesn't. It's Groundhog Day, and the world saw its shadow.

March 21, 2020

I am up early, as always, and I read the news, but I don't care anymore. Here is the headline. *"Everything is fucked, go back to bed".*

Wanda needs to get up soon to pick up her brother. I tell her I can't live like this, with fear and worry, and that despite everything going on, we need to keep living our lives. She agrees and our new mantra will be, "Live for the day", as it has been since I was in my twenties.

Tomorrow is Sunday and I am heading to the lake. I am looking forward to it, even though it will be cold. I need church. Wanda said our church will begin to have masses televised so we can watch them at home. The church is closed, but I can buy a fridge at Home Depot. Makes perfect sense.

March 22, 2020

End of the world update for Sunday, 3-22-20.
We are holding up well. We ate well over the past few days. We are learning to eat all our leftovers in rotation, in an effort not to waste food. Wanda has been a powerful ally in the face of confinement. I still look at her with the same zeal and passion as when we met. She has asked me to tone it down repeatedly.

I get to spend tons of time with my family. There was a time not too long ago when I was traveling the world, and I would briefly pass them on any given Sunday and give them a kiss and a hug in between packing for the next trip.

Now, I wake up early, get my coffee, let the dogs out and I write. Wanda and the kids eventually wake up and we have breakfast together. Wanda home schools and I do whatever it is I am doing these days, and we meet back in the middle for lunches and dinners.

I don't think our family has ever been closer than since I left my job. I am happy spending my days with them. You could say I was an early adopter of social distancing and quarantine. Self-imposed of course.

I used to be a CEO and now I am a hunter-forager. It is eerie sometimes, wandering in the early morning, wondering if in one moment all will change. And then I remind myself, that it already has.

I expect the next few days to be pivotal. I will also expect another blood bath on Wall Street. I will continue to remain hopeful that we recover from this but I'm counting my blessings and thanking God for every minute I am together with Wanda and the kids.

The Jackal (Formerly known as the "Jesus Jackal") is doing great. He is becoming a productive member of the family and continues to work on his urination skills outside the house. He still looks to the South, wondering where the beach is, but he is adapting to suburban life and is considering joining a hot yoga group.

All is well here. We hope your end of the world is relaxing and uneventful. Say some prayers.

March 23, 2020

End of the world update for 3-23.

The one good thing about being sequestered is that Amazon still delivers, and I can get all the projects I have been putting off completed. When life gives you lemons...

We surprised Ben with his first cellphone. He cried. He was shocked. It made me feel good to see him happy. We need more joy in the world, especially the kind that comes from bringing others happiness.

Wanda homeschooled, as usual. She is amazing. And super-hot, for an older woman. (She will kill me for that.)

Wanda implored me to take this situation and CDC guidelines more seriously and banned me from playing golf today due to a high exposure risk. I told her that this was nonsense and that I was going. She responded with, "Sure, go, but when you return you will be banished to the guest room, where you will shower, disinfect, and live in isolation for the next 14-21 days." Needless to say, I stayed home.

We shall see what today brings. The stock market is almost at the bottom. We closed with another day of losses at 18,591. I called the bottom at 18,500 and I passionately believe the bleeding will stop on news of stimulus help from the government. Get ready to buy! Hope you are all having a wonderful and secure end of the world.

March 24, 2020

It appears as if my premonition of a market rebound from 18,500 is holding true. The Dow bounced over 2000 points in a positive direction based on hope the government stimulus package will be approved. I want to buy but I have a limited amount of capital and I can't risk it like I could in the past when I was working. I estimate that I will miss a huge opportunity to make a lot of money.

I also received my new phone, a Samsung Galaxy Note 10+. It is gigantic and I pulled a hammy and aggravated my hernia just taking it from its massive box. I am breaking out my old Motorola razor just in case it can be used as a transporter. Beam me up, Scotty!

I will remain hopeful we are back on track and that the country will see a speedy recovery, a decline in new cases of the virus, and that Steven Spielberg was wrong when he wrote *The Stand.*

I miss the Rockland Bakery and the magical treats they baked. If I close my eyes, I can still imagine cannoli and cookies of rainbow and black and white. One day, I will tell my grandkids of these times.

Good day sir or madam.

March 25, 2020

Up early to see what I can find at the stores. Nothing much is going on today, other than the continued amazing climb of the stock market. I hope everything recovers, whether I make money or not. So many people lost money, it would be nice to see them trim some of their losses. The big news of our day is that I found 2 packages of toilet paper and two rolls of paper towels. In this new world, this is considered a bounty! Not the paper towel brand, as they only had generics.

March 26, 2020

I did stuff around the house today. Spent the evening in bed with Wanda watching *This is Us* and reading and playing with gadgets. I wanted to play with Wanda. I love her so much. My birthday wish will be the same as my Christmas wish. Time alone with her, even if her libido has died along with the dream I had of an active sex life.

March 27, 2020

We are out of creamer and iced tea, so I wake up early to fight zombies. I headed to Safeway. They do not have the Lindy's ice we like, which is disappointing as they have become my staple snack.

I have not eaten meat since the beginning of Lent. We are surviving our end of the world and Lent without red meat. Sometimes the menu choices are limited, but we made our commitment, and we intend to honor them.

Kiyoshi Tamura, my former partner in Japan, wrote me last night. How I miss my friends around the world. He has scaled back his operation to meet the demands of the virus, but he is ok. Out of all the people I have met in my travels, Kiyoshi-San has been one of the most instrumental in showing me how to run a business and live life. He is my Sensei.

I miss being the CEO of the old GMSI, The one before Heraeus. The one that put friendship and trust at the forefront of everything we did, with customers, vendors, employees, and contractors. We lived and worked the ideals of Pride, Accountability, and Focus. I am most proud of the cultures I created. We overcame massive adversity and thrived when we should not have.

We did this because we developed relationships. We had the trust of our clients, and we delivered where others could not. Not always, but consistently more than we failed, which is all anyone can ask for in life. It was exceedingly difficult, but we did what many could not do, and we did it as a team. I will always hold that as my greatest source of pride and accomplishment. We did what others could not, with fewer resources and less time, because we believed we could.

I hope I will have the opportunity to lead people again, or even better, to teach others what I have learned. Dr. Ron agrees that I should put a seminar together and do motivational speaking. I would like that. I will use this book as part of a platform.

March 28, 2020

It is a new day, and we are still alive. Day 18 of the end of the world saw a drop in the stock market of over 900 points. I still think there is much blood to give, with employment numbers and Q1 reporting due in the coming weeks. However, I believe we are going to stabilize and get through this.

Yesterday was a day of getting projects done. I know Wanda is not feeling tip-top right now, so I don't push the subject of romance. I love her for more than her body.

I am redirecting my lust for her into doing things for her around the house. Cooking, fixing, getting. These are all her love languages. Acts of Service. I am physical touch and words of affirmation. Wanda puts little importance on physical touch or words of affirmation unless it involves physically touching me in the form of strangulation! In the end, we make it work. Love makes it work.

A pandemic put a damper on what I was doing for InfinityGo or the GMSI deal, but I am taking it in stride and focusing on other things. Like the fact I get to spend so much time at home, a stark contrast to life over a year prior. I traveled the world monthly in the past, and now my travels take me to grocery stores and megastores. It is ok. I am happy.

"*I am happy.*"

It has taken me a long time to say those words.

I know I sound like an NBA star thanking God first after some great achievement, but as you may be aware, I am a pretty big fan of God and Jesus. They are my foundation. My faith is in a better place, a better way. And so, even in the face of these ends of times, I have faith.

We watched a beautiful mass at the Vatican with the Pope yesterday. The words were sound and thoughtful, and the message was clear. In times of great strife, faith is always the answer.

In God we trust. Or we should. Live and let live, but hopefully, in doing so, we can be tolerant of each other. That is the true test, to love others even when they do not agree with you, or like you. I have always tried to do this. Except Al Qaeda. How do you love the enemy? I am not sure, but Jesus knew something we did not.

In many ways, my dreams came true. Partly because I had to make them happen, but partly because I took a unique approach to life. I put my faith in God, and I pushed through with the faith that he was guiding me and that Jesus was with me every step of the way. And in the end, I accomplished what most told me was impossible.

There is something more that has guided me through this life. I PRAYED for the things I received, and for the support and guidance of the Lord when things were insurmountable. We overcame them. I asked for help, strength, support, safety, clarity, patience, forgiveness, and so many more things. I asked for the blessings of others, of friends and family, coworkers, and people I didn't even know. I asked for the pain of others to be lifted, for strength, and for the healing of those afflicted with cancer and other diseases. And many times, my prayers were answered, but sometimes, they were not. My dad and Stephen were a couple of those.

In so many instances I have sat in a plane, high over the world, talking to God. Asking him for his guidance, healing, or help in some situations. I believe I am being transformed. I have seen what is important in life. Part of that is due to my faith. Most of it is due to love. The love of others and the love I give to others. I am convinced that there is a God because love exists.

Many will judge the statements I make about faith and God. One size doesn't fit all, but you need to be willing to try it on first. Maybe, I will lead those who judge me to a better understanding, so they may choose to believe.

But *"Then again, maybe they won't."* Sorry, Judy Blume.

March 29, 2020

It's another day of the end of the world. We are still here. We have food, power, water, shelter, and Netflix. We will be ok.

I am trying to get into a routine again. I am not sure I want to, but my subconscious is ready for structure. I am getting an average of 6 hours of sleep per night.

I made a pot of sausages, peppers, and onions a la Denis. My dad loved this dish, and I love to eat it still. I miss my dad. I missed so much not having him around, but his memory feeds me. I am looking at his picture right now, and he is smiling back at me, so in his honor, I continue to push forward, as I have since that night I held his hand as he took his last breath. It is hard to grow up without a parent.

I have developed a scratchy throat and a little cough. I am not freaking out, but I am aware. It's funny, anyone who coughs or sneezes is now looked at as a possible carrier of this disease. We are living in scary times.

Coughing is the new leprosy.

March 30, 2020

Woke up at 4 AM coughing uncontrollably. Not Coronavirus, just seasonal allergies, I think. I will keep telling myself this fact until it is reality. So many people are sick across the world, the USA included. I am concerned the virus is uncontainable, and statistically speaking, it most surely looks like it is spiraling out of control. I have used statistical analysis most of my life, but question certain statistics, because they can be biased to support a specific output. I don't always trust the stats I read for this reason.

But there is one bright mind I do trust. Steven Millman, friend and noted statistician, has presented several charts detailing his analysis, and if he is correct, we are going to be faced with an outbreak of catastrophic proportions. Based on his numbers, and my own extrapolations, we could be looking at over 5 million people infected over the next 3 weeks, and if the totals track as predicted, global deaths of upwards of 1 million people, or more.

His chart presents the following data based on reported deaths, and the trend of newly infected cases. He says the height of this will be mid-April. I tend to agree. Steven prefaces the chart with this paragraph. The only thing that matters to me is his first sentence, as he just laid out a survival plan. He writes:

"Also, PLEASE REMEMBER that if we stop mitigation efforts, the rate will increase again. Lifting mitigation efforts before this curve flattens almost completely (will look horizontal) will be DISASTROUS. We are NOT going to be back to work by Easter. By Easter we will be at over a million confirmed cases in the US, many times that number actually infected, and over 50,000 dead at current rates. PLEASE stay home."

President Trump announced yesterday that he is extending the social distancing practices in place until April 30. I hope this will be enough to stop the deaths and infections, but my fear is many are going to get sick, and others infected will die. I pray for the world.

All this, and it's my 55th birthday tomorrow. "I am having a party, and you are all NOT invited" would be the message on my invitations. I will be staying home, as I promised Wanda I would stop taking unnecessary risks and exposing us to possible infection.

The irony of this situation for me is that I always had a plan. At GMSI or home, I had thought about what I was going to do, and we put it on the calendar and did it. Wanda too. But here we are, both of us schedulers and nothing to schedule. We cannot go anywhere.

I pray. A lot. Somehow, I do not think our prayers will be enough this time. I think God is mad, and he is going to share another side of what our lives could be like if we do not get our act together. I pray he will be merciful and will get bored of this exercise quickly.

March 31st, 2020 (The 55th year of my birth, the Day I admit I may have Covid 19)

I woke up early, coughing and hacking. "I am ok, I am ok!!" I keep telling myself that I will be ok, but I am starting to worry. I keep getting these weird, base-of-my-neck headaches. My elbows and joints are sore. And why is my throat so damn scratchy?

The day of my birth has always been a day I take off from work and go to the lake or stay home with Wanda and do something together. Today, I have the day off due to covid-induced exile. The end of the world is here, and I am alone with my family. That makes me happy.

I am feeling a little tired today, sluggish I guess is the word.

It is reported that there is a high likelihood the governor will impose a "stay at home" order, effectively tightening restrictions on movement around town, imposing a curfew, and probably shutting down all non-essential business even further. Happy birthday to me.

I make myself an everything bagel with salmon cream cheese and about 4 ounces of fresh Nova Salmon. A sandwich that would make a rabbi blush. I happily devour the sandwich but notice it is not as tasty as usual. I cannot put my finger on it. Something, well...like taste. The coffee I made tastes weird too.

As I eat, I read a slew of info on the Covid virus. One of the symptoms is now, neck pain. I have neck pain. A scratchy throat and dry cough. I have that too. A loss of taste? Wait, I am having this issue also. Oh God, I think I am getting sick. Not now God, please, my family needs me.

I read the CDC, WHO, and European accounts of people who had the virus and I am worried. I think I have Coronavirus. "I have to fight this!!", somehow trying to convince myself that I could overcome the fatigue, aches, and stiffness welling in my body. Sadly, I cannot. I am embarrassed and ashamed.

I fought Wanda and she was right. The worst part is I have put my wife and kids at risk of getting sick. I feel terrible. For the first time, I am aware that my actions affect others. I am feeling a little feverish but have no fever. I am worried. I started slamming vitamins, Amoxycillin, and doses of ibuprofen, acetaminophen, and Sudafedrin. I am standing at the medicine cabinet wondering what else I can take to rid myself of the plague I feel living inside of me. I seriously consider a mix of hormone pills, shaving products, and antacids, but pull myself back from the edge before things get weird.

Wanda decides she wants to give me a birthday massage. Normally, I would be expecting something a little more sexually oriented, you know, being my birthday and all, but before long, I fall asleep. Goodnight and a happy Covid birthday to me. For the first time in my life, I think there is a real possibility I may die soon.

The will to fight to live resides in all of us. It is only greater than the will to die by a few breaths.

11

April, 2020

April 1, 2020

It's Wanda's dad's birthday today. I really loved him, even though I only knew him for a short time. His death shocked all of us, and Wanda and her family still struggle with his untimely death.

I woke up and said a prayer, and then admitted to myself that my present health condition may have been misdiagnosed by me, Dr. "Duzentknowshit." I do not think this is seasonal allergies. I am not sure what I should do. I do not want to go to the hospital to get a tube shoved down my throat.

The real issue is I do not want to go because I don't want a health care professional to put a tube up my urethra. Yeah, mental note, when I am in such a physical condition that it requires a tube be inserted into the end of my penis, please knock me out by any means possible. A shot of morphine or a Jewish mother's pocketbook. Either will work effectively.

I have the chills and I tell Wanda, so she moves close and lets me hold her to warm up. She keeps telling me how hot I am, but she is talking about my body temp not my appearance. I drift to sleep, frequently coughing and feverish.

April 2, 2020

I did not sleep well. I took tons of meds and woke up early. I am sluggish but ready for golf. I am not really ready, but I am going anyway. It's my birthday golf and may be the last round I ever play.

I arrived at the golf course, but my heart isn't in it today. I tell Mike and Derek I am not feeling well, and that I think it's best if I take my own cart and keep my distance. No high fives or hugs, not that I feel I will do anything worthy of such revelry.

I golfed well in the beginning, but by the 9th hole, I am having trouble hitting the ball. My body is aching, and I think I have a fever. By the 15th hole, I am done. All I can think about is going home.

I have a fever. There, I said it out loud. I can't take a chance of getting my family sick, so I tell Wanda I am going into the guest room for a rest. I will end up there for the next 14 days or so. I am sick, and I am about to suffer what can only be described as torture. I feel for those dying from this virus. It's bad stuff. The fever and the aches are like having the flu, but it is "the cough" that is the real issue.

It is a deep and guttural cough, robbing me of air and paining my midsection into spasms. Once I finish the coughing fit, I lay wasted, gasping for air. I lay, about to die of suffocation. It is that kind of panic I have always feared. Being suffocated.

April 3, 2020, to April 11, 2020.

Alone and sick. I have something, the virus probably, but I do not die. I just feel like it. On April 4th, at 2:30 in the morning, I feel as if I am breathing my last breaths. I have been coughing nonstop for the past 2 days, and now, I am struggling to breathe. I am suffocating.

This is my worst fear. When I used to surf, my greatest fear wasn't sharks, it was drowning. And now, I am living this experience through every coughing fit I have. They are more frequent, and the dry, scratchy tickle in my throat continues to make me cough and wretch uncontrollably, robbing me of my ability to breathe in, and drowning me without any water. I am panicking as I struggle to breathe just enough to serve the next coughing fit. The pain of the body aches leaves me nearly paralyzed, so I can't move to get comfortable.

This continues for the next few hours as I pray deeply that God will spare me. "Please God, don't let me die. I have so much to live for. Wanda and the kids need me, and to make matters worse, I don't have life insurance anymore. You were my insurance, Lord; please renew my policy!"

In this dark moment, I took my phone off the charger and began to write to Wanda.

Dear Wanda,

You were right. If I die, it is because you were right. I should have taken more precautions and now, I am lying in the bed in our guestroom, and I am fighting for my life. I can't tell you this, because I don't want to scare you and it is the middle of the night. If I am to die, I would rather be here, with you guys, although I am crying at the thought of you or the kids finding my lifeless body here. I can't move though. I have no energy to get up anymore. I am scared.

I am writing this in case something happens to me. I have prayed, but I fear I am dying. I am sorry I didn't listen to you. Now, or many other times in the past. You are such a smart woman, and I should have listened to you more. Many times, you are right, but I am just too stubborn and thick-headed to accept that you may know more than me. I am sorry for that. I should have listened more, instead of speaking. I am sorry for that too.

I have loved you and been in love with you since the early days of our relationship. You were different, babe. You were everything I ever wanted, and because of that, I asked you to marry me, even though I swore that after my divorce, I would never get married again. I wanted to have a life with you. I wanted to have kids with you. I wanted to devote my love and life to you.

I have done my best to make your dreams come true, just like I promised you long ago. It has taken an enormous toll on me. I am so tired and broken. I tried to carry everyone on my shoulders, including you and our family, but now I am unable to carry myself to the bathroom. I gave everything I had. I have nothing left to give now. I feel like I let you down. Like I let everyone down. I am sorry about that too. Please tell everyone at GMSI and all my clients that I love them and appreciate every one. My mom and sisters too.

I just finished another coughing fit. I think I broke my rib or my diaphragm. I can't breathe. Just know that I love you, and I always will. You are my world, Wanda, and that's why I get so mad when we fight. I wanted to be close, so I quit my career to be with you and the kids. I have no life insurance anymore, but take all the money in the bank, my 401K, and sell all my stuff. Give my stuff to all the kids. Sell the house and start a new life. Just liquidate. The house and everything in it are just stuff. It doesn't matter. Live a happy life and know that despite all our fights and struggles, I was happiest with you and the kids in my life.

I am sorry for leaving you. I will always love you. Remember me.

I wrote those words in the middle of the night, thinking I would die in my sleep. Not a bad way to go. My anxiety was at an all-time high. I was struggling to breathe, fighting the urge to cough, and crying because I felt so guilty that I had let everything spiral out of control.

To my surprise and relief, I woke up the next day. Still extremely sick, but alive. Wanda came into my room and checked on me. I didn't tell her of the note, but I shared my agony. She knew. She had already spoken to my mom, who called my doctor and friend, Petar Novakovic. He immediately called me via video chat on my phone. He prescribed a Z Pak and Ivermectin and warned me that if I was unable to breathe, I would have to go to the hospital. I talked to them too. They assured me that unless my situation was life-threatening, please don't come. How comforting.

I followed the CDC guidelines and called an emergency hotline, where I was asked to answer 20 questions about my condition. I was instructed to stay home, away from people, and quarantine. They also suggested that if the symptoms became life-threatening, to go to the hospital.

For the next 3 days, I take the medication and suffer brutally. I endure countless hours of fitful coughing and pain, shortness of breath, and exhaustion. Nothing helps, no position is comfortable. The medicine helped my fever break on the 4th day, and my symptoms slowly began to subside. I am mentally and physically exhausted, but I believe I am healing.

I thank Wanda, my mom, and Dr. Novakovic for taking care of me. I am going to live, but this is the first time in my life I felt what it was like to die. I wonder if my father felt this way.

The difficult thing about all this is there is no known treatment currently. I could have easily died, but I didn't. Others will not be so lucky. I can see why this disease kills so many elderly people. I am a strong man, and this floored me.

In the days and weeks that follow, I will continue to struggle for air. Long conversations are out of the question, as I get winded too easily. Going up and down our stairs at the house leaves me breathless. I can't taste or smell anything. Food is tasteless. Drinks are tasteless and the lingering cough is less severe, but still there. It will take me 2 months to feel better.

My depression of the past months turns to renewal. Easter is coming; I am feeling a new and uplifting clarity. I don't want to die.

"I can't change many things, but I can change the way I deal with them."

I am going to be more patient with Wanda and the kids. I am going to stop worrying about things that aren't important. I can't change many things, but I can change the way I deal with them. And I am going to finish this book and make it a best seller.

I will find a way to get InfinityGo off the ground and I am going to focus on getting across the finish line in all aspects of my life.

Thank you, God, for listening, and for giving me a chance to finish telling my story.

April 12, 2020

Easter! He has risen! A time for joy and hope. I am immensely grateful to be writing these words, as a week ago, I couldn't even sit up, let alone write a single word, other than the note I struggled to write to Wanda.

The vet calls about Kino. He is going to be sick for the rest of his life. We wrestle with this, but it is suggested we consider euthanasia. We agree to give it more time. I was just given a new lease on life, and I don't want to be the judge and jury on our sick castaway.

We celebrate the resurrection of Christ on this day and struggle with the God-like decision we must make concerning the fate of the Jesus Jackal. This is the exact situation I wanted to avoid. We have endangered Wally and our kids, but Kino doesn't know any better. He is a street dog. We gave him a home, and we will try and save him.

We remain hopeful and continue to try and live as normal a life as possible. I still fear the worst is ahead of us. Not from the virus, but from the economic damage this has caused, and the unrest that will surely follow.

I think back to that week in Mexico. It looked different. It felt different. The vibe, the sky, the beach, the house, the weather. All of it. It felt like the end of the world, and then I came back to the USA to the reality that it was.

"I would like to create a culture within the corporate landscape that cradles my ideals. Pride, Accountability and Focus...determination and resilience, and above all, consideration of others."

This whole experience has changed me. I am not afraid anymore to live my way. I am putting my faith in God and my ability, and I don't want to be shackled to the confines of corporate slavery. I would like to create a culture within the corporate landscape that cradles my ideals. Pride, Accountability, and Focus. I am adding determination and resilience, and above all, consideration of others.

I missed that last part initially. I realized through my departure from GMSI and the months that followed, that the secret to keeping people moving forward had nothing to do with the things I thought it did. Cubby and Dr. Ron put things in perspective. They both said something identical. *They said that I cared.*

"In the end, EBITDA doesn't matter as much as people."

When I left GMSI, no longer did the relationships matter. Metrics, performance, goals, and projections were the primary drivers. Those things matter, but in the end, EBITDA doesn't matter as much as people.

Corporates focus on profit. Numbers over culture, dollars over feelings. That is not me. As I was told by one of the executives at 3M when they were a minority shareholder in GMSI, "You are a cog that doesn't mesh with the 3M wheel." It hurt me for many years, as I internalized this to mean that I was not good enough for 3M.

Recently though, I have made peace with the entire last decade, including this initially hurtful statement. As I had time to reflect, I realized he did me a favor. He identified the fact that I operate at a different level. I look beyond the numbers. I care. I had processed the original statement, the one that said I do not mesh, as a negative. It is just the opposite.

It defines and justifies that my way is not wrong, it's simply different. I had a large group of employees follow me, and an equally impressive list of big companies invest and trust in my vision. Even better is the fact that while I could call any of them a client, vendor, employee, shareholder, investor, banker, lawyer, or even competitor, is the fact that I could call most of them a friend.

GMSI transacted successfully with the semiconductor industry's biggest names, and in some cases, surpassed all the competition in our space. We created a technology platform built on excellence, but also on the fact that we genuinely cared about the success of our teammates, whether they be employees, vendors, or clients. I am immensely proud of that. I have 13+ International patents for our work. We didn't fail, we changed the game.

We defined who we were by living our conviction and commitment to treating others with kindness, respect, and appreciation. We made friends, we laughed, and we all carried each other.

April 13, 2020

There is so much to process these days. I have a beach Jackal that we may have to put down, I have an impending job offer for a position I don't want anymore, and my relationship with Wanda is a work in progress.

I listen as she tells me stories about her college days, the kids, a shopping list, or a movie she wants to see. I listen because I am grateful to be here, with her. I am alive, and 2 weeks ago, that wasn't guaranteed.

She is still amazing to me. My heart always fills with love and emotion when we are close. She used to make me feel invincible, but in the past year, I have seen a real degradation in the intimacy of our marriage. Maybe it's my fault because when I was the CEO, all my time was spent on work, on thinking about work, on doing work.

I don't anymore. I have a different feeling. Nostalgia. It is a longing for my friend and lover. The one who was present. We are not present lately, and phones, homeschooling, writing books, boating, consulting, parenting, and an end-of-the-world pandemic will certainly put a strain on any good relationship, marriage or otherwise.

I just listen to her voice and appreciate the moment. We used to go crazy for each other in a physical sense, and we were adventurous and passionate. We always missed each other. Then she got a hysterectomy and I quit my role as CEO and the wheels of romance fell off. Not for me, but we disconnected to some degree.

We have had 10 months together since I left work. In spending so much time together, I think we have both seen much more of each other in the past 10 months than in the past 10 years. You notice stuff. In each other and yourself. The one revelation for both of us? We are not as young as we used to be. Hair grows from places where hair never grew, things hurt that we do not understand, and we find that our energy plateaus.

We most likely will never return to the days of 2007, when love was new and sex was a daily occurrence, but we will find our middle ground, and in the end, as long as we are together, we will find our way.

Today we are just laying low, resting, and trying to get better. I am not 100%. I am not even 50%. Breathing is my greatest difficulty. I can't speak a few sentences without losing my breath. I have a conference call at 12:30 PM to talk to the executive team from a large company that wants to hire me. I can't even complete a sentence without coughing. I hope they have good health insurance.

Cubby just called me. One of the buyers is asking all the current employees if there is a management issue at GMSI. All the guys said, "What Management? We haven't had management or direction since Peter left". I am humbled.

I am not going from founding, funding, developing, transacting, and running GMSI to taking a backseat to the people I hired, and a new owner. And I am not working with people who don't understand the culture we built. I am going to be true to myself. I am finished giving to those who do not give back. Love should be a two-way street, but as I learned long ago, "In love, there is the loved and lover. The loved always has the upper hand."

April 14, 2020

Woke up to find our tax returns were accepted by the State and the Fed and that is good news to start the day. We are not getting any stimulus money, although we could use it, according to the accountant, we made too much in 2018, and 2019 will not count because we haven't filed yet. We are ok for now, even though I have not made any money in 10 months.

As I understand it, we will still receive a tax credit in 2020. If not, I would at least like the free toaster. (You would only get that joke if you were born between 1960 and 1970 when banks gave free toasters when you opened an account. I never understood the relationship between toast and money.)

I want to write as my new career. I have found a great outlet in writing. Writing this book, writing my thoughts on news sites, sharing my views, and creating dialogue on social media. Today, I am confused by the stock market. The S&P reached record levels while record unemployment was being reported. It was a paradigm that left me speechless. So, I shared a meme that showed the stats and stated, "Everything wrong in America, in one image".

16 million people lost their jobs in less than 3 weeks and the Dow had its best week since 1938. This is the new America. The land of the not-so-free and the home of the imprisoned.

Wanda posted a pic of our Easter in lockdown. Look how great everyone looks, except me. I look old. Sick, and rundown. I survived a near-death experience, and I am healing. The one constant medicine is time with my family. I love my family so much. Everything I do, I do for you. Except for boating, which I do for myself.

I have made no secret of my longing for the sea. Of wide-open spaces and journeys to find new places, people, and perspectives. I would like to sail away on a 40-foot sailboat one day.

I have a plan all mapped out, to sail from San Diego, around the Mexican coastline, up through the Sea of Cortez, back down to the Panama Canal and up through Columbia, into the Caribbean, and on to Puerto Rico, the Bahamas, Florida and up the coast to Northport, NY, and a place I once called home.

April 15, 2020

It's Tax Day, but it isn't anymore. In this new land, in these new times, Tax Day is now July 15th. I am ok with no taxes at all, but apparently, that is not an option.

I am upset with The Donald. An article states Mr. President would dictate when we opened back up, at his sole discretion. I take great issue with this. He shut the country down and that was the right decision at the time, but opening it before the pandemic has passed defeats the purpose of shutting down in the first place. I was angry, so I wrote an objection to the article on Facebook.

"Um, actually Donny, you don't have total authority and in case my fellow citizens have forgotten, all these elected crooks and liars on both sides are supposed to be working in our best interest and representing us in government.

Who feels justly represented right now? Not just by Trump, but across the board?

I care about you guys. Me. Our families. This country. What is happening in the world right now is a travesty and the worst is yet to come. Not health-wise, but economically.

At a time when we must truly rely on each other, big government will try and divide us. Do not listen. Do not comply. There is much more at stake here. Be savvy and remember, sheep go to slaughter willingly, and Americans fight.

Love to all and always wish you guys health, happiness, and peace.

I write this and smile. I don't care if anyone sees it; sometimes I just write for the sheer joy of presenting my opinion, even when it is unpopular.

After writing I jump in the shower and as soon as I twist the handle for the water, it spins 360 degrees, stripping the set screw and leaving the water in the on position. I will need to fix this now, but that poses some issues. Home Depot only allows a certain amount of people in the store at a time, so I must drive there, wait in line, go in, and wait some more, all the while keeping 6 feet from someone, and then pay for my merchandise without touching anything.

I turned the water main off and ventured forth to the Depot of Homes. A place where germs live and gather around barbecues, home appliances, and nuts and bolts. We wait in the sun with 50 other people, spaced 6 feet apart, just like the good little robots we are now. I am frustrated and annoyed with the level of compliance I am seeing. George Orwell was a visionary, and we should have paid more attention to his words.

I have never changed a shower cartridge before, but I am not intimidated. If I could help build a successful manufacturing company, I could certainly learn how to do this. That is until I read the instructions. They are written in a language spoken by aliens with illustrations that resemble the same.

I decided to use what I could from the directions and look for help on YouTube. I found a tutorial that tells you trying to fix this yourself could result in drowning, damage to your home, or death. "Better call a professional!" But after a few hours, I figured it out and fixed it.

I did. A non-professional. Suck it, internet naysayers!

Out front, I turn the water main on as Arielle follows me out. She looks at the lawn sign that says, "Seniors 2020". This is the new graduation thing; you post a sign for your graduate like you are selling your house or supporting a political candidate. She hates the sign. It reminds her of just how screwed up the world is right now.

Wanda pokes her head out the front door and calmly states, "You know the shower is running, right?" I had forgotten I was fixing the shower. This is my end of the world, plumbing for the survivors.

I ran back upstairs and made a few adjustments here and there, and the shower is good as new. I am proud of myself, and I take this time to share a lesson with the kids.

"Overcome obstacles by tackling them directly...No surrender, no failure. Life does not reward the coward. "

They are gathered around the shower, and I explain that fear never accomplishes anything but spreading more fear. Overcome your fear of the unknown by diving in and doing something you have never done before. They all look at me and nod. They don't get it; they just want me to stop talking. But I get it. Never quit. Overcome obstacles by tackling them directly. Head on. No surrender, no failure. Life does not reward the coward.

I hold my wrench up high. A job well done! I am happy but Arielle is not. She will miss graduation, prom, and every other highlight of her senior year. No senior celebrations. I love you, Arielle. I will make sure you get a nice graduation dinner. I hope you like takeout.

April 16, 2020

I lost a good friend today. He didn't die of Covid, but a heart attack and stroke. His name was Bill Coldwell, and when I first moved to

Arizona in 1983, he guided me through the ways of the Lakeway where we lived. He was such a cheerful guy, and always big-hearted. I will miss you, Billy. Thanks for the memories and I hope you are enjoying your new life, strolling the Lakeway's of heaven.

April 17, 2020

Steven Millman, a noted statistician, has my deepest respect and friendship. This is what an unbiased look at the current trajectory for Covid-19 deaths looks like. You won't see this on CNN or Fox News, but we should.

I would like to offer a simple thought. We don't know enough about the long-term spread of this virus, or the likelihood it would mutate, so please don't be so quick to push for a widespread re-opening of the country. It will be cataclysmic.

Economic damage was done long ago. It is irreversible but recoverable. A quick dismissal of stay-at-home orders could cause a 2nd and more deadly wave of infections, simply because we throw caution to the wind. There are other ways to get past this, other ways to help businesses, and other ways to help individuals. It requires concerted buy-in from banks, investment groups, the Fed, and others. But there are ways.

The only way we get out of this is by working together. By helping each other.

"Leadership doesn't push others down by force; true leadership lifts others up with praise, encouragement, education, and compassion. "

Leadership doesn't push others down by force; true leadership lifts others up with praise, encouragement, education, and compassion.

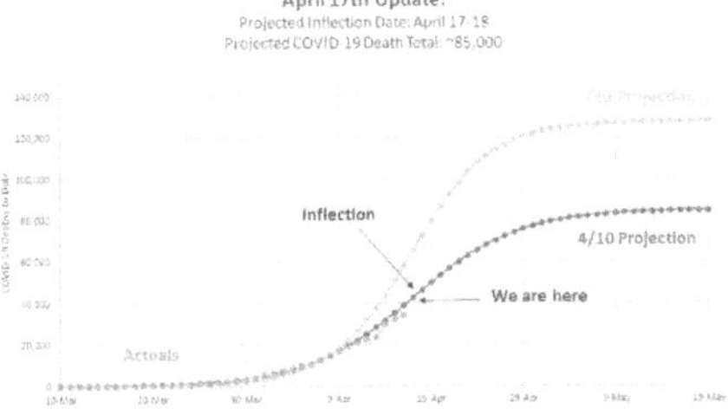

April 18, 2020

I am taking a break from writing about politics, the economy, and viruses. My boat, *The Red Barchetta*, is sick and in the boat hospital. That boat is almost as important to me as our kids or my drums. The truth is the boat is important to me because of its value to others. She is a vessel that brings joy to others. I drive them there, but she takes care of the rest.

April 19, 2020

This morning, I watched my drum videos from 2009. I made a series of live drum performances for YouTube and Facebook. Drums and I have had a long love affair. I have been playing since I was a kid. I still play daily.

When I was in my 20's and early 30's, I dedicated my life to the pursuit of a career in music. We played a lot of shows, practiced 3 nights a week and dedicated our lives to our craft. In the end, we had the good fortune of recording 7 albums together, and we played many shows, but made no money.

I always thought we would make it in the music business, but alas, there is always someone better positioned than you. What we failed to make in monetary gains we made in memories, and that suits me fine. I always played for the love of music, not the money. Anything you do out of love is never a waste of time.

April 20, 2020

This morning, I was asked to drive to the boat dealer to review the damage to the Red Barchetta. It's never a good sign when they want you to come talk in person. It's going to be almost $4000 for all the repairs necessary. I need a job to sustain this lifestyle, but for now, I will suck it up and pay the bill. I still have the jet skis to take people out to the lake. I derive my joy these days from bringing it to others. A broken boat won't stop that path.

April 21, 2020

From the beautiful mind of Steven Millman, who has been providing statistical analysis for all of us since the pandemic started. His chart today shows a clear picture that if the country doesn't follow social distancing rules, many will die. Many are dead already. Yesterday, over 2000 people died in a day. If this tracks to the statistical data, more will die from Covid than the Vietnam war.

I didn't take this as seriously as I should have when it started, and it almost killed me. I will make it my responsibility to share my story with others in the hopes I can shed light on how dangerous Covid really is. I am being careful and praying for Steven to be wrong, which he rarely ever is.

April 22, 2020

Happy Hump Day! Oil fell below zero the other day. Watching the devaluation of this commodity makes me grasp how worthless something is when no one wants it. The value we put on things and people are remarkably similar. Neither fare well when its value to others is diminished, and some days, I feel like Oil.

I haven't updated the progress with the sale of GMSI lately. The quick update is that I have no position in the sale anymore. As far as I know, the only buyer in the running is Applied Materials, and they want me to work with them as a consultant. I could make money, but I don't see myself going from the founder and leader of the company to a hired hand for a third party.

Normally, this would bother me in many ways, but I have a new sense of self, one that is not defined by what I did for GMSI or Heraeus. My worth is valued by my own interpretation, and I think I am priceless. I am the founder of InfinityGo, and hopefully with the release of this book, a published author and speaker. I want to share my stories with all of you. I have lived a very colorful life.

In the meantime, I am watching the world from the outside looking in. I spend much of my time at home, other than the occasional outing to a store for food or supplies. I have adopted a strict regimen of hand sanitizer, masks, and constant washing. Once bitten, twice shy.

There will be many more lessons as the coming weeks unravel. I expect a deep selloff in the market as previously discussed. I expect layoffs and many bankruptcy filings from both small and large businesses. And make no mistake, they will come. I fear many big names are at risk, and many small ones, which hurts, because small business feeds the American economy.

I will keep the world in my prayers and will keep looking for the silver linings. Take care of each other. That will be important as those we love may find themselves struggling in the coming months. Be empathetic. Be compassionate. Be kind.

Don't treat people like Oil; treat them like Gold. The returns are much more stable and valuable in the long run.

April 23, 2020

I read an article entitled, "The death of the Department Store". This is what I have been ranting about for weeks. The damage is already done and the "stimulus" you are seeing is only stimulating those who shouldn't get it.

I feel the days of big box stores and malls are gone forever. With the recent quarantine, big business has found they don't need the expense and overhead of a store for most products, as they can easily be sold via online offerings at the same price and delivered to your door. This cuts the middleman, passes shipping costs to the consumer and no one ever leaves the house.

A perfect business model if I ever saw one if we lived in 1980 Soviet Russia.

Bottom line, Retail is going to really struggle to recover. Next is the airlines, then car dealerships, aerospace (Boeing will go to $86 before rebounding), oil and gas and a slew of other technology companies and you have what I have been fearing and trying to explain for weeks.

People working from home will stay home. Not because Covid ends, but because many businesses have found they can operate quite efficiently outside the confines of the traditional office setting. 9-5 is a thing of the past, and video calls and work from home strategies are the new rush hour, only without a commute. As I see it, everyone wins except for commercial real estate, which I expect will see the pain of Covid in the next 12 months. My feeling is this will be a long, slow, and messy recovery. We haven't seen the bottom yet.

April 24, 2020

Another day in solitary. We are trying to make the best of it. Today I worked on an alternative to our current health insurance, one that includes public assistance. I don't want to do it, but Wanda is insistent. We paid into it, and bleeding our savings for health insurance is stupid.

Pride is misplaced as she explains it, and the government is handing it to us in the wake of the pandemic. We haven't worked since last June. It would only be temporary.

She is right, of course. We pay $1400 a month for health insurance, and it doesn't even give us a co-pay. Our insurance offers a discount, but we carry much of the burden out of pocket. This isn't sustainable.

Tomorrow is Arielle's 18th birthday, and like my birthday, there will be no social celebration. Last year, we surprised Arielle and flew down to Hermosillo where she was going to school. We went to the beach and had a great time! This year? Takeout and streaming video.

Wanda is having a video chat with her Mexican friends, and she is laughing and talking loudly in Spanish. I miss those days when we would have a house of happy Latinas, yacking and drinking and laughing loudly. I almost always saw a more amorous Wanda when we went to bed. Happiness and alcohol are great aphrodisiacs.

April 25, 2020

18. Our beautiful, sweet, funny, smart, mouthy, opinionated daughter, Arielle is 18 today.

I was not there when you were born, but I love you as if I were. We met when you were 4. The first time I brought you to my house with Mom, you just walked in and made yourself at home just like you owned the place. Truth is, you already knew you were home. And that made me happy.

I went from your mom's boyfriend to dad in a short period of time. I had never wanted to be anyone's husband or dad after my divorce, but you and Mom changed that. Your love and the love of your brothers and sisters changed me. I have been truly blessed to call you daughter and to celebrate all your birthdays since you were 5. Thanks for inviting me. :-)

It is another "end of the world birthday party" for us. First mine, now yours. If you are surrounded by the people who love you and you have all you need, you have everything. You will learn that lesson later in life.

We will make today as special as we can, as you make every day special for us. Thanks for being you and thank you for 18 wonderful years. I love you so much, Arielle. Happy 18th birthday!! Xox

Dad

April 26, 2020

I coerced the kids to take the first swim of the year. It feels good. Cold, but good. I am happy to see the summer again. We watch Mass on TV, and after, around 8 pm, I pick up Chinese food. I will be sick later for sure. I shouldn't eat after 6 PM, let alone 8, and I will pay dearly, or Wanda will.

April 27, 2020

Wanda and I didn't have a great night and I woke up angry. I am still upset about Wanda and her social distancing practices. Mainly, she is distancing herself socially from me.

I go downstairs and eat with Ben, and we hang out and talk. I love being home with him. Late in the day, I play Blackjack with Ben. He does not understand how I know which cards are coming. I tell him I am counting cards. I explain the premise of card counting. He is amazed. I am proud I taught Ben a useful skill he can use, but it doesn't work in Vegas. I know, I tried.

I waste the rest of the day away checking on bills and trying to figure out some other things related to finance. I find that the IRS is sending Wanda and me a stimulus check. We can use it. It's been almost a year without a salary and every bit helps. We aren't poor, but when your cash flow is only going out, you worry.

I go upstairs because I am tired and cranky and need a shower. The heat from the shower relaxes me. As I shower, I catch my reflection in the mirror outside the shower. I look at my 55-year-old body. I am tired of looking 55. I have been working out sporadically but as I gaze at my much rounder shape, I see my 40-year-old body still there. I commit to working out and getting back into shape. I need it. I will feel better about myself, maybe Wanda will like me better, and in the worst case, I will look good and feel healthy.

We go to bed early. There is not much chatter as I read the ever-increasing bad news related to Covid. I am tired of bad news. I decide to watch some surfing videos and watch a fisherman catch a 700 lb. Bluefin Tuna.

April 28, 2020

I wake up early after a fitful sleep and go for a long bike ride. It is a struggle at first, but I get into a rhythm and the miles get easier. I am winded by the time I arrive home, but I tell myself I still got it. I don't. I am large and aged, but I can fix one of those things, so all hope is not lost.

After the ride, I go to where my workout machine and weights are. The kids come out and marvel at my strength. They ask how I got so strong, and I tell them, "From carrying all your lazy asses for 12 years".

I am writing today. I need to get things organized. I am going to finish this book. I did not spend a year of writing and whining not to finish. I am hoping readers will appreciate my candid nature, and my willingness to bare all. It may be a huge mistake, especially the stories of Wanda and me, but I am committed to telling the real story of our lives, and those are the facts. Well, as Wanda would say, those are MY facts.

I have been given many employment opportunities lately. Some as CEO, some as consultants. I am not that interested; I just want to write books, drive boats, and hang out in Mexico every few months.

I spoke to Phillip Millman today regarding the state of the oil market. Phillip sent me a great analogy that put things into terms most men and women outside the financial and commodities market could understand. We use hookers and wives to better illustrate the principles of supply and demand and the futures contract.

From an oil futures trader buddy of mine. (Phil saying this) Here is an ... umm... interesting explanation of negative oil contracts and exceptionally low WTI prices.

(Feel free to use it, Peter Guercio)

This is how an oil-trading cowboy views things:

Imagine the following...you pay $500 today and commit to receiving an escort at your house in 15 days when your wife is traveling. This is called a futures contract. Unfortunately, lockdown came, and your wife will be home for the next 60 days. You do not want this escort to show up at your house at all now and you try to pass this futures contract to someone else. Only you cannot sell this commitment because nobody can receive the escort at home anymore. Everyone is in full storage with wives on duty.

To make matters worse, not even the pimp (Chicago Mercantile Exchange) has more room to receive girls because his house is crowded with other ho's. So, you will now pay anyone just to take the girl off your hands, on top of the $500 you already owe.

Do you now understand why oil has a negative price when the contract is delivered?

I know who really wrote this analogy, but we don't talk anymore. He and I had a falling out, a difference of opinion online. He was cyberbullying and I was real life disengaging. I miss him though. We grew up together and I loved our juvenile exchanges on all subjects.

Here is a tip for the day.

Don't go to bed angry. Say you are sorry, even if it is not your fault. Make peace where you can. Forgive and ask others to forgive you. The only thing worse than living a life of regret is dying from one.

April 29, 2020

The IRS says we will receive a stimulus check. I am shocked but pleasantly surprised. It's not like I haven't paid a large portion of my earnings to the government. We have been living off savings for a year. I could use the stimulation.

Speaking of stimulation, I feel President Trump lacks this talent. He has no power to motivate anyone anymore. I don't understand why. He rallied America 4 years ago; now he speaks and acts as if he injected himself with Lysol and the UV technology everyone made fun of him for.

I was writing a message to Phillip, but I wanted to share it with you in this book. My statement captures my true feelings as we emerge from COVID-induced slavery and capture. Phillip and I were talking about how things got so sideways. How did those in power reach this place where rich people decide the best way to get richer while leaving the rest of us destitute and confined to a prison of self-isolation and debt? The answer? We elected them.

Philip correctly states, "The election of Trump helped that abandonment. He is truly amoral and a ratings hound. He is slime and I hate to say that about another Queens boy".

I think about his words, and I respond, *"Yeah, I was sold by his message of change in the beginning, but now, I am just embarrassed. It is a horror show. I want him to stop talking because the more he talks, the less I want to hear. He is not a team builder or a leader as I see it. He has an insatiable appetite for praise and needs to be the hero or the problem solver to feed his narcissistic ego.*

I am a N.Y. boy too! I am from the island and Crown Heights/Prospect Park, with a minor in Bronx and Yonkers, but I spent most of my teenage years working at the "Bagel Oasis" on Horace Harding. (Queens). I am a longtime Mets fan and fiscally conservative for the most part. I look at the world today, and it's like I woke up from a long dream only to find my nightmares are real. It's crazy."

I talk with many people who justify this time of confinement as an extended vacation. I don't see it that way at all. We are watching the complete destruction of global economies, and the end of small businesses, and quite possibly, the middle class.

I am worried though. For the first time in my life, I do not trust the government. The message they are sending is, "We are mostly full of shit, all part of the same propaganda machine. We don't really know what we are doing, but whatever it is, we are going to do it to you, the American citizen. God Bless America". I trust a small circle; I know who my people are.

The thing that bothers me most about all this uncertainty in the USA, is that for most who have no savings, and no safety net, there will be little help. Jobs will be a struggle. LEI's (Leading Economic Indicators) are all the worst I have seen. Lending and credit will be the next casualty, then housing and banking.

If that happens, I fear the worst. Those with guns will take aggressive action. Civil unrest will blossom, and that is a tipping point that will involve the armed forces and law enforcement. In the end, those with guns will win.

The other issue is how our adversaries around the world view the activity in our country. Russia, China, and the Middle East all see our reactions to crisis, and they measure our readiness, and more so, our weakness. This is why leadership is so important. Strong leadership sends a message of strength, and poor leadership sends a message of opportunity.

I am scared for the life our wives and kids may endure.

April 30, 2020

The days and weeks are running together like a never-ending "Friends" episode called, *"The One with the Pandemic"*. I am tired of being a sloth, so I woke up early and did 9 miles on the bike. I am a fattish, middle-aged ex-jock, who has effectively let it all go. I huff and puff through the series of hills and terrains. I curse my lack of physical conditioning and blame marriage and parenthood, but it was a life of a sedentary existence of sitting on planes, trains, offices, and boardrooms.

Now, Wanda and I are both focused on getting in better shape. With the end of the world in our sights, I feel like being in shape will come in handy during a looting run or escaping the masses with guns and rage.

I received a consulting offer today to assist the new owners of GMSI. It looks very promising. I do not know all the mechanics, but I would work with the head of Global Sales and Marketing as a Business Development/IP consultant. I am sure it will lead me back to a leadership role within the company, but do I want it? I am not sure anymore. I want to do my own thing now, but I am keeping my options open.

The governor announced we are still locked down until May 15th; however, barring any unforeseen changes, will slowly re-open. Curbside retail will open first, so we can buy clothes we can't touch or try on, and then May 12th for social distancing restaurant night, which includes a sponge bath, a flea and tick dip, and your choice of soup or salad.

I have written my assessment of the country's state for the past weeks. I offered my predictions for the stock market, the economy, and the employment outlook. I have been consistently right. Yesterday, the reports came in that thirty million people filed for unemployment. I fear that is only the beginning, but I commit to writing something positive.

I end this chapter with a paragraph from one of my posts on social media. It reflects the desperation for items we once took for granted, and the humor with which I approach these end-of-day scenarios. I am still laughing, still grateful, and still hopeful.

End of the world problem for the day. While doing his chores, Ben left the top open on our only jar of Lysol wipes. I am looking for an underground connection on any shady disinfectant hook-up. I know many of our colleagues are huffing paint and sniffing glue, but I was hoping someone bought some intravenous Lysol from Trump and decided injections were a drastic idea.

I will treat any transaction with great discretion and the utmost privacy unless I write about it publicly, but let's cross that bridge when we come to it.

Message me or meet me at 7-11 at 7:11. I will be in the Beige Yugo, smoking a pipe and practicing my tantric yoga poses. Please knock first!

Good day to all. Happy March 63rd.

12

May, 2020

May 1, 2020

This morning, I went shopping. Hunter-gathering if you will. Later in the day, I have a call with Randy, the gentleman I would work with from Applied Materials.

I get what we need in less than 30 minutes. Not bad considering the restrictions in place. A year ago, I was flying around the world, and here we are a year later, and I am writing this book, not traveling for the first time in over 10 years and I am grocery shopping with an agenda for the day that includes writing this book, cooking for my family, and fielding job offers.

I never would have imagined this would be my life. I knew I wanted to leave last year, but I was scared. I will take many things from my journey at work and in my personal life, but this journey, the one where I got off the "stress express", has been the most fruitful in many ways.

I didn't make any money, but I got to spend time with my wife and kids, family, and friends. And...I wrote this book. This is the life I have always dreamed of.

I am grateful, most of all for my faith in God. I asked him to guide me, and he did. I found myself and my missing joy in these months. I can easily go back to the way things were, traveling constantly, working incessantly, and making money, but I think I may not.

I may choose joy. The joy that comes from writing, and spending time the way I choose, rather than strapped to the ideal that the only way to be happy is to have a respectable job, work for a big company, and do important things. There is a better way, and it's up to me how my story ends.

I headed upstairs to prepare for my call. This company has never been easy to work with. They have jerked me around for months. I am not sure what I am doing, but I know I don't want to go back to the way things were before I resigned. The dilemma is I must make money; the question is how.

Randy begins quite directly, saying, "Look, Peter, we want you on the team. Our offer considers your expenses and lack of insurance and accounts for that in your rate. Your verbal offer is $120 per hour. You cover expenses and we reimburse you. It has been well thought out and discussed, and so the offer comes non-negotiable as we are at the top of our range."

I let his words reverberate with me for a second or two, and then think of all the travel, the work, the stress, and giving up 28 years of knowledge for $120 per hour.

I answer with a calm I haven't felt in a long time, the calm of a person who is in control of his destiny, and I respond, "Well, that's quite a bit lower than my current rate. I had discussed this with your team before these discussions. My standard consulting rate is $300 per hour, plus expenses, and I told them I would be willing to consider less for a more permanent position. I appreciate your offer and I will consider it, along with several other opportunities. As you said, it is non-negotiable, so I will take a few days and get back to you by Wednesday of next week."

He is stunned. I expected that, and it's ok. I have some experience in negotiating deals and one important thing I learned--never say yes to something you aren't committed to, and no to something you haven't fully considered. In my maturing state, I choose to step back and think.

The bottom line, they flip-flopped so many times already, that I have lost my zeal and trust for their management teams. In plain English,

I am worth more. The knowledge I have gained, coupled with my experience, and IP, sits in a very niche market. This market generates billions of dollars in revenue per year, and as uses for it become more mainstream, and technology advances, the market will be worth tens of billions. In comparison to the market, they are offering me about $100K for 6 months of brain draining.

You get what you pay for, so invest in the people who bring you the greatest value and compensate them accordingly.

Last July, they wanted me to consult, but my former employer said no, citing the risk of disclosure. Then they suggested that they wanted me to be GM if they bought GMSI. I agreed. Then they changed their mind and offered a short-term contract with no benefits and no long-term commitment.

This type of indecision leaves me jaded, as it always has. I agreed to accept an employment offer as a Business Development Manager, as an employee, with benefits and security. A month later they came back with the offer of consulting, but at a rate 2.45 times less than my current consulting rate. That doesn't sound like much of a commitment to me.

I want to do something else. I do not want to go back to the way things were-- not even for $250k per year. I will think about this, but my gut says to say no.

I got a call from Frank, the service manager of the boat dealership. He called to let me know the boat should be fixed early next week. This is great news. I need to get on the water again. I pray, "Please God, help me find the path you want me on, and hopefully, the one that makes me happy too!"

Wanda and I meet in bed after 10 PM. It's been another long and emotional day, and as I read, I keep drifting off to sleep. She folds herself into me and we snuggle in the darkness. I want to write more, but I promised Wanda I would not expose our intimate details in print. Needless to say, she was the best part of my day and my night, as always.

May 2, 2020

After a great night with Wanda, I find it hard to wake up. No pun intended.

I know Wanda needs to sleep, so I slip out of bed and quietly go downstairs, feed the dogs, make coffee, and get ready for my morning bike ride. This fat kid is going to get in shape if it kills me, which it very well could.

This morning, I changed my route and tried something different. I am going to try a new way, which seems fitting as if it were a metaphor written to describe the current direction of my life. I am just going to see where things go.

This new trail is crowded and difficult, but I make a commitment to myself that unless I go into cardiac arrest, I am going to push myself to the limit, and in the end, I achieve my intended goal. As I ride, I think about the consulting offer.

I arrive at a difficult decision. I am not going to take the Applied Materials offer. This seems like going back to what I left to some degree. My gut is telling me no, and I am paying attention. I envision Dr. Ron, my spirit PhD, smiling in the background with approval.

Sure, I can make some money, but there is no guarantee of a future, and I will have effectively given all my knowledge and client contacts to them for a bargain. I am going to say no. I am going to finish this book and drive to make it a success, along with growing InfinityGo.

My reasoning is simple. I am banking on myself, and as my first boss, Mike Edelstein said the other day, "At my age, I don't worry. I make my own way and whatever happens, happens." I can live with that.

We choose the life we want to live, and I am going to choose a new path.

May 3, 2020

The light of the rising sun tickles my eyelids as I wake up. It's 6 AM and I have been thinking about my direction in life for most of the night. I am used to sleepless nights, but I slept for 44 minutes last night.

In considering the offer AMAT made, I realize I need to find something that makes me happy and excited, the way I used to feel at GMSI when we were growing. I need to lead people, to lift them up. This offer will not do that. It will mean traveling and stress and the value of their offer is unappealing for the return. It doesn't feel right, but I will talk with Wanda, and we can decide together.

Wanda and I are tasked with the decision of my employment, but we also need to discuss putting the Jesus Jackal down. I am saddened by this as I know everyone wanted this to work out. Three times the vet has suggested we put him down. I am not a killer by trade, but in this case, I feel like the executioner.

Today is Sunday, a day of church, virtually anyway, but first, I am making a roast. Sunday dinner, just like grandma used to make; only now, I am a grandma.

A new week beckons and everyone has something to do, even though we can't go anywhere to do it. The kids are tucked in around nine, and the house is locked. Wanda and I lay down in bed to watch *American Ultra*, which will turn out to be tonight's lullaby. Sleep well, world.

May 4, 2020

I have only one goal today--make LED light magic in my backyard. It may seem like a small task to many, but this is a special morning as life comes full circle. I am going to bring the very thing that got me here, LED technology, into my backyard.

You see, in 2008, when I began to pitch others that LED technology would replace all traditional lighting, investors didn't understand. In 1996, one of our clients, Lumileds, showed us the future, and I have been fascinated with the industry ever since.

LED lighting, or Solid-State Lighting (SSL) is hands down more efficient in every way compared to conventional lighting sources. Our team at GMSI had a part in bringing this technology to fruition.

In 2008, I told investors that LED technology would be the next "big" thing, and I was correct. Flash forward 12 years to 2020, and I dare you to find a place that does not utilize LED lighting of some sort. Try and buy an incandescent light bulb. I followed my gut, embraced my passion for technology, and helped make it a reality. And I hope to do that again in my new life.

But today, we are reaping what we sowed, and so, we will bring LED home to the Casa De Guercio, to the garden--light generated by the technology that GMSI had a part in producing. LED lights changed the world, and in turn my own.

In the middle of installing the lights, I take an InfinityGo call with Cort and Brad. Just as I saw the vision of LED lighting becoming mainstream, I have a new vision. It's a vision of connecting the world in a way that has never been done before. I am excited about everything going on, but most of all, for clarity. I am going to make my own way, and with the grace of God, I will find my path.

After 4 hours, I cautiously flick the switch on the lighting. The image before me is more than I could have imagined. Beautiful LED lights bathe the plants and walls of our backyard. I traveled the world in support of LED with one dream, to change the world. I didn't change the world, but I did change the world for the people around me and that is all a man could ever ask for.

May 5, 2020

I wake up early to ride my bike before the heat of the day, but Wanda pulls me back to bed. I am surprised, as she never wakes up this early. It is 6:13 AM. We snuggle and I rub her back in the morning quiet. It feels so delicious to be close to her. I am happily surprised, and she doesn't want me to leave. Alas, a fat boy needs to ride, so I tuck her in, and off I go.

I spend the early morning hours riding my bike and answering emails under the shade of a big mesquite tree along the way. One of the messages informs me that my former VP of Technology, Paul, will not be receiving an offer from the new owners of GMSI.

I am incredibly surprised. I say a prayer for him that he lands on his feet and that he finds his path, as I always pray that I will find mine. I tell God, "I don't want to be bitter, and I certainly don't wish ill will on him, but he did hurt me. I forgive him, Lord, so if you could, please make sure he finds his path as I pray that you will help me find mine." Amen.

As I scroll through the notifications on my phone, I see that Marco, the former CFO of Heraeus Quartz, confirms he is finally seeing the joys of slowing down, and he is finding his way. He reflects on the chaotic years he and I endured, and writes to me that he is happy, sitting in his garden, catching rays, and drinking a beer.

This message warms my heart in a way that no one will ever understand.

We earned this, Marco. You too, Heinz. We will find our path. In the meantime, let us all be happy we have not had to manage the group through Covid. We are home, relaxing with the people we love off the hamster wheel and running free.

May 6, 2020

I am exactly one month away from finishing this book, and fast approaching the 1st anniversary of my resignation. It is a difficult pill to swallow sometimes for me, and I am torn between the life I used to have and the one I have now.

I miss the role of leadership more than anything. I miss guiding my teams to successful places and working with others to overcome adversity. I miss traveling to faraway places to talk to faraway people about faraway topics. I miss overseeing a plan and managing our teams through the complexity of business.

But for everything I mentioned, there are things I don't miss, and I remind myself daily what they are. I don't miss the immense stress that comes with the responsibility of being the boss. I don't miss the constant international travel and I don't miss not being able to make everyone happy.

I do not miss my old life as much as I miss the people I interacted with. I miss a time when we were a small company with big aspirations and the camaraderie that propelled us. I miss the core group, with Rex, Aimee, Phil, and Mike. This is the foundation of what we became.

I miss all of you in the industry, my friends, and colleagues. I am immensely proud of the things we accomplished together. For me, GMSI will always be the core I mentioned, along with Cubby, Johnny, Eric, Logan, Paul, Nancy, and Andy.

I think about Paul, who was someone I considered a close friend, a confidant, and a partner. Despite everything that happened after I left; I will always wish him well. I am upset that he slandered me as soon as I gave him the keys to the castle, but not everyone is meant for the commitment and responsibility of leadership.

Being a good leader is not about what you want, or even what the clients want. It is about balancing the wants and needs of employees, vendors, clients, investors, and the industry while maintaining focus on the goals of the company. It is an extremely hard job and a delicate balancing act.

A title does not make you successful, but how you treat people does.

If I could give him a piece of managerial advice, I would ask him to keep in mind we are not more important than the whole of everything we manage. We need to lead by example, and that requires discipline, compassion, and sacrifice. We should not forget the sacrifice of others around us either, because they are as important as our own.

An effective leader doesn't demand or order people to do things; he brings them in, communicates the "why" before he asks for the executable, and gives them ownership and a clear direction. They do the rest. If you have the trust of your teammates, they will follow you into battle.

Good leadership is not about growing mushrooms, it's about letting the garden flourish. Do not keep people in the dark. Illuminate the path for them, and they will help you find your way too.

I could not have done anything I did without the buy-in and commitment from everyone on our team. I did not ask anyone to do anything I wasn't willing to do. They didn't do anything because I demanded them to; they did it because they were committed to the success of the team. I explained the goals and answered their questions; they scored the touchdowns.

We created a culture of excellence, and I am immensely proud of everyone. The greatest sorrow I harbor is not seeing all those great people for the past year. We lost some of them along the way, and our beloved Eddie Arroyo was one of them. Not everyone makes it to the finish line.

Be sensitive to the needs of others. There is no better feeling than to provide a solution to someone who is faced with what they see as an unsurmountable problem. Put yourself in the other person's shoes and they will be willing to walk in yours.

I hope this advice helps and I will continue to pray for soft landings for everyone.

My big accomplishment of the day turned out to be a pot of home-made spaghetti and meatballs that were slowly simmered for 5 hours. The meatballs were perfect, and I am grateful for the gift of meat. Looks like there will be many shortages in the wake of the Coronavirus, so I am counting my blessings now, as a future without meatballs sounds bleak.

I am taking Ben to golf tomorrow, so we are all going to bed early. Goodnight and God bless all of you. Yes Paul, to you as well.

May 7, 2020

The Guercio men are up early to play golf. The heat of summer has arrived. The day started fine, then drifted to comedic disaster status for Ben and me. What shook my game was an altercation with the ranger at the course, who was 900 years old and smelled of his sarcophagus.

Our exchange came after the group behind us hit their tee shots into our group, almost hitting Ben, and infuriating me. The ranger came to me and said, "You guys need to pick up the pace. Could you play a little faster?" I swear, as he spoke, the dust and debris from his burial wraps were spraying from his mouth. We ignored him, as you should when any mummy approaches you driving a golf cart.

"In a leadership position, you weigh the wants and needs of the team, and you do your best to keep morale up and the vision clear."

After golf, we drive to grab food for the family. I receive several calls regarding more job opportunities, but I can't react to them because I am stuck waiting in line at In and Out Burger for 45 minutes. I wanted to cook, but the kids wanted In and Out, so here I wait. That is what you do in a leadership position. You weigh the wants and needs of the team, and you do your best to keep morale up and the vision clear. I will just chalk this up to a team-building exercise.

The team bought me a "Double Double", protein style because leadership needs to eat too.

May 8, 2020

I don't really know what day it is anymore. A year of not working and a global pandemic has a way of really clearing the need for a calendar. The days run together, and Monday doesn't feel much different than Saturday. I like it. I still use my calendar, but more as a reference guide than a bible. I need to consider this as I am starting to receive offers of employment.

I mention this because today I will talk to Randy from Applied. I have been receiving other consulting offers, and I am going to continue to try and build InfinityGo.

I want to reach beyond my comfort zone, instead of settling for the familiar.

This morning, Wanda is taking Arielle to her *Max Headroom* Graduation. The premise is crazy. Arielle will green screen in holographic form for a virtual walk across the stage to receive her diploma. I never thought I would write those words, let alone live the experience. But here we are, in the uncharted territory of post-COVID-19 Armageddon, simulating graduation on green screens, in the seclusion of an empty Jr. High Auditorium.

This is the world we live in now, and I am very vocal in my social circles and social media postings about my disdain for the current direction of the globe, particularly the USA. I will pray for a better solution than isolation, food dumping, restricted travel, masks and gloves, hand sanitizer and anal probing at the Airport. Ok, that last part was for comedic purposes, but there is nothing funny about the rest of what I said.

Today, the stock market rose on the news that 14.7% Unemployment was better than 18.4%. This is the substance driving Wall Street enthusiasm, despite continued reporting of bankruptcy, insolvency, and the highest unemployment rate we have seen since the depression.

While Wanda and Arielle were virtually graduating, I received a call from a prominent tech company, letting me know they would like me to speak to their CTO about a position, or "other agreement", as they put it. I am very intrigued and interested. I am flattered they appreciate my expertise and experience.

The timing of this opportunity is good because I am about to turn down the offer from Applied Materials. In the past, I would have leaped at this opportunity, not thinking of the consequences, and diving in headlong. But I have seen the consequences of diving blindly, knowing sometimes the pool is not filled with water.

Randy and I make some small talk and then get right into the heart of the call. I let him know I was not interested in the position they offered. Yes, it is a significant amount of money, with the biggest Semiconductor OEM in the world, and yes, I would be able to directly affect the outcome and success of GMSI and AMAT. But deep down, I don't want to. My time has passed and it's time for me to say goodbye to the industry that was my home for almost 30 years.

Randy is surprised and asks me for my reasons. I am honest, and I tell him that I don't want to travel frequently, especially in the current climate; I want to be close to my family, especially if there is a risk of unrest over the coming months. I explain to him how I have soured with the indecision of the management regarding my role, and that I am going to focus on other leadership opportunities. The most attractive leadership role I am looking at is husband and father, both considered to be prominent positions.

As I stand in the parking lot at Lowes, baking in the late afternoon sun, I feel a profound sense of relief. I just gave up a 6-figure consulting offer, and the chance to manage my company again.

I am listening to Wanda's advice. Last night she said, "What does it matter if they offer you more money, or a different role if you don't want to do it?" She is right. And I told her she was. I am hanging on to the past. To move forward, I need to fully disengage from my former life.

GMSI died in March of 2017 when we sold our company to Heraeus. The spirit and passion of GMSI remained for a time, but the ideals and foundation were lost. Heart and determination, passion, and commitment were replaced by Lean Manufacturing, Factory 4.0, Efficiency ++, EBIT, Budget, 5S, EHS, and a slew of other reporting and metrics designed to measure the success of your business.

I appreciate the benefit of these tools, but a business runs on its heart, its products, and its commitment to the industry and its clients. All those other things are simply to measure how things are doing relative to someone else's standards. "Culture Eats Strategy for Breakfast!" Peter Drucker keeps repeating himself in my head.

"I just gave up an opportunity most would kill for, but I know this opportunity might kill me. "

I just gave up an opportunity most would kill for, but I know this opportunity might kill me. That is the difference between working for money and working with purpose. Working for money makes us put ourselves in dangerous physical and mental situations for the sake of the Benjamins.

Working with purpose allows you to say, "No, this isn't the best decision for me." I know the difference now. It does not make the "What ifs" any easier to reconcile in the dark of the night, lying sleepless and thinking about these decisions. That is the nature of decision-making. You choose, and then you hope you made the right choice, and you work to make sure you support the choice you made.

That is what sound leadership does. They carefully weigh options, look to others on their team for input, and then they give direction. No decision is still a decision. We choose our destiny every day. Choose wisely. Money shouldn't motivate us, but bettering ourselves should. The cash follows the courageous, just ask Elon Musk, Steve Jobs, Bill Gates, or Jeff Bezos.

May 9, 2020

I am up early this morning with the sole intention of getting Wanda flowers, and some goodies. It is Mother's Day tomorrow, and we are starting the celebration early.

Ben is working feverishly at his desk, "Shhh, I am making mom her present for Mother's Day." He is a kid who is wise beyond his years. I am happy he is mine. I have often been riddled with guilt about letting the first part of his life slide away while I worked feverishly to save and build GMSI. My family missed out on a lot of time together. I was absent for activities like family vacations, milestones, and holidays. I missed Mother's Days and other big events, because I was flying around the world, and they were living their lives. A life I helped give them, but one I couldn't be a part of. This paradox exists for many of us. We work to take care of families we don't get to spend time with.

I am incredibly grateful for the gift of this past year together. We had ups and downs, but I will forever cherish the time we have spent together, no matter what happens. My sincere hope is that this book is a success, and we can continue to build on this foundation of togetherness. I really enjoy writing, and while I am not an expert, I am willing to learn to be the best I can be.

I want to create public speaking engagements where I can hopefully inspire others with my unlikely "success" story, and at the very least, I would like to help others find their happy endings too. Not literally. That will be $5 extra.

Everyone deserves a shot at making their dreams come true, and I believe all any of us need is the confidence of someone who believes we can, and the tenacity to reach our goals. I had those people, and I appreciate their wisdom and friendship.

One of the stories I would tell at any speaking engagement would be a funny memory from the beginnings of GMSI. Aimee and Paul tried to figure out what earth signs all of us were. Aimee is water, flowing and moving. Paul was earth, grounded, and consistent. I was fire. I came in and "burned it all down!" as they put it, and Rex was air, fueling the fire. What I realize now is that even though we were different elements, we succeeded together. We needed each other to detonate, and when we did, we made magic happen.

With this memory in mind, I want to confess who I am. I have always been outside the norm. Not in a bad way, but certainly not a member of the "in" crowd.

I was the kid you knew but didn't hang out with. I had a small handful of people who were close to me, who knew the real me, and that was all I needed. I never cared about what other people thought of me; I accepted who I was, like it or not.

For those who collaborated with me, they know I don't like to waste time on frivolous details. I will drive the topic. If there is an issue, I believe in dealing with it, head on. Not always a sound strategy, but certainly an effective one. Dive in. Get it done!

I am fire, all-consuming and out of control as I was once described, or if you consider my view, fire can be renewing and cleansing.

May 10, 2020

Happy Mother's Day. I am trying to give Wanda a special Mother's Day weekend, as we are not going to see our family due to COVID-19 concerns. We have always gotten together with the whole family for Mother's Day. We gave her a card with money to go shopping, and last night we made her dinner and breakfast in bed. There were flowers, chocolate-covered strawberries, handmade pictures from the kids, and a few other treats. We will cater to her like the queen she thinks she is. I jest. She has told me she prefers the title of Princess.

This morning, before Wanda woke up, I drove to my mom's to surprise her with a bouquet of flowers. I had planned on dropping them at the door and running away, but as I got to the door, Rod opened it and said, "Come on in!!" So, in I went. Mom was happy and she said it made her day, which was my plan. Truth is, it made my day.

We spent the day making sure Wanda was relaxed and happy. Today was a day where every reason I wanted to leave my career was supported. I helped my family, I spent time with them, and I was able to be present in situations that I would normally be absent from. Physically or mentally.

In 2017, I missed Mother's Day because I was in Germany with my new Boss, Heinz. He shared his global strategy with me along with a historical experience, driving through the history of Germany.

I was appreciative of the experience, but all I could think about was that I missed Wanda and my mom. The family had a party, but I was not there. I felt terrible. As they barbecued and enjoyed the day, I stayed up late, every night, jetlagged and stressed, as I prepared to present GMSI to the executives and colleagues of Heraeus at the International Managers Meeting, or IMM.

I delivered a compelling and humorous presentation to my new company. They liked our story, the technology, and the direction I had for our business unit. But through all the accolades for my speech, and all the sites and experiences of those days in Germany, I just thought about that one thing. "I missed Mother's Day, and I can't go back in time and fix it."

The next year, I was asked to attend the IMM, but again, it was on Mother's Day, so I declined. Not a popular decision, but I swore I would never be absent in a family situation if it were preventable. And it was preventable by saying one word. No.

"I said no to being part of a machine that was chewing me up."

In time, I began to say no to other things that kept me away from my family or made me unhappy. This included saying no to being part of a machine that was chewing me up. I said no to money. No to good health insurance and a 401K. I said no to a future that would make me wealthy and unhappy, and when I finally said no to the things that I didn't want in my life, I found joy.

My advice is simple. Say no to things that prevent you from being happy and fulfilled. Your time is precious. Treat yourself with the same value as we treat others. You are worth it.

May 11, 2020

My mom has been having a bizarre problem with her phone. I have been a long-time "Techie", building PCs by hand, and ripping apart electronics to see how they work. I can admin a network, build the hardware, fix viruses, and corrupt DLL files, but this is a new one.

I go to her house early, and I am immediately attacked lovingly by her 5 dogs and 2 birds. I simu-hug her. I coined the phrase simu-hug, which is, according to the Covid dictionary of Peter, *"The act of air hugging, simulating a real hug, only with the end of the world, Pandemic style distancing. Simu-sex and simu-kiss also fall into these categories."*

I walk in and ask to see the patient.

"What patient? What the hell are you talking about?", she says, her Long Island/ Brooklyn Jewish princess, resonating in the way only other yentas can hear.

"Ma, the phone. I came to fix your phone!", I respond, laughing as she hits me playfully.

I love this woman! She is crazy, she talks a lot, and she drives me nuts sometimes, but this is the woman that bore me. That taught me. She loved me and took care of me as I broke my ankles, dislocated my wrists, and went through many sicknesses. She was always there for me and now, I want to be there for her.

After several hours, we were successful. I made her happy twice in a row. Once yesterday with the flowers, and once today fixing a problem no one could analyze. And THIS IS WHY I LEFT MY JOB!!! I wanted to be present in the lives of my aging family. I wanted to slow down. I wanted to see my kids grow up. I wanted to be there for my wife. I wanted to live my life, instead of living for work, and now, the people I love are my focus.

I worry about money, still, but my faith in God and in each other is all we need right now. I hope I can share this message with corporates around the world, that there is a better way to do things, a better way to coexist with our careers and our personal life.

I am making a lot of noise on social media; most of it is received negatively. I talk about the efficacy of masks, the likelihood that governments are covering up key facts about the virus, and a few other things that do not make sense. I am still doom and gloom on the stock market, but I am most likely wrong. If this is all one enormous power grab, rest assured the market will go up as aggressive hedge funds look at the opportunity to buy the market back up.

All I want is an open dialogue that keeps people thinking. Are we victims of a much bigger plan to gain control of the world? The jury is out for me, but I lean towards some sinister and very disturbing activity behind all this. I will pray for our survival and the health and safety of the world. And I will pray I am wrong about all this.

May 12, 2020

I leave for my morning bike ride. I make it a mile before running over a giant thorn, which punctures my front tire. I am convinced nature wants me to stay chubby. Walking back home with a flat tire gives me time to think about the day. I am going to speak with the CTO of a large European tech company about vertically integrating his critical supply chain, and that would include me working with their group in

Europe. I smile at the irony, as I just left a European tech company when I resigned.

Once home, I have a working breakfast. I eat my bowl of cereal while talking on the phone. First, Brad, Omer, and I discuss some development and financial slides regarding the growth of InfinityGo. If we can pull this off, InfinityGo could have a $2.3 Billion valuation within 5 years or less. I am encouraged by the numbers and my excitement continues to grow.

The only thing we need now, more than anything, is for the current travel restrictions to be lifted, allowing people to go out of their houses again. At the current juncture, it doesn't look promising that this is happening anytime soon.

I also turned down a position as CEO of a smaller manufacturing company. I advised the owner on how best to move forward, and he is grateful for my help and consideration. The sad truth, after reviewing his business case, is he may not have a company if the pandemic continues. That weighs prominently on my decision. I appreciate the offer, but there must be a company that survives to be the CEO. I fear this one will be one of many that don't make it.

Things have been moving in a mostly positive direction, but my son Adam called me a few minutes ago, he and his girlfriend are breaking up, and he has nowhere to go. I spoke to Wanda about his dilemma, and we agreed to let him stay here for a short time if he needs a place. Gustavo, Wanda's other brother, moved in with us a few days ago, until he can find his own place. So here we are, the end of the world, and we will have Adam living here, along with Gustavo. They need help and we have the means to open our door.

Many people helped me along the way, and I do my sincere best to help those along the way. *Kharmatic Resonance* is the term I coined. There is another word that means something similar--compassion.

So, a quick recap, it's the end of the world, the pandemic may kill us, if the lack of toilet paper doesn't. We are currently harboring Wanda, Arielle, Benny, Cailyn, Adam, Gustavo, Wally, me, and a beach jackal that may be Jesus. I have no job, no life insurance, crappy health insurance, investments and savings of a few years, and a global economy that could either tank or explode.

Folks, I was built for this. My whole life has been a dress rehearsal for my next chapter, and in truth, you couldn't write a better script if you meant to. Amid all this uncertainty, I will do the one thing that always centers me. I am going to the lake. If you know anyone looking for a slightly used beach dog who may be Jesus, do me a favor and give them my number.

May 13, 2020

What a glorious morning! Cubby and I greet each other the old-fashioned way. Peter's way, with an authentic hug, one not of the "simu" variety. The world may have ended but my love and care for my friends and family will never diminish. It is early and the sun is in my eyes, but I am not going on a plane or preparing a budget; I am just driving with my friend to one of the nicest places in the world.

Roosevelt Lake is over 21,000 acres with a total length of about twenty-two miles. This is a place where you can lose yourself in nature. Eagles and hawks fly overhead, bass jump in the reeds, and the temperature is 95 degrees. Water temperature, a refreshing 72 degrees.

We launch the Jet skis in calm water and ride for miles on water as smooth as glass. After a couple of hours, the wind picks up, creating a short period swell of 3 feet or more. We are exposed to the elements as we try and find protection.

We find a distant boat launch that is protected by the wind and waves and we tie off, exhausted and hungry. We eat sandwiches, feet dangling in the water, and have a couple of beers while we talk about life surrounded by the most breathtaking scenery you will ever see. This is what I want to do for the rest of my life, and InfintyGo will bring this possibility to others.

Cubby doesn't know this, but I recommended him as one of the key employees any buyer of GMSI would need to retain. He earned it. He has done what others would never do, and he is the most knowledgeable person left in the company concerning our core technology. My time as the head of GMSI is over, and it is his turn to shine. I already told AMAT I did not want to accept the consulting offer they tendered, but more importantly, I don't think I will work in my industry again. I would like to, but I don't think the industry has a place for me anymore.

None of that matters anyway. I want to write, and I want to develop InfinityGo. That's a direction, and that is what I have been praying for since that fateful day last June when I said my goodbye to a 28-year chapter of my life. As I sit here, with Cubby, I make peace with myself.

I will do something that makes me happy, makes others happy, and aligns me with my goals. Leadership, culture building, start-ups, business development, and executive management.

We will create something new with great people and I will bring my leadership and guidance to something we create together. Again. I do not need the accolades of my peers or fancy titles.

I just want to do something I like that gets me home in time for dinner with my family. In this decision, I made peace with the fact that I had reached the pinnacle of my career and gave it all up, with nothing behind it. Just my family and friends.

It has taken me the better part of 11 months, but I accept that I will define a new role and a new path for my life--one that I build with others, for others. The clarity I receive is simple. I thought I had given up this amazing life of travel and title, but the truth is, I still have all the most important things.

"I still have it all, but ALL is defined by ME."

I still have it all, but ALL is defined by ME. It is for all of us. If we look at our lives, chances are, you have everything you need. The people you love, a job that pays the bills, and a home and friends you love. This, by my definition, is having it all. Embrace the now.

We finish lunch and take a long cruise. The warm wind rushes past my face as the sun warms my soul. As I ride, I keep telling myself, "I am ok. I am going to be ok. It is ok to start over; don't be afraid. Look at where you are right now. This is a much better life than a boardroom or a plane. Share your joy!!"

I am listening to all this in my head as I watch the beautiful scenery go by. This is a much better place than a boardroom, making money for people who use me as a tool. I want to build a place where I would like to work, where demanding work is rewarded, and teams work together to reach their goals. I want to do something that brings others the same happiness I feel now.

I am choosing to follow my joy.

My heart is heading on a different path, and as I look back on my past 28 years of work, I realize the greatest gift I was given was not measured by dollars or achievements; it was the gift of the people I encountered along the way, all having a hand in shaping my life in mostly positive ways. Relationships were my greatest reward, and I am rich by these standards.

Goodbye GMSI. I will always love you and be most proud of what we accomplished. We did it our way, with a culture built on the ideals of pride, accountability, and focus. The principles of our business have become the principles of my life and the lives of many others we have interacted with.

Cubby told me on the way home, "You were never a boss to me. You were a mentor and a friend." That means so much to me. Others have made similar statements. Too bad I cannot use any comments from past employees on my resume. I feel very humbled that they believe I was a sound and fair leader, one who lifted others up rather than beat them down. I wanted everyone around me to benefit from the success of our company. I cared, and still do, genuinely about all those I have led and all those with which I have worked.

As we drive, Cubby and I reminisce about a time we had a major equipment failure during a process cycle, leaving both of us lying in a puddle of caustic water. The memory is so fresh, that I feel as if I can still smell the chlorine fumes.

Cubby had called me from the cleanroom that our main scrubber motor had failed during a run. A scrubber is a tool that "scrubs" caustic chemicals and gases from a process, neutralizing its harmful output. The main pump blew a seal, allowing hot, caustic water to escape from the cabinet.

This was a critical purification run, where we purified the materials we used before a secondary coating process. This process was designed to remove metallic impurities and run in a halogen environment above 1500 degrees Celsius. Not a place you want an equipment failure.

We had hired a maintenance person, Rick, who should have been able to fix this, but he was older and was just staring at the geyser of hot water and chlorine gas, a deer stuck in the headlights. I had given him a chance where others had not. Rick looked on helplessly.

I glared at him while lying in the soupy mess, asking him, "Rick, why are you just standing there while we are down here?! Do something; you are the maintenance tech!!"

He scurried away while Cubby and Johnny investigated the root cause and possible cure for the problem. Water was now pooling everywhere in the space we lay, and we needed to find a way to stop this. The problem was, we could not turn anything off, because if we did, the cooling water would not flow to the reactor, and it would melt down. The cost of a reactor is over $400k.

We needed to figure out how to change this pump, right now, and continue the process run without turning any of the vital cooling systems off. It was a significantly complex problem.

Out of the corner of my eye, I see Rick enter the room. He was carrying a mop and a bucket. The visual is akin to bailing out a sinking battleship with a dixie cup.

"Rick, what the hell are we going to do with a mop?", I screamed loudly over the noise of the broken pump and associated equipment.

He saw the solution to gushing pumps, spewing gallons of water per minute onto the service floors of our gray area as a mop and a bucket. Cubby, John Ford, and I all saw the only solution was to replace the pump, right now, to save the process run, save lives, and fix the leaking water and gas. And in a matter of 20 minutes, Cubby and John changed the failed pump in ankle-deep water. That is commitment and bravery-- and a bit stupid. But mostly bravery and commitment.

I turned to Rick as he stood there dumbfounded, and said, "Rick, you told me you had experience in maintaining semiconductor Fabs. Why didn't you jump in instead of Cubby? Why didn't you take measures to shut the water down or dive in and fix the pump yourself?"

He looked down and then up to me. Our eyes met and I could see the sorrow and embarrassment shine through his expression. "Well, there were other people who helped me in my previous jobs, and I may have slightly overstated my experience level."

"So, you lied?" I asked.

"Well, not like you think. I just had other people help me at my old job." He explained.

Cubby and I learned a valuable lesson. We let Rick go with severance, even though he only worked at our plant for a month. I felt bad for him. That is until he called me 2 weeks after he left asking me desperately for another 2 weeks of pay.

"Rick, you worked here a month, and we gave you 2 weeks' severance to help you, even though I had no legal responsibility to do so", I said, frustrated I was even having this conversation.

He responded, "I know, but I spent it, and I am going to get evicted!"

I have been there before. More times than I care to admit. Penniless and unable to find a solution to my plight. It was a horrible feeling of hopelessness, and I didn't want to be the guy who caused him to get evicted, so I wrote him another check. My executives told me I was crazy.

And I was, but I was driven by the need to help those around me, even if the things I did at the time may have been unpopular. I stood alone on my convictions, and sometimes you need to stand alone for what you believe is right.

We laugh at the Rick story because it illustrates the many things all of us did to keep our business running. It doesn't happen in any other company but ours. We were GMSI.

We had a saying when things went wrong or when others, who were outside our company made a reference to how we did something without proper resources. "Welcome to GMSI!" It was not a greeting; it was a statement of our acceptance that nothing was easy, and even though we didn't have everything we needed, we had each other.

We held each other up. I created that culture by leading them into battle, and they willingly followed me. All of them. Not because of the pay, but because we believed in each other, we helped each other, and we did not put our titles above our responsibility to run a successful company.

That is my greatest source of pride. I led, and they followed, and in the end, we accomplished everything others said we would fail at. That, my friends, isn't just teamwork. It is called "culture".

One team, One goal!

I developed a phrase after the Rick incident to better explain the job of a manager.

Some follow, some lead, and some show up to a Tsunami with a mop and a bucket. Management's role is to understand the difference between the three.

May 14, 2020

After turning down the role of CEO, I was asked to consult the owner of the local semiconductor company I was being recruited by. I agree to a face-to-face meeting with the owner and his investors. The meeting goes well until their main investor asks me why I am not willing to accept the role of CEO. I tell him the truth.

"Because without more money, and an end to the global pandemic, this company will go out of business", I say, in as calm and professional a manner as I can. Good news is easy to deliver, unwelcome news is always a more delicate conversation.

He appreciates my direct and honest approach and tells me he would like to mull this situation over. I shake his hand and as he walks me out, he gives me his card, saying, "I like your style. It's refreshing and I would like to get together with you on future business discussions".

I reply in the only way I know how. I daftly respond, "Cool!", and thank him and walk away, head held high. This is me, love me or leave me.

After the meeting, I drive to Phoenix to get the boat from the dealer. My happiness is bittersweet, as with the lakes closed, I do not know when I will use it, but $4500 later, I better find a way to make money with this thing.

Speaking of money, I sold my positions in the stock market, and I am cashing out my 401K. I am taking my chips off the table in many ways and getting stuck in a stock market correction seems like a good decision as the bad news keeps coming. I am sure I will regret this, but for now, it seems like a prudent decision for my family's welfare. I am risk averse, and cash is king.

I also spoke to Randy at AMAT, who informed me that their offer stands. I politely declined and thanked him. Randy tells me he appreciates my professionalism and honesty. I wish him and his team the best of luck and ask him to remember those people at GMSI are amazing people. I ask him to treat them that way. I secretly love Applied Materials, but they are another hamster wheel, and I can't get on those anymore.

As soon as I hang up the phone, my nagging angst comes back. I just turned down a significant amount of money to do nothing but consult. No benefits, no future, just a check, and I said no. Wanda supports this decision. She does not want me to kill myself trying to support our family, and that surprises me until I find out it is because she wants to kill me herself.

She has been an invaluable asset in my latest decision making and having her on the same page is a tremendous relief. I appreciate her support and I let her know I will move forward with InfinityGo and my writing, and with the grace of God, we will be ok.

May 15, 2020

Oh, precious sleep, why do you escape me?

My alarm is set for 5:30 AM but I am up at 4:45. I am picking up Gustavo to bring him to stay with us.

As soon as I drop him off, I leave to meet Brad for a morning round of golf. One key takeaway from this year is that my golf game has improved dramatically. The takeaway? If you want to improve your game, quit your job.

I played well today. Nice and relaxed, and in the middle of a good golf round, we can talk shop, and offer suggestions for the completion of our pitch deck for InfinityGo and some of the formation criteria. This is how to conduct business. The environment we work in definitely influences the outcome, which is why I am in favor of working from home if your company allows it. Close to the family, no commute, and no one standing over your shoulder.

After a productive day, the staff of Guercio Inc. opts for calzones and pizza. When I go to pick the food up, I am met with absolute chaos, as end-of-the-world COVID procedures are melting down faster than the cheese on our pizza. I hope this pandemic ends soon as it is driving people to insanity.

May 16, 2020

This day is dedicated to the formation of InfinityGo. In short, a business is born.

I filed the LLC paperwork with my attorney, and just like that, InfinityGo is a reality. Sure, we have no money, no app, and no pitch deck that is finished, but we have an LLC and a dream. This is how all great ideas are born. With hope and the belief that an idea can become an ideal.

Later, Wanda, Gustavo, and I pay a visit to the local Walmart. They are stunned by the lack of products, including meat, but as luck would have it, we arrive just in time for a fresh shipment of toilet paper and paper towels. I have never felt wealthier than toting a cart with an eight-pack of Quilted Northern and some store-brand paper towels. I fear we will never see Clorox wipes and hand sanitizer ever again.

May 17, 2020

After a delightful read on the toilet, I am compelled not to be fat. I jump on my bike and will cover about 8 miles this morning. Riding and thinking, panting and sweating. "How do I best convey long-term market strategy as it relates to revenue growth for InfinityGo?" Look at me. Thinking like a CEO again. It feels like it fits this time, and I am excited to see where Brad, Omer, and I take this thing.

I am looking forward to the end of this book, and the beginning of a new chapter in my life. I will stop writing this story in about 3 weeks. After that, an intensive series of edits, and hopefully, a publisher.

It is hard for me to comprehend that in a few short weeks, I will have been gone from the CEO seat for a year. I still have mixed emotions. I kept my promise to my family to be more present. I kept my promise to myself to focus on writing this book, and on myself. I will enjoy these last weeks before we set off to make InfinityGo a household name.

It will be in these last weeks that I finish my first book, a lifelong aspiration fulfilled. I have three more books behind this one, and in all honesty, I could write every day until I die. I just may do that. In the meantime, Wanda and I will guide our children on the path to being self-sufficient, productive members of society, even if that society is quarantined.

I hope Wanda will always be by my side, and I will do what I need to do to make sure she stays there. I will pray that my mom and Rod will stay healthy and that my family and friends will not suffer the deadly consequences of the COVID-19 virus. I will spend as much time as I can with all of them, but when they are gone, I will be heading to my place on the beach. To write, rest and think, and watch the water ebb and flow. I will watch starry nights, the kind that unveil the riches of the galaxies, planets, universes, and maybe if you look closely, heaven.

May 18, 2020

My good friend Don Scott and I are going to play a round of morning golf at The Raven in Phoenix. When I left the house this morning, I forgot something, but I can't remember what, and it annoyed me the entire round. I realize what I forgot. I forgot to save the file containing this book, and I fear one of the kids will accidentally come into my office and delete a year of my work.

I called home and let them know not to go to my office because I was having a moment of anxiety. They laugh and tell me they have already reformatted my hard drive. I don't think they are funny, but to them, it's hysterical.

Later in the evening, as the stars emerge from the darkening sky, I look up to the heavens and thank God for taking care of us. It's been a momentous year, despite all the setbacks and a global pandemic. We are blessed, by any definition.

May 19, 2020

Cailyn and I are up early to take the boat out. It is another gorgeous day in the desert, and my littlest crewmate is excited about going out with Dad. We are alone on the beach, as we fish and make videos, laugh, and swim. The boat is as good as new, and it is a perfect morning to be alive.

I am feeling super tired after the long day of sun and cooking, and as the sun sets, so do I. I am going to golf again in the morning, but I know these carefree days are coming to an end. Instead of feeling bad about that, I feel incredibly lucky to have had this time to reboot myself.

Every day isn't perfect, but most are better than I deserve.

"The best thing I ever did was resign. I gave up a lot, but I got more in return."

The best thing I ever did was resign. I would not have gained this perspective, or this time to reconnect with those I love if I had stayed at work. I gave up a lot, but I got more in return, and that's what I call a well-structured deal.

May 20, 2020

This morning, I am playing golf right across the street from our house at Trilogy Power Ranch. I am playing much better now, and I love the fact I am across the street from my house.

When I get home, Wanda and I do something we used to fantasize about. I take a shower, and afterward, I slide into bed and turn the lights down. We snuggle up and......watch a movie during the day! It seems like no big deal but for us, it was something we used to promise each other as I packed to go on a trip or came home late after a meeting or client dinner. Today, we made that wish come true. This is the beauty of what I have done. I still work but on my own terms. I put my title and my internal passion to drive my business on the shelf in favor of driving my relationships and mental well-being. The fruits of this labor are immeasurable.

After the movie, Wanda needs my help, so I do something I would have never done in the past. I stopped working to help her. In the past, I would have told her how I HAD to get this email done. What I was telling her was, "This is more important than you!" I have done this for most of our marriage.

Running a company is hard. It demands all your time and energy. The problem is your family needs time and energy too. Corporate America says they believe in "work-life balance," but they are unbelievably bad at enforcing this practice. I tried to make sure my team took days off or took their vacations because I wanted them to have a life outside of work.

I understood this, so I closed for Christmas every year since 1995. It was the right thing to do, despite the constant pushback I received from shareholders, investors, and other board members. I didn't care. My employees needed rest, and so did I.

"We are all expendable at work, but we are irreplaceable to our family. "

I learned a valuable lesson these past few years. Do not make work more important than your family. You can get fired at work, but your family will never throw you away. Make them your priority. Learn to say "No" at work. Leave time for the ones who love you most. We are all expendable at work, but we are irreplaceable to our family.

Arielle is graduating tomorrow. Let me clarify that--we will watch her virtual graduation tomorrow. Even though she can't graduate like those before her, we are trying to make it special. It breaks my heart to see Wanda and Arielle so upset that she cannot walk the podium to receive her well-earned diploma.

I am taking Arielle for a little end-of-the-world, pre-graduation lake trip in the morning. As I load the skis, I think about my life as it stands now. I have assumed a different role in my marriage. I am the woman of the house. Mr. Mom if you will, and I hate it and love it. I would be one fantastic stay-at-home spouse. I cook, I clean, and I am ready in the bedroom day or night.

Maybe some things are better left unsaid...

May 21, 2020

It's graduation day for Arielle. I am enormously proud. She is a good girl. She takes care of kids, she does her schoolwork, she works and in general is a joy to be around. Except when she is not.

We are having family over to watch her graduate. There is no football field with marching bands and fanfare. No graduates walking in a procession as they make their way to the seats on a one-hundred-degree-plus evening here in Arizona. No sitting in the stands for 4 hours. We are in the comfort of our living room, about to watch the first virtual graduation I have ever seen in my lifetime.

I am still in shock of what has transpired since March 7th, 2020. We went from leaving the USA as the land of the free, home of the brave, to returning to a pandemic, food shortages, an absolute vanishing of household cleaning products and toilet paper. This also included a mandatory period of hiding and the canceling of the school year, prom and ultimately, graduation.

It's a post-Covid landscape, full of cowards and know-it-alls who decide that the best course of action is to shop at big box retailers and E-tailers but to close small businesses, churches, and schools. The hypocrisy borders on lunacy, as Walmart, Target, Home Depot, Lowes, and Amazon should stay open and prosper, but small biz, Main Street, high schoolers, and churches should remain closed.

This logic is the most ill-conceived and deceitful act of government I have ever witnessed. Do you mean to tell me that it is safer in a crowded Walmart than sitting in the stands of an open-air field in the 100-degree weather, waiting for your kid's name to be called and watching them walk up to the podium? Six feet apart? I highly doubt it. We could have made something work.

I am quietly reflecting as I make sure coolers and life jackets are loaded prior to taking Arielle to her pre-graduation morning of jet skiing at the lake. It seems like a few months ago I met Wanda and Arielle. It was 2007. So many years, experiences, and changes have occurred since. I married Wanda. We had Ben and KK. We all became a family. Adam and Deveny moved. We moved. Adam moved back in, and Gustavo too.

Not only did I get the girl of my dreams in marrying Wanda, I received the added BONUS of a little sweet girl, who loved me and DECIDED to call me daddy. And that always made me happy.

"Labels are for cans of soup, not people."

I have always counted her as one of "my" five kids. Labels are for cans of soup, not people. I hate the prefix "step" anything. I don't have a stepkid; I have a daughter.

I surprise Arielle with a stop at Starbucks for a "Mocha Crapachino" with whipped cream. I wisely choose a non-lactose drink, remembering my last battle with a Vanilla Frappe and a roll of store-brand toilet paper. Jerry Baldwin built an empire on a lovely place to have a cup of coffee. The Starbucks model to me is one of the best. Simple and consistent. This is how you grow quickly and effectively.

As we drove the winding and twisting mountain road to the lake, my feeling of having to pee became overwhelming. We were in serious territory. It is the end of the world, the authorities have shut down most public facilities and I am here, twenty miles away from the lake, with an overflowing bladder. The odds were heavily in favor of me having an accident and I am not wearing underwear, just the mesh inside my swim trunks. God help us all!

As we got closer to the lake, Arielle took particular care to tell a story that she knew would make me laugh. The problem was my dam was breaking as we raced into the parking lot and its public restrooms.

I catch myself just as pee is going to come out. Arielle is in tears, laughing so hard she is cackling and then silent as she gasps for air to continue her laugh seizure. I lumber slowly to the "Shaque du toilettes.", walking as if a weight has been tied to my urethra. Arielle is laughing hysterically now; actually, she is pouring out of the truck in a stream of laughter and loss of muscle control. I am in full waddle now, with tunnel vision that leads towards the bathroom. I am not going to make it. Arielle is now taking a video of me as I am practically crawling towards the bathroom, writhing in pain. I made it at the last minute! (I didn't)

We skied, we laughed, I had a beer. We took pictures and enjoyed our solitary graduation. I can think of worse places to be on graduation day. After the skis are on the truck, I pull out onto the main road, and without warning Arielle shrieks with horror. jumps into the backseat of my truck, flinging the Starbucks drink over the front seats and floors. I stopped the truck and got out to find a bee in the towel she was sitting on. I have never seen her move so fast.

Arielle is ok but still in shock. Not because she got stung, but because she was shocked I acted so quickly and never yelled. I guess I am changing for the better. In the past, I would surely have been acting like a madman, screaming and out of control.

The rest of the day led up to the big moment. That time when we pass from student to adult with the turning of a tassel. We go from the confines of our parents' nest to the wide-open spaces of college, adulthood, and the workforce.

We start watching the virtual graduation, which can only be described as ridiculous. The scene is a backdrop that looks like the stage at a graduation. There are holograms of the principal and other key speakers, but the quality of the hologram is horrible. The whole thing is comical.

It is disorganized chaos and many times we are laughing and making jokes. The whole thing felt like a bad video from the 70's, poorly edited but entertaining for its dreadfulness.

But then, Arielle's name was called. She has always gone by Arielle Castro, but tonight and on her sign for last week, she chose Arielle Castro Guercio. She had never done this, but this gesture made me proud and happy. She is a Guercio and always will be. She has our spirit, but she also has the strength and character of a Castro. I guess in the end, we take the best pieces of ourselves and pass them to our kids. I hope she will take the good pieces of me and use them to achieve her goals.

I am so proud of her for her accomplishments. She is going to be ok. We all are. Virtually, digitally, and in real life. You finish one task, and you move on to the next. One foot in front of the other. We do this for the next 70 years or so until we can lay our heads back and look to the heavens and say, "My tasks are complete".

Happy Graduation my Arielle. I love you always. Make yourself proud!

May 22, 2020

5:30 AM. The alarm is ringing. I rolled out of bed and retired to my porcelain fortress. One constant in this book and my life--, when the sun wakes, so does my colon.

After conducting bathroom business, I look in the mirror and confirm I am still the fattest of fucks, so I jump on my bike to get a ride in. I am happy as the chilly air whips across my exposed shoulders.

"I complain that I left the C-Suite and gave up money and opportunity... this year will forever change my way of living... my way of managing people."

I complain that I left the C-Suite, and gave up money and opportunity, but the truth is, I am the happiest I have ever been. This year will forever change my way of thinking and my way of living, and if I am given the chance again, my way of managing people. I have work to do to get there again, but I am committed to this new life. I will do my best to bring the same culture of care to any new venture I am involved with, as I did in my other career as CEO of GMSI.

In the meantime, I am riding fast, soaking in every experience, and happily living life, despite the chaos around us. I am thankful and I let God know this daily.

I come back after 9 quick miles riding as hard as I can. I write for an hour or so this morning, and I am deep in thought when a little man comes into my office, wiping the sleep from his eyes as he climbs into my lap.

I have done more before 8:30 AM than most do in a day. Why am I still fat? This day is dedicated to catching up on this book and my mental health. It has been a remarkably busy few weeks, and it feels good to just sit and write, not worrying about the next place I must be.

Around 1:30 pm, Adam shows up with JoJo, my grandson. Adam is watching him today while his girlfriend looks for a job. My bet is she is not looking for one.

Since I have a full house now, I try and make dinners that feed an army. The kids are all in the pool, including Adam. I looked over at my large brood and found it hard to believe that 10 years ago, Adam would be a teenager; Ben would be a toddler and Cailyn would have just been born.

I am amazed at how quickly time has passed for us. 10 years in the blink of an eye. I used to comment that my global travel was akin to "time traveling." I look at my kids in the pool. They are growing up so quickly. This is one of the key reasons I left my job. I could have stayed for money and security, but the demands on my family would have only increased, and I never planned for a pandemic. This would have posed significant challenges for my staff and me, and while I would have confidently led us through these difficulties, it would have put more strain on my family, staff, and me.

"I never understood how little time we have, and how much of that time is wasted on things that do not matter."

I like to think I timed this break well. It was an eye-opening experience. I never understood how little time we have, and how much of that time is wasted on things that do not matter. Family, faith, self, and other people are where time should be spent. Yes, we all must work to make money, but we can CHOOSE the type of life we have with work.

We choose our destiny, our way of life, and the people we share it with. We choose to be happy or sad. These are the things I have learned over the past year. No one defines your life. You do that.

Do not give the power of choice to your need for money. Find your passion and follow it. It is scary, uncertain, and for some, an uncomfortable reality that others control their destiny. Take the power back. Make decisions that get you closer to where you want to be. Pursue the things that scare you and most of all, find the things that make you happy and pour all your energy into that. In the end, you will find the dividends are happiness, health, and prosperity.

May 23, 2020

I fell asleep watching *New Girl* reruns with Wanda. I love her so much, but I cannot stay awake past eleven lately. It could be the fact I wake up at 5 AM now. Anxiety, stress, and worry used to keep me awake at night; now I fall asleep fine, and wake up early, ready to face whatever is coming our way. Day by day, which is how we do things now. We plan, but the most essential element of our planning is how we do things together.

I used to be active, healthy, and in decent shape, but we tend to let some things go when we are comfortable in a relationship. At some point, you have to reel things in and make some positive changes. I have let my health go. Living in an office, on a plane, or in constant states of stress, flux, and intense travel will wear you down mentally and physically, and I fell apart in all those areas.

I am not willing to continue this way, so on the bike I go, 11 hard miles. I set off with doubt and a general sense of not wanting to, but I push myself. I make myself go harder. I fight the feelings of wanting to give up and quit, and I pedal harder.

Life and biking are similar. You try and set a pace that gives you the results you want that expends the least amount of energy. It is in our nature as humans to try and find convenience. But the truth is, the things we want the most require hard work, determination, and perseverance. Push yourself. Do the uncomfortable things and never, ever quit. Once you tell yourself that failure is not an option, you will find yourself doing things you never thought were possible. Push yourself past your comfort zone in all you do in life. Find your pace, and when the hills come, pedal harder.

Many are quick to blame others for their inability to reach a goal, but the truth is, we are the only ones to blame. If something or someone is standing in your way, you have two choices--knock it down or go around. The more intelligent and efficient way to overcome adversity is to simply go through it. Face it, fight it, and forget it. There will always be the next obstacle. The fastest way to get where you want to go is a straight line. Knock down the obstacle. You will find they fall easily once you are willing to take responsibility for your own path.

I have a meeting on Monday with another high-level person at the European company that has been recruiting me. So far, I like the way they look at things in their business and in the market. They ask good questions. I am hopeful we can find a way to position them in a place to succeed, and in that, make a place for myself.

Find your places. Figure out where you fit, and where you create value and build productivity. Be the person that others look to for guidance, support, and experience. Build your value and others will see it as well.

I do not know where I will end up in my career. I have already said no to Applied Materials, a CEO position with 2 Start-ups, and several other offers that didn't appeal to me. I am looking for something that makes me happy. I do not know what that is for sure. I need to be in charge of my own path, and I need to be able to directly impact a business. More so, impact people.

"It is ok to make money, but it's even better to provide a place for many to benefit,"

It is more important now to find my path, doing something that adds value not only to my life, the life of my family, and our bank accounts but impacts the lives of others. It is ok to make money, but it's even better to provide a place for many to benefit, and in that, lies my path.

I spoke with Adam last night about helping pay some bills and I laid down some ground rules. I am not thrilled that Adam and Gustavo are living with us, but I understand that for me to live the statement in the paragraph above, I must help lift the people around me up.

"The only time you fail is when you quit. "

I make a hearty breakfast, the kind that would make a rancher or lumberjack proud. I burned 960 calories on a 23-minute bike ride this morning and I ate 2300 calories 2 hours later. I need to check my math if I am to shed my girthy self. I have more faith that monkeys will fly from my ass, but still, I push ahead. The only time you fail is when you quit.

Later in the evening, Cailyn and I went out for a quick game on the putting green. It is a beautiful Arizona night, and I am happy. I am on our putting green with my daughter, teaching her how to putt. This is the stuff my dreams are made of, and I am in the REM state.

May 24, 2020

This morning, I slept in. Well, kind of. I woke at 5 AM but rolled over and went back to sleep until 7. It has been a while since I slept this late, but it does not feel any different when I sleep 7 hours vs. 5.

Over breakfast, Adam and I sit down and have a deep conversation about the trials and tribulations of Terraforming as it relates to space colonization. We agree it requires science we do not have yet. Thanks for the mind meld, Adam. Good talk!

Wanda has shown no intimacy or emotion towards me lately. I would never cheat on her, but I understand why people do. They look for something they are missing in their relationship--mostly the feeling of acceptance and desire by others.

Today is Sunday, and we watched church on TV because we couldn't get tickets to go to church in person. Just like a sold-out concert, if you don't have a ticket, you don't get inside.

God must hate the pandemic. It is cutting into the very fiber of organized religion. The reality that I can go to a big box store, because that's safe, but not church, is idiotic.

It is clear, the federal and state religion is...commerce.

May 25, 2020

Happy Birthday to my beautiful firstborn, my Deveny. 27 years ago, I became a dad. I love you so much Dev. I know we have not seen each other much since you moved back East, but I think of you every day. This pandemic really put a dent in our ability to see each other.

I haven't seen Deveny in over a year. The pandemic has distanced so many of us, and while the death count rises, I am sure this isolation will continue. This is the hardest part for many, the fact they cannot see the people they love. It isn't healthy, and it needs to stop.

The days run together now. Tuesday, Friday, Sunday. It doesn't matter, they all end in "Y". Many days, I don't know which day of the week it is without looking at a calendar. Despite all the inconvenience that comes with the pandemic, I know that I am fulfilling my destiny.

It does not matter anymore what day it is. We are alive. Every day we have is one more chance to do things right. And so, I focus on the goals.

This morning, I am having a business strategy session with the group in Europe. Normally, I would take the call in my office, but I don't want to wake anyone in the house, so I take the call on the bed of my truck, tucked under a shady tree.

We spent an hour and a half discussing technology trends in our market, and how my inclusion would help their team. Their team is pleasant and intelligent. They get "It". They are looking at the right things, and planning for success. I am more intrigued to see where this goes, but if it went nowhere, I would be fine. I have other options, and in all honesty, the more I talk to the professional community in the semiconductor world, the more I realize I want to write for a living. At least I am finding that path I keep praying for.

I decided to call my mom to see how she was doing. I write about isolation due to the pandemic, and my mom is one of those suffering. She has a variety of ailments, all of which could kill her, but her susceptibility to getting COVID-19 prevents her from leaving the house.

As we talk, I tell my mom about a conversation I had with Adam last week. I told Adam, "We keep talking about getting out on the lake, but we still haven't done it because every time I ask, there is always a reason you cannot. Do not put these things off, Adam. One day I will not be here for you. I missed all these opportunities with my dad. He died before we could do anything we planned on."

As I tell this story to my mother, she is uncharacteristically quiet. She is listening intently as I tell her something I never shared with her.

"I miss dad too, mom. Every day. I wish he could have seen what I accomplished. Not just professionally, because I know he would be proud but more so, what kind of man I became. I missed many things that others got to experience. I missed father/son golf, him being a grandpa to our kids, family barbecues, holidays and so many other things. I watched my friends grow older and go on outings with their fathers and I missed out on all of that. I had a dad who watched me grow up, but not mature. He missed my "launch".

I missed out on all the things I needed my dad for, and it hurts, deeply. I was a husband, a father, a friend, and a leader, so I pushed down these feelings for many years, but now, I have a lot of free time, and the gravity of how much I missed Dad is my fuel for spending so much time with the kids. And so, I let Adam move in when he broke up with his girlfriend. Because that is what you do. You try and give your kids all the tools to survive and then you hope you have done enough."

It hurts to lose your spouse or parent. There is no recovery. You just pick up the pieces and move forward with whatever fragments of yourself you can staple back together. Our pieces were more damaged than others because we watched my dad die slowly. The things we feel are likely very normal, but in these ends of days, where death is a more upfront topic, I see both of us facing our own mortality and trying to process the continued damage caused by the death of my dad, her husband.

At the end of the day, we remember loved ones in the brightest light and try and emulate the positive character traits they had in our own lives. Other than that, the wounds heal but the scars remain. You can cover them up, but they are always there.

I tell my mom I love her, and I sit in the truck in tears, remembering my father and the countless things I never got to experience with him. I don't want to go home to my family like this, and I am an expert at hiding my feelings related to the loss of my dad, so once again, I push the pain deep, to a place that hides my true emotions.

When I get home, I hug Wanda and the kids for a long time. They have no idea why, and I don't tell them. I just hold them and tell them all how much I love and appreciate them. I am sure they think I am dying.

It's about to get worse. Minneapolis Police murdered a man in custody by kneeling on his neck until he died. His name was George Floyd, and I was horrified as I watched the video.

Is this who we have become as a society? I am angry that this happened in 2020. We have learned nothing in the 50+ years since race riots and segregation, and we are about to learn another lesson, one that involves violent upheaval like we haven't seen since the Rodney King days.

Rest in peace Mr. Floyd, nothing you have done warrants the treatment you received at the hands of the police.

May 26, 2020

This morning Ben and I are playing golf with Grandpa and Mr. Jim at Shalimar Golf Course.

We tee off at 8 and it was a decent day, but the standout was Ben, just ripping some drives off the tee. He is getting better.

Everything was going well, until hole seven, when Ben's wheels fell off. Maybe it was the heat, or lack of water, or the 24-ounce AZ Green Tea, but he is suffering. It never dawned on me he was not feeling well, and it made me feel like a bad parent. He tells me he is going to pass out, so I drive him to the car. The cold AC in the truck along with some water did the trick. I am close to my mom's house, so I told him we should stop by so he can rest for a few.

The truth is that my mom asked us to come over when we were done to pick up some fresh tomatoes from her garden. As we walk into her house, the sounds of Pantera, the heavy metal band, are blaring. My mom is 76 years old. For years, I was a rock musician, and she was my biggest fan and PR person. But only now do I realize; that my mom is a metalhead.

After a long day, Wanda and I went to bed to watch a movie. As usual, I fell asleep halfway through the movie. When I wake up Wanda is snuggled up in my arms and has been for the entire movie. It is late, maybe 1 AM, but somehow, one thing leads to another, and we end up naked and breathless. I am shocked and elated. We fall asleep wrapped up in each other, and I am happy to be here, with her, for better or worse. We have had a lot of difficulties this past year, but she is my girl, and this is who I committed my life to.

I love you babe. Para toda la vida, mi cielo.

May 27, 2020

After an exceptionally late night with Wanda, I am up at 5:30 AM. I am so exhausted, but I need to get up because I promised Arielle and her friend a morning at the lake, and I intend to keep my word.

I kiss Wanda's head as she sleeps and gaze at her for a second. Ladies, I can absolutely quantify that if a man loves you, he sees the beauty in you that you never do. So, no matter how bad you think you look in the morning, remember the guy who loves you has X-ray vision and is partially blind.

Arielle's friend shows up late. The old me would be mad, aggravated by the delay, knowing my time was extremely limited, but the past year has taught me to be more patient. Not everything is critical, and I am learning to go with the flow in pretty much every situation I encounter.

It pains me to admit it, but I may be maturing, in more ways than my age.

We spend the morning whipping Arielle and her friends around on the 3-person tube attached to the back of the boat. They are all having a fantastic time, and the smiles are overflowing. This is what I want to do for the rest of my life--facilitate the joy in others.

On the way home, all the girls fell asleep while I drove. I have a truckload of teenage girls who passed out in varying states of disarray. I hope I don't get pulled over. It looks like I am a human trafficker.

Back home we are preparing to host JoJo's 2nd birthday, and we are having cake and presents. The little shindig goes well, and JoJo loves it. After Adam takes JoJo home, he asks me to have a beer. I just sat down to watch a movie with Wanda, but it feels like he needs me, so I agree. He lets me know his frustrations with his current situation and I listen empathetically. I have been there before. Sleeping on someone's floor because I had nowhere to go.

My life wasn't easy, and I relate my experience to him. He never knew of my struggles because I don't like to share them, but it reminds me how close any of us can be to losing it all, and how far I have come. I don't spend time looking back anymore. Everything important is in front of me.

May 28, 2020

As I make my morning coffee, I read my texts to find Brad has written more threatening texts to me regarding InfinityGo. He is frustrated we aren't moving faster, but he forgets we are in the middle of a global pandemic and our venture is based on travel and human interaction.

Over the past few months, Brad has sent me aggressive text messages, usually late at night after he has been out having some drinks. They are all rooted in his overarching frustration at not being able to move forward. It's a pandemic, people aren't investing in travel when they can't go anywhere. It's that simple, but to Brad, it's a hard pill to swallow. I remain patient and ignore most of the threats for what they are…idle.

I am the founder of InfinityGo, and over the years, I have taken a lot of bumps and bruises as I came up the ranks of management. Two important lessons I learned early on are to stand by your ethics and never be intimidated by anyone. Brad is no different.

As I clean up my mess, I get a call from Cubby. He is officially an AMAT employee. They all are, except for me. I assisted in critical discovery for this transaction since last July, but I doubt anyone will talk about me, or my influence in helping this along. It's ok, because I intended to make sure GMSI was saved, and the people I cared about had jobs, and I know I had a hand in that, and that is all the recognition I need.

We don't help people to be celebrated for our actions; we do it because it is the right thing to do. I may not have a place in the new direction of my old company, but in the end, I will be proud that I was able to steer the transaction to a place that left them whole. And now, the Heraeus chapter is complete, and so is the history of GMSI.

In the year since I left GMSI, the company went from success to failure, to being shut down, to being sold to one of the best and biggest companies in our sector. In the end, I will find my way, post-GMSI, post-CEO, post-C-Suite. I will be ok.

> ***"I stopped worrying about the "What ifs" and put my focus on the "'What could be".***

My head, heart, and body are all going in the right direction now, and my faith is firmly placed in myself and the blessings of God and Jesus. I stopped worrying about the "What if's" and put my focus on the "What could be".

I am going to cash out one of our 401K's for working capital for InfinityGo. The new stimulus package allows for the waiver of the early withdrawal penalty, and my accountants confirm that I have had no measurable income this year, so the tax implications should be minimal.

This should sustain us for the rest of the year and will help launch my new ventures and support the work I want to do around this book.

One day, I will have my place on the water, and I will cook delicious food for the people I love, while the sun sets golden on the sea. This is my life's goal now. I am just looking for a quiet existence where I can think, write, laugh, fish, golf, consult, and love my family. In that, are the true riches of life.

May 29, 2020

It will be 112 degrees today. Only the strong, drunk, and well-sunscreened will survive. Cubby and I will be taking Ben and KK to the lake for a morning of tubing.

For the first time since I left, Cubby has the security of a job in the field he excels in.

The mood is one of joviality and we are both smiling as the boat glides across the serene water. Joy is present and accounted for. Not Cubby's wife, whose name is Joy, but the emotion. The one I had lost many years ago, in a dark hospital room when my father died.

We drive back to the beach first, but there is an algae bloom in the lake, killing hundreds of fish, and making the water a murky brown color. Ben and Cailyn are pestering us to tow them in the tube. Dragging my children behind the boat in a death-defying fashion is the next best thing—even with the algae bloom. Guercios don't quit; they just pivot.

As I pull the boat away, Cubby drops the tow rope too early, and it immediately gets sucked into the jet engine. The engine I just spent $4500 to fix. Again, old Peter would have lost it, but I grabbed a fishing knife and dove into the murky water like a swashbuckling pirate. The rope has not only been sucked into the engine from underneath, but it has also wound itself around the impeller shaft, essentially locking the entire engine in place. We are dead in the water, literally.

We spend 45 minutes cutting out the rope on a disabled boat in forty feet of water that may or may not be the home to an elusive and deadly Lake Shark. I repeatedly dive UNDER the boat, holding my breath and cutting the rope from underwater. I am going to need counseling after this for sure. Through teamwork, we can get the last piece off the impeller. I start the boat and the engine fires to life. The kids are happy, and tubing, a disastrous situation averted.

This was how we managed our time together at GMSI. Through every obstacle, and every tangled rope, we worked together to find solutions. That is the ever-lasting legacy of my work as CEO. I untangled the ropes that held our team down, and together, we freed ourselves to fly.

May 30, 2020

Wow, did I have a horrible night of sleep. Between acid reflux, bad dreams, snoring, and farting, I feel like I haven't slept a wink. I am a real joy these days. No wonder Wanda doesn't want to sleep with me anymore. Lol! (Mental note; no more Mexican food at 9 PM.)

Our 12th Wedding anniversary is tomorrow. I want to do something special for Wanda, but our choices are limited. Most restaurants are only open for take-out, and movie theatres have been closed for months--not that there has been a new movie released since the pandemic started.

As I cut the lawn, nostalgia is flowing. I think of the many lawns I cut in my teen years to earn money. My mom and dad raised me well. They instilled a work ethic that stays with me to this day, through this book, and throughout everything I have ever done in my life. I was not a kid who had life handed to him. I worked hard for it. And while I can hire someone to cut my lawn and trim my bushes, I do it because it keeps me tied to my roots.

In days past, Wanda and I would travel to some exotic locale for a vacation and to celebrate our anniversary, but tonight, celebrating our "End of the World Anniversary", we are just eating at a little Indian food buffet in town that Wanda loves. We are together, and it feels just as good as being on a tropical island. After dinner, we headed to Target. I would rather be here with Wanda in Target after an Indian food meal than be without her anywhere else.

Wanda looks at me and says, "Want to go for a drive to watch the lights?"

We leave Target and head to the desert. The elevation allows for panoramic views of the southeast valley of Phoenix, including the fabled Superstition Mountains.

The rain has cleaned the desert air, and we are sitting on the back of my truck. It is a little scary and wildly romantic, and we are sitting close enjoying the solitude.

"Wanna fool around?", Wanda seductively says to me.

I do babe, always. Happy anniversary to you. I love you more than all the lights and all the stars combined. I love you past Infinity (Go).

May 31, 2020

We are having a sleepy morning on our 12th anniversary. Church is at 4, so today I think we will just take it easy. I am off to the store to get things to make Wanda breakfast in bed.

But first, I will ride my bike. I rode hard this morning, fifteen miles totaled. I sit on the bench at the park I rode to, looking at the water, at the families fishing, and at the many people jogging, walking, and riding their bikes. It is 7:30 in the morning and the park is bustling with activity, albeit without any contact. We are socially distancing as instructed, and to me, it looks just like any other day at the park.

Maybe the world is not ending after all. But of course, I must consider the pandemic, race wars, police brutality, rioting and looting, and a president who can't control the pulse of the country because he is not good at unifying.

Economics does not touch everyone like it does for the rich and well-to-do. No, for the rest of us, it is a news story that only plays out in our 401K and our investments. The stock market does not tell the whole story.

I wish the president could intervene in a peaceful and non-confrontational way. I wish he would say something that would quell anger, but he only fuels the fire. Leadership unites, not divides.

I ride home from the park vigorously, sweating and panting towards the end of my ride, but I feel great. I feel strong. I am alive. So, are you! Every day we are breathing is another day to change the world, and so, I ride with hope, for me, my family, our future, and the future of mankind.

As I near the final mile of my ride, I am reflecting on the past year. I never would have done any of this if I was still the CEO. I would be working on solutions for the business, the clients, and the employees. Solutions to keep jobs, create revenue, and propel the group to the next level.

Instead, I am thinking about the events of the past year. I wrote a book; I stopped working and stayed off the hamster wheel. I am out of my cage and running aimlessly.

Whatever transpires over the next year will be by my own design. I am nervous and excited, hopeful, and focused. I am rested and relaxed. Everything will be ok. I just want to have a voice and be able to impact the world around me in a positive way.

"I will create the reality I want to live, and in that, I hope I will find the balance in life I never had."

I am happy. It is our 12th anniversary, we are all together, and I have not stepped foot on a plane or in an airport since last October. It was an international flight, to Cancun, for the first real family vacation we ever took together with all the kids, and it was awesome. I want more of that. More time with the people I love. This will be my focus as I venture forth with new ideas, new opportunities, and renewed optimism. I will create the reality I want to live, and in that, I hope I will find the balance in life I never had.

We spent an enjoyable day together. We went to church at 4 pm. It is still by reservation only, just like heaven. I am always tempted to say, "Table for 5, no smoking please", but no one has a sense of humor anymore.

This is our new world. I hate it. I want the old one back. The one where we moved about freely and lived life on our terms, not on the new restrictive nature of our "Orwellian" existence.

I will remain hopeful and prayerful, and I will do my best to be the voice of reason, the voice of faith, and the voice of love and acceptance. I am not perfect, but I will do my best to help others around me be the best we can be.

It's not what you do to achieve your goals, but who you take with you to get there.

People can lift you up or pull you down. Choose a buoy, not an anchor.

13

June, 2020

June 1, 2020

It is a new day, a new week, a new month, and the final stretch for this book. I hope it properly conveys the joy, sorrow, happiness, and newfound enlightenment I have experienced over the past year. Most of all, I hope it helps others to step outside their comfort zones and focus on the things that are important to them, not fearful that they will make a mistake. The mistake is to let life slip by and look back with regret. I have minimal regrets.

I want to create a course where I can help others find their path. Public speaking is something I enjoy, so I will put an effort into supporting my books by creating public speaking engagements where I can share my experience with others, including business leaders and their employees.

We are getting Arielle's diploma. I am immensely proud and while her senior year did not pan out as we planned, we made it all work. We will look back at this with fond memories, of a time when the world was ending, and so was high school. It was not easy on any of the Seniors of 2020, but you are resilient and powerful. Help make the world a better place by drawing from this resilience as you begin to take your place in the world. Be the change you want to see.

I am getting nothing done today, but I am fine with that. Some days work out like this. I have learned to roll with the punches and keep moving forward.

June 2, 2020

In the wake of the murder of George Floyd, I am reading really disturbing posts on social media. There are riots, protests, civil unrest, and violence. I write the following as something to consider:

Racism is a subject that needs open conversation and action. But a thought about the current behavior nationwide:

MLK believed in peaceful, nonviolent protests. He would not have condoned looting a Target or the destruction of other people's property. He would have especially disliked the violence.

What I see happening right now isn't even about race or George Floyd. It's about stupid people taking advantage; it's about greed and political influence.

In Arizona, we are under a mandatory 8 pm curfew now due to violent protests and looting. This is Insanity. Everyone must get a grip and remember that 2 wrongs don't make a right. Be the change you want to see.

The country has gone mad. Between BLM, Antifa, QAnon, and a variety of other groups, there is mass hysteria and mass violence around the country. People are looting and burning the USA down, and I am not sure what can be done to quell the unrest.

As if the pandemic wasn't enough to deal with, now we are dealing with a strong racial divide and civil unrest. I had high hopes for 2020 on New Year's Eve, but those hopes diminished in March, and things are only getting worse.

I have a lot of errands to run today, along with the completion of the InfinityGo pitch deck for investors. I am antsy to get my work done concerning InfinityGo. I need to work again. This year has been great. It has nourished my soul and heart, aligned me with my family, and renewed my drive and ambition. However, I need to create. I need to impact people. I need to lead. It is who I have been all my life, and my restment is over. I am ready to move forward and grow.

I do not miss the elements of big company life, but I do miss the people, the employees, and my co-workers. They were my family, too. But I do not miss the deadlines, the stress, the constant travel, and most of all, the politics of a large company. In my new venture, I will strive to keep politics out of the day-to-day running of the business. It won't be easy; there will always be someone who won't be happy, and the challenge will be to create a cohesive environment to minimize this.

June 3, 2020

I am putting the finishing touches on the InfinityGo deck. I am proud of the work that we have done. I am feeling confident that InfinityGo will be a great success. I have good partners and good people around us. We will deliver a fun and pleasing experience. Most of all, I hope it will connect people to people in a way that has never been done before.

I am currently working on several projects, and I am busy. I am in a transitional phase. I am looking at many things, but I am most focused on how to create a revenue stream for my family that does not include me never being here, like before.

It is a hard-balancing act to juggle work and a life outside work. Work is not 8 hours at the C-Suite level. It is a 24/7 existence, which leaves little time for anything else. I learned a valuable lesson from working at a high level for almost 30 years. I learned that it is equally important to stop and spend time with family and yourself. This time is important to rejuvenate and critical to maintaining a healthy mental state.

"Time is the most precious commodity... Do not squander it; it will never come back."

Time is the greatest wealth we will ever have. It is not infinite, cannot be bought, and time, my friends, is the most precious commodity you can be given. Do not squander it; it will never come back, and its value is immeasurable, so use it wisely.

June 4, 2020

I wish I could sleep past 6 AM. Here I am, all the time in the world, to catch up on some sleep, and I have insomnia. The cruel irony of it all!

I got up and rode my bike for 8 miles this morning. I am just a few days away from my first anniversary of leaving work. I am unsure why we are so busy; we are not even working! Wanda will kill me for saying that. She works. Homeschooling is a full-time job, and I am grateful for her patience and dedication.

Later, I headed to the boatyard to grab the boat. I am going out early in the morning; just me, myself, and I. I am really looking forward to the quiet time. I need it. I have so many thoughts running through my head. It will be nice to get out in the wild, turn the noise off, and fish for a while.

As I hitch up the boat, I glance at my clock. The time is 8:35 PM, and I forgot that the governor imposed an extremely strict curfew to stave off the damage caused by looters and hooligans, not protesters. Protesters are not nocturnal. Protesters march during the day so their message is heard when people are awake. Looters, thieves, and vandals work in the shadows of darkness. I support the order that comes from making sure the only people out after dark are the cops.

In these end-of-world days, I am stunned that I agree with any impedance to my freedoms. Yet here we are, watching daily as we are restricted by local, State, and Federal Governments. These are crazy times in which we are living.

I quickly say a prayer and hop in the truck. I am nervous as I pull out onto the dark street that leads to the main road. Busted for curfew? I hope that does not involve a beating; I have very inadequate medical, dental, and vision insurance right now.

I should not joke. Police brutality is a choice the police make. A cop chooses to follow the protocols of the department he works for. Each cop chooses whether to use force, deadly or otherwise. I know many situations are predicated upon the belief that there is a viable threat, but when we talk about brutality, especially against Black people, you are talking about committing a crime as well.

Law enforcement officers have stun guns and rubber bullets, and while I understand the dangers that can threaten a cop, once an arrest is made, cuff them, read them their rights, and put them in the car. This is how you end police brutality. Follow protocol. Act responsibly. Be honorable. Respect all life. Protect and serve.

I drive white-knuckled through the dark streets of Queen Creek, trying to elude whatever cops are out. We are in the burbs, farm country before the houses and developers came in. It is quiet at night and I hope that the sheriffs are busy with something else. I am a mile away from the house, and I see lights behind the truck speeding towards me. I am not taking any chances, and I floor it, racing wildly to my home and the safety of my driveway. It's a place where I can "drop the soap," confident my netherworlds will remain untouched.

I sped home and put the boat and truck in the driveway. I went upstairs to find Wanda already in bed. She looked so beautiful, even though she would say, "You're crazy!" I am, babe; I am crazy for you.

We lay in bed and talked, and while I was asked not to provide intimate details of the rest of the evening, as Wanda's lawyer would surely send me a nasty letter, assume it ended happily.

June 5, 2020

On the lake by myself this morning. I needed this time away. The world is going crazy, and as I sit in the boat, floating alone at the lake, I take a second to post something on social media to address the laundry list of atrocities we face today.

Good morning, End of the Worlders,

As a kid I often wondered what it would take to bring down society. I was deep like that, always thinking about the future and scenarios that may never exist.

In my wildest dreams, I never would have thought that we would be dealing with a pandemic, civil unrest, tensions with China, race wars, a stock market that shines in the light of disaster, and an asteroid.

Since we're here and this is the reality we live in, I want to throw in a zombie apocalypse and coordinated shark attacks as the next disasters to befall 2020.

My message seems comical; however, it speaks for the human race's resilience.

If we can get past all those things, we can certainly recognize police brutality against black people and other social injustices, racially or otherwise. Then, we can find solutions and get over it.

I'm going to go ride my bike now. Have a great day.

My post is well received, and others add to the list of insanity we are dealing with right now. According to my social media following, I also failed to mention Yellowstone is about to erupt, there have been minor earthquakes in California, murder hornets are on US Soil, and the government just declassified a series of files relating to the existence of UFOs.

If the pandemic doesn't kill us, there is a long list of things that will. Just go back to bed!

June 6, 2020

Life is about perspective, and each of us reacts and responds to certain situations differently. Despite the United States reaching a critical tipping point, I continue to look at life and its offerings with a certain sense of humor and razor-sharp sarcasm. I am tired of the pandemic and its cataclysmic events, so I am writing a breakup letter:

Dear Covid,

We need to talk.

I know we have been together for a while now, but I think it's time we considered ending our affair. It's not me, it's you. I need space and a day without a mask or incessant hand washing. And honestly, I am tired of your face.

I am a giver, and you are a taker—a taker of life, liberty, and the pursuit of happiness. This has become a very one-sided relationship, and I want to break up.

Sure, you want to get me into bed, but for all the wrong reasons. I like monogamous relationships, and you are a dirty slut, bedding anyone you can get your hands on. I wonder if you were ever a musician here in Arizona during the 80's and early 90's.

So, listen, it's over. I don't love you, and you make everyone around me unhappy. Pack your stuff and leave your key.

I would say it's been real, but I would be lying. The best thing about our relationship is that you showed me what's really important in my life, and it turns out it's other people and toilet paper.

I don't know who you've been with, so I'm getting a shot. Hopefully, that will protect me from your unwanted advances. No means no!

It's been a good ride, but it really hasn't. My advice to you for the future? Intensive counseling and maybe some time in seclusion to get yourself right. Maybe go back to your roots as a common cold and stop being such a homewrecker.

Sincerely,

Humanity

June 7, 2020

Well, this is it, my friends, 365 days of life and the end of the line for this book. We have completed another trip around the sun, although I think we may have hit space junk along the way. I started this book on Saturday, June 8th, 2019, the day after my last day at GMSI, and today is officially one year since I left the C-Suite and the business I founded. The funny thing I realized as I write these last words is that the book should have been titled "366 days", as 2020 was a leap year. Of course it was!

This has been an amazing experience—leaving everything I knew for the unknown and trying to find my place in the world again. I have experienced so much in the past year since I left. I am filled with an array of emotions today: sadness, joy, pride, happiness, and a tinge of fear brought about by mild uncertainty.

I think of the employees and clients I left a year ago, and I wonder if I impacted them as a leader as they impacted me as my teammates. I think about my future. Will this book catch the attention of readers? Did it make you laugh, smile, or think about your own life and allow you to reflect on some "What if?" scenarios? I hope so.

It has been an eventful year, and I will never forget this time at home with my family. I will also never forget my former employees, clients, vendors, and the many investors who took a chance on us. I am forever grateful and truly blessed for the life I have been allowed to lead. I have lived a charming life, and the greatest gifts I ever received were love, health, and faith, not wealth, accolades, and fame. I understand the value of all those things now.

"Faith is the life jacket of life."

I thank God and Jesus for this incredible life I have been given. My faith has gotten me through the most difficult times, and at the end of the day, it helped me to remain positive, to stay focused, and to keep pushing forward. Faith is a personal thing, but faith in yourself, in a deity or in others is paramount to overcoming adversity. We cannot do anything alone. Faith is the life jacket of life.

My faith helped me to accomplish everything I have ever done. Faith in God helped me keep moving forward in the face of overwhelming odds. Faith in myself allowed me to push aside the doubts others cast upon me, ignore the pitfalls and speedbumps we encountered, and motivate others to have faith in what we were doing. Faith is essential to finding peace, happiness, success, and a stress-free life.

This morning, I woke up early—really early—3:45 AM, to be exact. I cannot sleep, and Wanda is next to me, snoring happily. We argue, fight, annoy each other, and sometimes want to strangle each other in our sleep, but there is absolutely no one else I would rather lay my head on at the end of the day. She is my best friend, my spouse, my partner in life.

"Our relationships define the direction of our life."

Remember, relationships are the key to everything. Whether it is business or love, parent or friend, our relationships define the direction of our life and the happiness contained therein.

I love you, Wanda, and I have loved you since the first days of our courtship. I went through hell in my first marriage, and you are my heaven on earth. I appreciate you, babe, and I thank you for the past year. Not every day was perfect, but they were all better because you were with me. Thank you for your love and support.

There is no better way to end this story than the way I spent many of my days on the water, sharing the joy of being in nature. I kiss Wanda and get out of bed to take care of my digestive business. After "dropping the kids off at the pool," I make the coffee. I am tired—like exhausted tired. This has been an exceptionally busy few months.

I think about this time next year. Where will I be? Will I still be here at all? God, I hope so. Will InfinityGo be a success? Will one of the other opportunities I am considering come to light?

Will Applied Materials change their offer to me? Will this book be successful? I do not have any of these answers. The only thing I know is I am sincerely grateful for everyone around me, everything we have, and all the people who have offered me jobs or consulting gigs.

"I have learned the value of stepping back and waiting."

Since I left my position as CEO, I have been given one beneficial gift: I do not worry so much anymore. I have learned to be patient. Impatience and impulsive behavior have been my downfalls on many occasions. Either I am getting older or smarter, but I have learned the value of stepping back and waiting. I have learned not to overreact, except when I do!!

The key element I have gotten rid of, the one that weighed on me the most, is stress. I do not stress out like I used to. I am calm and relaxed, and I can deal with chaos better in this new plane of existence. This will help me later as my brother-in-law Gustavo pushes us off from the docks for an early morning ride around Canyon Lake.

We see a fire around the edge of the lake. This reminds me of how some corporations work. They stifle creativity and innovation by stamping out the flames of those who do not fall within the lines of corporate expectations. Then, one by one, they put out the remaining smoldering ashes. This is not a concept I can accept. I want all the people I lead to shine, to burn with their passions. I will continue to try to get to a place where my voice can help others find their path and help companies better utilize the teams they create.

We continued to ride to the back of the lake in silence. No words were exchanged, and it was clear we were both reflecting on our lives and enjoying the scenery. The water was moving swiftly here, and they were letting water out of the dam above the lake. It was too turbulent here, at the Bronze Walls of Canyon Lake, so we pushed off after a quick swim and headed for deeper waters.

It is all trolling speed back here, but the force of the rushing water is so strong that it is pushing the boat backward. The rushing water continues to push the boat violently, and the boat is caught in a swirling whirlpool filled with debris, broken logs, and branches.

As I start the engines, I hear the unmistakable sound of a clogged jet port. I cannot get the engines to run, and we are now hopelessly getting carried in the rushing water and headed straight for the canyon walls. We are, quite literally, dead in the water.

I am in the middle of the canyon, with a beach on one side and cliffs on the other. I am using only one engine, which causes the boat to continue pushing to the starboard side, putting us dangerously close to the canyon walls. The situation is critical.

I do not let Gustavo know how serious the situation is; I focus on the goal and continue navigating the churning waters littered with logs. The "Old Peter" would have gotten upset, angry, and stressed. I would have yelled and, worse, created a more chaotic situation than we were already dealing with.

After 20 minutes of fighting the rushing water, debris, and winds, we find calmer conditions in a deeper, more sheltered part of the lake. There, I found a chunk of wood, about 6 inches long and 3 inches wide, wedged between the impeller and the impeller wall. The engine is locked, and we are drifting.

I ask God to help us, not to leave us stranded, and to help me stay calm in the face of adversity.

"Faith. It is the sincere belief that despite all is bad, good will prevail. "

I reach back into the long, narrow port of the jet cleanout, a place I have spent way too much time in the past year, and grab the chunk of wood. It is wedged hard, and we are ten feet from smashing into the canyon wall, but I focus on the task, tug with all my strength, and after a few seconds, the wood pops free. I show Gustavo the evidence; he smiles back at me and says, "Bro, that was right as I finished my prayer."

Faith. It is the sincere belief that despite all is bad, good will prevail.

I feel like my life was a chunk of wood, caught in the engine of my creativity. Leaving my position as CEO freed my powertrain to run at full capacity once again, and I will use this analogy many times in the coming months.

We fire up the engines and power away, free of the chains that bound us. Faith and patience carried us through.

As we speed along the now-crowded canyons, I reflect on a year ago today. I gave my last speech as CEO, making a presentation titled, "Goodbye. The past is just a shadow of the future".

Many considered it a sincere offering of what I had learned over 28 years. A year ago, I was the CEO of a multi-million-dollar German company's business unit. I was the head of Advanced Ceramics. I was the President and CEO of GMSI. I thought I was important, but on that day, as I looked out over the many faces listening to me tell my last story and provide my last piece of guidance, I realized I was nothing more than a human in a race nobody wins.

I created a culture of excellence, a team of experts who excelled in their respective fields, and I led a group of people who I can confidently say are the best in the business.

I have traveled the world countless times, bringing our message of faith to all corners of our industry. I have seen so many amazing and breathtaking sights around the world.

I was at the top of my game and the top of my field, but in the end, after all I had created, all I wanted was to go home and see my wife and kids.

And I did, For 366 glorious days.

Where will I go from here? Only God knows. I have faith in the path and in myself and those around me. I will create a new journey, one that keeps me close to Wanda and the kids and one that keeps me closer to my newfound piece of mind.

What can I take away from all this? Honestly, a lot more than I thought I would. I thought I just needed to catch my breath, but instead, I received a full lung transplant, diaphragm and all.

If I could leave you with one thought, it would be to ask yourself a simple question. "Are you happy?" If not, how will you find the peace and path you desire?

"Follow your heart and listen to those who love you the most."

My answer would be simple. Follow your heart and listen to those who love you the most. They know what is best for you. They are the reason we do what we do, work as hard as we work. The greatest gifts we will ever receive are the love of our family and friends, and time to experience the things that bring us Joy. If you can find a way to do that, you will be the richest person in your world.

After I went to the lake with Gustavo, I went home and took a long shower. Out of the shower, I go to my closet to grab my shorts. My travel items from when I was employed have been tucked away for over a year. An array of international chargers, travel bags, overnight bags, duffle bags, shoes, belts, suits, hats, jackets, and trench coats. I have five different backpacks and two different laptop cases. This was my life for many, many years. I lived out of an assortment of bags.

I can still feel the anxiety of last-minute travel details and readying presentation materials or whatever it was I was to be doing. I used to stand in my closet for an hour or more, trying to figure out how to pack the least amount of crap into the smallest suitcase for whatever journey I was heading on.

Wanda used to call it my travel anxiety. She was right, as she always is, but I never recognized it as such. It was just another one of the things I did automatically. I was a soldier preparing for battle. The suitcase and backpack were my survival gear. I do not miss this aspect of my past life.

I once traveled around the world with a small carry-on bag for a trip that would have me visit 6 countries in 9 days. I bought 2 suits, 2 shirts, 3 ties, one pair of dress shoes and one pair of comfy shoes. I added socks and undies for 9 days, and I went away. I would have the hotel dry clean my suits every third day and my dress shirts every other day. I was an expert in global travel. Today, I like to wear board shorts, no underwear, and flip-flops.

It is late afternoon here on Sunday, June 7, 2020. I have nowhere to go. I am finishing these last words in the air-conditioned comfort of my office. The kids are playing on their computers, Wanda is out shopping, and on these end-of-the-world days, I have found peace.

I am going to be ok no matter where I end up. I gained a vast amount of knowledge these past 30 years. I found the courage to stop the path of my unhappy life and find the hidden trail to a joyous one. It cost me, especially in the financial department, but I gained the wealth of being with my family for a year. I was given the gift of time to enjoy the life we made. I took time to slow down and assess what I was doing and found the peace I sought. Now, I want to share my blessings with others.

A quick end-of-the-book recap, if you will. First, I have no job yet. I am not looking too hard. Well, not at all. And I am ok with that for now. The stress of living on our life savings and investments weighs on me daily, but for now, I focus on finishing tasks like this book.

I formed a new company called "InfinityGo." We hope it will be the next big thing. If not, I will still try to make it successful. The pandemic is stifling this venture, but I remain faithful that the right path will find me. I have some other things in the works, but for now, it's Wanda, the kids and I, the unemployed former CEO.

I have to stop referring to myself as a "former CEO." I am just a guy—a guy who did a lot of cool stuff and overcame great adversity. I am a dad, husband, friend, son, brother, cousin. I am Peter "F-ing" Guercio, as I once screamed at a man giving Wanda a tough time at a Bon Jovi concert. The details aren't important, but the sentiment is. Be "F-ing" incredible. It's your middle name.

I need to go now. The kids are downstairs fighting about configuring Minecraft on VR. I will be patient, and with that newfound patience, I will go down and help them calmly. Never mind, they just fixed it themselves. See? I am learning. Empower others to take care of themselves through delegation and a hands-off approach. I am the steering committee in the corporation of my life.

In previous days, this interruption would have aggravated me. I would have yelled and gotten annoyed that the kids or Wanda were interrupting me.

Then, I would leave for a trip and miss them the whole time. This paradigm now seems ludicrous. Why would I get mad at them for asking for my time when, as soon as I left, that was all I wanted?

Because I did not understand the importance of time and the limited amount of time we are given on this globe, I have selected to use mine more responsibly. I hope you will find value in yours as well. Make time for yourself, your family, and your well-being.

Time is the greatest treasure; love is the sweetest treat. Birth is painful, and the truth shall set you free. I still have an "end of the world Jesus Jackal" living in our house. Please send help.

I do not know what tomorrow will bring, but I will focus on today and be thankful for my life, love, friendships, and experiences. Tomorrow is today, just a day later.

Everything you have ever dreamed of is on the other side of everything that terrifies you. Look before you leap, but leap boldly and with excitement, knowing you are not bounding into the unknown but into the possibility of the life you have always dreamed of.

THE END

Wait!!! Want more?
Visit Off the Hamster Wheel's official website for pictures, stories, and other goodies we couldn't fit in the book.

www.othwbook.com

14

Epilogue (4-15-2024)

"The End" means different things to different people. Nothing is "The End" other than death and divorce, and as I have stated, my hope is death isn't the end, it's just another chapter in our journey to heaven.

But surely, I digress. My editor and now friend, Barry Cohen, had suggested I tie up some loose ends being this is the technical "End" of this series of books. This is the third of three books I write in reverse chronological order, so, this epilogue needs to bring closure to the series.

Where do I start? First, let us talk about Wanda and me. We are still married, still in love, and ironically, still friends. As a matter of fact, she did the final edit of this book, and added some clarity I was missing from this time period. We learned from these experiences, and the many others over 16 years of marriage, and in that, we have learned how not to kill each other. Lol!! In truth, we are in a good place. I don't put so much emphasis on our intimacy as I did in 2020, and in turn, it's in a better place. She is still headstrong and immovable in many of her opinions, but in favor of more peace, I have learned a magical phrase that can be used to defuse any situation. I say, "Yes, dear." I love you, Wanda. You will always be my lobster.

Our kids are great. Deveny and Adam live in Ohio, Arielle is in her second year of college and working as a Case Worker for a state sponsored counseling group, and the "little" ones, Ben and Cailyn are still homeschooled by Wanda. Ben has blossomed into a brilliant young man, doing college work in many cases, and in all honesty, smarter than I was at his age. He takes after Wanda in many ways. He does have my warped sense of humor, and similar hair, so I still see me in him. Cailyn is the President of her school, and is an active member of everything she can get involved in. Most of all, she is still sensitive, kind, and funny, and she still likes going to the lake with her dad.

Kino, the "Jackal that may have been Jesus," sadly, was euthanized in 2022. It broke our hearts. We took him as far as we could, but he was getting weird around little kids, and unstable, and after the 3rd Vet told us to put him down, we listened. It broke our hearts, but Wanda and the kids found another little dog in Mexico that our sister-in-law rescued from a construction site, and they rescued him. By rescued, I mean they lied to me about everything and brought back a dog that was supposed to be quiet. He sits and barks at me early in the morning, much to my dismay, but he is cute, does not think he is Jesus, and is good around other kids and dogs. He too is practicing Hot Yoga and is currently dating the Yorkie up the street.

My golf game is as craptacular as ever, and we still spend mornings on the lake. We have yet to encounter the dreaded lake shark, but we remain vigilant, just in case.

What else? Oh yes, my restment. Well, first things first. The pandemic killed InfinityGo. It is ok, Brad and I were not getting along and in truth, I am not sure I wanted to be the CEO of a startup again. I took this as a sign from God, as I had been praying for my path, and the path for InfinityGo was littered with land mines and barbed wire. No worries, the concept is well structured and if I want to, I will do it with other people.

InfinityGo may not have come to fruition, but the restment ended. I asked God for a path, and it turns out, he found me one.

First as consultant, then as Executive VP and then...CEO. I know, I know, your first thought is, "You got back on the hamster wheel"? No, I did not. First, I consulted. I consulted middle market business leaders on M&A topics and on surviving the Pandemic. It was a wonderful experience, and it led me to another consulting gig with my longtime friend, James. He asked me to help him with his business, and I did, as an Executive VP. Then he asked me to sell it, and I was successful in doing that as well.

I functioned as interim CEO post transaction, and then...I fell in love. Not with another woman, but with a large group of them. Men too. Lol! I found a group of people who needed leadership. They needed to be part of a team. They needed a strong culture. And we built one together. We just finished our latest acquisition, and we continue to build a talented team. We also just finished another year of double-digit growth at > 20% EBITDA.

I am the Group CEO of a portfolio group of companies for the best Private Equity firm in the world. And to that end, the best companies in the world. It is not in Semiconductors or Advanced Ceramics. It's in the industrial markets, and I am happy. I am not stressed; I partner with awesome people in all aspects of the business, and we bring this amazing and collaborative culture to our acquisitions. We assimilate them, and then we make them part of our family. Relationships, people. It is the secret to everything in life. Good ones make you flourish, bad ones make you die. This will be my last job, and my sincere hope is to leave on a high note, one that brings joy, success and a one team, one goal culture.

And GMSI? Well, as I wrote, GMSI became Applied Materials, and Cubby is a leader in that division as the Director of Operations. He is still one of my closest friends. I see his life today compared to when we started, and I know the impact our relationship had on each other. I am also immensely proud that my technology lives with Applied Materials and serves the industry I loved so much. It is an enormous source of pride to know that what I built with the team at GMSI lives on to serve so many. It is called...a legacy.

The pandemic ended, but stupidity and manipulation remained. Drug companies, oil companies and politicians made billions and used fear and trust against the American people. We are still trying to get back to "normal," whatever that is, but we are transitioning as a society, and most days, I don't think we are moving in the right direction.

What do I know, though? I am just a guy who said he could change the world.

But now I know, I did change the world. I have patents for my work with GMSI, and these patents will live to serve as a timestamp in my life and the work we did as a team. We created technology that helped change the world.

I changed the world for many that collaborated with me, many that started as hourly workers who now work in executive roles. I changed their world, and they changed mine.

I was idealistic when I made the statement that I could "change the world," but as I look back on my career and my life, I realize that I did indeed change the world. Maybe not the entire world, but for many of the people I interacted with, and in that I can take great solace. The bigger takeaway is that they changed me too. For the better. I am who I am because of the people around me who called me family, coworker, client, supplier, husband, dad or friend.

I feel like I am forgetting something, but it doesn't matter. I am on to other things. I look back sometimes and remind myself where I came from, and I see that old life, the hamster wheel and its confines and cages. I do not look back with contempt. I look back with fondness to a time when we built the future.

I will not go back there though, because as I have learned, the only thing you really influence in life is your mood, the people around you, your attitude, and your direction. Don't look back, always look ahead, find your happiness, and your peace, which always leads to Joy.

What's next? I don't know. Hopefully a significant and profitable exit from this business for all involved, retirement and hopefully more books, if you like what I have to say. Even if you don't, I will write them anyway, because it's important to me, and in the end, we do the things that make us happy.

I must go now. It is bedtime and Cailyn is standing next to me waiting for me to finish writing. She said I have been writing long enough and she needs me to kiss her goodnight so she can dream of lake sharks and big waves.

15

About the Author

Peter J. Guercio is an accomplished business leader whose recent departure from the C-Suite is the subject of his new book *Off the Hamster Wheel,* a heartfelt and intimate story of self-discovery.

A wunderkind before he became a storyteller, Mr. Guercio launched the semiconductor darling, GMSI and led the company for 28 years as it developed state-of-the-art products in wide use today. He is responsible for multiple M&A transactions with publicly traded and private sector companies. Mr. Guercio is credited with thirteen international patents for his work.

A native New Yorker, Mr. Guercio was born in Manhattan and raised on Long Island. The son of a composite engineer and a hairdresser, he quips that he has a mind for the complex, and an eye for the perfect hairdo, even if he is bald.

Mr. Guercio graduated from high school with a New York State Board of Regents Diploma. After several forays into college life, he departed higher education for the music scene spending years as a professional drummer and earning multiple album credits to his name. He often attributes his tenacity and drive to his long tenure at the "School of Hard Knocks," where he graduated top of his class.

Traveling the globe for GMSI, Mr. Guercio logged more than 1 million miles over 20 years. In his spare time, he enjoys golf, boating, cooking, surfing, reading, video games, and time with his beautiful wife, Wanda, and their five children.

Mr. Guercio is completing a trilogy of novels and is currently the Group CEO of a portfolio group of companies owned by a Private Equity firm. He teaches culture, accountability, and the value of a "One team, one goal" philosophy.

Mr. Guercio's point of view is honest, intelligent, forthright, and refreshingly humorous with a touch of sarcasm.